COMMUNITY BY DESIGN

COMMUNITY BY DESIGN

The Olmsted Firm and the Development

of Brookline, Massachusetts

KEITH N. MORGAN

ELIZABETH HOPE CUSHING

ROGER G. REED

University of Massachusetts Press   Amherst and Boston

in association with

Library of American Landscape History   Amherst

ISBN 978-1-55849-976-8

Designed by Jonathan D. Lippincott
Set in Perpetua
Printed and bound by Thomson-Shore, Inc.

Library of Congress Cataloging-in-Publication Data
Morgan, Keith N.
    Community by design : the Olmsted firm and the development of Brookline,
Massachusetts / Keith N. Morgan, Elizabeth Hope Cushing, and Roger G. Reed.
        pages   cm
    Includes bibliographical references and index.
    ISBN 978-1-55849-976-8 (cloth : alk. paper) 1. City planning—Massachusetts—
Brookline—History. 2. Olmsted, Frederick Law, 1822–1903—Friends and
associates. 3. Brookline (Mass.)—Buildings, structures, etc. 4. Brookline
(Mass.)—History. I. Cushing, Elizabeth Hope, 1945– II. Reed, Roger G., 1950–
III. Title.
    NA9127.B68M67 2012
    307.1'216097447—dc23
                                                                                2012031167

British Library Cataloguing-in-Publication Data
A catalogue record for this book is available from the British Library.

Frontispiece: Aerial view of Brookline. Photograph by Alex McLean.

Dedicated to

Elizabeth C. Morgan

Greer Hardwicke

And the Two: Isabel Brewster Cushing and Alyce Margaret Cushing

Contents

Preface

The subject of this book is the development of Brookline, Massachusetts, a wealthy suburb of Boston that successfully resisted annexation by the expanding metropolis, unlike many other satellite communities. The story is noteworthy, owing both to the particular beauty of this place and the constellation of nationally prominent design practitioners who lived and worked here during a critical period of its growth. Among those based in Brookline, several talented protagonists stand out, including the horticulturalist Charles Sprague Sargent, the architect Henry Hobson Richardson, and the landscape architects Frederick Law Olmsted Sr., his son and namesake, Rick, and his stepson, John Charles.

A recently commissioned report for the Frederick Law Olmsted National Historic Site by Keith N. Morgan, Elizabeth Hope Cushing, and Roger G. Reed provided the basis for this book, which greatly enlarges our understanding of the role of these individuals in the history of town planning in Brookline and beyond. *Community by Design* also provides an analysis of the Brookline iteration of the Olmsted office, which was distinctly different from the one that preceded it in New York City. We see at close range how projects came into the office, how they were managed, and how a training program for new practitioners was established, in some measure influenced by the atelier system run by H. H. Richardson. This book thus constitutes a critical contribution to the Olmsted literature.

The authors argue that it was both Brookline and its inhabitants that drew Olmsted Sr. to a town that was widely regarded as one of America's loveliest. The charms of the suburb had been touted in a lot auction notice circulating forty years before Olmsted's move there in 1883, and they had not changed much in the interim. "The situation is delightful, commanding a full view of the city, and connected with a rural spot that is unequaled in the country." Olmsted also appreciated the efficiency of the Brookline city fathers—he claimed that he was sold when he observed the town's snow removal crew at work on a Saturday.

The authors make an equally persuasive case that the founder of the modern profession of landscape architecture was drawn to Brookline to be closer to H. H. Richardson, with whom he had enjoyed professional and personal ties for decades. Olmsted relished collaboration, and in Richardson he found a robust source of inspiration. The opposite was true as well. Neither man would have been the artist he eventually became without this relationship. The authors also document the Olmsted firm's work with many Brookline-based architects beyond Richardson and his successor firm, Shepley, Rutan & Coolidge.

Throughout, they demonstrate the myriad ways in which the Olmsted office used Brookline to test its emerging planning principles, helping guide the town in its sometimes fraught development, realized through new roads, housing enclaves, parks, estates, home grounds, and institutions, including The Country Club, one of the first in the nation. The practitioners employed by the firm—a roster that included (at various times) Charles Eliot, Henry Codman, Olmsted Sr., Olmsted Jr., John Charles Olmsted, Arthur Shurcliff, Warren H. Manning, and others—were among the nation's finest. The sources and inspirations for their work in Brookline and beyond will be much better understood as a result of this volume.

We are very grateful to the National Park Service for their cooperation in our transformation of the NPS report into a richly illustrated book. Myra Harrison and Lee Farrow Cook, superintendent and site manager of the Frederick Law Olmsted National Historic Site, enthusiastically helped throughout the publication process. We thank the Friends of Fairsted for their financial support from its earliest stages; LALH is honored to have been the first recipient of a Friends of Fairsted grant. We are also very grateful to the Graham Foundation for Advanced Studies in the Fine Arts, the Hubbard Educational Foundation, and Susan L. Klaus, a director of LALH, all of whom provided generous underwriting.

I am greatly indebted to the authors, Keith N. Morgan, Elizabeth Hope Cushing, and Roger G. Reed, for bringing this project to LALH and for their tireless work on securing illustrations for it. I also thank Amanda Heller for her editing of the revised manuscript and Jessica Dawson, special projects coordinator for LALH, who oversaw the administration of the illustration program. I thank Michele Clark, archivist at Fairsted, who supplied critical assistance in obtaining the scans of photographs and plans. I am grateful to Jonathan D. Lippincott for his inspired book design, Mary Bellino for her editorial management, Martin White for his fine index, and Carol Betsch for her deeply grounded perspective on publishing.

As LALH celebrates its twentieth anniversary, it is striking how far this organization has come since its founding in 1992. None of it would have been possible without the support of the LALH staff, authors, editors, photographers, book designers, advisers, board of directors—past and present—and the staff of the University of Massachusetts Press, particularly the director, Bruce Wilcox. It seems apt that we mark this milestone with a volume that illuminates the richness of collaboration, as well as the origins and influence of the nation's most important office.

Robin Karson
Executive Director
Library of American Landscape History

Acknowledgments

A project of this scale could not be accomplished without the advice, assistance, and guidance of many people. The authors would first thank the National Park Service for asking the questions that led to the report on which this book is based. In particular, we are indebted to Myra Harrison, Betsy Igleheart, Paul Weinbaum, Lee Farrow Cook, Alan Banks, Jill Trebbe, Michele Clark, and Michael Dosch. Susan Ferrentino of the Organization of American Historians attempted nobly to keep the project on track.

Greer Hardwicke of the Brookline Preservation Commission has been an invaluable and enthusiastic supporter of this effort. She constantly and happily answered questions and shared information from the archives of the commission and the files of the Brookline Public Library. The staff of the library was also very helpful, especially Anne Clark. At the Frederick Law Olmsted Papers in Washington, D.C., Charles Beveridge arranged for material to be reproduced and generously shared the knowledge of his lifelong scholarship on Frederick Law Olmsted Sr. and the Olmsted firm. Ethan Carr, associate editor of the volume of the Frederick Law Olmsted Papers addressing the Boston years, was also an important adviser and friend to this project. We are grateful, as always, to Mary Daniels at the Frances Loeb Library, Harvard University, for advice and assistance. Lorna Condon at Historic New England; Sheila Conner at the Arnold Arboretum; Mary Haegert at the Houghton Library, Harvard University; Carol Bundy in generously sharing photographs of Lowell's Sevels from her collection; Russell Flinchum at the Century Association Archives; Charlene Lawless at The Country Club, Brookline; and William Dwyer at the First Parish Church, Brookline, have all offered considerable help with the research and the illustrations. Eliza McClellen of Maps@Work provided the clear and accurate cartography.

Boston University students Natania Remba, Gilan Bilal-Gore, Jackson Miller, and Casey McNeill provided assistance with research and with the production of the book. Arleen Arzigian and Susan Rice of the Visual Resources Center were helpful throughout the process.

We are deeply grateful to Robin Karson and the Library of American Landscape History for choosing to publish this volume and for guiding its production so adroitly. The book has benefited from the excellent editorial services of Mary Bellino, the manuscript editing of Amanda Heller, the image management of Jessica Dawson, the proofreading of Carol Betsch, the indexing of Martin White, and the handsome design of Jonathan Lippincott, for all of which we are deeply grateful. We also wish to thank the University of Massachusetts staff, especially Boston editor Brian Halley, director Bruce Wilcox, and production manager Jack Harrison. Finally, we thank James F. O'Gorman and Susan Klaus for their detailed and helpful reviews. Having their support for this effort has meant a great deal to all three authors.

COMMUNITY BY DESIGN

INTRODUCTION

Initially commissioned by the Frederick Law Olmsted National Historic Site of the National Park Service through the Organization of American Historians, this volume examines the impact of the Olmsted firm of landscape architects on the development of Brookline, Massachusetts. Frederick Law Olmsted Sr. relocated his home and office from New York City to the Boston suburb of Brookline in 1883. Until the departure of his son and namesake, Frederick Law Olmsted Jr., for California in 1936, the firm played a dynamic and influential role in the physical changes of this elite suburb. This book focuses on the work of the firm during approximately a half century of involvement in and direction of public and private projects in the town. To assist the Park Service in the interpretation of the site and the firm, particular attention has been paid to the design work for friends and neighbors in the immediate vicinity of Fairsted, the Olmsted home and office at 99 Warren Street.

At the community scale, the chapters that follow assess the Olmsted office's contributions to town planning and the design of boulevards and parkways, residential subdivisions, institutional grounds, and private estates and gardens throughout Brookline. We selected the sites and projects that we felt were either influential or representative of broad patterns, or both. The archival base for such a study is rich and deep, including the firm's drawing and photograph collection housed at Fairsted and the Frederick Law Olmsted Sr. and Olmsted Associates collections of correspondence and reports at the Library of Congress. Because of the Olmsteds' close personal and professional ties to other designers and horticulturalists living in Brookline, a nexus of connections has been studied to see how the Olmsted office members and others in the Green Hill neighborhood and beyond influenced both Brookline, which defined itself as the richest town in the world in the late nineteenth century, and other communities across the Commonwealth of Massachusetts and the nation. The firm both reinforced a pattern of town management and landscape development that was established when Olmsted arrived in Brookline and assisted the town in accepting more intensive development in relation to the adjacent central city of Boston.

Suburbs matter in America. The 2000 United States Census documented that 50 percent of Americans were living in suburban communities.[1] The continued outward sprawl of most metropolitan areas has transformed the United States into a suburban nation, even as a housing-based recession and a continuing energy crisis have brought the viability of this paradigm into question and more intense urban development has become a leading trend. Scholarly and popular debate about the cultural significance and environmental impact of suburbia remains intense. Therefore, reexamining one of the country's most lauded and influential suburbs, and the role that the locally based and nationally dominant landscape architecture and planning firm founded by Frederick Law Olmsted and his successors had in its creation, is especially timely.

The history of Brookline as a suburb attracted much interest in the mid-1980s but has been little studied since then. The Boston historian Sam Bass Warner invigorated the field of urban history in 1962 with the publication of *Streetcar Suburb: The Process of Growth in Boston, 1870–1900,* although he focused on Roxbury, Dorchester, and West Roxbury, the corridor of communities extending south and east from central Boston and south of Brookline.[2] As the book's title suggests, he argued that new patterns of transportation—changing Boston from a walking city to one ultimately served by electrified trolley lines—facilitated metropolitan expansion and the evolution of the suburbs. He influenced a generation of historians who adopted his basic argument or attempted to refine it.

For Brookline, Ronald Dale Karr's 1981 dissertation, "The Evolution of an Elite Suburb: Community Structure and Control in Brookline, Massachusetts, 1770–1900," provides a wealth of information but is not generally available to the wider public.[3] In 1985 two scholars advanced the argument on the position of the suburb in American culture with contrasting works. Henry C. Binford's study *The First Suburbs: Residential Communities on the Boston Periphery, 1815–1860* carried on Warner's concern with the role of transportation methods and systems in the definition of suburbia, focusing on the early suburban elements of communities around the Boston basin, especially Cambridge and Somerville in the first half of the nineteenth century.[4] More comprehensive was Kenneth T. Jackson's *Crabgrass Frontier: The Suburbanization of the United States,* which paid close attention to the role that Brookline played as a model for other suburbanization efforts throughout the nineteenth century and well into the twentieth.[5] In 1986 the Brandeis University historian David Hackett Fischer edited an anthology of papers from his research seminar titled "Brookline: The Social History of a Suburban Town, 1705–1850," in which he argued for the distinctive nature of this "town within a city" which "from the very start . . . functioned as a tax shelter for affluent Bostonians."[6]

It seemed to many historians that the essential nature of the suburb, or at least the nineteenth-century suburb, had been defined in these works by the mid-1980s. More recent scholarship has focused on later suburban development, especially the nature of suburbia since the Second World War, and has sought to privilege the role of racial and ethnic minorities and of the poor in creating their own suburban domains. One notable exception is Michael Rawson's *Eden on the Charles: The Making of Boston* (2010), an excellent environmental history of nineteenth-century Boston.[7] In his chapter "Inventing the Suburbs," Rawson pairs Roxbury and Brookline as two similar suburban communities that made different choices: unlike Roxbury, Brookline opposed annexation to Boston, provided the same services as the central city, and invented a compromise form of representative town meeting that allowed closely held community control of its future.

Although Olmsted's national reputation was based in part on his pioneering work as a planner of model suburbs and subdivisions, relatively little attention has been devoted to these planning types within the Olmsted scholarship. Scholars have focused on the Olmsted firm's subdivision activities in suburbs whose planning it controlled totally. The design of Riverside, Illinois (1868–69), a suburban community that Olmsted planned with his then-partner Calvert Vaux, remains a widely recognized landmark in the history of city and regional planning.[8] Susan Klaus has published a monograph on Forest Hills Gardens, the work of Frederick Law Olmsted Jr. on Long Island, which documents the evolution of the Olmsted firm's ideas in response to the Garden City movement in England and other European planning concepts of the turn of the twentieth century.[9] For Frederick Law Olmsted Sr.'s role in the development of the various subdivision and public projects in Brookline, Cynthia Zaitzevsky provided an initial study in an essay published by the Brookline Historical Society in 1979.[10] Some prominent historians have assumed that Brookline at large was Olmsted's work. For example, Kenneth Jackson writes: "Olmsted, and his partner, Calvert Vaux, laid out sixteen suburbs, among them Brookline and Chestnut Hill in Massachusetts, Sudbrook and Roland Park in Maryland, and Yonkers and Tarrytown Heights in New York. His first and most influential residential creation was Riverside."[11] Even though this statement is technically inaccurate, Brookline is in many ways the work of Frederick Law Olmsted and his partners and successors. The Olmsted office, in its various incarnations, received over 150 commissions in Brookline from the early 1880s until 1936, when Frederick Law Olmsted Jr. moved to California.[12] These projects included planning studies, roadway corridors, subdivision plans, estate and garden projects, and institutional schemes that defined the character and qualities of Brookline as a place both physically and psychologically. To understand more deeply how central the Olmsted office was to the evolution of the community at large, this book seeks to read at close grain the seminal and typical examples of the work of the firm from its earliest Brookline projects until the period of the Great Depression.

There are other basic goals that this volume is designed to address. As part of the interpretation plan for the Fairsted property, the Park Service seeks to understand why Frederick Law Olmsted Sr. moved his family and his business from 209 West Forty-sixth Street in New York City to 99 Warren Street in Brookline. Henry Hobson Richardson has frequently been cited as the principal reason for the move. How closely did these men, their assistants, and their families interact both before and after they had relocated from New York to Brookline? What other motivations did Brookline and its extraordinary inhabitants provide for this change? How did the Green Hill neighborhood where they settled nurture the future of the firm, the family, and the profession of landscape architecture?

On a larger scale, how fully did the Olmsted office determine the development of Brookline during this crucial half century from 1880 to 1936? What networks of private individuals, public institutions, and municipal authorities embraced the Olmsted office members and enlisted their talents in the development of the town? How different is Brookline as a physical space because of the presence in the community of the nation's leading landscape designers? In what ways did the Olmsted office members' experiences in Brookline translate into designs, programs, and policies with impacts well beyond the borders of town? How did members of the firm not only design but also manage Brookline as an evolving model community? In asking these questions, we must remember that both the firm and the community changed substantially during the years being examined. The population of Brookline increased more than fivefold during these years, requiring the kind of careful planning that the Olmsted office constantly espoused. And the ideals of Frederick Law Olmsted Sr. were nurtured but significantly altered by his son, and by all of the interns, assistants, and partners who pursued the practice of landscape architecture at 99 Warren Street.

One

BROOKLINE BEFORE OLMSTED

rookline seems to have been predestined to become an influential suburb
and a likely home for Frederick Law Olmsted. From the colonial period
forward, circumstances of location, topography, and economic, political,
and social structure coalesced to create an environment in which the suburban
ideal emerged. By the late nineteenth century, as the home of the first country
club in the United States, Brookline could boast the status of a leading example for
America's affluent suburbs. Indeed, its staunch resistance to annexation by Boston
made it an island of privilege surrounded on three sides by Boston neighborhoods.
Nevertheless, the Brookline story is far from simple.

Surrounded originally by the Charles River estuary to the north and Boston's
saltwater Back Bay to the east, the land that would become Brookline was defined
by a series of seven drumlin hills left behind by the retreat of the last ice age. The
Muddy River was the principal waterway along the southern and eastern edge of
the area. This varied but gentle topography became desirable for agriculture, and
the riverine districts with their salt marsh hay ideal for raising cattle.

Leading members of the Massachusetts Bay Colony discovered the advantages
of this area, originally called Muddy River, almost immediately, claiming grants of
farmland here beginning in 1635. It remained, however, an agricultural extension
of Boston, as seventeenth-century farmers traveled to Roxbury to attend Puritan
meetings. After several unsuccessful efforts, a group of local residents persuaded
the Massachusetts Bay Colony to allow them to incorporate as a separate town,
named Brookline, in 1705.[1] The bridge at Muddy River (now Brookline Village)
attracted those wishing to escape the Shawmut Peninsula in the colonial period.
Here the Punch Bowl Tavern was the established focus of village life by the mid-
eighteenth century. Just as the Muddy River crossing defined the commercial

heart of the community, the civic and religious functions were removed in 1711 to a meetinghouse at Warren and Walnut streets, which became the official town center.

During the colonial period, a number of prominent families emerged as the principal owners of farmland, leaders of the established church, and influential figures in local politics. According to the historian Ronald Karr, three families—the Gardners, the Whites, and the Winchesters—became the core of the economic and political establishment in the seventeenth and eighteenth centuries.[2] By 1770, 10 percent of the property owners in Brookline controlled nearly half of the taxable assets of the town, indicating the emergence of an ensconced upper class.[3] These families depended on farming as the chief source of their wealth, although immigrants to Brookline from Boston and beyond established summer residences in a slowly developing pattern of external wealth controlling a substantial proportion of local real estate.

The transition from a subsistence agricultural economy to agriculture and horticulture as a gentlemanly avocation began to occur in Brookline even before the American Revolution.[4] As one historian notes: "By the second decade of the nineteenth century, . . . some form of rural pursuits seemed almost de rigueur for the elite. One Bostonian after another purchased a rural residence. Probably the most popular location for a country seat was the little town of Brookline, which quickly became, according to one Bostonian, a neighborhood of 'tasteful pleasure grounds . . . occupied by a cluster of refined and cultured families.'"[5] In 1792, when the Massachusetts Society for Promoting Agriculture was established, many leaders of the organization resided in Brookline, including estate owners George Cabot, Thomas Handasyd Perkins, Stephen Higginson, Thomas C. Amory, Richard Sullivan, Thomas Lee, Nathaniel Ingersoll, and Theodore Lyman Jr., all of whom had made their money in Boston or elsewhere.[6] Sullivan, for example, who served the society as recording secretary (1811–12), corresponding secretary (1823–1827 and 1830–1835), and trustee (1828–29), purchased a Brookline estate in about 1810.[7] The gentlemen farmers used their Brookline estates for personal pleasure and to pursue agriculture in a scientific manner that they hoped would benefit their fellow citizens by example.[8] This trend was reinforced by the founding in 1829 of the Massachusetts Horticultural Society; Brookline farmers and estate owners again served as leaders in this enterprise.[9] For those who were especially interested in fruit trees and ornamental gardening, the society provided information and a network of fellow enthusiasts.

One of the institutions that maintained an upper-class Protestant status quo throughout the first half of the nineteenth century was First Parish Church, with its long-serving minister, the Reverend John Pierce, from 1796 to 1849. Even after the disestablishment of the Congregational Church in 1833, Pierce used his pulpit to maintain core values and community structure. Parishioners were encouraged to pursue "compulsory excellence" and to practice restraint in their personal and business dealings.[10] Pierce extended the influence of First Parish and the ideals of his flock to public institutions and the political realm. He also carefully balanced the interests of Brookline's elite, who were primarily summer residents, with those of the more locally focused upper middle class. Whereas a small number of long-term local farming families of substantial wealth had determined town policies throughout the colonial period, from the federal period onward the elite class, with its attachments to Boston, were not as interested in local politics. Instead, a class composed of successful farmers, businessmen, and professionals came to dominate the political vacuum left by the retreating colonial families. They maintained a uniform point of view and community objectives into the twentieth century. These were the forces who controlled town hall, the public school system, and all elements of public life. They also worked hard to control new development.

The establishment of a more general suburban mentality coalesced early in Brookline. The construction of a milldam across the Back Bay in 1821 facilitated the exodus from Boston of those who could afford a daily commute. Key financial backers of this enterprise also purchased the Sewell Farm at the Brookline end of the milldam causeway and held the land for future development.[11] A stage line connecting Brookline Village to Boston began operating in 1816, and omnibus service twice a day was added by 1839.[12] In the 1830s Boston became the national leader in the popularization of the railroad, with the Boston and Worcester line passing along Brookline's northern edge. A station was not constructed in Brookline until 1845 at Cottage Farm, with a spur line to Brookline Village finally opened in 1848. These methods of public transportation were actually quite expensive, so they served primarily successful businessmen who had the funds and the time for the commute into the city. Nevertheless, they encouraged development along the corridors served by these systems.

At around this time Brookline gained its first planned subdivision, possibly the first in the nation,[13] when Thomas Aspinwall Davis (1798–1845) developed Linden Place (now Linden Street), commissioning Alexander Wadsworth, a noted civil engineer, to lay out the streets, lots, and parks on twenty acres of his property, a farm just outside Brookline Village off Harvard Street. He sold twenty-four of the twenty-seven lots at auction in 1843. Expensive houses were built here, including Davis's own residence, and it remained a desirable address until the 1880s, when properties were further subdivided and multiple-family houses were built. The original auction notice described the potential of the development: "The situation is delightful, commanding a full view of the city, and connected with a rural spot that is unequaled in the country. In connection with the retired and beautiful location, is the consideration of the short distance from the city, affording to

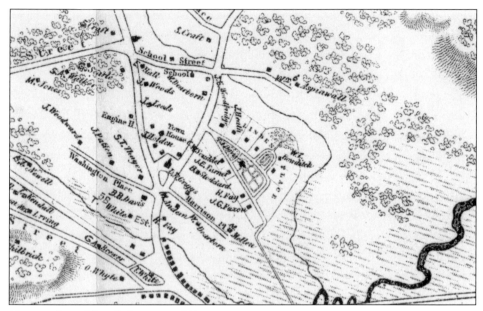

Fig. 1.1. Plan of the Lindens, Brookline, 1843. Courtesy Brookline Preservation Commission.

the man of business an agreeable ride after the duties of the day, and a pleasing exercise to the gentleman of leisure. Omnibuses run at accommodating hours."[14] Wadsworth's plan included a triangular park near Harvard Street and a horseshoe-shaped park at the center of the subdivision (fig. 1.1). Davis, who was elected mayor of Boston the following year, attracted prominent business leaders to his real estate development. Although the lots were sold at public auction, the Lindens was a very restrictive environment. Karr notes, "The deed received by the buyers at Linden Place in 1843 required that all buildings be erected at least thirty feet away from the street and 'that the only buildings to be erected or placed upon said parcels shall be dwelling houses and their appurtenances exclusive of all yards, shops, or other conveniences for manufacturing or mechanical purposes.'"[15]

Subdivision of former farmland would remain the common pattern for suburban development in Brookline and across the country. Before the establishment of zoning legislation, the desire to control those who bought the land and how they used it could be realized only through deed covenants. Hiring a civil engineer or landscape gardener to lay out the property as Wadsworth did in this instance would also become a common procedure. An owner building a residence for himself was typical of the general trend as well. Thus the Lindens codified the pattern of subdivision that would be refined, expanded, and repeated across the evolving landscape.

More expansive than the Lindens were two planned suburban communities in the northeast corner of Brookline at Longwood (1849) and Cottage Farm (1850), developed by the Sears and Lawrence families (fig. 1.2). [16] David Sears, one of the wealthiest property owners in Boston, recognized the potential for development of this marshy area of Brookline due to its close proximity to the city. He purchased a section of the former Sewell Farm in the early 1820s, eventually amassing land stretching from the Muddy River to the Charles River, incorporating five hundred acres. Sears chose the name Longwood, after Longue Bois, Napoleon's last prison on St. Helena,[17] and modeled it on English precedents in urban planning. He proceeded slowly with his plans for development and eventually hired Alexander Wadsworth to assist with the scheme.

Sears, "a man of vision, wealth, and taste," according to Linda Olson Pehlke, set a standard that was to persist in the large estate grounds and suburban developments in Brookline.[18] According to the horticulturalist Charles Sprague Sargent, during Sears's "numerous and often long visits in Europe . . . [he] learned the importance of planting trees."[19] Sears, among other large landholders, not only established a handsome private estate but set another precedent as well: between 1826 and 1838 he laid out streets and "four squares or small parks," one of them being the Longwood Mall, three hundred yards long by thirty-five yards wide,

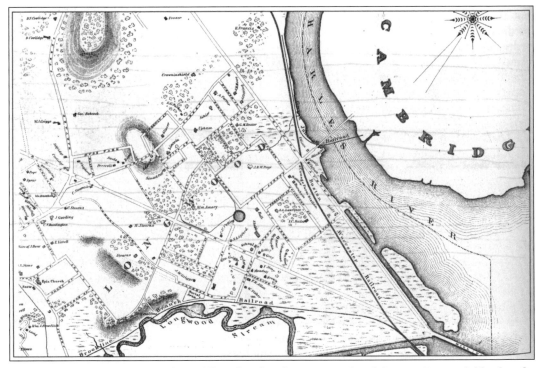

Fig. 1.2. Detail of an 1855 map of Brookline showing the Longwood and Cottage Farm neighborhoods. Note the connection of the milldam to Boston in the lower right corner, the Boston and Albany Railroad line along the Charles River shores, and the branch line to Brookline Village along the bottom of the plan. Courtesy Brookline Preservation Commission.

allowing for the possibility of discreet and seemly residential development.[20] At one point Sears noted, "In addition to 14,000 trees planted at Longwood I have ordered Messrs. Cunningham & Sons in Liverpool, England, to ship me in February next 300 European Sycamore, 3000 English and Dutch Elms, 1000 Oaks assorted and 1000 Norway Maple."[21] Although many of Sears's trees have disappeared through natural and man-induced attrition, the Longwood Mall retains some of his original large and handsome European beech trees. "These," according to Sargent, writing in 1925, "are the finest exotic trees which have been planted in Greater Boston and probably form the finest grove of the European Beech in the United States."[22] In 1982 Cornelia Hanna McMurtrie observed, "These impressive . . . trees are informally grouped, creating spaces of varying sizes and allowing passage and viewing throughout the area."[23]

Sears built a house for himself at Longwood in 1842–43 and gave lots to and constructed houses for his six children here. He even erected a nondenominational union church, Christ's Church, Longwood, to the designs of Arthur Gilman in 1860–61. As at Linden Place, deed restrictions prevented unwanted development, including the prohibition of sale to any "negro or native of Ireland."[24]

North of Beacon Street and the Longwood district, Amos A. Lawrence, head of one of Boston's most influential industrial families, acquired land in 1850 for a country home with an easy commute to the city.[25] He called his suburban retreat Cottage Farm and hired George Dexter to build a stone Gothic Revival residence there (fig. 1.3). Across the street Dexter built a smaller Gothic house for Lawrence's daughter Emily and her husband, Thomas Hall. He retired from practice after completing these houses, perhaps his most important surviving commissions.

Nearby Frederick Sears erected a third stone cottage (fig. 1.4) in 1850–51 on land given him by his father, David Sears. The architect is unknown, but the house resembles the demolished David Sears house (1843) by Edward Shaw. Though also constructed of stone, the Frederick Sears house characterizes more fully the American interpretations of the Gothic Revival than did the earlier buildings by Dexter.

Amos Lawrence built several brick single-family houses for rental purposes in the vicinity of his own house, such as the early (1853) example of the mansard style at 96 Ivy Street and the Gothic Revival cottage at 89 Carlton Street. He was not pleased with the nondenominational church built by Sears and hired Alexander Esty to design a stone Gothic Revival Episcopal church, the Church of Our Saviour, in 1867–68 at the corner of Carlton and Monmouth streets. By the 1870s Lawrence had accepted the desirability of denser development and erected four five–row house units. His civil engineer, Ernest Bowditch, created a small green mall in the center of Monmouth Court, the cul-de-sac off Monmouth Street. After Lawrence's death in 1885, prominent turn-of-the-century firms designed many houses in the Cottage Farm neighborhood. In the case of both the Sears develop-

Fig. 1.3. Amos Lawrence house, Cottage Farm, 1850, George Dexter, architect. Courtesy Historic New England.

Fig. 1.4. Frederick Sears house, Cottage Farm, 1850– 51. *Godey's Lady's Book.*

ment of Longwood and the Lawrence development of Cottage Farm, the owners built their own rural retreats, constructed houses for their children, and sold other lots to associates. Sears began to sell to others under covenants sooner than Lawrence, who controlled most of his land until his death.

On land adjacent to where Frederick Law Olmsted and his family would settle in 1883, another early planned real estate venture arose on Fairmount, a hillside south of the Brookline Reservoir, which was completed in 1849. The construction of the reservoir was actually the motivation for this subdivision, which enjoyed views over the water. A group of speculators, including Charles Stearns and William Dearborn, laid out two streets, Hillside Place and Lakeside Place, which formed a gentle oval across the property (fig. 1.5). Limitations on commercial development may have been included with the early deeds.[26] The owners of nearby estates acquired some of the lots for residences for their servants.[27] Although no public landscape features were included in this scheme, the adjacent public reservoir made such amenities unnecessary.

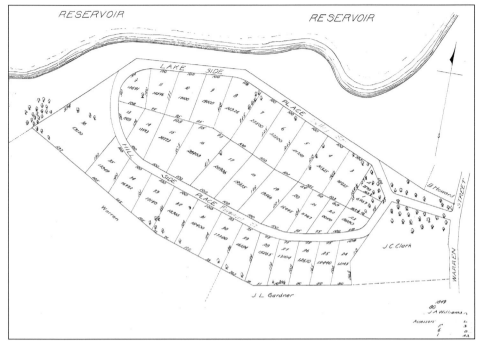

Fig. 1.5. Plan of the Fairmount subdivision overlooking the Brookline Reservoir, 1849.
Courtesy Brookline Preservation Commission.

While these four early subdivision examples begun in the 1840s and 1850s established important precedents for the future, most of the community, beyond developments surrounding the commercial core at Brookline Village, remained rural and agricultural. Diverging from the suburbanization story of many Boston area communities, Brookline did not develop many local industries, and wealthy residents continued to divide their time between Boston and Brookline throughout most of the nineteenth century. With the arrival of the railroad and omnibus service, however, a group of new arrivals to Brookline began to upset the carefully controlled environment inherited from the colonial era. The Irish potato famine of the mid-1840s brought many immigrants to Boston, and they began to seek work on the farms of Brookline. In addition to living on various estates and farms, both as day laborers and as household servants, the Irish immigrants were forced into two small areas near Brookline Village—Whiskey Point, off Cypress Street west of Brookline Village, and the Marsh, between the railroad line and Western Avenue. Their numbers grew rapidly at mid-century, and Brookline soon started to exhibit a demographic mix of extremes in wealth and poverty.[28] The town continued to grow in size, more than tripling in population between 1850 and 1885, through both working-class immigration and the attraction of new upper-income residents.[29]

In response to this pressure, a new phase in real estate subdivision created consortiums of multiple owners buying land as a shared investment. An early example was the Brookline Land Company, a group of individuals from Brookline, Boston, and Roxbury who purchased an eighty-acre farm south of Brookline Village in 1860 and proceeded to develop the property over the next two and a half decades. Though lacking the single-proprietor role of a Davis, Sears, or Lawrence, this group still exercised great caution in the sale of the lots to individuals and institutions. Often, investors continued to build residences for themselves on the land. The development of the Brookline Land Company proceeded slowly enough—interrupted by both the Civil War and the recession of 1873—that ultimately Olmsted played a role in the design of the final stages of this area, especially the connection to the Riverway and Leverett Pond sections of his Boston park system scheme and the initial siting of the grounds of the Free Hospital for Women to coordinate with the adjacent parkway and Leverett Pond. Later development corporations in Brookline, many initially envisioned before Olmsted came to town, frequently turned to the landscape architect for guidance, either alone or in consultation with other established civil engineers such as Alexander Wadsworth, Ernest Bowditch, or the firm of Aspinwall & Lincoln. These included the Aspinwall Land Company, the Goddard Land Company, the Fisher Hill Land Company, and the Chestnut Hill Land Company (see chapter 6). Olmsted certainly changed the physical character of these projects—creating a comprehensive system that ties into surrounding districts and introducing a more natural pattern of road design to coordinate with the varied topography—in comparison with the orthogonal schemes undertaken before his arrival, but the business and political systems for subdivision had been firmly established decades before he moved to 99 Warren Street. While the scions of old Brookline families controlled most of these land development firms, their shares traded openly on the Boston Stock Exchange.

Opening new land for subdivision and carefully controlled development required close coordination and cooperation with the local political establishment. As Karr observes: "During the second half of the nineteenth century the upper middle class dominated Brookline. Accounting for a third of the town's households, this class largely controlled the political and economic life of the town, as well as set the standards that many of lesser status also followed. Drawn almost exclusively from old Protestant Yankee stock, the members of the upper middle class shared a common culture and traditions that clearly set them apart from the Irish Catholic working class with whom they shared the town."[30] The upper middle class achieved a political balance with the Brahmin elite and with the Irish Catholic working class, who generally voted as their employers instructed. Those in charge of town government worked closely with individuals who wished to subdivide their land, underscoring the common assumptions that kept Brookline an exclusive and well-controlled community for the wealthy. As new developments proliferated, additional members of the upper middle class or the professional community settled there, reinforcing the existing social and political structure.

This unanimity of vision helped preserve Brookline from annexation to the neighboring metropolis. Between 1868 and 1873 Boston aggressively acquired surrounding communities. Offering economies in the provision of municipal services such as water, sewer, and electricity, Boston brought Roxbury, Dorchester, Charlestown, West Roxbury, and Brighton within its political control during these years. As the adjacent suburbs cast off their independence, pressure grew in Brookline to join the common pattern. In 1872 the first of many campaigns was launched to annex Brookline to Boston. It was soundly defeated then and again in 1873, 1875, 1879, and 1880, when the desire of the majority to remain a separate incorporated town was fully accepted by even the most ardent annexationist. The role of future subdivision was apparent in the pattern of who proposed and who opposed annexation. Large property owners in the northern sections of the city saw annexation as a logical step in providing the services required to make their land ready for sale and development. The Brahmins and their working-class dependents supported the political establishment in opposing this dramatic step. Those who were against annexation were not necessarily anti-growth; they simply wanted to control new development, as had their Brookline predecessors.

By the 1870s, when local newspapers began to appear as a voice for these discussions, most Brookline residents admired the form and character of the community while remaining anxious about its future development. As one resident noted in the *Brookline Chronicle* of August 16, 1879: "Brookline is often called the Garden of Boston, so cultivated, shady, and floral, so rich in broad estates and tasteful in its residences. Many years ago it was all this, and more, for it then was not as now injured by Progress (so called), which stretches its mercenary hands over the country, leveling hills, filling valleys, destroying trees, blasting rocks, longing to transform all that is valuable in nature to its own uninteresting level." This critic continued, complaining about the streets "defaced . . . by . . . ordinary wooden buildings, packed close together and filled to overflowing," lamenting, "There seems to be a mania for destroying everything that is old and beautiful or natural among a certain class of minds."[31]

One frequently observed problem was the disparity of wealth in the community and the lack of a solid middle class. George W. Carnes, a Brookline resident, remarked in the *Brookline Chronicle* of May 29, 1875:

> The composition of the people of Brookline is somewhat peculiar. I think
> it will be readily admitted that the extremes of classification in society are

more apparent in our town than in most of the other towns on our borders. Those who are accounted wealthy, on the one hand, and the hardworking laboring class on the other. . . . [T]is true, we have in our midst many who are accounted neither rich nor poor, but of this middle class, I think will be a general agreement that the relative proportion or percentage of this class, is much less in Brookline than elsewhere.[32]

An economically divided but politically unified Brookline managed to negotiate growth in a manner that reinforced the status quo at both extremes. Referring to Brookline as a "Boston suburb with grandiose pretensions," the "self-styled 'richest town in the world,'" Kenneth Jackson summarizes the social contrasts there in the late nineteenth century:

> As the most prominent of the region's independent suburbs, Brookline attracted a galaxy of the rich and famous—architect Henry Hobson Richardson, landscape gardener Frederick Law Olmsted, financial publisher Henry V. Poor, and poet Amy Lowell, among them. Alongside these prosperous members of the upper crust, however, lived a poor, blue-collar, first-generation Irish Catholic community. In 1870, when 10 percent of Brookline taxpayers controlled more than 70 percent of the assessed property, less than 25 percent of the populace was in executive, professional or managerial positions. The unskilled Irishmen found plenty of work hauling lumber, grading streets, tending lawns, and digging trenches.[33]

By now two Brooklines had emerged geographically as well: a northern district of more intensive development and a southern zone of larger estates, roughly divided by Boylston Street (Route 9). As elsewhere, streetcar lines brought linear growth to the northern community. The West End Street Railway (1889) opened Beacon Street, the dominant east-west boulevard of the northern section of Brookline, to more intensive development, including row houses and apartment buildings along a corridor to be laid out by Frederick Law Olmsted. Although single-family homes predominated, some two-family and three-decker enclaves sprang up to serve other clienteles. The ethnic mix also increased as first Irish and later Jewish families moved into northern Brookline. Meanwhile, The Country Club became the symbol of southern Brookline and the focus of large private property holdings in the surrounding areas. Substantial lots with professionally designed landscapes complemented houses of exceptional scale and architectural quality. As the passage of the graduated income tax (1913) and restrictions on immigration in the 1920s made servants harder to find and maintain, the estates gradually shrank in size or were divided for institutional uses.

But in the early 1880s, when Frederick Law Olmsted decided to move his family and his landscape architecture practice from New York City to suburban Brookline, a community still existed that was ideally suited to his personal and professional interests. Like his friend Henry Hobson Richardson, who had made a similar migration nearly a decade before, Olmsted was a professional, a member of the dominant upper middle class, even if many of his clients, some of whom would be his immediate neighbors, were drawn from the elite. He arrived in a community that would provide continuous and diverse opportunities. Brookline understood the lessons that Olmsted had been preaching as a landscape architect in New York and was ready for the sophisticated practices of planning, design, and horticulture that he would bring to his commissions. He had been raised in the same privileged Congregationalist environment as his neighbors in the Green Hill area and beyond. Even though he was an advocate for the advantages of democracy, he did not oppose the policies of class control or racial and ethnic exclusion that were ingrained among the elite and in the political status quo of the town.[34] He would find immediate social access to a wide range of clients and an environment that suited his personal and professional needs.

Two

OLMSTED BEFORE BROOKLINE

Among the many salient features that enhance the city of Boston, not least is the enviable amount of green space that characterizes it. In part this rich resource is the consequence of the cultural evolution that left areas such as the Boston Common open to public access despite steadily advancing development from the late seventeenth century on. The large swath of open land encircling the municipal area was, however, the result of a concerted effort on the part of nineteenth-century city fathers who understood the growing importance of urban recreational areas and green space in a rapidly expanding and increasingly inhabited urban core.

In this effort they were aided by the enlightened expertise of an outsider brought in to orchestrate the process—the first professional "landscape architect" in America, Frederick Law Olmsted (1822–1903). Olmsted's eventual move from New York to Brookline brought with it a gently seismic change in the way the citizens of Boston and the surrounding areas, including Brookline, viewed issues of open space, development, and planning. In Brookline this change was seen among the established social elite, the new financial forces, and last but not least, the general population, who were to profit from the social concerns woven into his theories of landscape.

Olmsted was an established professional long before he was first called upon to aid in the creation of an encompassing park system for Boston in the late 1860s.[1] His preparation for becoming a landscape architect, however, proved diverse and convoluted. The experiences of childhood and a formal education truncated by physical problems left him with one inviolate guiding force: his deep and abiding affection for rural scenery and the natural world around him.[2] This predilection was instilled from an early age by his parents, John and Mary Ann Olmsted, and reinforced by years of meanderings in the natural world around his home in

Fig. 2.1. Frederick Law Olmsted (*seated, right*), John Hull Olmsted (*standing, right*), and friends from Yale University. Courtesy Historic New England.

Hartford, Connecticut, family trips in rural New York, as well as forays into the White Mountains of New Hampshire.[3] "He was instinctively, persistently a rambler," wrote his friend the contemporary architectural and landscape critic Mariana Griswold Van Rensselaer (1851–1934), "spending all the time he could in long, solitary walks, when he forgot why he carried rod or gun, and was never tempted into any scientific study, but gave himself up to the silent influence of wood and field, hillside, brook, and cloud."[4]

Years after that peripatetic youth Olmsted himself observed, "The root of all my work has been an early respect for and enjoyment of scenery, and extraordinary opportunities for cultivating susceptibility to its power."[5] His parents introduced him to the English concept of the picturesque, and he pursued its theories through the writings of the eighteenth-century landscape critics and writers William Gilpin and Uvedale Price.[6] His innate predilection for the natural landscape was reinforced by contemporary conviction regarding the superiority of "naturalistic" scenery. Throughout his life Olmsted continued reading autodidactically in diverse areas, propelled by an active intellectual curiosity nourished by a lively intelligence (fig. 2.1).

Frustrated in his hopes for traditional academic training, Olmsted turned to the field of engineering. For three years he worked with the Reverend Frederick

Augustus Barton at the Phillips Academy in Andover, Massachusetts, where he learned "some of the rudiments of surveying, but spent most of his time fishing, hunting, or collecting rocks and plants," according to the historian Charles McLaughlin. "He also amused himself by drawing plans of hypothetical towns and cities. It was a period of his life which he enjoyed recalling later, maintaining that the instruction in surveying, the town planning, and the outdoor life were unwitting preparation for his later career as a landscape architect."[7]

After a brief apprenticeship in business in New York City, the twenty-one-year-old Olmsted set to sea in 1843, sailing to China.[8] The grueling conditions of his year-long voyage as an apprentice seaman ruled out a maritime vocation. His reflections on the ill-treatment of sailors hint at the social analysis that infuses his later writings. Here, too, in the eloquence of letters home, one sees the dawning of the journalistic path he was to pursue.[9]

Perhaps Olmsted's recurring medical difficulties explain John Olmsted's infinite patience with his son's mercurial professional schemes. Upon his return from China, Frederick Olmsted decided to take up scientific farming, apprenticing himself to a gentleman in Waterbury, Connecticut. In farming, Olmsted felt that he might combine his growing interest in science with his lifelong affection for the outdoors. Next he decamped to study under the agriculturist George Geddes in Syracuse. After Olmsted's apprenticeship with the enlightened and knowledgeable Geddes, his father bought him his own farm near Hartford, eventually purchasing a larger one for him in 1847 on Staten Island (fig. 2.2).

In typical fashion, the twenty-five-year-old threw himself headlong into the work, learning firsthand about the planting of crops and the practical tending of a farm. He was already displaying the ingenuity and organizational skills that would be perfected during his future professional experiences. He systematized the workers on his farm and immersed himself in local agricultural organizations, becoming secretary of the Richmond County Agricultural Society. He made innovations in matters of proper farm drainage and improved transport roads.

Fig. 2.2. The farmhouse at Staten Island, 1848, possibly drawn by Frederick Law Olmsted. Laura Roper, *FLO: A Biography* (1973).

According to McLaughlin, Olmsted read extensively during this period, being determined to transform his "dirty and somewhat disagreeable spot into a gentleman's country seat" (fig. 2.3).[10] In this he was no doubt influenced by his reading of Andrew Jackson Downing (1815–1852), the well-known Newburgh, New York, nurseryman and landscape designer whose writings on picturesque architecture and landscape—and whose assertion that landscape architecture was "an expressive, harmonious, and refined imitation" of nature—widely introduced the concept in America and made him a major tastemaker of his time.[11] Olmsted met him coincidently while visiting in Newburgh, and it was Downing who first published the young farmer in his magazine the *Horticulturist*. Olmsted, writes McLaughlin, "took to heart Downing's plea that his fellow citizens should tastefully arrange and embellish their dwellings and property for both convenience and beauty."[12]

Downing, in fact, was something of a crusader for the popularization of good taste, evincing an undying belief that it could and should be extended to all levels of society. According to his biographer David Schuyler, he "advocated the establishment of institutions of popular refinement—parks and gardens, museums,

Fig. 2.3. The Staten Island farm, ca. 1900. Courtesy Frances Loeb Library, Harvard Graduate School of Design.

libraries, and other repositories of 'intellectual and moral culture'—that would be attractive to and accessible by all citizens. Downing thus posited a vision of a society in which gentility was universal, where even the poorest working man could benefit from 'the higher realms of art, letters, science, social recreations, and enjoyments.'"[13] It should come as no surprise that Downing's democratization of culture would attract Olmsted. During his sojourn on the farm he was also reading another tastemaker of enormous importance, the English art and social critic John Ruskin (1819–1900), as well as deepening his understanding of Ralph Waldo Emerson, Thomas Carlyle, and Thomas Babington Macaulay.[14]

For two more years Olmsted devoted himself exclusively to his farm, importing fruit trees and establishing a nursery business that specialized in ornamental and shade trees. Six years away from the China voyage, however, restlessness overtook him once again. In 1850, when his brother John and a friend, Charles Loring Brace, decided to take a walking tour of England, Olmsted, overcome with envy, implored his father to send him along. The indulgent John Olmsted agreed. The impact that the trip had on Olmsted's life and career is incalculable. From the moment of the trio's spring departure, Olmsted kept extensive journals and notes on what he saw in the British Isles. He wrote animated letters home, his observations leaping off the page, combining the aesthetically compelling with the socially conscious.

The three walked in England, Scotland, and Ireland, then moved on to France, Germany, Holland, and Belgium, not returning until the autumn of 1850.[15] Almost from the moment they first docked at Liverpool, Olmsted noted and began assessing English social stratification and comparing it to social conditions in America. The dramatic discrepancy between the wealthy and the poor and the arduous lot of those without money or position increasingly occupied his thoughts as he traveled through England and the Continent.

Olmsted fell hard for the English countryside. "We stood dumb-stricken by its loveliness," he records, a sentiment he never relinquished.[16] Nowhere in all his travels, he later wrote, had he been "so charmed" as he was "continually while walking through those parts of England least distinguished and commonly least remarked upon by travelers as beautiful."[17] This "commonplace scenery," however, was difficult to capture. "Beauty, grandeur, impressiveness . . . is not often to be found in a few prominent, distinguishable features," he observed toward the end of his walking trip, "but in the manner and the unobserved materials with which these are connected and combined."[18] This subtle interaction among landscape, materials, and atmosphere would be characteristic of his own approach to landscape creation, in both large-scale public works and designs for private estates.

Years later he continued to advocate for the enduring power of the natural landscape, telling the architect Charles Platt's younger brother William, then training under Olmsted and heading off on a tour of Italy, that the formal Italian gardens did not enchant him. However, he added, "I am enthusiastic in my enjoyment of much roadside foreground scenery there in which nature contends with and is gaining upon the art of man," urging Platt to "hunt for beauty in commonplace and pleasant conditions . . . and all such things as are made lovely by growths that seem to be natural and spontaneous to the place."[19] He later wrote Andrew Jackson Downing that he had experienced "the best parts of England, spending two months travelling through it on foot, seeing the country of course to great advantage, so that I feel as if I had not merely seen the rural character but lived it, and made it *part* of me."[20]

It was in England that Olmsted had his first landscape epiphanies. Across the Mersey River from the busy port of Liverpool lay the industrial suburb of Birkenhead, and within its limits Birkenhead Park, designed by Joseph Paxton in 1843 and opened in 1847 (fig. 2.4).[21] Many of the parklands of England would impress the young American, but none did so with the force of this urban space designed and executed specifically for public use. In his 1852 publication *Walks and Talks of an American Farmer in England,* he writes of his response: "Five minutes of admiration, . . . and I was ready to admit that in democratic America there was nothing to be thought of as comparable with this People's Garden. Indeed, gardening, had here reached a perfection that I had never before dreamed of. I cannot undertake to describe the effect of so much taste and skill as had evidently been employed."

He was also gratified to observe that "the privileges of the garden were enjoyed

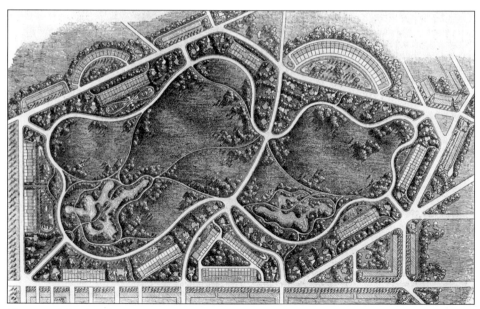

Fig. 2.4. Birkenhead Park, Birkenhead, England, 1847, designed by Joseph Paxton. It was a major influence on Olmsted's first park design. Private collection.

about equally by all classes."[22] The keen social observation he bent on England never ceased: "All this magnificent pleasure-ground is entirely, unreservedly, and for ever the people's own. The poorest British peasant is as free to enjoy it in all its parts as the British queen. More than that, the baker of Birkenhead has the pride of an OWNER of it. Is it not a grand good thing?"[23] Nevertheless, his biographer Laura Wood Roper writes that Olmsted was far from "an uncritical Anglophile." He was deeply shocked by the poverty of the underprivileged classes compared with the comfort of the well-to-do, and he had "no use, then or later, for the doctrine of laissez faire. The idea that the depressed classes should be left undisturbed in their 'degradation and supine misery' was repugnant to him."[24]

The park was not the only portion of Birkenhead that interested Olmsted. Noting that the community itself, which he called the "most important suburb of Liverpool," was growing at an unparalleled rate, he concluded, "this is greatly owning to the very liberal and enterprising policy of the land-owners," an example he recommended for "many of our own large towns. There are several public squares, and the streets and places are broad, and well paved and lighted. A considerable part of the town has been built with reference to general effect."[25] Planned suburban space was a relatively new concept, and Olmsted was on the alert.

Upon his reluctant return in October, the mantle of farmer weighed heavily on his shoulders. He began organizing his letters and journals with the intention of writing a book about his travels abroad. In the meantime, he published an article about Birkenhead Park in Downing's *Horticulturist*. Ambition to have his say asserted itself. "The fever to write had . . . attacked [him]," Roper writes. "He wanted the influence he did not command and thought he deserved."[26] He was befriended by his Staten Island neighbor, the highly respected publisher George Palmer Putnam, who introduced him into New York literary society.

Olmsted next formulated a plan to tour the South and write about it for the *New York Daily Times,* and by the end of the following year he was off on a four-month trip through the slave states. Although he opposed the Fugitive Slave Act, he was not much of an abolitionist before his departure. His was to be a dispassionate examination of the economic merits of slave labor. The conclusions he reached proved to be the very theses he had left with: that slavery was more expensive than free labor, and that the very institution deprived the laborers of any incentive, hence decreasing their productivity and well-being. It was a question not of a fundamental inferiority in blacks, as some argued, but of the conditions of their fettered lives. Furthermore, "not only was slavery doing nothing to elevate the Negro race, but it was demoralizing the white. A man could not have absolute power over others without its impairing his sense of justice."[27]

Vowing neutrality at the beginning of his journey, Olmsted could still claim in his last installment for the *Times,* "I have declared myself not to be an Abolitionist," but by that he was referring to his support for manumission as the only viable and humane solution.[28] Slavery, he had decided by the end of his tour, "*as it is*, in the vast majority of cases, is shamefully cruel, selfish and wicked. It is incredible that the tyrannical laws and customs to which the slave is *everywhere*, and *under every master*, subject, are necessary for any but the most meanly selfish and wholly ungenerous purposes."[29] He therefore concluded that there was no alternative but to abolish it: "The north must demolish the bulwark of this stronghold of evil . . . by letting the negro have a fair chance to prove his own case, to prove himself a man, entitled to the inalienable rights of a man."[30] His championing of the underclasses appears to have been color-blind. Nothing could have honed his critical skills quite as sharply as this long and extensively chronicled journey.

Back on Staten Island by the spring of 1853, he was joined by his brother John, John's wife, Mary, and their small son, who settled on the farm in hopes of ameliorating John's advancing tuberculosis. To his great joy, when the *New York Daily Times* suggested sending Olmsted back south to Texas, John came along as his companion. When Olmsted returned after nine months of travel, he immediately began writing the first of his three books on his southern journeys.[31]

Meanwhile he was acquiring a literary reputation. His old walking companion Charles Brace was now established as the director of the Children's Aid Society in New York, and through him Olmsted was further introduced into literary circles in the city. When the opportunity to buy a one-third partnership in an established and admired journal, *Putnam's Monthly Magazine*, arose, Olmsted leaped at it, his father footing the bill once again. He turned over the title of the Staten Island farm to his ailing and agriculturally hapless brother and was off to rented rooms in Manhattan. His farming days were over.

For the next two years Olmsted devoted himself to his writings and to being a partner in the publishing firm of Dix, Edwards & Company. While he gained valuable experience, both in his own literary efforts (two of his southern travels books were published during this period) and in business negotiations in the larger publishing world, Dix, Edwards eventually slid into bankruptcy, leaving Olmsted once again without regular employment.[32] Thirty-four years old, still financially dependent on his aging father, his beloved younger brother's health slipping away, he was at a low ebb.

His weary, defeated removal to an inn in rural Connecticut for the summer of 1857, ostensibly to work on his third southern travels volume, proved a transformative moment. While talking casually with Charles Wyllys Elliot, a member of the newly formed commission for Central Park in New York City, Olmsted learned that there was an opening for a superintendent to oversee its construction. Elliot suggested that he apply for the job. That Olmsted did so, won it, and subsequently went on to join forces with the immigrant English architect Cal-

Fig. 2.5. Olmsted around the time he began
work on Central Park. Courtesy National Park
Service, Frederick Law Olmsted National Historic Site.

vert Vaux to create a plan for the park is well-documented history.[33] There was
as yet, however, little obvious demonstration of the capabilities the job was to
bring out in him. Roper writes: "Nothing in his record—a farmer who had not
made his farms pay, a writer who had made nothing but reputation, a publisher
who had gone bankrupt—suggested his capacities. . . . A thoughtful reader
of Olmsted's books, however, might have suspected their writer of the vision
to grasp complex problems, the acuity to analyze them, the balance to see the
whole and the parts in proportion, and the discipline and imagination to devise
solutions" (fig. 2.5).[34]

Over the following years every aspect of Olmsted's previous preparation was
put to the test. With the invaluable partnership of Vaux, who had formal architectural training, Olmsted turned his intellectual musings about landscape into an
innovative and elegant design that reflected his observations of European parks and
synthesized all the aesthetic information he had been absorbing since youth (fig.
2.6).[35] Charles Sprague Sargent, director of Harvard University's Arnold Arboretum, characterized the site of what would become Olmsted's world-famous design
as "a rocky piece of land hardly worthy of the name park."[36] Here Olmsted learned
to supervise thousands of workers and to create and manage large budgets. He
mastered the convoluted, exacting, and sometimes exasperating art of threading
his way through the labyrinth of New York City politics, a process that left him

FIG. 103.—View of Water Terrace in Central Park.

FIG. 104.—The original condition of the ground.

Fig. 2.6. Central Park, before and after views. A. J. Downing, *A Treatise on the Theory and Practice of Landscape Gardening* (1859). Courtesy Boston Athenaeum.

jaded but conferred an enduring ability to negotiate the inevitable issues that arose in public as well as private projects while maintaining his own integrity. (Sharpening his "executive skills," however, proved a lifetime challenge, according to Van Rensselaer.)[37]

The initial period of his Central Park work proved a transformative time in Olmsted's private life as well. His brother John succumbed to tuberculosis in 1857; two years later Frederick Olmsted married his widow, taking charge of her and of his brother's children, John Charles, Charlotte, and Owen. Their union produced two more children, Marion and Frederick Law Jr.

At the outbreak of the Civil War, his work on the park substantially reduced and his health still problematic, Olmsted cast about for the manner in which he could be useful to the Union cause.[38] When the United States Sanitary Commission approached him to serve as its executive secretary, he accepted with alacrity. He found a relatively powerless commission thrown into a disorganized and decidedly unsanitary situation. Drawing on the skills he had learned supervising the Central Park project, he once again threw himself into creating order out of the chaos of army camps and military hospitals in filth and disarray, incomplete and inadequate food distribution to the troops, and a general lack of organized methods for keeping them healthy and well supplied with food, medicine, and vital camp supplies. By early 1862 the commission was running more smoothly, "sending relief agents and stores to camps, battlefields and hospitals, and coordinating the efforts of 7,000 aid societies in northern cities and towns."[39] Like every other aspect of the Civil War experience, however, the position was fraught with political snares and perils. By 1863, his political capital at the commission spent and his health nearly broken once again, Olmsted was ready to move on.

His release came in the form of the Mariposa Mining Estate, a seventy-square-mile tract in the Yosemite Valley of California. A letter arrived offering him the job of superintendent of the entire mining operation, now in the hands of new eastern owners and appearing to be a highly profitable enterprise. When Olmsted accepted, those who had observed his work for the Sanitary Commission were dismayed. Charles Eliot Norton (1827–1908), the Cambridge author, translator, social critic, and Harvard's first professor of fine arts, who had just met Olmsted, "regretted that he should have to exchange civilization for barbarism."[40] Unitarian minister Henry W. Bellows, his acquaintance from Central Park days, wrote Olmsted, "I don't know a half dozen men in the whole North whose influence in the next five years I should think more critically important to the Nation," although Bellows confessed that he didn't know how this influence was "to come in—whether by means of the Newspaper . . . or by means of public office."[41] Olmsted hesitated, writes Roper, then, "for the second and last time in his life, he made the mistake of committing himself to a commercial venture."[42] Rife with deception and mismanagement, the Mariposa Company, despite valiant efforts on Olmsted's part, foundered and eventually failed. By 1865 he was ready to move his family back East and start afresh.

Mercifully, however, his time in California had not been wasted. On the basis of his Central Park reputation, clients consulted him about various projects, including plans for a cemetery, a few private estates, and the creation of a campus for the College of California, complete with an academic village. For the college, drawing on his knowledge of A. J. Davis's Llewellyn Park in New Jersey, Olmsted designed for the existing topography, integrating the campus and residential space and providing outdoor living spaces appropriate to the mild California climate. He also devised a planting scheme exploiting native species of trees and plants, making water provision in the dry climate virtually unnecessary. Aspects of these designs were incorporated in his later designs, including those in Brookline.

Olmsted was also hired to serve on a commission to administer Yosemite Valley and Big Tree Grove, great tracts of land set aside by the United States government and ceded to the state of California to be preserved in perpetuity for public use.[43] During this time he wrote an impassioned preservation report for the California legislature, parts of which were later used for further preservation efforts at Yosemite Valley in 1872 and in drafting the National Park Act of 1916. "In this document," Roper writes, "Olmsted elaborated for the first time in America, the policy underlying the reservation by government to the public of a particular and fine scenic area; and he gave it a general application. In short, he formulated the philosophic base for the establishment of state and national parks."[44] Before he left California, he also made a report and drew up a plan for a park in San Francisco, complete with excellent suggestions for town planning, all of which were ignored.

Early in 1865 Calvert Vaux had written to Olmsted proposing that they collaborate on a new park in Brooklyn. By this time it was clear that while Vaux considered himself an artist, for Olmsted, Roper writes, "beauty, convenience, and appropriateness in landscape and architectural arrangements were not ends in themselves but devices to secure moral aims . . . his view of the profession and the art of landscape architecture, a view fundamental and Ruskinian . . . [was that] it was not a means of self-expression; it was a means of manipulating human surroundings to promote human betterment, both physical and spiritual."[45] Despite these divergent philosophies, Olmsted accepted Vaux's invitation. In addition, a long-standing plan to start a weekly magazine, *The Nation* (with Edwin L. Godkin serving as editor), was at last coming to fruition, and Olmsted wanted to be part of it. Vaux and Olmsted had been reappointed as landscape architects for Central Park as well.

In November of that year Olmsted arrived back in New York City, healthy and eager to engage in the work set out for him. He and Vaux formalized their partnership establishing the firm of Olmsted, Vaux & Company in preparation for taking on the new commission. The Brooklyn site of what was to become Prospect Park was infinitely more hospitable to the arcadian ideal of beauty that Vaux and Olmsted sought in their work than had been what McLaughlin calls the "rocky spine of Manhattan Island."[46] The site was diamond-shaped, complete with rolling hills, meadows, and a plethora of mature trees for the creation of woodland groves. In the end it was declared to be an even more successful design than Central Park, all of its parts perfectly integrated (fig. 2.7). According to the historian Witold Rybczynski, the landscape architect Laurie Olin "describes Prospect Park as 'a meditation on post–Civil War America': a transcendental vision of a unified, peaceful country, in which the meadows represent agriculture, the wooded terrain is the American wilderness, and the lakeside terrace and its more refined architecture, civilization."[47] It was a compelling reflection of Vaux and Olmsted's increased expertise and sophistication in landscape design, demonstrating "with startling clarity both variety *and* unity."[48] In the 1866 report that Olmsted wrote for the Brooklyn park commissioners, he fortified that expertise with a long and reasoned articulation of enlightened city planning and street design.

As an associate editor at the *Nation,* Olmsted contributed articles and collabo-

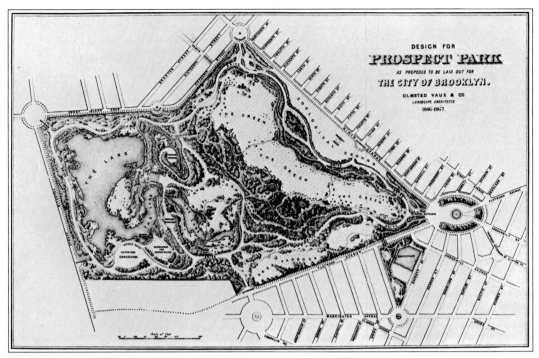

Fig. 2.7. Olmsted and Vaux, plan of Prospect Park, Brooklyn, 1866. Courtesy National Park Service, Frederick Law Olmsted National Historic Site.

rated with the editors, but his relationship with the magazine was short-lived. By the summer of 1866 he had parted amicably with his colleagues (continuing to write occasional articles and maintaining a small share in the company until 1871) and withdrawn permanently from executive engagement in the field of journalism. He had his hands full with the burgeoning practice of landscape architecture. The most important event of 1866 was his meeting a young architect named Henry Hobson Richardson, who would become a neighbor—first on Staten Island and later in Brookline—and a frequent collaborator on design projects (see chapter 3).

In 1868 the firm was hired to plan a park for Buffalo. In addition, they began working with the Riverside Improvement Company in Chicago on what the editors of Olmsted's collected papers consider "the most extensive and fully realized of any of his community designs."[49] With its gently curving streets and the judicious use of trees and greens, Olmsted and Vaux sought to "suggest and imply leisure, contemplativeness and happy tranquility."[50] It was, according to Rybczynski, "a compromise between private and public, between domesticity and community, between the city and the country,"[51] and it was the forerunner of the sort of work the Olmsted firm was to carry out later in Brookline. That same year they were hired to design a park for Chicago as well.

Between 1868 and 1872 the firm of Olmsted, Vaux & Company prepared plans and made studies for Fairmont Park in Philadelphia and built parks in Fall River, Massachusetts, and New Britain, Connecticut. Parks in Albany and Hartford were in the planning stages, and reports had been written on subdivisions in Needham, Massachusetts, and Tarrytown Heights, New York, when, in October 1872, Olmsted and Vaux terminated their seven-year partnership. Despite tensions over the years, theirs was a reasonably amicable parting.[52] Also in 1872 the Olmsteds moved permanently from Staten Island to Manhattan.

The following year, John Olmsted died quietly in his bed. Just after that came the financial panic of 1873, temporarily reducing Olmsted's workload. The depressed economic situation did not, however, prevent a heartening demonstration of Olmsted's growing stature in the profession of landscape architecture. He was invited to assume responsibility for designing the forty-five acres surrounding the United States Capitol in Washington, D.C., a task he willingly took up, feeling that it was his duty "to form and train the tastes of the Nation."[53] It was a commission that was to go on for many years.

A year later he was engaged to plan his first park design since the dissolution of his partnership with Vaux: Mount Royal, in Montreal. His second commission came in 1881 from the city of Detroit, for Belle Isle. While elements of each were accomplished, neither plan was followed to completion.

Between 1873 and 1878 Olmsted was working hard on Central Park and designing the new Riverside Park in New York City;[54] yet again, however, terrible political struggles were building, and scurrilous attacks were launched against him. Olmsted was losing heart. After a brief respite in Europe in the spring of 1878, a trip he took with his stepson John Charles, Olmsted returned home to the certain knowledge that his work in Central Park was over.[55]

Depression ensued, causing Olmsted and his family to seek respite in Cambridge, Massachusetts, for the summer with his trusted friend from the *Nation* Edwin Godkin, a sojourn repeated for two more summers.[56] There he collaborated with Richardson, who had relocated to Brookline in 1874, and helped his friend Charles Sprague Sargent, then director of the Harvard University Botanical Gardens and a Brookline resident, establish Harvard's Arnold Arboretum.[57] Olmsted also pursued his friendship with the highly cultivated Charles Eliot Norton, a fellow founder of the *Nation* and an unparalleled aesthete.[58] It was this healing combination of friendship and collegial collaboration that drew Olmsted to the Boston area. The commencement of a major project induced him to consider staying.

Boston passed its Park Act in 1875, "the last of the older great cities of the United States to become alive to the necessity of public parks," observed the journalist and parks advocate Sylvester Baxter in 1897. "The reason for this lay in the park-like beauty of its suburbs, with woods and fields easily accessible to the population, and in the existence of the large, old-fashioned Common, and the more recent Public Garden, in the very heart of the town. But with the expansion of the city, and the consequent gradual disappearance of rural charms, the necessity for the preservation of areas of open space within convenient reach became apparent."[59]

Shortly after passage of the Parks Act, the chairman of the newly appointed three-man Park Commission, Charles H. Dalton, invited Olmsted to come on a tour of various proposed park sites.[60] Again in the spring of 1876 Dalton requested his opinions concerning the placement of the various parks. Although no formal request to design the proposed system was proffered to the puzzled landscape architect, Olmsted nevertheless responded favorably to the concept, and to the land already set aside in West Roxbury for the main jewel in what was to become Boston's Emerald Necklace: Franklin Park, a 527-acre tract,[61] and two proposed satellite parks, the Charles River Embankment and Jamaica Pond. Still no contract was offered to Olmsted, and in the meantime Dalton himself came out with the first park report. "The general plan included a series of inner-city parks, a series of 'suburban' parks in the newly annexed areas, several connecting parkways, and widening and extensions of existing streets," writes Cynthia Zaitzevsky. "The sites in the inner city were selected primarily because they were located near densely populated sections where, in most cases, parks would alleviate actual or potential sanitary nuisances."[62]

Next the park commissioners, hampered by insufficient funds,[63] purchased about one hundred acres of malodorous tidal swamp at the western edge of the Back Bay. To Olmsted's surprise and dismay, they held a design competition while he was in Europe. The results were sufficiently disastrous that within months the commissioners called upon him once again, requesting that he make studies for the proposed park in the Fens. Olmsted, fresh from a vigorous tour of European parks, accepted with alacrity. Over the following year, still in his capacity as a New York–based consultant, he worked on what he called the Back Bay Fens.

In 1879 the park commissioners designated Olmsted landscape adviser, his "Proposed Improvement of Back Bay" providing his first published report to them (fig. 2.8). From 1878 through 1883 Olmsted and his stepson John Charles rented various properties, first in Cambridge and then in the Town Green district of Brookline, to work on plans for the Boston municipal park system and the Arnold Arboretum. In the winter of 1881 Olmsted visited his friend Richardson and was impressed by the physical beauty of the neighborhood and the organization of the community of Brookline.[64] After town crews began to clear snow from the roads the morning after a heavy storm, Olmsted announced to Richardson: "This is a civilized community. I am going to live here."[65] Having become quite fond of Brookline, he rented a house there, close to his friend. "I

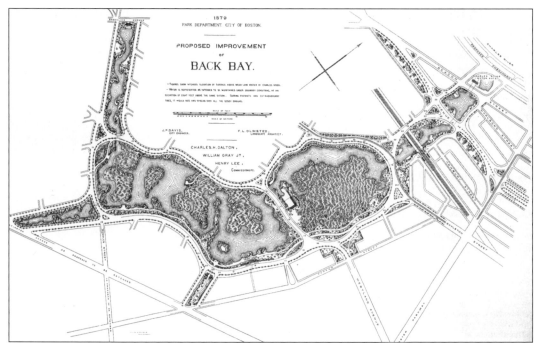

Fig. 2.8. Olmsted's plan for the Back Bay Fens, Boston, 1879. Courtesy National Park Service, Frederick Law Olmsted National Historic Site.

enjoy this suburban country beyond expression," he wrote his old walking companion Charles Brace.[66] According to the *Brookline Chronicle,* his admiration for the snow removal assured Olmsted that "there was a higher order of civilization here than anywhere else in the world. His satisfaction with the town increased with every year."[67] "As with many New England towns," Zaitzevsky notes,

> Brookline's fundamental nature was forged over two centuries by geography, population growth, economic conditions, and modes of transportation. Brookline was different, however, in its degree of civic consciousness, almost an Athenian sense of superiority in the face of mighty Boston. On the whole Brookline managed to retain this strong civic personality and much of its old-time rural character, even as it dealt with the challenges posed by the twentieth century. The town maneuvered to remain sufficiently exclusive to attract the well-off commuter and sufficiently democratic to provide the public services of which it was so proud.[68]

It was the perfect combination for Olmsted, who valued carefully preserved open space and the notion of community responsibility. "With Brookline," he said approvingly to the Brookline Club about their tangible support of the Sanitary Commission during the Civil War, "it is deeds, not words."[69] His Manhattan house and offices were maintained for two more years, John Charles, by now a trusted member of the firm, manning them while the rest of the Olmsteds rented two separate houses in Brookline.

The Boston Park Commission formalized Olmsted's position as landscape adviser for the design of the entire park system in 1883. With a three-year contract secured, he finally felt confident enough in his position to sever ties with New York. Olmsted wanted to establish himself near Richardson. The architect at first attempted to persuade his friend to build on land adjacent to the house he rented on Cottage Street and offered to design the house (fig. 2.9). He wrote to Olmsted: "What do you say to building on my lot (or Hooper's). I think I may own the place in a year and have arranged with Hooper or can (he is with me) to have you build at once. . . . It may be advantageous to both of us," noting a location for "your future home, a beautiful thing in shingles."[70] The Olmsteds, however, ultimately negotiated the purchase of the Clark family's ancestral home at 99 Warren Street, a five-minute walk from Richardson, as their home and office, naming it Fairsted. Olmsted expanded the house with mushrooming attached offices.[71] Like Richard-

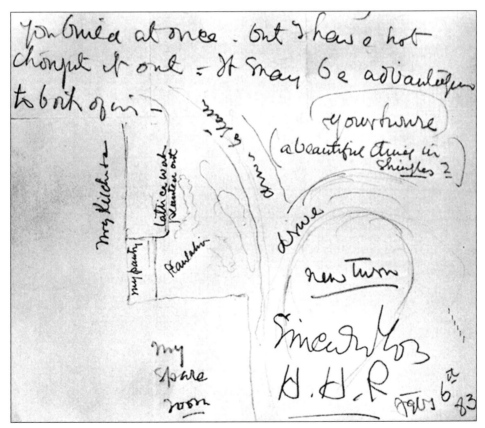

Fig. 2.9. H. H. Richardson's sketch of a site for Olmsted's proposed house in Brookline.
Courtesy Library of Congress, Manuscript Division, Frederick Law Olmsted Papers.

son, who has been described as "a thoroughly domestic man [who] loved his house above all other earthly things," Olmsted relished the interweaving of his domestic and professional life.[72]

To help induce the unmarried Clark sisters to sell their home, Olmsted proposed building a handsome shingled cottage, perhaps inspired by Richardson's proposal, at the rear of the property (eventually designed by John Charles Olmsted) where the sisters would live rent free for the remainder of their lives. Thus the Olmsteds' relocation to Brookline followed the same pattern as that of the Richardson's almost a decade earlier: a substantial commission allowed and encouraged the move from New York. It is perhaps ironic, however, that Olmsted never worked on the landscape of the Richardson property and that Richardson never consulted on the changes that Olmsted made at Fairsted, at least as documented by surviving records. Nevertheless, they learned much from each other during their frequent collaborations on projects for clients.

The grounds of Fairsted were arranged in a riot of greenery—"a veritable little bower of a place . . . a perfect maze of wild beauty," according to Hazel Collins in her 1903 description.[73] Indeed, Olmsted purposely designed and kept the grounds in a state of organized blowsy disarray, with vines spilling over and off the man-made elements, and the plantings reflecting what Zaitzevsky calls "the somewhat negligent charm" of the overall landscape (fig. 2.10). She hypothesizes that it was a section of his own property he referred to when he

Fig. 2.10. Fairsted, with Olmsted's "wildness and disorder." Courtesy National Park Service, Frederick Law Olmsted National Historic Site.

wrote to his stepson John Charles, "Less wildness and disorder I object to."[74] By 1896 a Chicago journalist could write that the home of "the father of landscape architecture in this country and the chief exponent of the art in the world today" was "as beautiful, as thoroughly in accord with all of nature's happiest little dreams—her grander ideals, her quaint delightful notions—as the great park in the center of the Nation's metropolis." He went on to describe the offices, noting, "Everything is order and system, and upon the large tables young artists are working busily over acres of grades and walks, and drives, and cunningly devised effects for nature's development."[75]

Here Olmsted settled with his family, living and working, with up to twenty assistants, together with Henry Sargent Codman and Charles Eliot, the two extraordinarily gifted associates who became partners before their premature deaths in the 1890s,[76] and continuing with his sons, John Charles and Frederick Law Olmsted Jr.,[77] for the next dozen years, on hundreds of projects, large and small, not the least of which was the Boston park system.[78] As Olmsted increasingly required assistance in his work, he inadvertently took on the job of training the next generation of landscape architects. Always self-conscious about his own deficiencies in formal training, he was exceedingly rigorous in his approach to landscape education; with his stepson and his son he was exacting.[79]

By 1881 the Boston parks design had been thoroughly conceived as a series of green spaces that included the connected Boston Common, Public Garden, and Commonwealth Avenue, linked to the newly established Back Bay Fens, the Muddy River (including the upper valley of Jamaica Pond and the Arnold Arboretum), and rural Franklin Park in West Roxbury. "It was a grand concept," writes Roper, "the most sweeping Olmsted had yet devised."[80] Between 1881 and 1895, according to Zaitzevsky, "the plan of the Boston park system as a whole was gradually altered and elaborated until it showed only a general resemblance to the park commissioners' 1876 plan. Some of the elements of that plan were kept; others were dropped. New parks were added, often because of pressure from local residents. Still other sites were suggested, considered for a while, and then rejected, generally on Olmsted's advice. The connections between parks were worked out with particular care."[81]

Charles Beveridge writes that along with Calvert Vaux, Olmsted "set the pattern for the urban park in America, provided a concept and rationale for the urban park system, designed and named the parkway, and created the country's first significant examples of greenways."[82] Indeed, Beveridge contends that the concept of the parkway was Olmsted and Vaux's innovation.[83] Unlike in New York, with its fixed gridiron configuration, in Boston the natural topography could be honored. It was, according to Sylvester Baxter, writing in 1897,

fortunately situated . . . a maritime city lying upon an island-studded bay, with estuaries penetrating a strikingly diversified landscape; a region not modeled upon a grand scale, . . . but with a broad and liberal consciousness in the charmingly picturesque commingling of hills and valleys, woodlands and marsh levels, with many ponds and various clear streams, and margined by the sea. . . . Much of this has been ruthlessly mutilated, and conspicuous areas are hopeless wrecks of former beauty. But much yet remains unspoiled, and the city, with such landscapes laying upon nearly every side, has been enabled to take good advantage of its natural endowment.

And, he concludes, "Boston had the good fortune to obtain the services of Mr. Frederick Law Olmsted at the outset."[84]

The innovative parkway system called for following stream and river courses rather than taking the time and expense of suppressing waterways underground.[85] Thus the Riverway was born, the Muddy River improvement that ran from Brookline Avenue to Tremont Street (now Huntington Avenue), and the Jamaicaway

Fig. 2.11. Franklin Park, Roxbury, Massachusetts, 1885. Courtesy National Park Service, Frederick Law Olmsted National Historic Site.

Fig. 2.12. Olmsted at the height of his career. *Century Magazine* (October 1893). Courtesy Boston Atheneum.

from Jamaica Pond to the arboretum and on to Franklin Park, where it is called the Arborway.[86] With the design of Boston's Emerald Necklace, Olmsted completed his triad of extraordinary large urban recreational spaces: Central, Prospect, and Franklin parks (fig. 2.11).

The next decade was to see a steady increase in work for Olmsted, with the consequent burgeoning of office and practice. In part this remarkable productivity may have been based on the fact that after years of economic and professional instability, moving from residence to residence and job to job, Olmsted was at last happily ensconced in a house that was endowed, according to one observer, with the "luxurious coziness and cheerful restfulness that make so much of a perfect home."[87]

The high-strung, sensitive artist was settled into a situation of economic security, in an aesthetically pleasing community he respected, surrounded by family, friends, and colleagues, doing work he loved (fig. 2.12). That work included exerting significant influence throughout the Boston area, not least in his adopted home of Brookline.

Three

HENRY HOBSON RICHARDSON

rederick Law Olmsted and his family moved to Brookline in 1883 primarily because of their personal and professional connections to Henry Hobson Richardson (1838–1886) and his family. With Olmsted's move from New York City, the nation's leading landscape architect and its most prominent architect were near neighbors in this suburban enclave. Although both men moved their homes and offices because of major commissions in Boston, it was suburban Brookline that became the site of their residences, their businesses, and their efforts in training the next generation of their professions. From the Green Hill neighborhood, until Richardson's early death in 1886, they carried on a series of collaborations that not only defined their work together but also influenced design ideals throughout the country. Thus Green Hill became a center for the evolution of architectural and landscape architectural practice and education in the United States at large.

Olmsted first met Richardson when the dashing young architect moved into Olmsted's neighborhood on Staten Island in 1866. The rapport between them appears to have been instantaneous. Olmsted later told the art and architectural critic Mariana Griswold Van Rensselaer that during Richardson's first visit to his house, he took one look at Olmsted's drawing board and stated that "the most beguiling and dangerous of all an architect's appliances was the T-square, and the most valuable were tracing-paper and india-rubber. . . . Never, never, till the thing was in stone beyond recovery, should the slightest indisposition be indulged to review, reconsider, and revise every particle of his work, to throw away his most enjoyed drawing the moment he felt it in him to better its design."[1]

Olmsted and Richardson shared this "passion for perfection" and "a profuse inventiveness" that bonded them instantly.[2] Van Rensselaer notes: "Mr. Richardson

. . . was constantly turning to Mr. Olmsted for advice, even in those cases where it seemed as though it could have little practical bearing upon his design. And where it could have more conspicuous bearing he worked with him as a brother-artist of equal rank and of equal rights with himself."[3]

"Many of Richardson's most successful works were designed in concert with Olmsted," writes Richardson expert James F. O'Gorman, confirming her observation:

> [Olmsted] thought in terms of regions, not isolated parks or structures, and consequently relied upon others to give specific architectural interpretation to aspects of his sweeping concepts. Richardson would seem to have been most favored among the others. It takes nothing away from Richardson's stature as an architect to envision him as part of a group of interacting individuals who together contributed to the work we for convenience call his. His place in the group was central. And his crowning achievement lay in his ability to focus in the most direct and lasting architectural terms the currents of nineteenth-century theory which found broader expression in his lifetime in the panoramic landscape of Olmsted's vision.[4]

In return, writes Olmsted biographer Witold Rybczynski, "Olmsted's taste for rusticity influenced the architect, who incorporated rough glacial boulders into some of his buildings. This made it hard to know exactly where the building stopped and the landscape began, an effect that Olmsted often sought. Richardson's habit, acquired when he was a student at the [École des] Beaux-Arts, was to cogitate a design problem before setting pencil to paper. Olmsted was his sounding board."[5]

Richardson (fig. 3.1) was born on September 29, 1838, at the Priestly Plantation in Louisiana and spent the first eighteen years of his life there and in New Orleans until he entered Harvard College in 1856. More interested in his social than his academic achievements, Richardson left Harvard with important contacts that would eventually lure him back to the Boston area. In 1859 he traveled to Paris, where he entered the École des Beaux-Arts to train as an architect for the next five years, roughly the period of the American Civil War. Richardson became the second American, after Richard Morris Hunt, to attend the Paris school, perpetuating a pattern that would soon become more common for American architects. At the conclusion of the war in 1865, Richardson returned to the United States and settled in New York City. In 1867 he joined Charles Gambrill in architectural practice and married Julia Gorham Hayden of Boston. The newlyweds lived on Staten Island, first in a rented house and then in 1869 in one of Richardson's own

Fig. 3.1. Richardson dressed as a medieval monk, early 1880s, George Collins Cox, photographer. Courtesy Houghton Library, Harvard University.

design at 45 McLean Avenue, which they called Arrochar. In 1865 Olmsted and his family had returned to New York and Staten Island from California at the urging of Calvert Vaux, his former partner on the creation of Central Park, to submit the final competition design for Prospect Park in Brooklyn and to form the partnership of Olmsted, Vaux & Company in November.

The Olmsted and Richardson families established a pattern on Staten Island in 1867 that they would later repeat in Brookline. Here Richardson lived until his eventual relocation to the Green Hill neighborhood of Brookline in 1874. Olmsted's residence and career path became more peripatetic than Richardson's, although the New York City area remained his major base of operations until his move to Brookline in 1880. Linking their design experience, Olmsted and Richardson also joined in efforts to plan for the intelligent development of Staten Island, serving as two of the four authors of an 1870 report from the Staten Island Improvement Corporation.[6]

Before their joint efforts on Staten Island, Olmsted and Richardson may have initially met through the Century Association, a private men's club in Manhattan founded to promote "the advancement of art and literature by establishing and maintaining a library, reading room and gallery of art, and by such other means as shall be expedient and proper for that purpose."[7] Olmsted was elected to the Century Club in 1859 on the basis of his work as a journalist and as the superintendent and one of the designers of Central Park. Thomas P. Rossiter, the landscape artist and a founder of the Century Association, proposed both Olmsted and his father-in-law, Charles L. Perkins, for membership. Olmsted was elected on June 4, 1859; his business partner, Calvert Vaux, also became a member at that meeting.[8] Richardson was nominated for membership in 1866, the year after his return from Paris and Olmsted's return from California. His sponsors included his cousin John Priestley, editor of the *American Whig Review,* and A. C. Haseltine, a member of a Philadelphia family of artists and collectors, as well as his future architectural partner Charles Gambrill, who had become a member in 1859, the same year as Olmsted.[9] Assuming they first met in 1866 when Richardson was nominated for membership in the Century Association, Olmsted would have been forty-four and Richardson only twenty-eight.

While neighbors on Staten Island and fellow Centurions, Olmsted and Richardson embarked almost immediately on a series of collaborations that would continue for the remainder of Richardson's life. (See appendix D for a chronological list of Richardson and Olmsted collaborations.) Beginning in 1867, they joined forces on a monument for Alexander Dallas Bache in the Congressional Cemetery in Washington, D.C. Bache, a grandson of Benjamin Franklin and former professor of natural history at the University of Pennsylvania, was the superintendent of the United States Coast Survey from 1843 to 1867. He served with Olmsted on the U.S. Sanitary Commission during the Civil War. Because of this association with Bache, C. P. Patterson of the Coast Survey asked Olmsted to help with a monument to Bache. Olmsted generously suggested that Richardson be invited to participate on this project too. Constructed in late 1868 and early 1869, the Bache memorial played a key role in launching this relationship of national significance. Though quite modest in relation to their later collaborations, the $2,800 granite monument to Bache indicates that the more established and older Olmsted saw Richardson as someone who shared his aesthetic precepts and could become an important partner for larger projects. It certainly would have been more logical for Olmsted to turn to his architectural partner Calvert Vaux. Inviting Richardson instead of Vaux signals an interest in nurturing the career of his new friend and neighbor and also perhaps underscores the ongoing tensions between Olmsted and Vaux that would eventually lead to the dissolution of their partnership in 1872. In any case, in encouraging Richardson's participation on the Bache monument, Olmsted was serving as a mentor for the younger man, who was relatively newly arrived in New York City.

Another member of the Century Association became an early and powerful client for both designers. William E. Dorsheimer, a successful lawyer and community advocate in Buffalo, New York, had joined the association in 1864. Two years later Olmsted and Dorsheimer began to correspond about the possibility of creating a new park for Buffalo, and in August 1868 Olmsted met with Dorsheimer in Buffalo to discuss a location.[10] This marked the beginning of a long-term project for the Buffalo Park Commission, which became one of the most significant for Olmsted, Vaux & Company. Although they had introduced the concept of landscaped parkways in their work on Prospect Park, in Buffalo the partners expanded that concept into a system of parks, parkways, landscaped boulevards, and public institutional projects that provided a civilizing armature for this expanding industrial city.[11] Olmsted may also have recommended Richardson to Dorsheimer as the architect for a house the attorney planned to build in Buffalo.[12] If so, that would again be surprising, given the fact that Olmsted and Vaux were still partners. In any event, Dorsheimer contacted Richardson in October, three months after Olmsted's initial visit, and Richardson's substantial brick mansarded residence for Dorsheimer was completed by 1871. The Dorsheimer commission allowed Richardson to translate contemporary French patterns of suburban architecture to an American setting.[13] At the time of the commission, Richardson could boast only his own house on Staten Island and a town house for a Harvard contemporary, Benjamin Crowninshield, then under construction in Boston as examples of his domestic work. Perhaps Dorsheimer was impressed by Richardson's training in Paris; but the chronology of the Olmsted and Richardson projects in Buffalo makes it hard to avoid the assumption that the landscape architect promoted the work of his new young friend. Dorsheimer would soon become an important figure for other Richardson and Olmsted commissions.

Beginning in 1869, Richardson was able to return the professional favor to Olmsted. That year he began to consult with Dr. John P. Gray about the design of a new state mental hospital on land given by the City of Buffalo to the State of New York. Richardson's plans for the Buffalo State Asylum were approved on August 25, 1870, and he consulted Olmsted the following year about the siting of the hospital and the development of the grounds. Political involvements complicated its construction, which began in 1872 but was not fully realized until 1895.[14] When Dr. Gray selected Richardson for this important public commission, he was choosing a newcomer over established designers of buildings and grounds for insane asylums. But in Dorsheimer's opinion, "no one used architectural forms with so much originality, no one with so much grace and tenderness, no one with such strength as Richardson," according to the Buffalo architectural historian Francis Kowsky, who suggests, "Perhaps it was Dorsheimer, the chief promoter of the innovative park system that Frederick Law Olmsted and Calvert Vaux had proposed for Buffalo, who got Richardson the job to design the mammoth hospital."[15] Olmsted had prior experience with designing the grounds of the private Hartford Retreat in his native Hartford, Connecticut, in 1860, where Vaux and his architectural partner Frederick Clarke Withers renovated the complex in 1868. Vaux alone provided the design for the private Shepherd Asylum outside Baltimore in 1861, although the building was not completed and opened until 1891. Vaux and Withers, with consultation from Olmsted, also designed the massive Hudson River State Hospital in Poughkeepsie, New York, in 1867.[16] Nevertheless, Gray turned to the unproven Richardson for the important Buffalo commission; in turn, Richardson invited Olmsted to develop the grounds and to connect the hospital to the Buffalo park

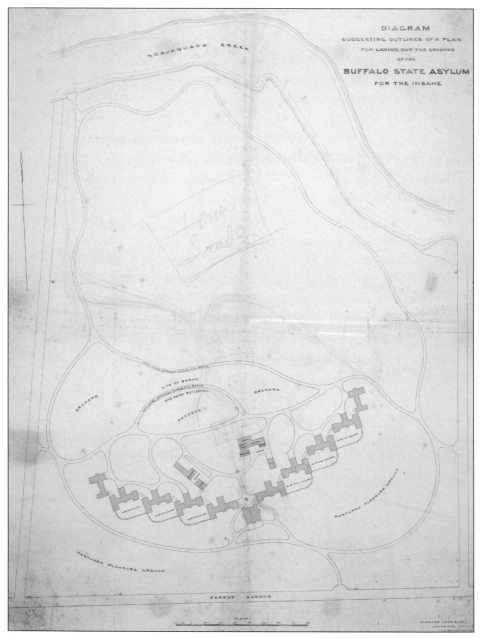

Fig. 3.2. Landscape plan for Buffalo State Asylum for the Insane, 1871, inscribed "F. L. Olmsted." Courtesy Houghton Library, Harvard University.

and parkway system. Richardson's massive brick and brownstone campus (fig. 3.2) of linked pavilions organized in the spread-V format of the Kirkbride plan for mental hospitals was the architect's largest single commission.

At the opposite end of New York State, Richardson and Olmsted collaborated on another large public building, the New York State Capitol at Albany, beginning in 1875, through the intervention once again of William Dorsheimer. Ottawa architect Thomas Fuller originally designed the new capitol in 1867, but construction proceeded slowly and was stopped in 1874 for a lack of funds. A new Capitol Commission, chaired by Dorsheimer, now the state's lieutenant governor, invited Olmsted, Richardson, and New York architect Leopold Eidlitz (1823–1906) on July 15, 1871, to form an advisory board to consider questions of plan, design, and construction. The committee's proposed alterations met with both professional and legislative criticism, but the Capitol Commission accepted the modified plans in 1876 and retained the committee as the new architects and landscape architect. The complex history of the building and the involvement of changing administrations meant that the ultimate completion of the capitol dragged on until the end of the century.[17]

With his college ties and a wife from Boston, Richardson was also focused on architectural opportunities in Massachusetts from an early moment in his career. Indeed, his earliest surviving building is Grace Episcopal Church (1867–1869) in Medford, another Boston suburb. Its nubby boulder construction shows the sensitivity to nature and to geology that made Richardson so attractive to Olmsted as a collaborator. In 1870 Richardson entered a competition for the design of a new town hall in Brookline.[18] His handsome design, pyramidal in massing with a five-bay arcaded entrance porch, did not convince the selection committee. Although he lost the opportunity to connect with the community where he would eventually make his home, he had by then been successful in receiving commissions for a wide range of projects throughout Massachusetts. On many of these Richardson collaborated with Olmsted. One of the most significant of Richardson's Massachusetts successes was his winning the 1872 competition for the design of Trinity Church in Copley Square, Boston. After inaugurating construction on his design for the church, Richardson moved to Brookline in 1874, reconnecting with friends from his undergraduate years at Harvard and with the Boston relatives of his wife. He rented a house from a former college classmate, Edward William ("Ned") Hooper, treasurer of Harvard College, at 25 Cottage Street, Brookline, where he would live for the remainder of his life.

The Brookline that Richardson moved to was an unusually beautiful rolling stretch, nestled between the city of Boston and the countryside beyond, with eight thousand residents who cherished the green and wooded beauty of their town. "His choice of residence was no accident," according to O'Gorman. That area of Brookline "was in the nineteenth century, as it is today, a landscape of rolling hills dotted with large houses inhabited by men of wealth, achievement and influence."[19] In an 1886 obituary for Richardson, the New York architect Peter B. Wight states that the great architect moved to Brookline because it was "one of the most picturesque suburbs of Boston, where he was surrounded by the friends of his wife and the refined and cultured society whose association and sympathy he craved."[20] Olmsted was a frequent visitor while working on his early plans for the Boston parks and the Arnold Arboretum.

When the Olmsteds decided to move to Brookline in 1883, they followed the same pattern as the Richardsons nearly a decade before. A substantial Boston commission allowed and encouraged the move from New York to Brookline. Living only a short walk from each other, the two families intermingled constantly. As Frederick Law Olmsted Jr. recalled the relationship with Richardson during his youth, "I was in and out of his house and office all the time, with father and with the Richardson children."[21]

Throughout the late 1870s and early 1880s Richardson and Olmsted found more opportunities to collaborate on projects in the vicinity of Boston and beyond. Their chief long-term patrons were members of the Ames family of North Easton and Boston. The Ames fortune was based on the manufacture of shovels, starting in 1803 in North Easton and expanding during the Civil War. Family involvement with the railroads began in 1855 and was augmented by investments in railroad construction after the war. At North Easton and elsewhere, Olmsted and Richardson developed five projects either financed or commissioned by the Ames family.[22] As a group, these buildings demonstrate most strongly the ways in which the two men learned from each other. The buildings grow naturally from their Olmsted landscapes and project an even greater sense of "rootedness" than is found in almost any of their other collaborations.

The initial Ames project in North Easton was the Oliver Ames Free Public Library (fig. 3.3). The commission entered the Richardson office in September 1877, and the library was completed two years later but not officially opened until 1883. Oliver Ames II had left $50,000 in trust at his death in 1877 for the development of a privately owned public library in North Easton. His children Frederick Lathrop Ames and Helen Angier Ames oversaw the project. Frederick Ames's intense interest in horticulture may have led to Olmsted's involvement. Richardson had recently celebrated the dedication of Trinity Church in Boston and was working at the time on another suburban public library in Woburn, outside Boston, making him a logical candidate for the design of the building. Olmsted had a national reputation, but he had not yet received the permanent commission for

Fig. 3.3. Oliver Ames Free Public Library, North Easton, Massachusetts, 1877–1883, H. H. Richardson. Mariana Griswold Van Rensselaer, *Henry Hobson Richardson and His Work* (1888). Courtesy Richard W. Cheek.

the Boston park system. The Ames Library was the first of three public libraries in Boston suburbs on which Richardson and Olmsted collaborated. In 1880–1882 Richardson designed the Thomas Crane Memorial Library in Quincy, considered by many to be the finest of this group. Olmsted designed the landscape in 1881–82.[23] The Converse Memorial Library in Malden followed in 1883–1885 with Olmsted collaborating in 1884–85.[24] All of these buildings, which were private gifts from leading philanthropists to their native towns, signify the importance of books and education for Massachusetts at this time.[25] Set confidently on a hillside site, the Ames building in North Easton rises in legible massing, with the horizontal stack wing to the left, a stairwell marked by a tower, and the cavelike entrance masking the reception area and reading room. The warm granite and sandstone facade grows from a broader water table and is markedly horizontal in emphasis.[26]

Immediately adjacent to the Oliver Ames Free Library stands the Oakes Ames Memorial Hall, erected in memory of Oliver's older brother and business partner. Richardson began work on the design of the memorial hall in 1879 on a commission from the children of Oakes Ames (1804–1873), who had been a member of Congress from 1862 to 1873. At the request of Abraham Lincoln, Ames assisted with the financing of the Union Pacific Railroad through the Crédit Mobilier company, beginning in 1867. His efforts led to the completion of the transcontinental

Fig. 3.4. Oakes Ames Memorial Hall, North Easton, Massachusetts, 1879, H. H. Richardson and Frederick Law Olmsted. Courtesy National Park Service, Frederick Law Olmsted National Historic Site.

railroad by 1869. Three years later, questions about the financial practices of Crédit Mobilier led to Ames's censure by Congress. Oakes Ames, who always maintained his innocence, died suddenly in 1873. His children used this commission as a way to guarantee a more positive memory of their father. The less resolved design of the memorial hall results from a program that was less homogeneous than that of the adjacent library.[27] Here, however, Olmsted played a more dramatic role in the development of the project, capitalizing on the natural rock outcroppings of the site as the rationale for a broad and irregular stairway (fig. 3.4) climbing from the street to the ground-floor arcade of the building.[28] Following the dedication of Memorial Hall, Olmsted continued to work on the development of the landscape, designing a small triangular plot of land south of the building and across the street. Here he designed later in 1881 and erected in the summer and fall of 1882 rock-work (figs. 3.5 and 3.6) that provided a central nucleus for the village and a further extension of the terraces spilling down from Memorial Hall.[29]

In a somewhat similar manner, both brothers were memorialized in a monument erected at Sherman, Wyoming, to mark the meeting of the eastern and western branches of the Union Pacific Railroad. During the debate over the censure of Oakes Ames, one of his congressional defenders suggested that the government should be building a monument to him, not accusing him of financial wrongdoing. The Union Pacific stockholders agreed, approving funds for a memorial in 1875, although action was delayed until 1879 because of continuing litigation. Frederick Ames again assumed supervision of the project, both for the family and for the railroad. Since Oliver Ames II had also served as president of the railroad, his contributions were celebrated in this monument too. Though built in a barren western landscape and responsive to the natural conditions of the region, the Ames

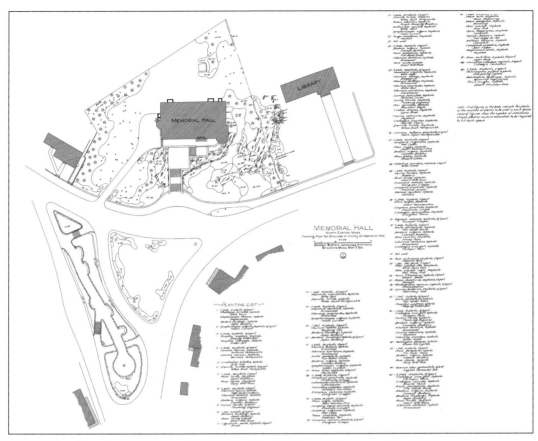

Fig. 3.5. Planting plan for Memorial Hall showing the Ames Library and the Rockery. Courtesy National Park Service, Frederick Law Olmsted National Historic Site.

Fig. 3.6. Rockwork tunnel in the Rockery landscape, North Easton, Massachusetts, 1882–1886. Courtesy National Park Service, Frederick Law Olmsted National Historic Site.

monument (fig. 3.7) still speaks to Bostonians' expectations. A stunted pyramid of changing profile with portrait busts of the Ames brothers on two principal facades, the monument resembles a drumlin of natural boulders regularized by civilization. Olmsted praised the design, but he played no direct role in the development of this project. The primitive naturalism of the monument owes much to the environmental sensitivity Olmsted instilled in Richardson throughout their many collaborations.[30]

Back in North Easton, a project that somewhat resembles in spirit the monument in Wyoming is the Ames Gate Lodge (fig. 3.8) for Langwater, the estate of Frederick Lathrop Ames.[31] A yawning arch that springs up from the ground spans the entrance drive to the estate, interrupting a horizontal mass that looks like a pile of boulders capped by a flowing terracotta tile roof. To the left of the arch, Richardson allocated space for a large potting shed; to the right he placed quarters for bachelor members of the family and guests. The boulder walls, laid in decreasing scale from bottom to top, are dressed with Longmeadow sandstone at the openings. Eyebrow dormers gently lift the plane of the roof. Even though he had been involved in the initial discussions of this project, Olmsted did not develop the landscape here until 1886–87, well after the gate lodge was completed.[32] He gently merged the primordial-looking rock pile with the rolling landscape that slides down to the adjacent millpond.

The final project of Richardson and Olmsted in North Easton created a new home for the Old Colony railroad station.[33] Once again the Ames family provided the funding and chose the architects. Designed and constructed between 1881 and 1884, the Old Colony station is one of the finest examples of a building-landscape type that Richardson and Olmsted helped to define for the Boston region and beyond. The expansive arches of the porte cochere and of the main building firmly root the structure in the ground. The long hip-roofed extensions over the train platforms reemphasize the horizontality of the design. As in other railroad sta-

Fig. 3.8. Ames Gate Lodge, Langwater, North Easton, Massachusetts, 1880–81, H. H. Richardson and Frederick Law Olmsted. Courtesy National Park Service, Frederick Law Olmsted Nationa Historic Site for Harvard College Library.

tion collaborations (two examples by Richardson's successors are discussed later in this chapter), the Old Colony was embowered in a public landscape intended to blend the building into its environment and to present the best possible community image for the arriving passengers.[34]

Another important area of collaboration between Richardson and Olmsted was in the latter's work for the Boston municipal park system, and especially the Back Bay Fens, the initial element of his comprehensive scheme for the city. Olmsted designed the Fens as both a public park and a flood control district. Here the freshwater Muddy River and Stony Brook merged with the tidal estuary of the Charles River. To naturalize this work of hydraulic engineering, he created a fen, a low-lying zone with a stream meandering through the center of the park and meeting water gates at the conjunctions of the riverways. Needing bridges and buildings that would complement the character of his landscape forms, in 1880 Olmsted requested that the Park Commission retain Richardson's services. Under Olmsted's close supervision, Richardson provided designs for two bridges, the now demolished iron-truss Charlesgate West Bridge over the Boston and Albany railroad tracks and the Boylston Street Bridge, the more important of the two, which fortunately survives.[35] Olmsted wanted more substantial bridges at these sites because Boylston Street was one of the major entrances to the Back Bay Fens from the city. For the Boylston Street bridge he requested the single-arch masonry form, but Richardson added the tourelles (small semicircular towers rising from the banks of the Muddy River, which flows beneath the bridge) and extended one retaining wall to connect this bridge to the one over the adjacent railroad line. The designs were finalized in 1882, and the bridges were completed in 1884. Olmsted also required a building to conceal the floodgate between Stony Brook and the Muddy River, for which Richardson submitted a design in July 1881. Built of Roxbury puddingstone, a local conglomerate widely used throughout Boston at this time, the hip-roofed structure and a nearby clone of 1910 continue to serve their original purpose.[36]

In addition to their highly visible but modest (from Richardson's perspective) work for the Boston Park Commission, the neighbors continued to execute projects throughout the Boston area. An exceptionally important collaboration was the Waltham country house of Robert Treat Paine, the chairman of the building committee at Trinity Church. Somewhat similar in feeling to the Ames Gate Lodge, Stonehurst, as the Paines called their retreat, was built on land acquired from Paine's father-in-law, George Williams Lyman, whose inherited estate, called The Vale, was nearby on lower land.[37] The Paines had built a country house on this property in 1866 to a design by Gridley J. F. Bryant. With the expansion of their family and the death of Lyman, they decided to enlarge the house and invited Richardson and Olmsted to collaborate on it in 1883.[38] The addition ultimately overwhelmed the original mansarded building. Richardson used boulders for the first level, surmounted by shingles for the upper stories and roof, except for double-level boulder towers at the corners of the garden elevation and near the entrance. Olmsted designed an ample terrace across the rear of the property (fig. 3.9) with boulders defining the outer wall and broad ramps leading down into the landscape.[39]

Even before the Olmsteds moved to Brookline, they had a family reason for wanting to relocate. On October 15, 1878, their daughter Charlotte married Dr. John Bryant of Boston. Two years later the young couple approached Olmsted and Richardson to design a house in Cohasset, on the South Shore of Boston, where Bryant's father, Dr. Henry Bryant, was already a summer resident.[40] Olmsted, naturally, was consulted about the siting of this new house, picturesquely located on rocky outcroppings along the ocean shore. Richardson chose shingles as the natural response to the oceanfront location, a building material used in coastal New England from the earliest settlement. The main house was basically rectangular with a service wing projecting at an angle over the entrance drive. Here the Olmsted family, the medical community, Olmsted, and Richardson come together in a symbol of the long-term alliances that would soon be consolidated with the landscape architect's move to Brookline.[41]

Fig. 3.9. Rear terrace of Stonehurst, Robert Treat Paine House, Waltham, Massachusetts, 1883–1886, H. H. Richardson and Frederick Law Olmsted. Courtesy Paul Rocheleau.

The final collaboration to which we must turn was a commission from another physician, and Richardson's only domestic project in Brookline. Dr. Walter Channing invited the architect to design a residence on Chestnut Hill Avenue near Boylston Street in 1883. As with the Bryant house in Cohasset, Richardson restricted himself to shingles for the exterior envelope, including the roof. This uniformity of massing and material was characteristic of his designs at the time. Atypically, the Olmsted office did not become involved with this project until 1899, when Olmsted Brothers developed plans for the subdivision of the property for Dr. Channing.[42] On March 27, 1899, French & Bryant, civil engineers, produced a topographical plan (fig. 3.10) for the property, which shows the Channing house at the north edge and the much larger Francis Fisher house (1852), which Channing had acquired in 1879 and expanded as a private psychiatric hospital.[43] When Channing decided to move the hospital to Wellesley and sell the land, a new Channing Street was cut through to provide lots for development. By April 22, 1899, the Olmsted firm had plotted a "preliminary sketch for subdivision of the property" into twenty-six building lots, ranging in size from 6,784 square feet to 23,404 square feet.[44] This scheme, which paral-

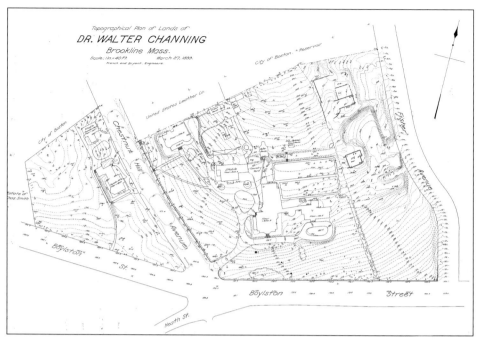

Fig. 3.10. Topographical plan of the Walter Channing estate, Brookline, 1899, French & Bryant, showing the Channing Psychiatric Hospital at the center, the Walter Channing house at the top center, and another house owned by Channing across Chestnut Hill Avenue. Courtesy National Park Service, Frederick Law Olmsted National Historic Site.

leled the adjacent development of Fisher Hill by a group of property owners to a master plan devised by the Olmsted office, sadly included the demolition of the Channing house in 1935, a sign of the rapid pace of Brookline real estate development in the early twentieth century. This section of Brookline, along Boylston Street and overlooking the reservoir to the south, was a district in which the Olmsted office worked with private clients, Richardson's successor firm, and other architects during the 1880s in creating private estates and then dividing the properties for more intensive development. Although the Channing house is the only project in Brookline that Richardson completed, his association with the Olmsted office ironically resulted in its eventual destruction. In contrast to Richardson's limited direct impact on Brookline, Frederick Law Olmsted and his office received more than three hundred commissions in Brookline over the duration of the firm. Admittedly, Richardson's early death from Bright's disease in 1886 makes the comparison somewhat uneven and unfair.

Professional education was another element that connected the Richardson and Olmsted house-offices in Brookline. First the Richardson and later the Olmsted offices became nationally important as training centers for a new generation of architects and landscape architects. The basic model for Richardson's office was the atelier system of the École des Beaux-Arts in Paris, where he had studied.[45] Similarly, beginning in 1883 Olmsted accepted into his residence at 99 Warren Street a series of apprentices who would become the leaders of his own firm in future years and of the profession of landscape architecture, which he had been the first to define and name.

Richardson may have chosen the house at 25 Cottage Street because of its resemblance to the monumentally porticoed southern plantations of his youth, but he developed his residence into a full-scale office, where ranks of architects who would rise to prominence enjoyed the benefit of his criticism and careful supervision. In addition to the atelier life in Paris, Richardson may have been inspired by Richard Morris Hunt's office-atelier in his Tenth Street Studio in New York City, where contemporary French ideas and methods of education were introduced to the United States.[46] Before leaving New York, Richardson and his partner Charles Gambrill, a former student at the Hunt atelier, had conducted their business from an office in lower Manhattan, although Richardson often needed to work from his Staten Island residence for health reasons. When Richardson relocated to Brookline in 1874, he worked from home, sending sketches to New York to be developed into drawings or summoning a member of the New York staff, such as Stanford White, to Brookline for consultation. After the dissolution of the partnership in 1878, Richardson expanded and converted his rental property at 25 Cottage Street into a mélange of private residence, professional office, and architectural academy. What was significantly different, of course, was the fact that the office was an extension of his home and that it was located in a suburban community.

When Frederick Law Olmsted likewise moved from New York to Brookline, he quickly adopted Richardson's habit of bringing the office into the home. Of course, Olmsted had worked from his various residences in New York and elsewhere over the years, but he did not have a coterie of young acolytes until his move to Brookline. There were significant distinctions between the two office environments and educational settings. Most of the young architects hired by Richardson had the advantage of training in an academic program in architecture at the Massachusetts Institute of Technology, which established the first American school of architecture in 1867.[47] Olmsted, by contrast, was filling a more obvious vacuum, since the first academic program for training landscape architects would not be created until 1900 at Harvard University. Not surprisingly, it was members of the Olmsted office who would take the lead in that new enterprise.

Entrance into the Richardson office was a highly attractive prize for young architecture graduates from MIT.[48] Here they worked with one of the dominant figures in the profession, observing his design process, participating in the social life of the office, and studying the collection of books, drawings, and artifacts with which Richardson surrounded himself. One columnist for *American Architect and Building News* wrote of Richardson and his atelier in 1884: "Starting out with the assumption that an architect will produce the best work if he treats his profession as an art to be lived and known . . . and not as a business to be locked up and left 'down-town' each evening . . . Mr. Richardson has established his own office at a house two miles from the railroad station of a small suburban town, without thought or care whether clients may find such an arrangement as convenient for themselves as most usually adopted by the profession."[49] Here Richardson enticed clients with fine meals and an exotic environment embellished with his professional library (fig. 3.11), architectural drawings, and objects acquired in his European travels.[50] The sensuous and personal aura of the artist at home distinguished Richardson's studio from the office his friend created nearby at 99 Warren Street. Frederick Law Olmsted Jr. recalled the contrast between the two: "Richardson consciously and deliberately expressed his personality by a very distinctive and impressive room-of-his-own in his office, while father was uninterested in 'expressing his personality' either in his office or in his executed works of landscape architecture, which he approached as solutions of other people's problems

Fig. 3.11. Photograph of Richardson's private study and library at 25 Cottage Street, Brookline, ca. 1886, where he entertained clients and educated his young apprentices, who had access to his collection of books, drawings, and objects.
Courtesy Historic New England.

Fig. 3.12. The central space adjacent to "the coops," the drafting rooms in the Richardson office in Brookline, ca. 1886. Courtesy Historic New England.

and definitely not as opportunities for 'self-expression' for himself."[51] Olmsted also maintained a stronger barrier between the office and his personal and family space.

By comparison, between Richardson's main residence and his private study he constructed two very simple ranges of drafting rooms, called "the coops" because of their similarity to chicken coops, flanking a central drafting room / exhibition space (fig. 3.12). There were notable differences between the Richardson office in Brookline, the studio run by Hunt in New York, and the ateliers of the École des Beaux-Arts which inspired both. For one thing, Hunt never lived in his studio building, nor did the masters of the Parisian ateliers, unlike Richardson, who merged his home and his office after his move to Brookline. Unlike Hunt's assistants, Richardson's generally arrived with academic training in architecture, although he accepted some students as well. His office provided more of a postgraduate education, an opportunity to apply academic knowledge to current commissions within a professionally nurturing environment. When students left the Richardson office, they were prepared to launch themselves as highly competitive professionals. The roll call of Richardson alumni is long and prestigious; several became important figures in architectural education in more institutional settings.[52]

Landscape architecture education in the United States had its origins in the office of Frederick Law Olmsted. While still based in New York, Olmsted began the edu-

Fig. 3.13. John Charles Olmsted in the offices at 99 Warren Street. Courtesy National Park Service, Frederick Law Olmsted National Historic Site.

cation of his nephew and stepson John Charles Olmsted (fig. 3.13), who was employed by the firm beginning in 1872 and admitted to partial partnership in 1878. One year after the relocation of the family and office to Brookline, the firm changed its name to F. L. & J. C. Olmsted. John Charles took on increasing responsibilities, especially as the health of his aging stepfather began to decline.

Almost as soon as the firm was reestablished at 99 Warren Street in 1883, Charles Eliot (1859–1897) became the first official intern in the office.[53] His father was Charles W. Eliot, the president of Harvard College, who, speaking of himself in the third person, later recounted the process of having young Charles presented to Olmsted: "During the winter [of 1882] his father had opportunities at the Saturday Club of talking with Mr. Frederick Law Olmsted about the means of preparing a young man for Mr. Olmsted's profession; and Professor [Charles Eliot] Norton, who had formed a good opinion of Charles's capacity, had also opportunities of interesting Mr. Olmsted in him. Finally, on the 22nd April, 1883, his uncle, Robert S. Peabody, introduced him to Mr. Olmsted at Brookline."[54] It seems likely that the pattern of office education that Richardson was actively pursuing was what inspired Peabody to approach Olmsted on behalf of his nephew, although Eliot and the other interns who followed him at Fairsted came with much less basic knowledge of their desired profession than was the case with most of the students at 25 Cottage Street. After his graduation from Harvard College, Eliot (fig. 3.14) briefly pursued relevant courses at the Bussey Institute of Harvard College before joining the Olmsted office. Eliot spent the years from April 29, 1883, until April 1, 1885, learning the profession by observing Frederick Law Olmsted and John Charles Olmsted. Fortunately his journals from this period survive, detailing his daily patterns, assigned duties, and office frustrations.[55] Olmsted recommended a course of reading and relied on the young man to travel with him and assist in the production of drawings and reports. Eliot left Olmsted in 1885 to travel in the United States and Europe. Wanting to pursue his own commissions, he declined an invitation to rejoin the Olmsted firm, instead establishing his own practice as a landscape architect upon his return to Boston in late 1886.

Following a very similar pattern, the second intern was Henry Sargent Codman, who entered the office in 1884 on the recommendation of his architect uncle John H. Sturgis and his horticulturalist uncle Charles Sprague Sargent, Olmsted's neighbor and the first director of the Arnold Arboretum.[56] Because of the press of business, both Eliot and Codman were rapidly given broad responsibilities. Among other projects, they assisted Olmsted with his plans for the arboretum. Like Eliot, Codman followed his internship with a period of professional travel, but he then returned to the Olmsted office, where he became a partner. Codman's death following an appendectomy on January 13, 1893, while he was supervising the firm's plans for the World's Columbian Exposition in Chicago was a severe blow to both Olmsted and the office. As a result of this loss, Olmsted

Fig. 3.14. Charles Eliot at the time of his graduation from Harvard College, 1882, one year before he began his internship in the Olmsted office. Courtesy family of Carola Eliot Goriansky.

persuaded Charles Eliot to rejoin the firm and form a new partnership, Olmsted, Olmsted & Eliot.

In the meantime, other interns and junior office members (fig. 3.15) had expanded the ranks at 99 Warren Street. Noteworthy among these were Warren Manning, who supervised the planting programs, and Edward D. Bolton, who oversaw construction projects. In 1897 Frederick Law Olmsted Jr. also entered the firm, becoming a partner with his half-brother in 1903. By that point the informal education of landscape architects at Fairsted had been institutionalized by the creation of the first academic program in landscape architecture at Harvard University, under the direction of Frederick Law Olmsted Jr. and Arthur A. Shurcliff, another former intern and junior member of the firm. The training of landscape architects at Fairsted bore little resemblance to the clublike atmosphere of Richardson's studio. Unlike Richardson, the boisterous former Harvard clubman, Olmsted had no wish to create a Parisian atelier–like environment, complete with office dinners, athletic competitions, and other forms of social life, like that at the architectural firm. The Fairsted assistants certainly enjoyed moments of levity, but the office culture was much more serious and decidedly less sociable. Admittedly the Richardson office became more like that at Fairsted as the architect's health grew more fragile and the press of office business greater.

Fig. 3.15. Office members posed outside the drafting rooms added to the rear of 99 Warren Street. Courtesy National Park Service, Frederick Law Olmsted National Historic Site.

Thus the friendship between the country's leading architect, Richardson, and landscape architect, Olmsted, produced an environment in which the two firms thrived, enjoying close proximity and frequent collaboration. Both offices also became launching pads for key figures in succeeding generations of these professions and laboratories for advancing methods in professional education and enrichment. Brookline, and specifically the neighborhood between 25 Cottage and 99 Warren streets, became the most fertile soil for the American design professions at the time, bearing fruit locally and beyond for many years to come.

The final stage of the relationship between Olmsted and Richardson was defined by the landscape architect's role in the production of a monograph on Richardson after the architect's death in 1886. Two other figures were central to this story. One was Charles Sprague Sargent, a Green Hill neighbor and friend of both Richardson and Olmsted.[57] The other was the author of Richardson's biography, Mariana Griswold Van Rensselaer, one the first influential writers on American art, architecture, landscape architecture, and garden art. She was an associate of the three Brookline men, and these relationships became a base for advancing her activities as a critic and historian.

In the months following Richardson's death on April 27, 1886, Olmsted and Sargent began to think about organizing a memorial volume that would summarize the accomplishments and importance of their friend and neighbor. They selected a young and promising woman critic whose principal works to date had been in the field of art criticism. Mariana Ally Griswold (1851–1934) came from a wealthy mercantile family in New York. She met fellow American Schuyler Van Rensselaer while studying in Germany and married him in 1873. After the birth of their first child in 1875, she started to write for periodicals. *American Architect and Building News,* the country's first professional architectural journal, founded in Boston in 1876, published her first essay in architectural criticism that year. In 1884 Schuyler Van Rensselaer died, and Mariana moved from New Brunswick, New Jersey, to New York City to pursue her writing. Her essays on recent American architecture in *Century Magazine* from 1884 to 1886 introduced Richardson's work to a larger audience than *American Architect and Building News* could claim. In 1886 she published two volumes, *Book of American Figure Painting* and *American Etcher,* which signaled her arrival as a major voice in art criticism. It is not surprising, therefore, that Olmsted and Sargent approached her about writing a monograph on Richardson after his death. Van Rensselaer had traveled to Brookline in 1883 to meet with Richardson about her articles on his buildings, but she was not a close personal friend of the architect. When Olmsted wrote to her in August 1886 about the monograph, however, he observed: "It is not desirable that you should have been nearer Mr. Richardson than you have been. It would be better in order to make a thoroughly discriminating, candid historical view that you should stand further away."[58] Although she was not an insider, she was chosen for this commission because of the impressive record of her previous writings.

Henry Hobson Richardson and His Works (fig. 3.16) appeared in 1888 as the first professional monograph, more than a simple memoir, published on an American architect. Frederick Law Olmsted provided guidance, and Charles Sprague Sargent offered a subvention for the illustrations to the edition of five hundred. Sargent consequently assumed responsibility for choosing the illustrations.[59] Houghton Mifflin, the publisher of the monograph, referred to it in internal documents as the "Richardson Memorial" and sold the deluxe book at $20 a copy to the East Coast intelligentsia for whom Richardson and Olmsted had worked. It remained the key document on the architect's career for half a century. In the 1930s Lewis Mumford revived interest in the work of Richardson and Olmsted. In the same decade, Henry-Russell Hitchcock published a new monograph, *Henry Hobson Richardson and His Times* (1936), in which he declared that the Van Rensselaer monograph was the foundation of all

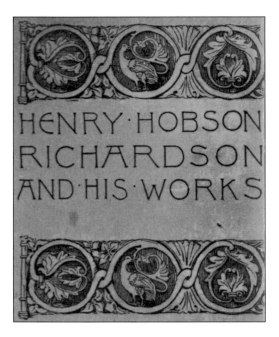

Fig. 3.16. Title block on cover, Mariana Griswold Van Rensselaer, *Henry Hobson Richardson and His Works* (1888). Courtesy Richard W. Cheek.

scholarship on the architect. Thus Olmsted and his neighbor Sargent influenced the future reputation of their recently deceased friend both in commissioning the volume and in encouraging Van Rensselaer's career as a critic and historian of American architecture and landscape architecture. Although she never lived in Brookline, Van Rensselaer became an important fellow traveler with Olmsted, Sargent, and Richardson's reputation. She would also soon emerge as a dominant advocate for the principles of landscape architecture.

In 1886, the year of Richardson's death, Sargent and Olmsted became involved with the creation of a new periodical, *Garden and Forest,* which for the next decade remained the forum for discussing the evolution of the profession of landscape architecture in the United States. While William A. Stiles edited the journal in New York City, Sargent directed the periodical from Brookline. Olmsted and members of his staff, especially his young partner Charles Eliot, used the periodical as an organ for presenting new ideas on landscape architecture and related matters. Van Rensselaer, however, became the most frequent contributor, penning more than fifty articles during the life of the journal.[60] In addition to reporting trends in landscape architecture, *Garden and Forest* also charted the progress of American interest in landscape conservation, city and regional planning, horticulture and botany, and garden making.

Although the amount of time that Olmsted and Richardson enjoyed as new neighbors before the latter's early death was brief—only three years—their intimate

Fig. 3.17. "A Glimpse of North Easton" from Van Rensselaer, *Henry Hobson Richardson and His Work* **(1888).** Courtesy W.E.B. DuBois Library, University of Massachusetts Amherst.

collaboration had grown from their first acquaintance and would continue through the joint work of the Olmsted office and Richardson's successor firm, Shepley, Rutan & Coolidge, and the work of other architects trained in the Richardson office. Olmsted had provided a guiding hand for his young friend from their early years in New York City on.[61] The two men learned from each other and generously shared commissions and design opportunities. The great park-maker inspired the thread of Richardson's production that emphasized geology and land-hugging form (fig. 3.17). Similarly, the close friendship of Olmsted, Richardson, and Sargent would continue, owing to the sponsorship of the Richardson memorial monograph and the ongoing association that Sargent and Olmsted maintained after Richardson's passing.

Both the architect and the landscape architect had established by 1886 clear patterns of education and professional practice that would inform their respective fields through the next generation, which they had trained, and through their examples to the broader design communities as well. Few places have ever been as central to the emerging worlds of American architecture, landscape architecture, and horticulture as the bucolic Green Hill neighborhood in the early 1880s.

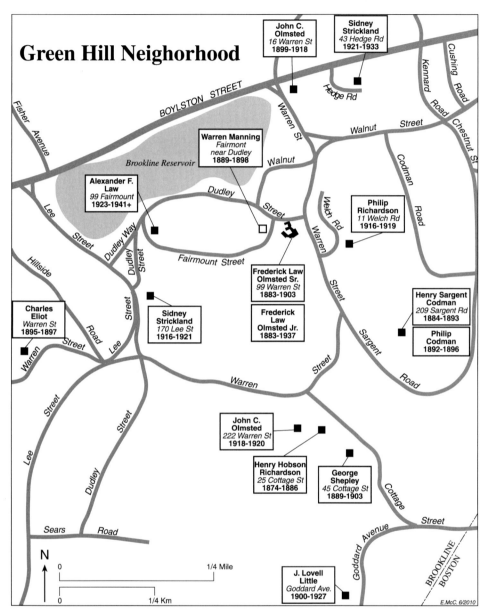

Green Hill Neighorhood

John C. Olmsted
16 Warren St
1899-1918

Sidney Strickland
43 Hedge Rd
1921-1933

BOYLSTON STREET

Warren St

Hedge Rd

Walnut Street

Kennard Road

Cushing Road

Chestnut St

Fisher Avenue

Brookline Reservoir

Warren Manning
Fairmont near Dudley
1889-1898

Walnut

Alexander F. Law
99 Fairmount
1923-1941+

Dudley

Codman Road

Welch Rd

Philip Richardson
11 Welch Rd
1916-1919

Lee Street

Dudley Way

Dudley Street

Street

Warren

Fairmount Street

Frederick Law Olmsted Sr.
99 Warren St
1883-1903

Hillside

Street

Charles Eliot
Warren St
1895-1897

Road

Lee

Sidney Strickland
170 Lee St
1916-1921

Frederick Law Olmsted Jr.
1883-1937

Street

Sargent Road

Henry Sargent Codman
209 Sargent Rd
1884-1893

Philip Codman
1892-1896

Warren

Street

Warren

Street

Street

Dudley

Street

John C. Olmsted
222 Warren St
1918-1920

Henry Hobson Richardson
25 Cottage St
1874-1886

George Shepley
45 Cottage St
1889-1903

Cottage Street

Lee

Sears Road

N

0 — 1/4 Mile

0 — 1/4 Km

Goddard Avenue

BROOKLINE
BOSTON

J. Lovell Little
Goddard Ave.
1900-1927

E.McC. 6/2010

Fig. 4.1. Map of the Green Hill neighborhood showing the locations of the residences of architects and landscape architects who interacted with the Olmsted office. Map by Eliza McClellen.

Four

THE DESIGN COMMUNITY

Perhaps the most important and most obvious network that extended from Fairsted into the surrounding neighborhoods and the community of Brookline at large was the collective of architects, landscape architects, civil engineers, horticulturalists, and other professionals who shared interests with the Olmsted family and the firm's office staff. Some of these connections began before Olmsted relocated to Brookline and continue, in some ways, into our own time. The Richardson-Olmsted matrix has already been discussed; the association of Olmsted with Charles Sprague Sargent will be examined in the next chapter. On a more general level, many of the leading members of these professions in the Boston area in the late nineteenth and early twentieth centuries lived in Brookline and had significant personal and professional ties to the Olmsted family and office.[1] The largest of these groups, and one of the most central to the production of the Fairsted office, consisted of the architects who lived in the community and who collaborated with the Olmsted firm on a range of projects, both locally and throughout the country.

Mapping the locations of architects' residences in Brookline clarifies the range of networks within which Fairsted operated. Not surprisingly, one dominant node was the Green Hill–Town Green neighborhood (fig. 4.1), where Fairsted is located. Of course, the immediate architectural counterpoint to Fairsted was the H. H. Richardson house and studio at 25 Cottage Street, a short walk from the Olmsted office at 99 Warren Street. From these two points, connections extended to members of other architectural and design firms. Members of the Olmsted office resided nearby if they could find and afford housing. John Charles Olmsted initially lived a short walk away at number 16 Warren Street; Warren Manning found a place on Fairmount Street near Dudley Street; and Charles Eliot rented a house for his family on

Warren Street near Walnut in the final years of his life. Similarly, Henry Sargent Codman and Philip Codman lived nearby at their parents' home, 208 Sargent Road, during the brief period when they were interns and members of the Olmsted office. Frederick Law Olmsted Jr., known as Rick, continued to live at Fairsted after the death of his mother until his departure for California in the 1930s.

Among the architects, George F. Shepley, the head draftsman for the Richardson office, acquired the property at 45 Cottage Street, near the residence of his former mentor at number 25. On the opposite side of Richardson's property,

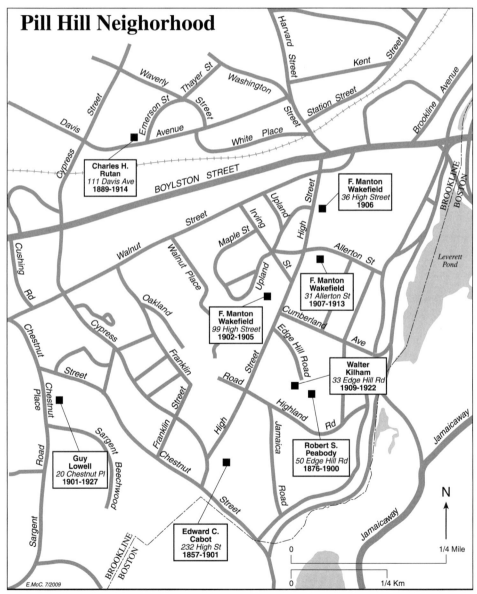

Fig. 4.2. Detail of the map of Brookline showing the concentrations of architects' residences in the High Street Hill (Pill Hill) neighborhood. Map by Eliza McClellen.

John Charles Olmsted lived at 222 Warren Street from 1918 to 1920. Architect J. Randolph Coolidge lived at 24 Cottage Street. Also in this immediate neighborhood Sidney Strickland of Strickland, Blodgett & Law built two houses, first at 43 Hedge Road and later at 170 Dudley Street. The home of his partner Alexander Law was between those two locations at 99 Fairmount Street. Nearby at 50 Fisher Avenue was Robert D. Andrews, nephew of Robert S. Peabody, former member of the Richardson office and partner at Andrews, Jaques & Rantoul. Not far from Andrews were the homes of Arthur Rotch and William H. Dabney, two outstanding architects whose careers were cut short by their early deaths.[2]

Another significant cell of designers emerged in the district that came to be known as Pill Hill (fig. 4.2), where many doctors and other professionals lived in close proximity to the Free Hospital for Women (see chapter 7), a collaboration between the Olmsted firm and George Dexter. Edward Clark Cabot, a leader of the earlier generation of Boston architects, lived at 232 High Street. In 1876 Robert S. Peabody designed and built a house at 50 Edgehill Road. Walter Kilham of Kilham & Hopkins lived at 33 Edgehill Road, and F. Manton Wakefield, one of the most prolific Brookline architects at the turn of the century, resided at 99 and later at 36 High Street. Other architects, landscape architects, and related professionals purchased or designed houses throughout Brookline.

Following Richardson's death in 1886, a series of other firms, both those created by Richardson's former assistants and those of competitors who had never worked with Richardson, became key collaborators with the Olmsted office. By this time Olmsted's work with the Boston Park Commission had provided a level of visibility and credibility that made the firm an obvious choice for a range of landscape projects, in Brookline and beyond. To consider the relations of the Olmsted office to this expanded circle of architectural firms, we first focus on domestic projects in Brookline, an element of the Olmsted office production that remains understudied. In later sections of this book, the collaborations in the fields of public landscape design and institutional or public architecture are addressed.

As a framework for understanding the collaborative process, both with clients and with architects, the "Circular as to Professional Methods and Charges," published by the office of Olmsted, Olmsted & Eliot in January 1894 and later revised by the Olmsted brothers in January 1902, clarifies the steps that the firm pursued in developing domestic landscapes in Brookline.[3] In general, this circular sought to instill in the minds of clients and architects that the Olmsted office functioned in the manner of professional architects. There is even a citation from the "Schedule of Minimum Charges" established by the American Institute of Architects as a footnote in this document. The professional approach represented by this advisory statement is not surprising for a firm headed by a man who sought to redefine the field of landscape gardening as the profession of landscape architecture. From the time of Central Park and his service with the United States Sanitary Commission, Olmsted was widely recognized as a professional who believed in clear patterns of responsibility and performance. Charles Eliot, who joined the new partnership in 1893, may also have pushed for a statement that clarified procedures and working patterns. By this time the senior partner was seventy-two and was himself trying to establish general standards for the future of his firm and of the profession.

The circular lays down a series of steps through which the firm would pass in its relations with "owners, architects, engineers and gardeners" as they supplied "professional advice with respect to the arrangement of land and landscape for use, convenience and enjoyment." Although the document refers to the work of the firm in "the arrangement and planting of public parks and squares, of private grounds and gardens, of land sub-divisions and street," it was probably most useful as a guide to private clients who would have been less familiar than public officials with professional design services. The first step was the "preliminary visit" to the grounds and, if appropriate, the development of a "preliminary plan," which would be critiqued and revised. A topographical plan, usually supplied by a civil engineer under the firm's direction, would be necessary for development of the preliminary plan. The firm advised that "the suggestion embodied in our preliminary plan should influence the architect in his design. It is therefore often important that our design should precede that of the architect." Not only was the firm to be seen as providing professional advice, but also its suggestions should precede and inform the work of the architect.

The next step was the development of the "General Plan showing the outlines of the principal constructive features, the controlling figures of elevation, and the general disposition of plantations and isolated trees." Frequently accompanied by an explanatory report, the general plan would allow the owner and the contractor to proceed with execution. If the general plan was to be executed by contract, the Olmsted firm would provide "Working Drawings, Specifications and Supervision as required." The circular notes, "In supervising work done either by contract or by the day, our practice precisely corresponds to that of an architect." Although the firm would provide "Planting Plans in all necessary detail," the landscape architects were "not dealers in plants, and we take no commission on purchases."

Clarity about expenses was also addressed: "For a Preliminary Visit our fee is ordinarily one hundred dollars . . . ; for private grounds, of varying acreage, a general plan may cost from one hundred to one thousand or more dollars." Owners were encouraged to have the firm continue to inspect the plantings for several years: "For such subsequent annual supervision, —as we wish to encourage it, —

we make, in addition to cost of assistants, about half our charge for planting and supervision the first year."

A comparison of the Olmsted office documents with the earlier "H. H. Richardson Circular for Intending Clients: Used during the Latter Part of His Life" provides a useful basis for evaluation.[4] At the request of a potential client, Richardson wrote to explain his firm's charges and "the responsibilities which, as an architect, I undertake." His basic charge was 5 percent of the cost of construction, 8 percent for projects in excess of $10,000, which was often the case. For interior decoration—such as mantels, paneling and ceilings, or furnishings and other movable elements of the design—his charge could be as high as 50 percent. (These higher fees reflect Richardson's eminence in the profession. As the architectural historian Mary Woods observes, "at a time when most architects could not collect the AIA [American Institute of Architects] standard charge of 5 percent, Richardson got 8 percent.")[5] Richardson promised to use his best judgment in issues of design, although he could not guarantee that the completed project would conform to his client's "ideas of beauty or taste, or indeed to those of any person or school." Aesthetics, taste, and expenses remained his primary concerns.

In contrast, the Olmsted, Olmsted & Eliot circular, while alluding to the American Institute of Architects standards, carefully explains the peculiar professional practices of the landscape architecture field. The longer document was committed to educating the client or consumer so that he or she could understand the necessary steps and processes in producing a design. Narrative justifications for various courses of action—either in correspondence with the client or in the production of a formal report—were built into the professional-client relationship. Also, the document was designed to be read by other professionals who might be participating in a project, such as architects, engineers, and land surveyors. It stressed the central organizing role of the landscape architects, who would ideally be the first to be consulted and would remain involved as appropriate in all decisions. The circular also stressed the significance of different types of plans that would be drawn up at specific stages or under particular circumstances. As a result, it gives the impression of a firm with an institutional character, expressing not the personal artistic vision of a single individual but the well-coordinated work of a team of experts.

When Olmsted's relationship with his friend and frequent collaborator ended with Richardson's death, the partners, apprentices, and interns of the Olmsted firm needed a structure to help them deal with a range of architectural offices, most of which were also increasing in scale and complexity in the later 1880s and 1890s. After the death of Eliot and the retirement of Frederick Law Olmsted Sr., Olmsted Brothers released a new statement of professional methods and charges on January 1, 1902 (appendix C). The firm altered the list of types of commissions for which it would provide plans and supervision to include "suburban neighbor-hoods, town sites . . . and parkways," indicating the expansion of the firm and of the profession into the new discipline of town and regional planning. Much of the language remains the same as in the 1894 document, although more didactic headings were placed throughout the three-page text to help the client navigate it: "Preliminary," "Preliminary and General Plans," "Working Drawings and Supervision," "Planting Plans and Supervision," and "Charges." As in the earlier document, the charges are given as suggested dollar figures for specific types of planning or supervision rather than as the percentage of total project cost adopted by the architectural profession. In the 1894 circular, the fees are often projected in relation to the number of acres involved: "Our experience has taught us that we can make such plans for parks for from ten to twenty dollars per acres [sic]; for sub-division of properties of large areas into building sites and roads, our ordinary charge is from five to ten dollars per acres; for private grounds, of varying acreage, a general plan may cost from one hundred to one thousand or more dollars." Surprisingly, the estimated dollar figures for basic services did not change from 1894 to 1902. Most of the discussion of fees and charges, however, is masked in indefinite language ("we charge a professional fee, plus expenses"), also noting that the firm controlled the reproduction of plans.

With this schema of professional practice in place, we can explore a range of domestic environments in Brookline created by the Olmsted office with representative locally based architects.

SHEPLEY, RUTAN & COOLIDGE

After the early death of H. H. Richardson, Olmsted maintained a close relationship with his friend's successor firm, Shepley, Rutan & Coolidge. George Shepley and Charles Rutan continued to live in Brookline after the death of their mentor.[6] Unlike Richardson, two of his successors invited the Olmsted firm to make changes and additions to the landscapes of their Brookline residences. A significant number of the houses designed by the firm in Brookline were augmented by landscapes developed by the various iterations of the Olmsted office.[7]

Richardson had selected his three successors personally. On the day of his death he dictated a memorandum naming "Messrs. Shepley, Coolidge and Rutan" to carry on his professional business. The document continues, "As to the execution of my designs the final decision must rest with Mr. George F. Shepley whom I hereby appoint as my personal representative."[8] Shepley took the lead in forming the new firm with his contemporary Charles A. Coolidge and an older member of the Richardson office, the engineer Charles Rutan. Although the young partners moved the practice from Cottage Street to downtown Boston, the successor firm remained a family operation in many ways. George Shepley married Julia Richardson, the daughter of the architect, on June 30, 1886; three years later Charles Coolidge married Shepley's sister. The firm carefully maintained ties to Richardson's widow; she continued to receive financial benefit from the work of the young partners (Shepley was twenty-six, Coolidge twenty-five, and Rutan thirty-five), who inherited approximately twenty-five incomplete projects at the time of their mentor's death.

George F. Shepley (1860–1903), a native of Saint Louis, came to Boston to attend the Massachusetts Institute of Technology after graduating from Washington University in his native city in 1880. That Ware & Van Brunt initially hired him after he graduated from MIT indicates how well his teacher, William Robert Ware, thought of him. Within the year, he moved on to the Richardson office, clearly the most coveted post on the local architectural scene. Charles Allerton Coolidge (1858–1936) was from Boston and attended Harvard, graduating in 1881. Like Shepley, he attended MIT and entered the Ware & Van Brunt office briefly before moving to the Richardson atelier. There Shepley and Coolidge met Charles Hercules Rutan (1851–1914), who had been hired by Richardson in 1869, when the Gambrill & Richardson practice was still based in New York. Rutan became the office engineer and a trusted adviser to Richardson. Very rapidly the firm began fulfilling commissions that might well have gone to Richardson if he had not died so young. In this section we explore representative commissions for houses and subdivisions in Brookline on which the Shepley and Olmsted offices worked together.

Both Shepley and Rutan lived in Brookline, and both sought landscape advice from the Olmsted firm. George Shepley lived at 45 Cottage Street, adjacent to the former Richardson residence and studio at number 25.[9] In January 1888 the Olmsted office proposed a planting plan for the Shepley property, which was refined and executed in the spring and early summer of the following year, with Frederick Law Olmsted Sr. giving personal attention to the project.[10] Though the lot was relatively modest by Brookline standards, the Shepley garden nevertheless included 123 species of plants; the Olmsted firm revised the design in 1902, including a particularly fine formal flower garden for the property (fig. 4.3). Rutan lived at 111 Davis Avenue in Brookline on a rather narrow lot in a modest residence he designed in 1889 (fig. 4.4); the Olmsted firm developed the planting plan in 1905.

More representative of the collaborations between the two firms was the two-stage development of a suburban residence for George Armstrong (fig. 4.5) at 1405 Beacon Street, a boulevard planned by the Olmsted office for the West End Street Railroad. Now two hundred feet in width and with a trolley line in the center, Beacon Street was originally a fifty-foot-wide country lane laid out in 1850. It

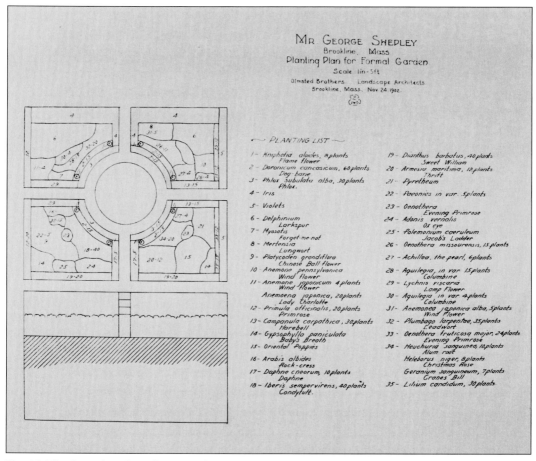

Fig. 4.3. The formal garden of George Shepley, 1902, Olmsted Brothers. Note the geometric form in the garden, typical of American patterns in garden making at this time. Courtesy National Park Service, Frederick Law Olmsted National Historic Site.

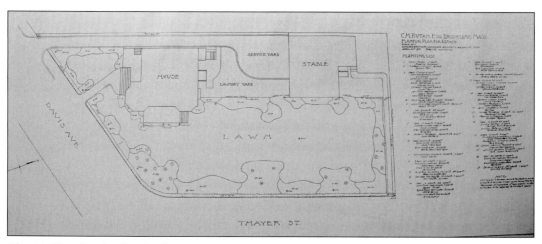

Fig. 4.4. Site plan for the Charles Rutan property, 111 Davis Street, Brookline, 1905. Courtesy National Park Service, Frederick Law Olmsted National Historic Site.

was redeveloped beginning in 1886 by the Olmsted firm for Henry M. Whitney, president of the railway, a Brookline park commissioner, and a member of the town's Tree Planting Committee.[11] At the same time this redevelopment was taking place, Armstrong invited the Shepley and Olmsted firms to oversee the design of his property. The civil engineer Alexis H. French generated a boundary plan for the property on June 9, 1887, and F. L. & J. C. Olmsted made their preliminary plan for the property by June 23 (fig. 4.6). The planting plan for the lot between Beacon and Marion streets remained under review in August of the following year.

Fig. 4.5. George Armstrong house, 1405 Beacon Street, 1887, Shepley, Rutan & Coolidge, published in *American Architect and Building News* (1887). Courtesy Brookline Preservation Commission.

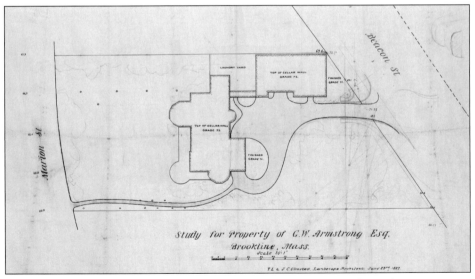

Fig. 4.6. Study for property of George Armstrong, 1887, F. L. & J. C. Olmsted. Courtesy National Park Service, Frederick Law Olmsted National Historic Site.

More than a decade later, the Olmsted office provided a new landscape plan (fig. 4.7) when Armstrong purchased an adjacent lot to the north and expanded his house, connecting it to a new stable entered from Marion Street. Between August 1899 and April 1901, the Olmsted firm and Armstrong considered new schemes to extend and alter the earlier landscape. Shepley, Rutan & Coolidge designed the original house in 1887 as the firm's first project in Brookline and oversaw the expansion of the property in 1899. The architects provided a shingled design with conical projecting towers, reminiscent of the houses of H. H. Richardson, who had died the year before. The property has since been demolished.

Closer to the Boston border and south of the Beacon Street corridor, Shepley, Rutan & Coolidge designed a red brick and limestone Classical Revival mansion in 1901 for George H. Wightman at 43 Hawes Street, overlooking the Longwood Mall. By this time the firm had embraced an emerging national interest in reviving the classical style. Wightman had served as an executive of the Carnegie Steel Corporation, and when he retired in 1899, he relocated to Brookline.[12] His substantial mansion dominated one corner of the Longwood Mall. The Olmsted firm developed the landscape plan for this property, although the rear gardens have been replaced by later additions for institutional uses.[13]

Monmouth Street bordered the Wightman house on the north, and Wightman owned property across the street, which he began to develop to designs by Shepley,

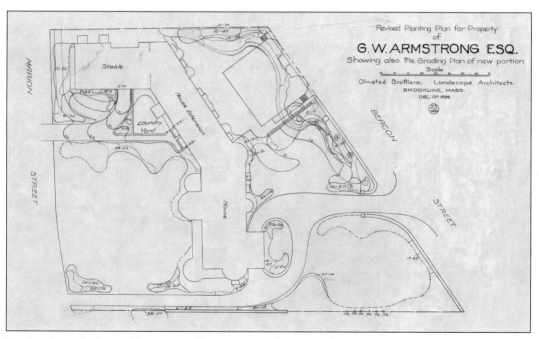

Fig. 4.7. Second phase of Armstrong development, 1899. Note the footprint in the upper right corner of an adjacent house that was demolished to make way for the expansion of the gardens. Courtesy National Park Service, Frederick Law Olmsted National Historic Site.

Rutan & Coolidge and by Olmsted Brothers in 1905. The second of these houses, 16 Monmouth Street, was planned by the architects for Wightman's daughter Elizabeth Pope in 1911, and once again the Olmsted firm developed the landscape. The value of considering this property derives from the more modest scale of the house and grounds within the collaborations of these two firms. Just as Olmsted would have wished, Wightman approached the landscape architect in advance of requesting plans from the architect. A topographical survey by Aspinwall & Lincoln, dated May 26, 1910, provided the basic information for the preliminary site visit the following month.[14] By February 6, 1911, a planting plan (fig. 4.8) had been developed with a list of fifty-two species to be used in creating the gardens. Olmsted Brothers provided naturalized planting beds along the western, northern, and eastern edges of the property to screen the house from its neighbors. No garage or carriage house was constructed, but a square vegetable garden and a space for the "clothes reel" behind the house suggest the need to capitalize on the small scale of the lot. A grading plan of June 11, 1911, noted that the house had to be moved eight and three-quarters inches to the west to accommodate changes in the design.

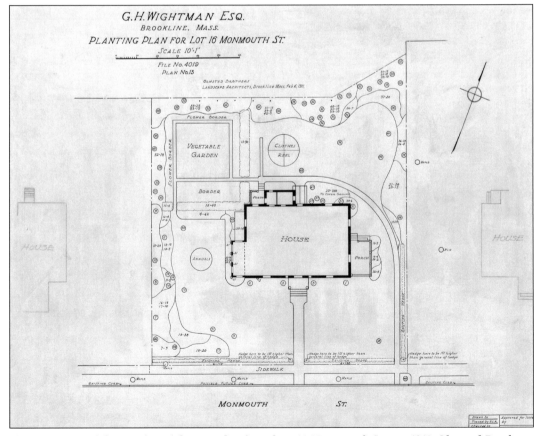

Fig. 4.8. G. H. Wightman (Pope) house, planting plan, 16 Monmouth Street, 1911, Olmsted Brothers.
Courtesy National Park Service, Frederick Law Olmsted National Historic Site.

Lawns across the front and compartmentalized service and garden areas to the rear provided a compact solution to the requirements of suburban landscape space for this brick Colonial Revival residence.

Shepley, Rutan & Coolidge would continue to work with the Olmsted firms throughout the period covered by this chapter. We return later to other collaborative projects, both schemes in which the Shepley office worked on estates planned initially by other firms and public projects with significant landscapes such as the suburban railroad stations for the Boston and Albany line or the First Parish Church at Town Green.

PEABODY & STEARNS

After the death of H. H. Richardson, the Boston firm of Peabody & Stearns, whose partners both lived in Brookline, rose to a position of dominance on the Boston architectural scene. While Shepley, Rutan & Coolidge remained very productive and well respected, Peabody & Stearns gained more attention in the architectural press and a more interesting range of clients. Important lines of connection ran between Richardson and the slightly younger Peabody and Stearns, but they were more a product of the Boston architectural environment.

Evaluating the firm's significance, Wheaton Holden, an early scholar of the firm, writes that before Richardson's death, Peabody & Stearns, "although widely patronized and admired, was clearly eclipsed by Richardson among Boston's architects. But after 1886, in spite of the accelerated output of Richardson's successor firm, Shepley, Rutan & Coolidge, Peabody & Stearns rose to preeminence in Boston occupying for some years a position commensurate to that of McKim, Mead & White in New York City."[15] On the local level, Peabody & Stearns executed seventy-two projects in Brookline between 1871 and 1917, while Shepley, Rutan & Coolidge handled forty-two commissions between 1887 and 1917. (See appendixes E, F, G, and H for further information on collaborative projects with the Olmsted office and other projects in Brookline.) The fact that Peabody & Stearns had been one of the three local architectural firms invited to submit designs for the Trinity Church competition in 1872, only two years after the partnership was established, indicates how quickly the firm had risen into the first rank on the Boston scene. Holden also emphasizes the selection of Peabody & Stearns to design the Machinery Hall and the Massachusetts State Pavilion for the Chicago World's Columbian Exposition of 1893 as validation of their ascendancy to dominance in Boston architecture. Frederick Law Olmsted was chosen to design the landscape master plan for the fair. Whether the Olmsted office was consulted about the selection of the principal architects for the exhibition is unknown.

Robert Swain Peabody (1845–1917) was the design member of the firm and the man primarily responsible for its architectural reputation. The son of the Reverend Ephraim Peabody, Robert was born in New Bedford, Massachusetts, where his father served a Unitarian congregation. Soon after Robert's birth, the Reverend Peabody was called to the pulpit of King's Chapel in Boston, one of the most prominent and influential churches in the city and in the denomination. Robert's mother was Mary Jane Derby of the Salem Derbys, a family known for its economic and political success. His sister was Ellen Derby Peabody Eliot, the wife of Professor Charles W. Eliot, who became the president of Harvard College in 1869, the year his wife died. These and other family connections would prove enormously helpful in launching the young firm. Robert attended Harvard College, graduating in 1866, seven years after Richardson. Following graduation he briefly worked with Gridley J. F. Bryant, the Boston architectural leader of the previous generation, and then studied with Henry Van Brunt, one of the dominant figures on the architectural scene at the time.[16] Like his predecessor at Harvard, Peabody went to Paris to study at the École des Beaux-Arts, joining the Atelier Daumet by the end of 1867, where he met fellow Americans Frank W. Chandler and Charles Follen McKim. When he returned to Boston in 1870, he formed a partnership with John Goddard Stearns Jr. with offices at 14 Devonshire Street, not in a suburban office-atelier such as Richardson and Olmsted maintained.

John Goddard Stearns Jr. (1843–1917) was born in New York City, although his father was originally from Brookline, to which the family returned eventually. In 1861 Stearns entered Harvard College, receiving a B.S. degree from the Lawrence Scientific School in 1863, three years senior to Peabody. After graduating, Stearns joined the Boston architectural practice of William Ware and Henry Van Brunt, where he remained for seven years, becoming the firm's chief draftsman. These were important years for American architectural education. In 1866 the Massachusetts Institute of Technology invited Ware to oversee the creation of the country's first academic program in architecture.[17] Although Stearns did not have Peabody's advantage of a period of study in Paris, he would have been introduced to an international dialogue in contemporary architecture through both of the partners in Ware & Van Brunt. In formulating his plans for MIT, Ware traveled in England and France, and the architectural curriculum he proposed was heavily indebted to the scheme of the École des Beaux-Arts. From a different perspective, Van Brunt would have exposed Stearns to the writings of Eugène-Emmanuel Viollet-le-Duc, the dominant French theorist of architectural technology and new materials, whose writings Ware was then translating for publication. Peabody had also briefly been a student of Ware's before his departure for Paris, and to this knowledge of contemporary French architectural practice, Peabody added an awareness of activities in England and a personal interest in historic American buildings to inform the firm's new architecture. Stearns and Peabody eventually became collaborators with the Olmsted office, both in the vicinity of Brookline, where they lived, and beyond.

The Peabody & Stearns firm provides a useful counterpoint to the structure, scale, and practice of the offices maintained by Richardson and Olmsted. In 1874, when Richardson moved from Staten Island to Brookline, Peabody & Stearns moved to new quarters at 40 Devonshire Street and invited Peabody's nephew Robert Day Andrews to become an office boy. In 1917, the year when both principals died, Andrews reflected in the *Architectural Review* on the organization and character of the Peabody & Stearns office: "In those days, it was easier than it is now to recognize the work of each architect. The offices were much smaller and the personal tastes of the chiefs counted for more. Also, it was a period of greater eclecticism. The profession and public alike were passing through a stage of experimentation."[18] Andrews went from serving as office boy for Peabody & Stearns to MIT and then joined the Richardson office in Brookline. Interestingly, Peabody helped another of his nephews enter the design professions when he recommended Charles Eliot as the first intern in the Olmsted office in 1883, soon after Olmsted's move to Brookline.

In their early work, Peabody and Stearns frequently collaborated with Ernest Bowditch, a Brookline-based landscape architect and civil engineer, on the landscape development of their projects, a relationship that was challenged by Olmsted's arrival in Brookline.[19] This collaboration was especially important for larger country estates and summer cottages, where significant landscapes were expected. Two centers for impressive country estates were Newport, Rhode Island, and Lenox, Massachusetts, where Peabody & Stearns developed a broad reputation and where designs were incorporated into substantial landscape plans, executed by either Bowditch or Olmsted. Wheaton Holden emphasized the importance of Newport, and especially the 1877–78 commission from Pierre Lorillard for his summer cottage, The Breakers, in establishing the national reputation of the firm.[20] Studies of country estates in Lenox also provide insights into the competition between the two landscape architects in their collaborations with Peabody & Stearns.[21]

Soon after creating the firm, both partners moved to houses in Brookline which they designed. Stearns's house was built on family land at 24 Pleasant Street in the Coolidge Corner district of Brookline in 1875. The house at 50 Edgehill Road in the newly fashionable neighborhood of Pill Hill that Peabody built the following year was a model of the Queen Anne style, which he would soon discuss in architectural journals and exhibit in his contemporary work.[22] Pill Hill also boasted another Peabody design next door at 44 Edgehill Road, built for Moorfield Storrey in 1877. With irregular massing, especially a diagonally projecting wing, the Peabody house exuded variety in the red brick, cut-brick, and shingle envelope terminating in numerous gables, dormers, and chimneys.[23] Peabody read a paper before the meeting of the Boston Society of Architects in April 1877 titled "A Talk about 'Queen Anne,'" in which he connected the current interest in late medieval and eighteenth-century vernacular forms as inspiration in British architecture to an emerging American focus on colonial buildings as a foundation for a national style of architecture.[24] He expanded on these principles in a two-part article, "Georgian Houses of New England," published in *American Architect and Building News* in October 1877 and February 1878.[25]

One of the most substantial projects that Peabody & Stearns completed in Brookline was the compound of houses for the brothers Joseph H. and Jonathan H. White on adjacent lots overlooking Boylston Street and the Brookline Reservoir. The Olmsted office oversaw the development and redevelopment of these properties, while Shepley, Rutan & Coolidge also played a role. Joseph and Jonathan were the brothers of R. H. White, whose Boston department store Peabody & Stearns had designed in 1877.[26] Like his sibling, Joseph was president of a Boston dry goods business, White, Payson & Company, which eventually became Joseph H. White & Company. Presumably R. H. recommended Peabody & Stearns when Joseph embarked on the development of property he had purchased from William P. Perkins on Fisher Hill. Peabody & Stearns designed for Joseph White a twenty-five-room house (fig. 4.9), then the largest on Fisher Hill, in 1880.[27] Over a red brick mass trimmed in granite, Peabody added shingles for parts of the second story and the dormer gables, some of which were ornamented with half-timbering. Tall ribbed chimneys animated the silhouette of the house. At a much larger scale than his own residence, the White house projected the Queen Anne formula that Peabody had been developing for several years.

The entrance drive from Boylston Street passed through a porte cochere on the

Fig. 4.9. Joseph H. White house, Boylston Street, 1880–81, Peabody & Stearns; property developed and altered by the Olmsted firm from 1880 on. *L'Architecture Americaine* (1886).

Fig. 4.10. Photograph looking toward Fairmount Hill across the Brookline Reservoir from near the Joseph H. White property. Courtesy Brookline Preservation Commission.

north side of the house. A broad terrace across the southern facade provided panoramic views over the Brookline Reservoir (fig. 4.10). The earliest evidence of the Olmsted firm's involvement in the estate is a "Plan Showing the Proposed Changes in the Boundary Line between the Estates of Joseph H. White and Henry Lee," dated May 23, 1880.[28] Already this plan records twenty projected lots for development east of Catlin Street, intersected by Seaver Street, Hyslop Road, and Leicester Street. By June 25, 1881, Olmsted had developed a planting scheme for the gardens above the house, and a plan for the entrance and approach road followed on December 2.[29] As noted, plans to subdivide the property for future development had been under discussion from an early moment in Olmsted's involvement. In December 1884 Joseph White joined with four neighbors and the Goddard Land Company to publish the Olmsted firm's "General Plan for Subdivision of Property on Brookline Hill."[30] F. L. & J. C. Olmsted proposed 296 lots for development of Brookline Hill, now known as Fisher Hill. Although most of this land was still undeveloped, White and a few of the owners had constructed houses here. (A fuller discussion of the Fisher Hill development can be found in chapter 6.)

With this future template in mind, both Joseph and Jonathan White commissioned further projects from Olmsted and from Peabody & Stearns on Fisher Hill. Immediately east of Joseph's property, Jonathan purchased land bounded by Buckminster Road to the east. For Jonathan White, Peabody & Stearns designed a more modest but still substantial residence at 45 Buckminster in 1888. The Olmsted archives include a plan for the Jonathan White house (fig. 4.11), directly east of the Joseph White house, drawn on November 7, 1887.[31] The civil engineer Alexis H.

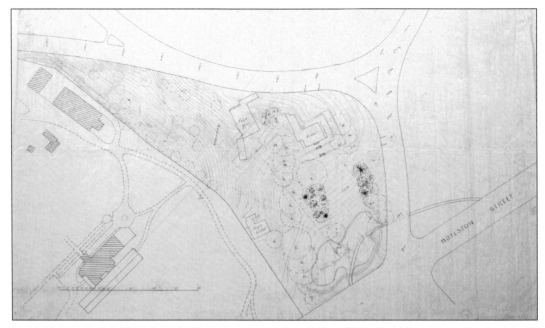

Fig. 4.11. Plan for the Jonathan H. White property, Brookline, 1887. Note also the earlier Joseph H. White house at the lower left and an earlier barn-stable group in the upper left corner. Courtesy National Park Service, Frederick Law Olmsted National Historic Site.

French had produced a plan of the estate by January 2, 1888.[32] Various studies for approach roads, walls and gates, and planting schemes followed, as the scale of the house increased in the planning.

While Jonathan White developed his property, Joseph turned to the Olmsted office to consider a series of possible construction projects on his adjacent land. These resulted in three houses, including two for White family members, one directly east and one north and west of the original house. The first of these (fig. 4.12) sat immediately adjacent to the original house, bordering on the Jonathan White property line. For its architect, in 1891 Joseph White turned from Peabody & Stearns to Shepley, Rutan & Coolidge.[33] The Olmsted firm provided a planting scheme for the property in April 1892. Like its larger neighbor, the house, built for one of Joseph White's daughters,[34] included a porte cochere on the uphill side of the building and a broad terrace across the south and east facades to capitalize on the view from this elevated location. Plans showing a vista path in the gardens connecting the original Joseph White house, this addition to the compound, and the Jonathan White house underscore the family connections.[35]

Two years later, for a second house on the property built for another daughter and her husband, the Batchelder house (fig. 4.13) at 80 Seaver Street, Joseph White again selected Shepley, Rutan & Coolidge. The architects placed the house on a brick

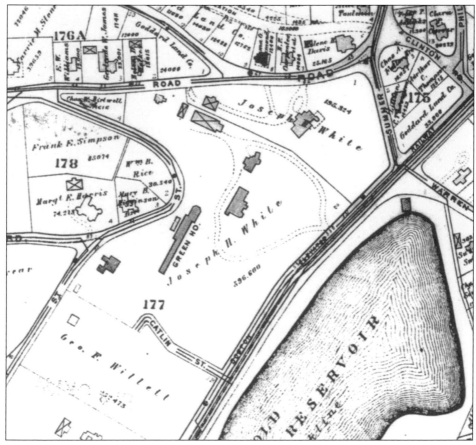

Fig. 4.12. Detail of the 1907 *Atlas of the Town of Brookline* showing the relationship of the Jonathan White house (top, incorrectly labeled "Joseph H. White") to the Joseph White houses (below). Courtesy Brookline Preservation Commission.

terrace overlooking the Brookline Reservoir, the larger Joseph White residence, and the greenhouses for the estate. Knit into the landscape scheme of the adjacent White properties, the Batchelder residence displays the same red brick material and multiple bays of the original White house but is more regular in massing and in plan. The entrance drive from Seaver Street allowed for privacy from the other residences in the compound. In the same year, 1894, Shepley, Rutan & Coolidge also designed a house for the White estate's gardener at 104 Buckminster Road.

It is interesting to observe how compressed the development pattern of the White properties was. In 1881 Joseph White built the largest house on Fisher Hill to designs by Peabody & Stearns and a landscape laid out by Olmsted. By 1884 his brother Jonathan had built a smaller house on the property immediately to the east. In the same year, Joseph commissioned a study of the potential development of his land for residential subdivision. In 1892 he and several neighbors approved a comprehensive development proposal conceived by the Olmsted firm for the creation of nearly three

Fig. 4.13. Perspective drawing of the third Joseph H. White (Batchelder) house, 1894, Peabody & Stearns. Courtesy National Park Services, Frederick Law Olmsted National Historic Site.

hundred lots on their combined property. Indeed, Joseph White may have been a client for a "show map," Charles Eliot's term for a document drawn up to illustrate the proposed subdivision of a larger estate.[36] Admittedly, even after the cutting up of the land, the White family members lived on generous parcels with excellent views. Although lots along Boylston Street were suggested on these plans, that land was not sold for development. In 1924 Mr. and Mrs. Galen L. Stone purchased the Joseph White estate and again requested the advice of the Olmsted firm in the modification of the gardens.[37] Sold for institutional uses in 1948, the property was not fully developed until the 1980s, with a series of condominium units built along the Boylston Street corridor and elsewhere on the grounds.

Peabody & Stearns remained an important collaborator in other activities of the Olmsted office, which are addressed in later chapters of this book. Like the Olmsteds, the two architects were invited to advise on projects for the Town of Brookline and its public school system, among other points of professional interface. In 1909 Robert Swain Peabody, who had moved from Brookline to Boston in 1902, was appointed chairman of the Boston Park Commission, a position that he held almost continuously until his death in 1917. Having worked closely with the Olmsted firm for many years, including the period when his nephew Charles Eliot was a partner in the firm, he was an ideal collaborator in the continued development and maintenance of the Boston park system. The deaths of both Peabody and Stearns in 1917 marked the end of an era in Boston architecture.

ANDREWS, JAQUES & RANTOUL

The third prominent architectural firm of late-nineteenth-century Boston was Andrews, Jaques & Rantoul. Both Robert D. Andrews and Herbert Jaques were

Brookline residents, and the firm worked closely with the Olmsted office on multiple projects. Robert Day Andrews (1857–1928) was born in Hartford, Connecticut, and educated for two years at the Massachusetts Institute of Technology. He trained in several Boston offices, including that of his uncle Robert Swain Peabody before a period of travel in Europe. Upon his return, he joined the office of H. H. Richardson. In 1885 he entered a partnership with Herbert Jaques (1857–1916) and Augustus Neal Rantoul (1864–1934). Jaques was another alumnus of the Richardson office and had accompanied his mentor on a tour of Europe in 1882.[38] The firm established a reputation both in Brookline and nationally, with fifty-six

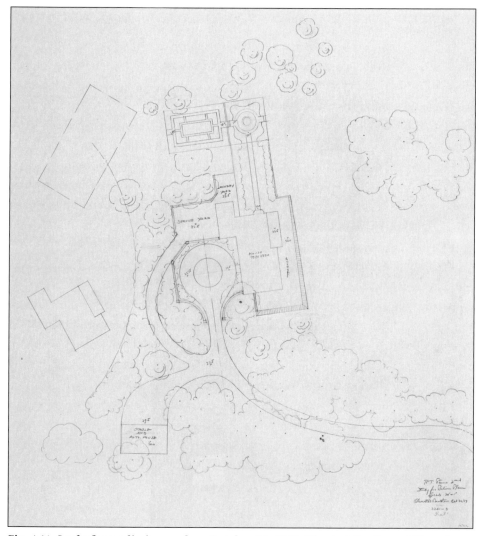

Fig. 4.14. Study for preliminary plan, October 30, 1907, Olmsted Brothers. Other drawings from this period emphasize the importance of vista corridors to the east from this desirable location on the top of Singletree Hill. Courtesy National Park Service, Frederick Law Olmsted National Historic Site.

local projects. (See appendix G for a list of collaborative projects by Olmsted and the Andrews firm in Brookline.) Among these were additions to The Country Club, addressed later in this book.

One domestic project in the Singletree Hill (Heath Street) section of Brookline was an estate on which both Andrews, Jaques & Rantoul and the Olmsted firm worked, if not always in tandem. In the eighteenth century, this area of Brookline consisted of large parcels held by a small number of families.[39] At 400 Heath Street, Andrews, Jaques & Rantoul created a country house for William Cox in 1890 that revealed the partners' training in the firm of H. H. Richardson. Across the road, Walter Channing Cabot purchased the property at 325 Heath Street and commissioned Andrews, Jaques & Rantoul to devise an impressive residence in 1893 for his daughter Ruth Cabot Paine, the wife of Robert Treat Paine II.[40] The Paines invited Olmsted Brothers to work on the redevelopment of the landscape in 1907.[41] Grading and topographical plans indicate several opposing possibilities for the location of a new "stable and auto house" as well as an evolving series of formal gardens. The more architectonic gardens (fig. 4.14) of this generation are a distinct departure from the work of Frederick Law Olmsted, who had died two years before this commission. Even the hand of the draftsman (initials R.B.W.) reveals a new, freer approach to the presentation of architectural and landscape space typical of early-twentieth-century design.

The Paine estate was adjacent to Hillfields, the Joseph Randolph Coolidge estate, which bridged the hill from Boylston Street on the north to Heath Street on the south. Here the Olmsted firm worked from 1885 to 1890 designing the grounds to complement the main residence, designed by C. Howard Walker in 1885–86.[42] On part of that estate Coolidge's son, the architect J. Randolph Coolidge Jr., lived and designed buildings. In general, the large estate district of Singletree Hill was prime territory for the work of the Olmsted office, which found active employment here for several decades.

OTHER BROOKLINE ARCHITECTS

The list of prominent architects who chose to live in Brookline and who requested the assistance of the Olmsteds extends well beyond these three dominant firms. For example, Edward C. Cabot, a neighbor of Robert Peabody, designed several houses in Brookline with his partner Frank Chandler, a close friend of Peabody's, along High Street and Edgehill Road in the Pill Hill neighborhood. In 1882–83 Cabot & Chandler collaborated with the Olmsted office on the Charles Storrow house, located at 112 High Street on Pill Hill.[43] Cabot lived in his family's house at the south end of High Street; Storrow, a merchant in the China and India trade who had raised a volunteer regiment to fight for the Union cause, was married to Cabot's daughter Martha.

The Storrow house is a classic example of Shingle Style design, with a brick first story and various patterns of wooden shingles originally on the second story and roof. The Olmsted firm and the architects took great care in siting the house and merging the architecture with the gardens (fig. 4.15). More than two dozen

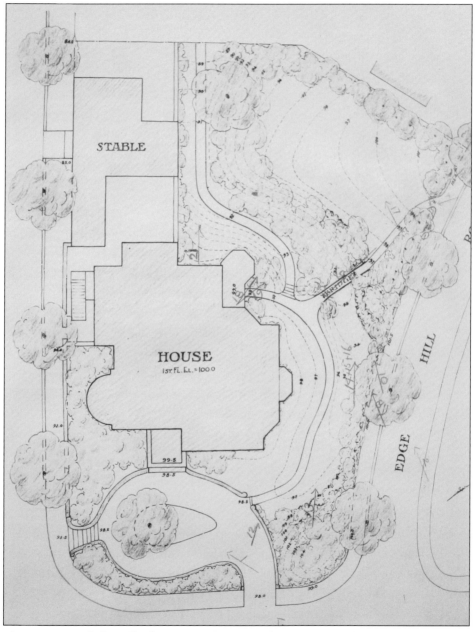

Fig. 4.15. General plan, Charles Storrow house, High Street, Brookline. Courtesy National Park Service, Frederick Law Olmsted National Historic Site.

Fig. 4.16. Entrance drive and perimeter boulder wall for the Charles Storrow house.
Courtesy National Park Service, Frederick Law Olmsted National Historic Site.

schemes were developed for the entrance drive and walkways at the corner of High Street and Cumberland Avenue. Fortunately, significant elements of this scheme survive.

The Olmsteds made multiple studies for the naturalistic landscape development of the property. A low wall of large-scale boulders marks the periphery of the property (fig. 4.16), serpentine walls of boulders extend from the house into the garden, and a small boulder bridge arches over a stream (fig. 4.17); a cutting and vegetable garden originally occupied a lower section of the property. The Olmsted firm also developed a plan for the subdivision of part of the property. The garden project, which was begun in 1882 before the move of the firm to Brookline, helped to demonstrate what a lucrative market Brookline would be for the Olmsted office through many decades to come.

A large number of other Brookline-based architects interacted with the Olmsteds. Guy Lowell, who developed a national reputation as both an architect and a garden designer; Horace Frazer, a partner in the firm of Chapman & Frazer; and J. Lovell Little all lived in Brookline and had professional connections to the Fairsted office. A large landscape design for the home of John G. Wright in 1896, located across Heath Street from Horace Frazer's own house, marked an important collaboration between Olmsted and Chapman & Frazer.[44] (Portions of the landscape, though not the house, survive as a recreation area owned by the town.) In a later generation, both Walter Kilham, principal partner in Kilham & Hopkins, and J. Randolph Coolidge Jr. served with Frederick Law Olmsted Jr. on the first Brookline Planning Commission, of which Olmsted was the chairman from 1914

Fig. 4.17. Path and bridge along the Edge Hill Road side of the Charles Storrow property. Courtesy National Park Service, Frederick Law Olmsted National Historic Site.

to 1916. Those volunteer activities not only benefited the community but also led to collaborative projects between their firms, such as the public housing projects on which the Olmsteds and Kilham & Hopkins cooperated during the First World War, and Brookline High School, where the two firms planned developments from the 1920s through the 1940s. Both Alexander Law and Sidney Strickland, principals in the firm of Strickland, Blodgett & Law, lived in Brookline and executed many projects with the Olmsted firm there and elsewhere. F. Manton Wakefield, who was trained by Richardson, also lived in Brookline, designed many houses in the community, and worked frequently with the Olmsted office.

Brookline remained a magnet for the design community from the 1880s to the 1930s. The physical beauty of the area, the professional management of the town, and the presence of both the Richardson and Olmsted offices were initially the principal reasons for this surprising concentration of design professionals. There was a significant difference, however, in the impact that the two firms exerted. Richardson trained many architects who opened offices of their own and often lived in Brookline. Most of the apprentices of the Olmsted office, by contrast, remained in the employ of the Olmsted firm, so there was not as large a local community of competing landscape architects. Rather it was the impact of the Olmsted firm on the development of Brookline, its landscape and townscape, that continued to attract designers.

The relationship of the Olmsted office to the Brookline-based architects changed subtly but significantly during the period under study. The long-term and intimate association of Henry Hobson Richardson and Frederick Law Olmsted, begun decades earlier in New York, ensured that their joint projects were true collaborations. Indeed, Olmsted may have exerted the dominant influence on Richardson's sense of environmental design. The selection of boulders, granite, brownstone, and shingles, often massed and treated in a natural manner, gave Richardson's buildings an immediate connection to both the character of the site and the manner in which Olmsted developed the surrounding landscape. Although a distinguished and cohesive group of projects from both designers can be identified and traced, none of these was located in Brookline, where many of the designs were generated. Nevertheless, the qualities that drew both Richardson and Olmsted to Brookline infused the work they completed in tandem and influenced many of their contemporaries in Brookline and throughout the country. At Richardson's early death, this continuity was severed.

Admittedly, the early work of Shepley, Rutan & Coolidge revealed the lingering influence of Richardson and his intellectual partnership with Olmsted. Within a very few years, however, as documented by the Brookline examples, this second-generation firm had begun to embrace national trends that were more dependent on classicizing, European architectural models and less derived from the nature of the site and natural materials. This change also occurred in the work of the Olmsted office, especially following the 1893 World's Columbian Exposition in Chicago and the collaboration with the Paris-trained architect Richard Morris Hunt on Biltmore, the massive George Washington Vanderbilt estate in Asheville, North Carolina, in the early 1890s. Because the younger members of the Shepley firm were not close personal friends of Olmsted's, they retreated to a more formal and professional manner of operation that often brought the landscape architects to the project later than might have been the case with Richardson. Indeed, the removal of the Shepley, Rutan & Coolidge office from Cottage Street to downtown Boston broke the pattern of a suburban, domestic environment that was also a professional office and an informal academy of architecture.

The same patterns are observable in the relationship of the Olmsted office to both the Peabody & Stearns and the Andrews, Jaques & Rantoul firms. Both sets of architects had personal or family connections to Fairsted, and the principals continued to live in Brookline. But their offices were in town, and they chose to interact with more than one landscape architect or civil engineer, depending on the needs of a project and the interests of their clients. Although Peabody and Stearns were both of a generation only slightly removed from that of Richardson and Olmsted, they did not share the same career path or close personal friendships. Both the Peabody firm and the Andrews office were disbanded in 1917 with the deaths of the principals, ending a second generation of architectural dominance in Brookline and beyond.

On the other side of the equation, the promulgation of the "Circular as to Professional Methods and Charges" in 1894 shows that the Olmsted office was also moving into a new phase of operation at that point. As Frederick Law Olmsted entered his seventh decade, the scale of his operation expanded, and the number of employees increased, he also needed to establish clear professional procedures for design development and implementation, and this removed the level of direct collaboration that he had enjoyed with Richardson. When Charles Eliot joined the partnership in 1893, he pushed for patterns and office practices that paralleled the standardization that was also emerging in the architectural field. John Charles Olmsted, as the bridge between his stepfather's and his stepbrother's generations of the firm, had acquired habits of discipline and order that were necessary for such wide-ranging projects. Since he and Charles Eliot were often on the road throughout much of the 1890s, there had to be a system in place that would allow a changing and growing office roster to fulfill expectations with predictability. After Eliot's early death in 1897, Olmsted Jr. had to step into the family business more fully. While John Charles continued to control the practice until his death in 1920, Rick was partially deflected into helping establish the program in landscape architecture at Harvard in 1900. He rose quickly to prominence, especially after his appointment to the McMillan Commission on the redevelopment of the national capital in 1901. He also became a major force in the emergence of city, town, and regional planning both as a component of landscape architecture and as a parallel profession in the opening decades of the twentieth century.

But it was in Brookline that all the generations of the Olmsted firm chose to make their homes and continued to find significant employment. Just looking at the understudied work in domestic architecture—both the houses and their landscapes—which exemplifies the interactions of the Olmsted firms with the community of local architects reinforces how very exceptional Brookline remained as a community and as a physical environment. The citizens of "the richest town in the world" considered designers essential colleagues in crafting and maintaining an attractive community. Like the Olmsted office members, many of these professionals also achieved regional or national reputations, often based in part on the quality of the projects they executed in Brookline.

Five

CHARLES SPRAGUE SARGENT

Frederick Law Olmsted's prominence in Brookline is unquestionable, and the prevailing wisdom has always decreed that Henry Hobson Richardson's presence drew people to the Warren Street neighborhood, in particular Olmsted himself. Historically, however, there has been an unrecognized third element in what turns out to be an important triad in the history of architecture, landscape architecture, and horticulture in Brookline and in the larger world: Charles Sprague Sargent, director of the Arnold Arboretum and longtime Brookline resident. Sargent's presence, his wealth, social standing, and familial connections, combined with his own considerable contribution to the fields of horticulture and dendrology, figure significantly in Brookline's stature within the Boston area and beyond. Indeed, as has already been observed both by Peter B. Wight in 1886 and by James O'Gorman almost one hundred years later, Richardson's choice of residences reflected "social and professional aspirations," and the "refined and cultured society whose association and sympathy he craved."[1]

Olmsted, visiting Richardson, followed suit. Sargent would certainly have been among those he sought out, because of his social and professional stature, but also because his estate, Holm Lea, reflected not only his own landscape ideals but also those promoted by Olmsted and admired by Richardson. As we shall see, Sargent's professional position as director of the Arnold Arboretum brought him both regional and international renown, but he was also active and influential in his own town. These three men were admiring colleagues; their work and their collaborations significantly affected the community they lived in, the larger metropolis of Boston, and beyond that, national policies, particularly in regard to Olmsted and Sargent. Brookline's bucolic character provided the perfect setting for these men to inhabit and interact in, their personal and professional lives constantly and effortlessly interweaving.

Crucial to Sargent's development was the environment in which he grew up—not only the Brookline estate so lovingly established by his father, Ignatius Sargent, but also the aura of horticultural and design practices that permeated the large estates dotting the verdant landscape. It has already been well established that from the seventeenth century on, Brookline's environment was rural in nature. Early allotment farmlands, originally apportioned to citizens of Boston in the hamlet of Muddy River, passed over the next century into the settled farming community of Brookline (incorporated in 1705). Toward the end of the eighteenth century and early in the nineteenth, with the opening of thoroughfares between Boston and Brookline, wealthy Boston merchants began purchasing large farms or piecing smaller ones together to form significant estates, chiefly inhabited in the warmer months.[2] "For the fashionable gentleman," observes Ronald Dale Karr, "a country estate was mandatory; but in the best English tradition, a nearby urban townhouse was of equal necessity. Most of these genteel newcomers therefore retained Boston addresses and only occupied their Brookline estates from April to October."[3] These men, by and large well traveled, especially in Europe, brought back sophisticated and cultured design concepts as well as horticultural practices directly resulting from their travel observations. The importation and introduction of plants and trees were the inevitable result. It is important to remember in thinking about the various properties in Brookline that many of the species that seem commonplace today were exotics in the nineteenth century, including the rhododendrons and kalmias that eventually became ubiquitous landscape material.

Early on, in 1792, prominent Bostonians established the Massachusetts Society for Promoting Agriculture, a group consisting of one-third "merchants; another third lawyer-statesmen; and the rest a mix of physicians and ministers," who banded together to acquire and disseminate information about and promote agriculture in Massachusetts.[4] Later, in 1829, many of these same citizens created the Massachusetts Horticultural Society (based on the Horticultural Society of London, later the Royal Horticultural Society) as a means of advancing horticultural knowledge, but also, according to Tamara Plakins Thornton, because "identification with horticulture . . . assured Boston's industrialists and merchants that the historical stage of materialism was a thing of the past. The very practice of horticulture was evidence of an advanced civilization and the formation of a horticultural society an emblem of cultural refinement."[5] Many of these early large landholders in Brookline were either founders or active members of the Massachusetts Horticultural Society, both supporting it and exhibiting the products of their elaborate cultivating in its numerous exhibitions.

Among its initiators was Colonel Thomas Handasyd Perkins (1764–1854), a wealthy Boston merchant trader who bought up large tracts of land and built a summer home sited atop one of Brookline's rolling hills, artificially elevated to provide an "uninterrupted view of Boston," writes Harriet F. Woods in her 1874 *Historical Sketches of Brookline, Mass.,* "and Colonel Perkins so planned his house as to command the fine prospect from his parlor windows [fig. 5.1]. The whole line of the Mill-dam, and the beautiful expanse of Charles River and Back Bay were included in this extensive panorama."[6] Initially what he called his "Brooklyne Farm" was a working farm, but by 1818, taking advantage of his numerous ships sailing around the world, he began importing an assortment of trees. According to Andrew Jackson Downing, writing in 1849, Perkins's estate was "one of the most interesting in this neighborhood. The very beautiful lawn . . . abounds with exquisite trees, finely disposed; among them, some larches and Norway firs, and with many other rare trees of uncommon beauty and form."[7]

Toward the end of his life Perkins was particularly interested in rhododendrons and azaleas.[8] "He was naturally a lover of the beautiful both in nature and art," notes Woods, "and spared no pains in the importing and cultivating of choice plants and trees on his beautiful place in Warren Street, which was quite a resort for visitors from many places."[9] Those visitors included President James Monroe

Fig. 5.1. The house of Thomas Handasyd Perkins, located on an artificially created hilltop.
Carl Seaberg and Stanley Paterson, *Merchant Prince of Boston* (1971).

in 1817, the marquis de Lafayette during his 1824–25 tour, and John James Audubon in 1836.[10] Frequent trips abroad brought visits to private estates, botanical gardens, and plant nurseries, and his professional correspondence is laced with requests for seeds from exotic places. His library contained a significant collection of agricultural and garden books.[11]

Perkins kept extensive glasshouses, said to be among the earliest in the Boston area. These three-hundred-foot-long greenhouses were devoted to grapes, peaches, and nectarines, as well as exotic fruits and flowers, especially camellias, for which he was renowned.[12] Marshall Pinckney Wilder, himself the owner of a substantial estate in Dorchester called Hawthorn Grove, wrote of Perkins in the *Memorial History of Boston, 1630–1880,* that his "residence in France and other foreign lands, where he had seen fine fruits and flowers, stimulated his natural taste, and induced him to purchase this estate in 1800, when he began to build his house, to lay out his grounds, and to erect greenhouses and glass structures for the cultivation of fruits and flowers. . . . For fifty years Colonel Perkins's estate was kept in the best manner by experienced foreign gardeners, and at an expense of more than ten thousand dollars annually."

The article confirms that Perkins spared no expense, importing trees and plants from Europe and exhibiting their "products" at the Massachusetts Horticultural Society. In 1840, Wilder concludes, "he introduced the Victoria Hamburg, West St. Peter's and Cannon Hall Muscat grape-vines, presented to him by Sir Joseph Paxton, gardener to the Duke of Devonshire."[13] In the 1880 *History of the Massachusetts Horticultural Society,* Perkins is frequently mentioned for his exhibitions of fine specimens. At the first anniversary dinner, held in 1830, he was among the group singled out who had "by precept and example, assiduously fostered a taste for cultivation, and successfully promoted developments in all the various branches of rural economy."[14]

Colonel Perkins's brother and business partner James Perkins (1761–1822) maintained an equally fine estate at nearby Pine Bank in Jamaica Plain. "The [James] Perkins estate," writes Downing,

on the border of Jamaica lake, is one of the most beautiful residences near Boston. The natural surface of the ground is exceedingly flowing and graceful, and it is varied by two or three singular little dimples, or hollows, which add to its effect. The perfect order of the grounds; the beauty of the walks, sometimes skirting the smooth open lawn, enriched by rare plants and shrubs, and then winding by the shadowy banks of the water; the soft and quiet character of the lake itself . . . all these features make this place a little gem of natural and artistical harmony, and beauty.[15]

Harriet Whitcomb described it in 1897 as having "a broad, winding avenue, beneath noble pines and larches," affording "many rich landscape features" that won the estate admiration for its "grandeur and nobility."[16]

Across Jamaica Pond, industrialist Thomas Lee (1779–1867) became a resident of Brookline in 1845, along with his wife, Eliza Buckminster Lee (1794–1864), the author of *Sketches of New England* (1837) and *Naomi* (1848), "with its beautiful descriptions of colonial Brookline" (fig. 5.2).[17] Once again Harriet Woods waxes lyrical about the landscape, revealing not only that the local landowners imported trees and shrubs, but also that some, like Lee, were interested in retaining and nurturing native landscape features. Although he was a frequent traveler in Europe, "Mr. Lee was a great lover of natural beauty, and preserved the forest trees which adorned his place, and admired the natural rocks with their wild mosses and vines about them, too much to permit them to be removed by blasting. What a man of less taste would have regarded as blemishes, he looked upon with the true eye of one who lived close to the heart of Nature, and won from her many a secret."[18]

Downing's earlier praise enlarges upon Woods's observations: "Enthusiastically fond of botany, and gardening in all its configurations, Mr. Lee has here formed a residence of as much variety and interest as we ever saw in so moderate a compass—about 20 acres. It is, indeed, not only a most instructive place to the ama-

Fig. 5.2. The home of Thomas and Eliza Lee; the landscape was noted for its emphasis on native plants. Courtesy Historic New England.

teur of landscape gardening, but to the naturalist and lover of plants. Every shrub
seems placed precisely in the soil and aspect it likes best, and native and foreign
Rhododendrons, Kalmias, and other rare shrubs, are seen here in finest condition." Reinforcing Woods's comments about the natural aspects of Lee's place, he
goes on: "There is a great deal of variety in the surface here, and while the lawn-
front of the house has a polished and graceful air, one or two other portions are
quite picturesque. Near the entrance gate is an English oak, only fourteen years
planted, now forty feet high."[19] Robert Manning describes Lee as a "lover and cul-
tivator of our native flowering plants." In 1839, before his move to Brookline, Lee,
a founding member of the Massachusetts Horticultural Society, funded a prize
specifically designed to encourage the cultivation of native flora.[20]

Slightly later, a small but highly cultivated nine-and-one-half-acre place in
Brookline was developed by Augustus Lowell (1830–1900), long associated with
the manufacture of cotton and the East India trade as well as the Lowell Institute.[21]
Lowell came by his interest in horticulture naturally. His grandfather, the industrialist John Lowell, a founder and president of the Massachusetts Society for Promoting Agriculture, was an avocational horticulturist with a handsome country
estate in Roxbury called Bromley Vale. The first orchids known in America graced
his greenhouses.[22] Lowell's son John Amory Lowell, himself a founding member
of the Massachusetts Horticultural Society, continued those traditions at Bromley

Fig. 5.3. Sevenels, the estate developed by Augustus Lowell beginning in 1866. Collection of Carol Bundy.

Vale. According to his grandson the astronomer Percival Lowell (1855–1916), he was an avid horticulturist: "As a botanist he was known not only at home but abroad, and was on terms of correspondence, not to say criticism, with botanists of his day."[23] Although Augustus Lowell became active in the field later in life, horticulture proved, according to son Percival, "a very deep-seated passion" which "became his most pronounced avocation."[24] Returning in 1866 from almost three years abroad with his family, Lowell cast about for a country place for himself, his wife, and (eventually) their seven children.[25] He found it in Brookline, in a place he named "Sevenels," in honor of his progeny (fig. 5.3).

The property already had an unspecified form of garden and two greenhouses, begun in 1800 when Boston merchant Stephen Higginson (1743–1828) purchased the land for "what was then a large country seat in Brookline," according to his grandson Thomas Wentworth Higginson.[26] "It is fair to presume that Mr. Higginson brought back [from England] a love of smooth lawns and patterned gardens, for here they are and here ever since, through successive ownerships, have they remained," adds Lowell's daughter, the poet Amy Lowell.[27] In these gardens, writes Percival Lowell, the emotionally remote Augustus Lowell "centered his affections, greenhouse and garden dividing the year between them."[28] The family decamped for Brookline each April and did not return to Boston until November; the children, in the academic interim, were driven to school by horse and carriage every day by Augustus Lowell, just as he had been driven by his father from Roxbury. The children thought of Sevenels as their real home.

"Two hot-houses of grapes helped to shield the [garden], which lay in a hollow open to the south," Percival Lowell continues. "Natural embankments enclosed it on the east and west, and a raised roadway, shut off from view, made artificial protection on the north. Clipped evergreens stood for sentinels along a terraced path, ending in an arbor which fringed one side of it, and a corresponding row faced them upon the slope opposite. In this sheltered spot he spent much of his time" (fig. 5.4). Of horticultural inclinations, Percival Lowell writes that his father's was "botany . . . of the old-fashioned kind," and he goes on to observe that "he did not pursue it as a science, but cultivated it as an art. . . . Pretty much every tree upon his place (and it included some rare ones) was personally known to him. . . . He was constantly importing new plants and then watching them succeed. Though he made no parade of knowledge or of success, he not infrequently had plants which knew no rival in the neighborhood."[29] For the Brookline of that period, this is a powerful statement. Lowell packed the property with trees and plants, but he did so in such a skillful manner that it suggested a much larger estate (fig. 5.5). In his hothouses he raised hundreds of plants to be tried out on his grounds.

When Amy Lowell inherited Sevenels upon her father's death in 1900, she

Fig. 5.4. Pathway leading to the hothouses at Sevenels. Collection of Carol Bundy.

continued the cultivation of gardens and grounds in the same configurations and with equally tender affections. "The love of flowers has persisted in our family for many years," she wrote, "and on Mr. Higginson's admirable ground-plan my father raised up such spaces of flowering beauty as few children can have the good fortune to look back upon (fig. 5.6)."[30] In an essay titled "Sevenels" she describes the estate in detail, with its dense arrangements of trees, shrubs, and plants, and an open meadow, thick with daisies and buttercups in June. The land beyond the meadow became a grove, "a little handful of land so cunningly cut by paths and with trees so artfully disposed that one can wander happily among them and almost believe that one is walking in a real wood." She goes on:

> The house itself stands in the midst of lawns and grass terraces. The South Lawn, fringed by trees and bordered with hybrid rhododendron and azaleas, drops sheerly down to a path, at one end of which is an old-fashioned arbour covered with wisteria and trumpet vine, and two flights of stone steps lead into a formal sunken garden. . . . On the other side of the house, lawns,

Fig. 5.5. Lowell planted hundreds of specimen trees, grouped gracefully around the grounds of Sevenels. Collection of Carol Bundy.

Fig. 5.6. Beds of flowers were planted along paths that led to artfully placed groves of trees. Collection of Carol Bundy.

shrubberies of magnolia and lilac, and a pine plantation lead to the hot beds (so called because they are cold frames) which is really a cutting and vegetable garden; and a fruit-garden runs up the side of the hill where grow apples and pear trees, more vegetables, strawberries, and all the thousand and one experiments to be set out near the house later on.

It remained "an old-fashioned garden," and, she avers, "it has been my pleasure to keep in it many old-fashioned flowers."[31] The Sevenels flower gardens figure significantly in her poetry.

The Lowells were hardly alone in showering attention, affection, and taste on their country retreat. "The environs of Boston are more highly cultivated than those of any other city in North America," wrote Downing. "There are here whole rural neighborhoods of pretty cottages and villas, admirably cultivated, and, in many cases, tastefully laid out and planted."[32] Indeed, his decided enthusiasm for Brookline reflects his intense appreciation of the town's general ambiance—its unusual combination of the "natural," picturesque scenery he so energetically espoused with the sophisticated horticultural collections and knowledgeable understanding cloaked in deceptively simple designs.

> The whole of this neighborhood of Brookline is a kind of landscape garden, and there is nothing in America, of the sort, so inexpressibly charming as the lands which lead from one cottage, or villa to another. No animals are allowed to run at large, and the open gates, with tempting vistas and glimpses under the pendent boughs, give it quite an Arcadian air of rural freedom and enjoyment. These lanes are clothed with a profusion of trees and wild shrubbery, often almost to the carriage tracks, and curve and wind about, in a manner quite bewildering to the stranger who attempts to thread them alone; and there are more hints here for the lover of the picturesque lanes, than we ever saw assembled together in so small a compass.[33]

Although Brookline stubbornly, and successfully, resisted incorporation into the city of Boston (the final vote for permanent independent status came in 1874, thus allowing Brookline to "remain aloof from the rest of the metropolis"),[34] slowly, through the nineteenth century, the town was transformed into a suburban commuting community. Many of the Boston-based large estate owners made the transition to full-time residents of Brookline. By 1888 the guidebook *Boston and Its Suburbs* could declare that the town had "long enjoyed the preeminent reputation of being the wealthiest in the United States. Its whole territory, which is quite large, is covered with beautiful and costly villas and magnificent estates, on the elaborate improvement of which great sums of money have been used. Drive where one will throughout the town, new and beautiful vistas are continually surprising us. It is said to more resemble an English country landscape than any other place in America."[35]

One of the Bostonians who arrived as a seasonal resident in 1847, in order to be closer to his good friends and colleagues the Perkinses, was the banker Ignatius Sargent (1800–1884). He retired from business in 1844, and the following year began purchasing land; in 1852 he became a year-round Brookline resident. By 1873 his handsome property, called Holm Lea from the Scandinavian words meaning "inland island pasture," consisted of 150 acres, including the 20-acre property of Thomas Lee (by then deceased), purchased in 1871. Ignatius Sargent, a member of the Massachusetts Horticultural Society from 1865, carried on improving his estate for fifty years, planting in a Downingesque manner, "transforming the rolling terrain into handsome parkland and gardens," and carrying on Lee's naturalistic design (fig. 5.7).[36] The *Gardener's Monthly and Horticulturist* wrote at his death that he had taken up "a piece of an old grazing farm, celebrated for nothing but good hunting ground for woodcock, and made of it a perfect horticultural paradise."[37]

In 1841 his second son, Charles Sprague Sargent (1841–1927), was born. Eleven years old when the family took up permanent residence at Holm Lea, he

Fig. 5.7. Ignatius Sargent's handsome Italianate house, banked with rhododendron. Copyright © President and Fellows of Harvard College. Arnold Arboretum Archives.

grew to manhood on a property that would both shape him and, later, prove a testing ground for his future profession. The young Sargent was an indifferent student, showing no particular affinity for the natural sciences or any other subject for that matter. He graduated at the bottom of his Harvard class in 1862 and immediately enlisted in the Union Army, serving until the end of the war. In 1865 he left for three years of wandering in Europe. There is no systematic record of his travels, or of any effect the constant exposure to the landscapes and great gardens in Europe may have had on him, but immediately upon returning in 1868, for lack of any other plan, he took over the management of Holm Lea, embarking on a botanical and horticultural adventure that would transform his life and the world of dendrology.

It would be difficult to overstate the importance of Sargent's Brookline environs in his personal and professional development. Consistent exposure to the aforementioned estates, as well as the general countrified ambiance, what Ronald Karr calls the "romantic ruralism" of Brookline,[38] significantly shaped not only the development of his own property but also in many ways his evolving philosophy about public spaces. Ida Hay reinforces this observation, writing: "These scenic and cultivated lands shaped Charles S. Sargent's boyhood. His father's grapes waxing almost fabulous in size and weight, the crystal depths of Jamaica Pond, the heights of Moss Hill—wild woodland and pasture, rose garden, grapery, planted grove—all were elements of the boy's landscape. The seriousness with which the adult cultivators pursued their plant collecting and horticultural experimentation deeply influenced Sargent in his future management of the Arboretum."[39]

Charles Sprague Sargent continued to develop the estate in the natural manner employed by his father and by Thomas Lee before him. In this, both men were influenced by Downing, of course, and by two other men, one Ignatius Sargent's first cousin Henry Winthrop Sargent (1810–1882) and the other their good friend Horatio Hollis Hunnewell (1810–1902). The former lived on his beautifully developed estate Wodenethe in Fishkill Landing, New York, characterized by his neighbor and friend Andrew Jackson Downing as "a bijou full of interest for the lover of rural beauty; abounding in rare trees, shrubs, and plants" (fig. 5.8).[40] Downing's leisure moments, according to J. J. Smith in his 1856 article "Visits to Country Places," were "never more thoroughly enjoyed" than when he was "pacing with [Sargent] around the new grounds, suggesting an effect here, an opening vista through yonder lofty grove, or advising about the hothouses and graperies."[41]

William Howard Adams describes Wodenethe as having "formal beds near the house, long allées, temples, greenhouses, and kitchen gardens spread out on rolling hills overlooking the river."[42] Sargent experimented with plants from the American West, Europe, and Asia to see what could survive within his climate range, methods Charles Sprague Sargent would later emulate on his own estate and in his

Fig. 5.8. Henry Winthrop Sargent's estate, Wodenethe, in Fishkill, N.Y. Illustration from A. J. Downing, *A Treatise on the Theory and Practice of Landscape Gardening* (1859). Courtesy Boston Athenaeum.

professional practice. Wodenethe became known not only as an elegantly designed landscape but also for its outstanding plant collection.[43]

There was another reason for Sargent's significance as well. According to J. E. Spingarn, writing in *Landscape Architecture,* Sargent consciously chose to have a small estate, only twenty-two-acres, and refused to "add a square yard to it during his forty-one years of residence there," because he felt strongly that Americans should not be endeavoring to attain the effects of large English estates, particularly in terms of size. Thus Sargent "is important not merely because he developed a beautiful country place, but because he built it on a scale that could be directly useful to the average American, and because he made it an experiment station in horticulture for all America."[44] Certainly that was the prevailing mode in Brookline, with major horticultural influences rippling out from its borders.

Horatio Hunnewell was cousin to Henry Winthrop Sargent and a friend of the Ignatius Sargent family. His estate, called Wellesley, became a horticultural and design showcase.[45] Particularly well known was his "Italian Garden," a seven-tiered display of topiaried conifers begun in 1866 and based on one at Elvaston Castle in Derbyshire, England (fig. 5.9).[46] His extensive grounds, exquisitely laid out in a naturalistic style, were packed with specimen trees and plants. He was a serious collector of conifers and rhododendrons. These men interacted with both Ignatius Sargent and his son, counseling the latter on what gardens and estates to visit during his three-year sojourn in Europe, and later by example during his visits to both gardens.[47] Charles Sprague Sargent affirmed the effect on him:

Fig. 5.9. "Italian Garden" at the H. H. Hunnewell estate, Wellesley, Massachusetts. Copyright © President and Fellows of Harvard College. Arnold Arboretum Archives.

> Personally I was greatly influenced by my cousin Henry Winthrop Sargent. Some of the best horticultural lessons in my life I learned at Wodenethe. Without his help and advice (my own place) Holm Lea (at Brookline, Mass.) would never have amounted to anything. And I am sure that without the knowledge and inspiration which I got at Wodenethe the making of the Arnold Arboretum would never have been entrusted to me. . . . If Wellesley (H. H. Hunnewell's place at Wellesley, Mass.), Holm Lea, and the Arnold Arboretum stand for anything in American horticulture, their influence can be traced to the inspiration and help of Henry Winthrop Sargent.[48]

During the time he managed Holm Lea and throughout the next fifty-nine years, after he had married and settled into his own house on the property (located on the site of Thomas Lee's former house and expanded by the newly married couple),[49] Charles Sprague Sargent looked upon it not only as his cherished home but also as a horticultural laboratory for his professional projects.[50]

Having spent four years concentrating on horticulture at Holm Lea, in particular on trees and shrubs, in 1872 Sargent was appointed director of the Harvard

Botanic Gardens in Cambridge, serving for a while with the renowned botanist Asa Gray. "There, being full of ideas, he at first dismayed Dr. Asa Gray by the decisive changes he undertook to make; but the elder botanist was soon convinced that everything the younger one did was for the advantage of the place, since from the first he showed unusual breadth of view and ability," Mary Caroline Robbins firmly declared in 1893.[51] Stephen A. Spongberg, a curatorial taxonomist at Arnold Arboretum in the 1980s, was less convinced, writing: "the opportunity to work in close association with the country's foremost botanist, to say nothing of an appointment as director of the Harvard Botanical Garden and professor of horticulture, was surely beyond Sargent's rightful expectations. . . . [N]evertheless, he was offered the post and . . . [t]aking up his new responsibilities with the energy and dedication that would characterize his career, the young aristocrat began to educate himself more fully" (fig. 5.10).[52] On this unlikely appointment Walter Muir Whitehill speculates: "Although the evidence is only circumstantial, I firmly believe that [the eminent historian and horticulturalist Francis] Parkman must have played a crucial part in the selection. . . . Otherwise how would a young man who had stood eighty-eighth in his class of ninety on his graduation have reappeared ten years later on the Harvard scene as Professor of Horticulture?"[53]

Sargent held the directorship until 1879, when further professional duties he assumed precluded his continuing. During that time he significantly rearranged the gardens, beginning the experiments in organization that he would later bring to fruition.[54] At the same time that he took the directorship, he became the Arnold

Fig. 5.10. Sargent about the time he was appointed director of the Harvard Botanic Gardens. *Century Magazine* (April 1893). Courtesy Boston Atheneum.

Professor of Dendrology at the Bussey Institute of Harvard University, although his austere nature prevented him from ever actually lecturing. He educated through his writings, which were prolific.

The university was already in possession of over three hundred acres of land in West Roxbury, left in 1842 by the wealthy Boston merchant Benjamin Bussey to be used for "the creation of an institution for instruction in farming, horticulture, botany and related fields."[55] Bussey, another founding member of the Massachusetts Horticultural Society, had assembled several farms there between 1806 and 1837, creating his estate Woodland Hill, in order to pursue his avocational interest in scientific farming as well as his desire to establish and preserve scenic landscape features. By 1871 the Bussey Institute was established, complete with a large, handsome Gothic Revival building. Just three years before, in 1868, Harvard had received a bequest of $100,000 from James Arnold specifically for the advancement of agriculture or horticulture. The combination of these two bequests and a thoughtful interpretation of their intended purposes led to an agreement between Harvard and the estates' trustees that an arboretum should be established on 125 of Bussey's acres, to contain "every tree and shrub able to endure the climate of Massachusetts."[56]

In 1873 Sargent, already a professor at the institution, was appointed the Arnold Arboretum's first director. "It is safe to say," he wrote dryly in 1917, "that none of the men directly engaged in making this agreement had any idea what an Arboretum might be, or what it was going to cost in time and money to carry out the agreement . . . and certainly none of them were more ignorant on these subjects than the person selected to see that this agreement was carried out. He found himself provided with a worn-out farm partly covered with native woods nearly ruined by pasturage and neglect."[57] Robbins elaborates: "This land was partly peat-bog and meadow, and partly scantily wooded upland, where were a few fine trees, a stretch of pasture, and a noble grove of hemlocks crowning a hill."[58] Sargent quickly learned that only a fraction of Arnold's money could be extracted from the university.[59]

By that time Frederick Law Olmsted was working on the park system in Boston, and he and Sargent, who served on the Brookline Park Commission from 1880 until his death in 1927, had become friends and colleagues. Sargent called in Olmsted to help plan the arboretum in 1878, suggesting, in the face of economic stringency, that a partnership between Harvard University and the City of Boston be established so that the arboretum might become part of the Boston park system. Olmsted's response was cautious; he would have to see the site first, he wrote Sargent. "Indeed a park and an arboretum seem to be so far unlike in purpose that I do not feel sure that I could combine them satisfactorily. I certainly would not undertake to do so in this case without your cooperation and I think it would be better and more proper that the plan should be made by you with my aid rather than by me with yours."[60] Furthermore, wrote Sargent later with obvious distaste, "this plan met with little favor and was strongly opposed by the University and the Park Commission of the City, and it took five years of exceedingly disagreeable semipolitical work to bring it about."[61] But bring it about he did, having convinced Olmsted of the worthiness of the proposal. Indeed, the landscape architect came to champion the plan, and in later years even Sargent became convinced it was originally Olmsted's idea.

As early as 1874 Olmsted drew up a tentative plan, and a published one by 1880 (fig. 5.11). During his transition from New York to Boston, he spent the summer of 1878 in Cambridge "in order to work out plans for the Arnold Arboretum with Professors Gray and Sargent."[62] In 1882 the Massachusetts state legislature agreed to the proposal, and a contract was drawn up that allowed the city to seize the land by eminent domain and then lease it back to Harvard for one thousand years. The city was required to build roads and walks designed to Olmsted's plans and maintain them permanently. Boston police would protect the grounds, and the city would provide water and assume any tax burdens that might arise. In return, Harvard agreed to arrange, plant, and maintain the grounds and collections. The arboretum was required to be open to the public every day of the year from dawn until sunset. Not until 1885 did the city complete the roadways and the planting commence.

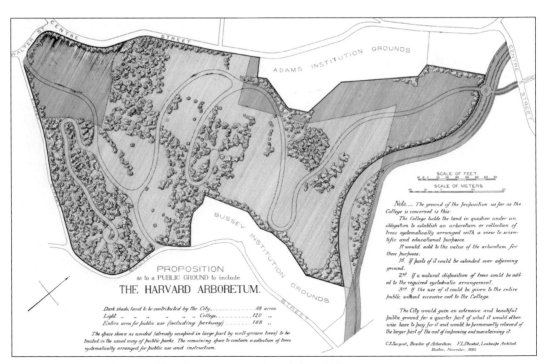

Fig. 5.11. Plan for the Arnold Arboretum, Jamaica Plain, 1880. Courtesy National Park Service, Frederick Law Olmsted National Historic Site.

Meanwhile, Sargent carefully worked out the planting program for what he described as his "Tree Museum," consulting with Olmsted, who drew up several "Studies for the Distribution/Planting" between 1879 and 1880. John Charles Olmsted and interns Charles Eliot and Henry Sargent Codman, Sargent's nephew, assisted Olmsted in that work.[63] Plant collector and succeeding arboretum director Ernest H. Wilson confirms that the Olmsted office planned the system of carriage drives and footpaths. Writing of Sargent's "artistic treatment of the . . . roadways," he notes, "native woody plants of low growth have been largely used, together with bold clumps of taller shrubs in relief."[64]

Although there is no question that the arboretum was to be a man-made landscape, Sargent was determined to incorporate existing elements of the original topography, the most widely known being Hemlock Hill. Initially preserved by Benjamin Bussey, whose estate lay close by Brookline, it is a steep rocky hill topped by a splendid stand of old forest hemlocks, still extant today. "Bussey's Woods" was already a popular destination for Bostonians in search of attractive scenery and fresh air. "During Mr. Bussey's life, and for years after, the public enjoyed the freedom of these charming grounds," wrote Harriet Whitcomb. "There were lovely wood paths, carefully kept, in all directions. Here was a rustic bridge spanning the jocund brook; there a willow-bordered pond, the home of gold and silver fish. This path wound back and forth to the summit of Hemlock Mountain, where was an arbor with seats for resting, surrounded by majestic trees, and where lovely vistas of the distant hills and nearer valley could be enjoyed."[65] Among its visitors was the Transcendentalist Margaret Fuller, who lived in Jamaica Plain for three years and walked regularly among Bussey's glades and vales, complete with burbling brook (fig. 5.12).

Sargent called upon his friend Hunnewell for counsel in the planting of the arboretum. The *Memorial History of Boston* records that Hunnewell's estate contained a "collection of hardy trees and plants, natives not only of our country, but also such of California, Japan, and other lands as would endure our climate," and that the avenues were lined with "the most beautiful pines, spruces, beeches, maples, magnolias, and other trees, intermixed here and there with the rarest and costliest conifers, rhododendrons, azaleas, and other flowering shrubs."[66] His great-grandson Walter Hunnewell observed: "In the beginning, the Arboretum got a lot of good advice from my great-grandfather. He and Professor Sargent were good friends. My great-grandfather was the older of the two and had started first—twenty years, and Hunnewell gave a lot of good advice to Sargent."[67]

Sargent, however, consistently maintained a firm grip on the project. "I shall group the trees in their rational sequence along the principal drive (in loose) generic groups," he wrote in 1875, "thus giving the visitor ideas of arborescent vegetation of the North Temperate Zone without leaving his carriage." That is to say, he planted the trees according to family and genus by the Bentham and Hooker

Fig. 5.12. Bussey's Brook (originally known as Sawmill Brook) in the Arnold Arboretum.
Century Magazine (April 1893). Courtesy Boston Athenaeum.

classification system, still maintained today. Significantly, he goes on to state that he wished to avoid the "stiff and formal lines of the conventional botanic garden," combining science and art to arrive, in both a Downingesque and an Olmstedian fashion, at a "comprehension of the study of the collection in scientific and pictur-esque effects."[68]

Aesthetic considerations should never dominate, however, Sargent assured the president and fellows of Harvard College in the same year. "Everything should be subservient to the collections, and the ease with which these can be reached and studied; and none of those considerations of mere landscape effect . . . should be allowed to interfere with these essential requirements of a scientific garden."[69] By 1880 there were 2,500 species of trees and shrubs growing.[70] Ultimately, writes William Trelease, "Sargent lived to see the saplings that he planted between 1882 and 1885 grow into stately and shapely trees—isolated so that they might attain their maximum symmetry, and elsewhere so massed that the grouped effect of each species might take its part in a landscape of beauty."[71]

By 1893 Robbins could report with confidence that "already there are numerous students at the Arboretum, and in the flowering season classes are conducted about the grounds by teachers, to familiarize them with the habits and appearance of the various trees and shrubs." Beyond its scientific uses, which she acknowledged were "the most important, as a part of the park system of Boston the Arboretum has its charm as a pleasure-ground. Its broad graveled driveways and footpaths, edged with low flowering shrubs, so well simulate nature that one is constantly reminded of picturesque country roads with their tangle of verdure" (fig. 5.13).[72]

Sargent's objective of combining scientific exactitude and aesthetic pleasure had been fully achieved. Thirty years later Mariana Griswold Van Rensselaer wrote a whole chapter about the arboretum and that successful commingling in her *Art Out-of-Doors:* "There is no collection of trees in America that rivals it," she contended, "and nowhere has it a rival as a *tree-garden,* for although in the actual arrangement of its specimen trees and shrubs as well as its purpose it is a scientific garden, in aspect it is one of the most delightful and most individual of naturalistic parks, and in spring and summer becomes a great informal flower-garden of amazing splendor."[73] Early on Sargent had provided Van Rensselaer with a venue for her writings on landscape architecture in the popular magazine he edited, *Garden and Forest.* There is little doubt that her friendship with him and with Olmsted influenced her dedication to the naturalistic style.[74]

Writing in 1917 in *Youth's Companion,* Sargent confirms definitively his inten-

Fig. 5.13. Arnold Arboretum with the beautifying treatment of roads described by E. H. Wilson. Here the famous swath of lilacs is in full bloom. Copyright © President and Fellows of Harvard College. Arnold Arboretum Archives.

tion of combining aesthetics and science in the arboretum. Observing that "beauty is a powerful influence in a garden devoted to study," he writes: "In arranging the museum of living plants, every effort has been made to do the work in such a way that the natural appearance of the native woods and the individual native trees shall be as little changed as possible. A stranger driving through the Arboretum for the first time might well believe that he was in a bit of native New England and not in one of the great botanical collections of the world."[75] Sargent's conviction, pride, and sense of accomplishment are evident. His pupil and friend Beatrix Farrand wrote admiringly in 1946, "Years of close observation and study of landscape composition convinced him that plant material could not only be displayed correctly from the botanist's point of view but also as part of a design."[76] Cynthia Zaitzevsky, in *Frederick Law Olmsted and the Boston Park System,* arrives at "the almost inescapable conclusion" that Sargent was "as much codesigner as client,"[77] a judgment earlier confirmed by Van Rensselaer: "Everything has been done according to his decisions and under his eye. In the truest sense the Arboretum is his creation," and "in the truest sense it is a great work of art."[78] The techniques he employed flowed constantly between the arboretum and Holm Lea, the place where he spent those "years of close observation and study."

Farrand was apparently the exception to the distance Sargent generally kept from his students. It happened, she writes, that she had "a fortunate meeting" with Mrs. Sargent at just about the time she was deciding to pursue landscape gardening. Herself a member of New York society, Farrand (a niece of the author Edith Wharton) and Sargent traveled in similar social circles; she was embraced into the Sargent family, living with them for several months, during which time Sargent educated her in his own garden as well as at the arboretum. Farrand's biographer Jane Brown explains this mentoring by attributing to him "that Brahmin tendency to give a serious-minded woman encouragement, and just perhaps, she appeared at the right moment, with her brightness and enthusiasm, to fill the gap left by the death of his former protégé, Henry Sargent Codman, in early 1893."[79]

Ever afterward Farrand credited Sargent, whom she affectionately called "Chief," for her thorough knowledge of horticulture. In fact, like Sargent, she used plants as a design element, providing her landscapes with structure, form, texture, color, and depth.[80] He advised her to adopt a landscape design principle he clearly adhered to himself in his two major landscapes, Holm Lea and the arboretum, the antithesis of Olmsted's frequent reshaping of terrain. One should always, Sargent informed her, be ready to "make the plan fit the ground and not to twist the ground to fit the plan."[81] Likely modeling her practices on Sargent's at Holm Lea, Farrand maintained an extensive living collection of rare plants at Reef Point, her home in Bar Harbor, Maine, along with an herbarium and a significant horticultural library. Farrand went on to become a prominent landscape architect in her own right. She was one of the founding members (and the sole female) of the American Society of Landscape Architects in 1899. In 1946 she was called back to the arboretum to consult on restoration and renovation of the grounds, and she responded to the invitation with delight, deeming it "a chance to show my gratitude and appreciation of what the Arnold Arboretum has meant to me individually and to my fellow workers in landscape art."[82]

At the beginning, the arboretum's library was based on Sargent's private botanical library of 6,000 volumes. He worked as director from his home until 1892, a process that indelibly wove the affairs of the arboretum into the fabric of Holm Lea. That year H. H. Hunnewell provided funds for a large brick administration building called The Museum, and Sargent moved his office, the library, and the herbarium from Dwight House, the cottage on his estate where he kept the latter two, donating his entire collection to the arboretum.[83] Throughout his tenure as director, he increased the library's holdings to 36,000 volumes, 8,000 pamphlets, and 12,000 photographs, and created 300,000 sheets of mounted specimens for the herbarium, almost all at his own expense.[84] By 1925 the library was the largest existing collection of books in the Western world relating to trees and their cultivation, second only to that of the British Museum in the number of fifteenth- and sixteenth-century volumes included.[85]

At the same time that he was making plans for the arboretum, in 1879 Sargent was asked by the United States government to head the research for and to write the "Tenth Census: A Report on the Forest Wealth and the Forest Trees of the United States." Resigning his post as director of the Harvard Botanical Gardens, Sargent traveled around the country, creating in the process a vast network of colleagues who helped him fill the arboretum with rare trees and shrubs and to compile specimens for the nascent herbarium.[86] "Out of it," William Trelease wrote of the census the year after Sargent's death, "has emerged a national policy of intelligent forest conservation and utilization, of salvaging the relicts of lumbering, and of preserving for future generations samples of Nature's own great arboretum in the form of national parks."[87]

Albert Benson, author of the *History of the Massachusetts Horticultural Society,* has high praise for Sargent's significance in forest preservation: "It was Sargent who laid the foundations of the New York State forestry work and saved the mountain woods, and who led the movement which preserved the giant redwood forests on the Pacific Coast. Thirty years before the Glacier National Park was set aside, he made the first proposal for its reservation; and he was Chairman of the National Academy of Science Commission which through its study brought about the establishment of the National Forest Policy." He was a leader in encouraging President

Cleveland to reserve 21 million acres, and when President McKinley was under pressure to return the forests to the public domain, he used all his powers of persuasion to keep the land protected.[88]

His government position significantly bolstered his status as a dendrologist and led to the creation of his magnum opus, the fourteen-volume *Silva of North America,* produced over eleven years (1891–1902).[89] Sargent's travels for the census expanded, taking him to Europe, Asia, and South America (fig. 5.14). In 1888 he began publication of *Garden and Forest,* an influential periodical that ran for a decade, until 1897, significantly popularizing landscape issues and reflecting what Stephen Spongberg calls "Sargent's interest in educating the public and in bringing the important environmental issues of his day to its attention."[90] Sargent, Olmsted, Charles Eliot, and Van Rensselaer were frequent contributors to the magazine. It should not be forgotten that Eliot's letters to *Garden and Forest* led to one of his "happiest accomplishments: creation of the Trustees of Public Reservations,"[91] the earliest private American institution for the preservation and improvement of scenery for public use and enjoyment.

Sargent became a world-renowned authority on trees and shrubs, and his work became nearly all-consuming. His daughter Mary Sargent Potter recalled after his

Fig. 5.14. Sargent, at left, with fellow census researchers, including his Brookline neighbor Francis Skinner, a volunteer (center). Copyright © President and Fellows of Harvard College. Arnold Arboretum Archives.

death, "Sundays and holidays, Christmas and Easter, as well as the working week found him at his desk."[92] A reticent man, even by cold-roast Bostonian standards, he was considered remote and unsociable by nature. Although his 1873 marriage to the gracious and vivacious Mary Allen Robeson mitigated that image somewhat, Potter nevertheless described her father as "a stern, silent, domineering New Englander. His determinations were inflexible and until softened by age and by my mother's influence he inspired fear rather than love."[93] His arboretum colleague Alfred Rehder modified that assessment somewhat in the obituary he wrote after Sargent died: "To those who knew him little his manner might have appeared abrupt or often aloof, but those who knew him better were aware he had a warm heart. It was not easy to win his confidences, but those whom he trusted could trust in him."[94]

In 1899 the renowned English plant explorer Ernest Henry Wilson (1876–1930), also known as "Chinese" Wilson, passed through Boston en route to China, seed collecting for the British nursery firm James Veitch & Sons. Arnold Arboretum was by this time an important stop for any horticultural expert. Like many people, Wilson was initially put off by Sargent's brusque manner. "After formal greetings he pulled out his watch and said 'I am busy now, but at 10 o'clock next Thursday I shall be glad to see you.' I voted him autocrat of the autocrats," he wrote, "but when our next interview took place I found him the kindliest of autocrats."[95] Not only did Sargent meet with Wilson during his five-day stay, he also made sure that the explorer was apprised of techniques for safely shipping seeds and plants.

As arboretum director, Sargent had already established relationships with plant collectors, including William S. Clark, as early as 1876. Clark, who resigned as president of Amherst College in order to establish an agricultural college in Japan, sent seeds for the arboretum. In 1902 Sargent commissioned Walther Siehe, "a collector living in Smyrna," to acquire seeds for him as well.[96] Even his old Brookline neighbor Percival Lowell, who by the 1890s had migrated to Flagstaff, Arizona, was pressed into service, sending exotic plants "from his garden and the surrounding desert and mountains" for Sargent's collections.[97]

By 1906 Sargent persuaded Wilson to leave England and Veitch to collect in China for the arboretum, raising funds for the trip from friends and arboretum members as well as contributing his own share. Through the years Wilson went on numerous expeditions, gathering specimens, photographs, herbarium species, seeds, grafts, and cuttings, ultimately introducing thousands of new species to the Western world.[98] "When Wilson's discoveries domesticated themselves happily at the Arboretum, and proved suitable for decorative planting," writes Walter Muir Whitehill, "Professor Sargent would make stock available to nurserymen for propagation and sale."[99] Over the years, more than five hundred varieties of ornamental trees and shrubs made their way into American gardens, including those in

Fig. 5.15. Sargent (left) and Wilson standing in the arboretum. Copyright © President and Fellows of Harvard College. Arnold Arboretum Archives.

Fig. 5.16. Jackson Thornton Dawson, the long-lived and cherished chief propagator at the Arnold Arboretum. Copyright © President and Fellows of Harvard College. Arnold Arboretum Archives.

Brookline.[100] Wilson wrote extensively, publishing his most significant work, *Plantae Wilsonianae* in 1917, with Sargent serving as editor.[101] In 1919 the seventy-eight-year-old Sargent sent Wilson on a world tour to make connections with other botanical garden officials and establish lasting relationships between them and the arboretum. Sargent, as always, was seeking to solidify the arboretum's position as a major horticultural institution (fig. 5.15).

Significantly less high-profile, but equally important to the arboretum and Holm Lea, was the English-born plantsman and propagator Jackson Thornton Dawson (fig. 5.16).[102] The same year Sargent was appointed director, he spirited Dawson away from the Bussey Institute as the arboretum's first staff member. Trained from youth in his uncle's nursery and greenhouse in Andover, Massachusetts, Dawson went on to apprentice himself to C. M. Hovey, a Cambridgeport nurseryman, following service in the United States Army and the Sanitary Commission, headed by Frederick Law Olmsted, during the Civil War. Never forgetting his love of horticulture, throughout his travels during that time he carefully packaged seeds and rare plants from the southern states and sent them home to Massachusetts.[103]

When the Bussey Institute, a school of agriculture and horticulture in Jamaica Plain, was launched by Harvard in 1871, the historian and horticulturist Francis Parkman, who had been appointed its first professor of horticulture, hired Dawson as head gardener. Parkman himself was a member of the Massachusetts Horticultural Society and a part-time resident of a home near Jamaica Pond, approximately one mile from the institution. There he cultivated his three and a half acres, primarily in roses and Japanese plants, growing and hybridizing his increasing collection.[104]

For the next fifteen years Dawson and his family lived at the institution, notwithstanding the transition in employers.[105] Although the arboretum was still in the planning stages, the new director immediately set Dawson to work collecting woody flora in eastern New England. "In one year I collected 50,000 native shrubs to plant in the Arboretum. I also collected laurels and yews," Dawson noted.[106] After years of delay, by 1886 Sargent reported that Dawson had been able to collect and plant 62,000 shrubs from different wooded areas of New England.[107] In 1980, 15 to 20 percent of the arboretum's living collections could be attributed to Dawson's labors.

Throughout the years when Sargent's herbarium and library were still in Dwight House, the cottage at Holm Lea, Dawson doubtless interacted with him there. Dawson's eldest child, William, worked at Dwight House from 1880 until the move to the museum; his third son, Charles, worked at the Bussey Institute as a gardener and went on to found Eastern Nurseries. James Frederick Dawson, his fourth son, became a landscape architect and joined the Olmsted firm in 1896, becoming a full partner by 1922.

Everyone who worked with Jackson Dawson was influenced by his generosity, humor, enthusiasm, and grace, but foremost by his phenomenal skill at propagation and planting. Even the taciturn Sargent waxed sentimental over Dawson's talents in 1916, close to the end of the master propagator's career. "Knowledge and skill he has acquired by patient practice and by loving the things with which he works," Sargent wrote. "Plants seem to respond to affection, and he has that affection in large measure. In addition to the great number of trees and plants he has raised here, no one can tell how many hundreds of thousands he has sent to every part of the United States and to all the countries of Europe."[108]

In 1910 the very first Massachusetts Horticultural Society Gold Medal was awarded to Charles Sprague Sargent. The second, in the same year, went to Jackson Thornton Dawson, for advancing "the interest of horticulture in its broadest sense." After his death in 1916, the society established a medal in his honor, given for excellence in the hybridization of hardy woody plants. Dawson was indeed an integral part of the successful establishment of the Arnold Arboretum, a fact readily acknowledged by an appreciative Sargent. Extensively memorialized in words, Dawson lives on in the arboretum plantings as well. At the time of his death, writes Albert Benson, "there stood oaks fifty feet high which had grown from the acorns he had planted."[109]

When the Brookline Park Commission was established in 1880, as in so many communities surrounding Boston, it was in part a response to the central city's Park Act of 1875. The legislation that established the Boston Park Commission invited the cities and towns adjacent to Boston to lay out parks in conjunction with the city's efforts. Brookline was the only community to take the city up on its offer.[110] The Muddy River, running between Brookline and Boston, originally flowed unimpeded, draining thousands of acres from Brookline, Roxbury, and Dorchester into the Back Bay salt marsh which later became the site of the first gem in Olmsted's Emerald Necklace, the Back Bay Fens. Begun in 1880, that park was as much a sanitation project as a recreational facility, for by that time the Muddy River, what Cynthia Zaitzevsky calls that "inoffensive little stream," had evolved into a full-blown health hazard, pouring odoriferous sewage from burgeoning communities into the filtering marshes of the Fens and putrefying a site that tidal rhythms could no longer purify.[111]

Although Brookline had long been known for its enlightened attitude toward town planning, according to Zaitzevsky, neither Boston nor Brookline made "any effort either to preserve the natural features of the Muddy River valley or to develop it according to a comprehensive plan. . . . The haphazard and unattractive development along the Muddy River was atypical and a matter of considerable concern."[112] In point of fact, writes Charles Beveridge, "this project gave Olmsted his first opportunity to preserve streamways in the midst of built-up areas, as he and Vaux had proposed many times during their partnership."[113]

Who better to take on the question of a river park than longtime Brookline resident and park advocate Charles Sprague Sargent? He was promptly appointed one of three commissioners for the newly formed Park Commission, a post he held uninterrupted from that time until his death in 1927.[114] The other members of the commission were hardly shrinking violets, but "there is no question that Sargent's word was law on park matters," writes Zaitzevsky. "The other members deferred to him to such an extent that the commission effectively stopped functioning when Sargent was out of town."[115]

Upon the creation of their own park commission, the voters of Brookline

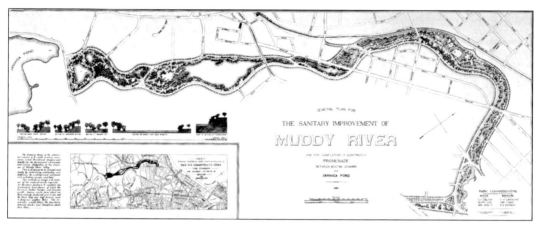

Fig. 5.17. Olmsted's first plan for the Muddy River improvement, 1880. Courtesy National Park Service, Frederick Law Olmsted National Historic Site.

immediately began discussing the improvement and landscaping of the Muddy River area. By December 1880 Olmsted had submitted "Suggestions for the Improvement of Muddy River" to both the Boston and Brookline park commissioners, since the river bordered both municipalities and any decisions made would require cooperation. In effect, the site was to be developed as an integral part of the emerging Emerald Necklace. Olmsted's first design, delivered the following year, suggested "a gently winding stream [replacing] the erratic wigglings of the existing tidal river," and the conversion of a cattail swamp into a large pond (fig. 5.17).[116] These, together with smaller ponds scattered along the river's route, were to be fed by local streams.

In this plan, "the drainage difficulties of Back Bay were," according to Olmsted, "proposed to be met by forming a part of it into a basin in which water would, under ordinary circumstances, be maintained at a nearly uniform level, but in which, when an unusually high tide would for a few hours prevent outflow, a larger amount could be harmlessly stored. Public roads were to be laid out around and across this basin, and its banks to be planted and otherwise treated picturesquely." Olmsted describes the lower part of the river being transformed by the Back Bay Fens park, noting that when such a major change takes place, the rivers feeding into the altered area often come "to be regarded as a nuisance; and radical measures, such as the construction of a great underground channel, and the filling of the valley, are urged as the only adequate remedy." His 1880 plan, however, lays out an extensively different approach for the Muddy River. "As an alternative to such a possible course the policy now suggested for Muddy river would look to the preservation of the present channel with certain modifications and improvements adapted to make it permanently attractive and wholesome, and an element of constantly increasing advantage to the neighborhood." The valley would be reduced in width by artificial banks "so that the river with its shores would everywhere have a general character"; the water would be kept at a uniform level and "guarded from defilement by intercepting sewers and otherwise."[117]

Employing his usual skill at synthesizing multiple advantages—aesthetic, recreational, and sanitary—into a single project, Olmsted enumerates the manifold rewards of the project. On the Boston side there would be a ten-foot artificial elevation, on which would be laid out a ninety-foot-wide "public way," built to accommodate "foot, carriage and saddle courses, and designed to serve as a public promenade along the river bank, as well as a trunk line giving an element of continuity to the street system of the neighborhood. The Brookline side would consist of a broadened base for the existing railroad embankment, screened by a "woody thicket." The proposed parkway threading along the riverway was to extend to Jamaica Pond. The whole would be "all of natural and in some degree picturesque outline, with banks wooded and easily to be furnished with verdure and foliage throughout." In Olmsted's opinion, with the exception of one spot along the river where there were a number of insignificant buildings, "the whole would be formed on land of little value, occupied by no buildings, and for no productive purposes, and all of it now in a condition hazardous to public health."[118]

Upon its completion, and "taken in connection with the mall upon Commonwealth avenue, the Public Garden and the Common, the park-way would complete a pleasure route from the heart of the city a distance of six miles into the suburbs. These older pleasure-grounds, while continuing to serve equally well all their present purposes, would, by becoming part of an extended system, acquire increased importance and value." Bringing his argument full circle he concludes, "They would be of larger use, be more effective as appliances for public health, and every dollar expended for their maintenance would return a larger dividend."[119]

The Boston and Brookline park commissioners jointly authorized further work on the parkway. The Town of Brookline had already borrowed $200,000 to acquire adequate parkland for the project, and a list of "Owners, and Approximate Areas of Land Proposed to Be Taken for the Muddy River Improvement" was drawn up. Everything looked simple and straightforward, but the project would consume the next fifteen years of the Park Commission's attention.

Large landowners were in general behind the plan, but several smaller holders immediately held out for financial gain. The commissioners also found over the next year that significant portions of the required land lay within the jurisdiction of Boston, not Brookline. Funding for the Boston portion of the project proved elusive at best, a fact that hindered Brookline officials from moving forward. By 1884 they were reporting with a certain amount of pique that "in many cases . . . the owners are holding their lands at prices far exceeding the assessed valuation. . . . It is therefore probable that many of these negotiations will fail, in which case we shall be obliged to wait until the Boston commissioners are prepared to join us in taking the whole territory not previously acquired by purchase, under the authority given us by chap. 185, acts of 1875."[120]

In 1885 the commissioners again reported their frustration with the remaining unsecured land for what they called the Riverdale Park, "divided among some fourteen small estates, which are held at prices which make their purchase improbable. . . . We are of the opinion that we have acquired nearly, if not all, the land which can be taken by private sale, and that the remainder must be taken under the Park Act." They were therefore "ready to commence the preliminary work of construction whenever the Boston Park Commissioners are in a position to co-operate with us, but it is impossible for us to say at present when that time will come."[121] And it continued impossible to predict. In 1886 they reported, "The Boston Park Commissioners being compelled, by want of appropriations, to defer plans and specifications, with estimates of the whole cost of construction of their portion of the park, we are still obliged to wait for their cooperation."[122] The following year they were "not able to report much progress on the Riverdale Park improvement, owning to the want of co-operation on the part of Boston authorities." They observed that the project they longed to complete did not appear to have priority in the Boston system: "The Park Commissioners of Boston have bought a comparatively small portion of the land needed, as they have not sufficient money for the purpose, and the large sums which they have for construction will be used for their other parks."[123] Wearily, in 1888 they noted that they were "still waiting for the Boston Commissioners to join us in laying out the Park."[124]

Finally, in complete exasperation, in 1889 the town voted to ask the park commissioners "whether the Brookline portion of the Parkway can be constructed independently of Boston."[125] The commissioners responded in the affirmative and engaged the Olmsted office to reconsider the Muddy River improvement plan. The reply came immediately: "The original plan would have required land to be taken on the west side of Pond Avenue which, since the design was made, has had several houses placed upon it. The revised plan will effect a considerable saving by rendering it unnecessary to take these properties. We are also aiming to shape a project to be submitted to you for improvement of the plan in the vicinity of Longwood and Chapel stations."[126]

Eighteen ninety proved to be a banner year for the Brookline Park Commission. Olmsted submitted a long and detailed letter outlining the changes necessitated by an eight-year lapse since the 1881 plan, citing the increased wealth and population of Brookline, the improved means of communication between Brookline and Boston, including electric street railways and steam railroad services, and the extension of the Back Bay residential district into the Back Bay Fens.

It appears, however, that Boston's years of stalling had diminished the general enthusiasm for the project in Brookline, for Olmsted spent significant time proclaiming the merits of the larger park system. The new parkland, he argued, was diminished by conceiving of it as a local Brookline park: "A habit of thinking of it in this way tends to maintain an absurdly low estimate of its probable value to the town. So much of the proposed pleasure-ground simply as will lie directly open to the town, under view from roads and from houses wholly within the town, will be of three times the extent of the area which the town has contributed to it, and the cost of this part to Boston will be more than three times as much as it will be to Brookline."[127]

The report contextualizes the river park by once again describing the sinuous flow of the Emerald Necklace, beginning at the Boston Common and moving through "stretches out the broad, dignified, urban parkway" of Commonwealth Avenue to the Back Bay Fens, a portion of the park system "overlooked on both sides by tree-shaded drives and walks," to be "carried on past the Back Bay Fens, a broad walk secluded from city sights as far as possible, by trees and shrubbery," on to the south end of Jamaica Pond. There "the type of scenery will be that of a small, placid stream, with quietly sloping, grassy and reedy banks, planted with such trees and shrubs as are natural under the circumstances in New England." Toward Jamaica Pond, the "waters widen out into pools and ponds, connected by a rapid brook, and besides the usual slopes, there are here meadows and higher banks, giving the scenery a more varied, secluded, and rural aspect." Last of all, the parkway would sweep on "by curving courses to the Arnold Arboretum and thence to Franklin Park." The eventual goal for the system was a seaside pleasure ground at Dorchester Point. In short, "Brookline is not undertaking to prepare in the Muddy River District an isolated local park of limited extent and value, but, at comparatively small cost, is taking to itself a partnership advantage in a long chain of truly metropolitan pleasure-grounds of extraordinary variety, extent, and interest."[128]

From here Olmsted moves on to the particulars of the Brookline portion. The changes would need to reflect the economic reality of 1890 Brookline, including increased land values and enlarged tax bases. The Boston and Albany Railroad planned a replacement railway station, with a new street between Chapel and Longwood stations designed to provide better access in both directions. The walkway between the Muddy River and the tracks would be shielded by mounding and plantings.[129] The widening of Beacon Street would necessitate shifting the two carriageways proposed, placing them at different levels. A swamp south of Tremont Street would be turned into a pond, combined with a meadow and "a graceful little hill commanding views of all this part of the valley." A section of the waterway was to be set aside for a zoological park, a concept never finalized.[130] Adjustments in the curving of the river and parkway were made, and an additional access way to the park was made available. Small areas of land would have to be exchanged between Boston and Brookline. Olmsted ends his report by stating that the Boston City Council had allocated $600,000 to purchase land, and that the Boston park commissioners had "passed upon a plan of operations to be pursued the coming summer," which included the part of the scheme that lay "between the already nearly completed work of the Fens and the Brookline boundary."[131]

The Brookline park commissioners were cautiously on their way. Their 1890 report concluded with the firm admonition, "We believe that it is important that the work of construction should be carried on with sufficient rapidity, when once begun, to insure its completion within two years; first, in order that the work may be done in the most economical manner possible; and second, that we may be able to include the whole cost of construction in the assessment of betterments, which must be laid within two years of formal laying out."[132] A revised plan was drawn (fig. 5.18). At last, in 1891, Alexis H. French, the civil engineer in charge of operations, was able to report not only on the progress on the Brookline portion of the river park but also that "the Boston Park Commissioners have put under contract their work on the Improvement, and the contractors of the adjoining sections are working harmoniously, and to the mutual advantage of all concerned."[133]

In typical Olmstedian fashion, the site was transformed with considerable alterations of the terrain in the name of naturalistic scenery. A portion of the estate of David Sears (1787–1871), an early Brookline landowner, had been purchased for the park, and a vista cut to Christ Church, located in the Longwood section of Sears's land, became a "picturesque element" in the design.[134]

The following year, construction of what was still referred to as the Riverdale Park continued apace. "The excavation, filling, grading, loaming and manuring are nearly completed. The ground is prepared for planting, the trees and shrubs have been contracted for, and the work of planting will be begun early in the spring," reported the commissioners (fig. 5.19).[135] According to Norman Newton, "a good start had been made, through the purchase of adjacent parcels of land, toward elimination of scores of squalid shacks and a dump that had come to border the

Fig. 5.18. The revised plan for the Muddy River improvement provided by Olmsted Brothers, 1890.
Courtesy National Park Service, Frederick Law Olmsted National Historic Site.

stream and endanger public health." Specifically, "the slopes were minutely plotted, staked, and graveled against slumping, and footpaths were laid out on both sides of the stream and a carriage road on the Boston side." The railroad, "which ran beside the lower part of Muddy River on the Brookline side, was blocked out visually by means of a continuous mound of heavy planting, and several sinuous islands were built in the stream at this point as an additional screening measure."[136]

Fig. 5.19. Views from the Longwood Bridge of the Muddy River improvement during construction (ca. 1892, top) and after plantings had matured (1907, bottom). Top courtesy Brookline Public Library; bottom courtesy National Park Service, Frederick Law Olmsted National Historic Site.

The plantings, almost exclusively native materials, included nearly 24,000 trees, noted French, and "the largest part of the trees set out consisted of the different varieties of oaks, this being the variety that naturally predominates in the Muddy River Valley. Besides oaks, a considerable number of beeches, ashes, American elms, maples and other trees were planted."[137] Zaitzevsky discusses the issue at length, for although planting plans for the Emerald Necklace are spotty, those of the Muddy River improvement project proved more complete than most.

These plantings, it turns out, occasioned an unusual rift in the long-standing relationship between the Olmsted firm and Sargent. Olmsted first selected plants native to New England for the Muddy River but included a few of foreign origin, apparently much to the displeasure of Sargent, a man confident in his knowledge of horticulture and accustomed to having his way. Immediately after Olmsted left for a six-month stay in Europe, having approved all the plant lists and planting plans, Sargent arrived at the Olmsted offices, confronted John Charles Olmsted, and crossed out one-third of the trees and a quarter of the shrubs in the plans. "Practically all of the foreign trees and shrubs, all of what Sargent considered 'garden' plants, (most of which were also foreign), and all shrubs with showy flowers were struck out. A few items were eliminated because of their susceptibility to diseases and pests," writes Zaitzevsky.[138]

John Charles Olmsted, ever dutiful and compliant, allowed for modification but refused to accept such extensive changes, and Sargent, ever the autocrat, responded that if the plants were not removed, the services of the firm would no longer be required. His own nephew, Henry Sargent Codman, advised his colleagues at Olmsted's firm, "It will probably be best to resign our position rather than allow our design to be so injured and cut to pieces as Professor Sargent proposes."[139] John Charles Olmsted produced an altered but still basically intact planting plan. Sargent made no further comment but quietly went about ordering large quantities of the plants he wanted used. The only foreign species he conceded to were Japanese barberry and European brier rose. It was Sargent's list that was planted. It seems impossible that such a row would have occurred if the senior Olmsted had been present. Nevertheless, as to the matter of Sargent's triumph, Zaitzevsky concludes that in the end, "the Brookline planting is somewhat more monotonous than it would have been—a result that was largely, although not entirely, independent of the native/foreign controversy."[140]

Meanwhile, bridges, "designed by Richardson's successors from sketches by the Olmsteds, were thrown across [the river] at several points."[141] Culverts, macadamizing, and curbing were all well under way, and the expectation was that within a matter of months the park construction would be concluded.[142] And so it was; apart from certain construction details, the project was completed. The Brookline park commissioners requested an annual maintenance fee of $5,500.[143] Once again in 1894 some construction work remained to be done, but the overall plan had indeed been executed.

Charles Sprague Sargent's dedication to public open space has already been attested to in his work on national parks. He invested time and effort in his position on the Brookline Park Commission as well, writing that park commissioners bore a great responsibility to be "serious and enlightened" in their role as park advocates and guardians.[144] Brookline's commitment to parks for its own community, however, was initially desultory at best. An 1876 *Chronicle* article claimed that public parks were essential to "crowded cities, not to suburban towns like Brookline. . . . Brookline itself is a park."[145] Indeed, in 1889, years after Olmsted had moved to Brookline, he was asked during a talk at the Brookline Club if the town should be acquiring land for a park. "He thought it ought not," according to the *Chronicle* report, although he added that "it might be profitable . . . to secure small tracts in various parts of the town."[146] Through the years the park commission did just that, adding a municipal golf course and playgrounds. The main addition to the park system, after the all-consuming Muddy River project, occurred in 1902 with the acquisition of the four squares belonging to the David Sears estate. Longwood Mall, with some of its magnificent European beeches still extant, Mason Square, Winthrop Square, and Knyvet Square were all donated to the town by Sears's descendants to serve as public parks for the pleasure of all. The town held a special meeting on June 19, 1902, to approve their incorporation.

Sargent figured large in the deliberations and actions of the commission during his long tenure. After his death in 1927, the Board of Park Commissioners attested that throughout his forty-seven-year association, "he gave to the town largely of his time, his expert knowledge of everything having to do with arboriculture and his money, for many of the fine and rare trees and shrubs, which now adorn the town, were his gifts. In large measure, the town owes its many beauty spots to him, and generations to come will be grateful to him for what he did for them."[147]

Throughout the time he was establishing and running the arboretum and attending to the various other duties associated with his professional and civic obligations, Sargent continued to transform Holm Lea into a horticultural testing ground in the form of a model gentleman's estate. By 1897 Van Rensselaer called it "the most beautiful suburban country place that I know," observing that "the traditions of Holm Lea have remained unbroken and its spirit unchanged" from the time of Thomas Lee.[148] In Brookline, writes Van Rensselaer, "every place has a personality, and plays its part in a panorama of perpetually changing charm. But the most beautiful and most interesting of all is Mr. Sargent's. It is larger than any other, it is very diversified in surface, and it has been treated with exceptional artistic skill."[149] Sargent used the natural terrain to good advantage. One scholar observes, "In accordance with Downing's emphasis on vistas, the rolling hills were used to create visual changes in texture."[150] Cows grazed in the five-acre pasture, save in the springtime, when thousands of "poet's narcissi" nodded amidst the grass (fig. 5.20). As at most country places of the era, there was at least a hint of self-sufficiency at Holm Lea, including farm buildings (dairies, stables, and a barn) and some livestock. These were augmented by greenhouses, cold pits where azaleas were wintered, and a large kitchen garden.[151] Many of these efforts were carried over from the days of Ignatius Sargent, who not only kept a herd of Jersey cows and a pen full of pigs but also maintained an extensive apple orchard.[152]

There was a two-acre man-made pond, with *Pseudacorus* iris and purple loose-strife dotting its borders, water lilies floating about, and willow and tupelo trees hanging over its banks.[153] A "rockery" stood nearby, replete with alpine plants. Hazel Collins described it in 1903: "One of the prettiest little spots on the estate is the rock-garden hidden from the avenue by tall shrubbery and partially concealed

Fig. 5.20. Poet's narcissi beside the two-acre man-made pond at Sargent's Holm Lea. In the distance is Sargent's house. Copyright © President and Fellows of Harvard College. Arnold Arboretum Archives.

Fig. 5.21. Sargent ringed the pond with a handsome collection of rhododendrons. Copyright © President and Fellows of Harvard College. Arnold Arboretum Archives.

from the pond by the old willow tree, like a gem too beautiful for the vulgar gaze. Foot-paths and steps lead through and around it and all sorts of little alpine and other plants fill every crack between the rocks. At its foot nestles the old moss covered pump house, as much a part of the natural scene as though never built by the hand of man."[154] The aesthetics of the rock garden did not preclude its role as a scientific breeding ground for alpine plants of all kinds.

Large, abundant rhododendrons ringed the pond, creating the finest "rhodo-dendron plantation" around, according to Van Rensselaer (fig. 5.21). "All those of defective form or with blossoms of unpleasant color have been weeded out so that no discordant note mars their blaze of purple, crimson, and white."[155] Azaleas pro-liferated as well. The place, according to the horticulturist and author Wilhelm Miller, was amply endowed with "open pastoral views" and generally unencum-bered by flowerbeds, although naturalized flowers abounded.[156]

On visiting Holm Lea in 1893, the renowned California naturalist John Muir wrote his wife, "This is the finest mansion and ground I ever saw," depicting the landscape in admiring detail, including the "lawns, groves, wild woods of pine, hemlock, maple beech, hickory, etc. and all kinds of underbrush and wild flowers and cultivated flowers—acres of rhododendrons twelve feet high in full bloom, and a pond covered with lilies, etc., all ground waving, hill and dale, and clad in full summer dress of the region, trimmed with exquisite taste" (fig. 5.22).[157] In the tradition of the early Brookline residents before him, Sargent had planted rare

Fig. 5.22. Flowers were naturalized along the many pathways threading through Holm Lea. Copyright © President and Fellows of Harvard College. Arnold Arboretum Archives.

trees in profusion. Muir, not much given to veneration of material things, wrote a glowing review of "Sargent's silva," for the July 1903 *Atlantic Monthly,* acknowledging Sargent's seriousness of purpose. "While all his surroundings were drawing him toward a life of fine pleasure, and the cultivation of the family fortune, he chose to live laborious days in God's forests, studying, cultivating the whole continent as his garden," he wrote admiringly.[158] The informal, uninhibited, and outgoing Muir formed an unexpected friendship with the starchy, remote Brahmin. In 1903 he even accompanied Sargent and his son on one of their trips abroad.

Sargent frequently used his and his friends' grounds to test the viability of plants he gathered or was sent from faraway places for the arboretum. H. H. Hunnewell's Wellesley provided one setting, as did Rockweld, the one-thousand-acre Dedham country place of Stephen Minot Weld, a Boston industrialist. Weld's gardens contained over five hundred varieties of flowering plants, including rhododendrons and azaleas that he and Hunnewell clubbed together to bring up from the South by the train car full. He also created a significant rock garden. Plant distribution lists from the arboretum indicate that Rockweld was used as a test site for plant and tree specimens, in particular for the tiny alpines Sargent brought from Switzerland "to test in the Rock Garden in Dedham."[159]

Fig. 5.23. Mary Robeson Sargent. Copyright © President and Fellows of Harvard College. Arnold Arboretum Archives.

Holm Lea was not simply a testing ground; it was a classroom and showcase. Visitors flocked from all over the world to visit Sargent and his garden. His daughter was convinced that the private estate complemented and even enhanced the arboretum. Particularly in springtime, during peak blossoming, "year after year a constant procession of visitors from all parts of the world—scientist, amateurs, students, public spirited citizens, travelers—gathered at lunch or took tea on the long terraces during an interim in their enthusiastic inspections of outdoor beauties," wrote Mary Sargent Potter of her parents' estate. "I feel confident that interest in the Arboretum was enhanced by the memories of Holm Lea and of its presiding genius."[160] Mary Robeson Sargent's contribution to the welcome that was extended to visitors should not be underestimated (fig. 5.23). Her grace and hospitality were fondly recalled upon her death, in particular her generosity in sharing Holm Lea. In the words of one typical reminiscence: "Her home and estate were for others to enjoy and on Saturday afternoons and Sundays thousands of people, families from Brookline, Jamaica Plain, Dorchester and Boston wandered over the lawns, sat upon the verandas and took possession. That was her pleasure, to watch them enjoying the beauties which were so dear to her."[161]

Marshall Pinckney Wilder reserves his highest praise for the Sargent property, "the most extensive and elegant estate in Brookline." He describes both Sargent's embellishments and the role Holm Lea played in his educational efforts: "Under the supervision of Professor Sargent, this place, with its magnificent landscape, its conservatories of plants, and its extensive collection . . . is every year thrown open to the public. With its extensive and rare collection of native and foreign trees and shrubs . . . this estate is one of great interest for the study of landscape and ornamental culture."[162]

For over fifty years Sargent stood firmly at the helm of the Arnold Arboretum, and for even longer he was passionately committed to his beloved landscape at Holm Lea. Seldom in poor health, at eighty-five he succumbed to influenza on March 22, 1927, after a brief illness. Awards and encomiums were liberally awarded him during his long career. As William Trelease stated after his death, "publicity was not of Sargent's seeking, but he did not escape many and highly prized recognitions of his talent and accomplishment."[163] He was the recipient of an honorary LL.D. degree from Harvard University (1901), the Veitch Memorial Medal (1895), the Loder Rhododendron Cup from the Royal Horticultural Society of England (1924), and medals of honor from the Société Nationale d'Agriculture de France (1893), the Massachusetts Horticultural Society (1910)—where he was library chairman for thirty-four years and a vice president for fifty—the Garden Club of America (1920), and the American Genetic Association (1923).[164] Above all, according to members of the Brookline Park Commission, Charles Sprague Sargent was "always unassuming and exemplified the finest type of American citizen."[165] Albert Emerson Benson declared that for the Massachusetts Horticultural Society, which Sargent had joined in 1870, he was "a strength and a safeguard—a powerful oak—a mountain."[166]

And powerful he was. Frederick Law Olmsted Jr.'s 1927 memorial may have summed up Sargent's character most honestly. He characterized Sargent's nature as compounding three types of men: one the diffident scientist who maintains a "lifelong constancy of aim and persistence of devotion to a single chosen field"; another the steely businessman who drives forward toward his goals with "a disregard of opposing points of view," a type "often described as ruthless"; and finally, a man capable of "a deep and strong emotional capacity—utterly undemonstrative and usually masked behind brusque manners—for personal affection and personal loyalty, binding those who feel its presence to a lifelong devotion."[167]

It was fitting that his memorial service should be held at Arnold Arboretum in the valley at Bussey Brook, where, in Harvard president A. Lawrence Lowell's words, Sargent had " 'built his thoughts into' the lovely landscape that surrounded the mourners," according to Ida Hay. "Behind them grew forty-foot hemlocks planted by Sargent in the 1880s, and beyond those stood the cherished native stand on Hemlock Hill."[168] It was even more fitting that he had died at his beloved Holm Lea, the Brookline haven he husbanded throughout his life.

What becomes clear on closer examination of Sargent's lifelong efforts, both at Holm Lea and at the Arnold Arboretum, is how pivotal his role was in advancing the free-flowing, naturalistic planting and design approach that came down to him through the writings of Andrew Jackson Downing, and through the picturesque traditions so lovingly interpreted in the Brookline estates that surrounded Sargent during his formative years and adulthood. His private estate was the epitome of beauty and horticultural endeavor. Creator of an aesthetically conceived, world-class arboretum, he achieved a national and international reputation for his work in and his writing on dendrology. Sargent was admired and his counsel sought by the community he lived in, his most significant contribution on the Park Commission being the long years of establishing the Muddy River section of the Emerald Necklace. He influenced numerous landscape architects, for the arboretum was a field study resource for Harvard's landscape architecture school (founded in 1900) as well as for MIT's short-lived program in landscape architecture (1900–1909), headed by his son-in-law, the architect Guy Lowell.[169] One of his two sons, Andrew Robeson Sargent—a frequent traveling companion on Sargent's far-flung travels—was a successful landscape gardener associated with his brother-in-law's architectural office until his death in 1918.[170]

Sargent's wealth and social position contributed to his stature as well. Certainly that, combined with his outstanding aesthetic contributions, might easily have added to Brookline's appeal for the likes of Henry Hobson Richardson and Frederick Law Olmsted. His status as an old guard Bostonian and a long-standing member of the Brookline community provided entrée for both Olmsted and Richardson. His presence in Brookline decades after the other two were gone contributed to his long-lasting influence on the development of that community.

One of the founders of the Brookline Park Commission, and chairman until his death, Sargent represented the public face of horticulture and landscape design to his fellow residents. His business connections, including his influential position on the board of the Boston and Albany Railroad, helped secure important commissions for Olmsted and Richardson. His founding and editing of *Garden and Forest,* the first significant American periodical devoted to the fields of horticulture, botany, landscape architecture, land conservation, and forestry, allowed ideas generated within Brookline, including articles written by his friends and fellow residents, to be disseminated among a far-reaching public. His role in encouraging and directing the landscape development of key institutions in Brookline such as the Free Hospital for Women, where his wife served on the board of advisers, and above all in establishing, designing, and directing the Arnold Arboretum in nearby Jamaica Plain, afforded him the opportunity to preserve and improve the physical world he inhabited and, by extension, the fields of horticulture, dendrology, and design at home and abroad.

Mariana Griswold Van Rensselaer, friend and admirer of Sargent, Olmsted, and Richardson, dedicated the 1925 edition of her influential book *Art Out-of-Doors* "To the Friends in Brookline Who Taught Me to Care for the Art Which Stands Nearest to Nature." The existence of that dynamic triad, colleagues and friends living within walking distance of one another, fashioned a creative force field seldom seen in American design. Sargent's role in the process was pivotal. Among the visionary forces at work in Brookline in the late nineteenth and early twentieth centuries, Sargent's influence is evident and his place secure.

Six

THE PLANNING CONTEXT

O n February 25, 1889, Frederick Law Olmsted gave a talk at the Brookline
Club about the history of roads and parkways, beginning with the earliest
periods of Western civilization. According to the local newspaper,
Olmsted related his reasons for moving to Brookline, remarking that it was an
attractive place to live, efficiently managed, and very unlikely to be developed
by "commercial interests," adding, "How to preserve the topographical condition
of the town is the most critical question of the time." In what was presumably
the central point of his talk, Olmsted "laid particular stress to the importance of
laying out streets with an eye to the future and in advance of present needs."[1]

The desire to preserve the residential character of Brookline by directing development is reflected in the firm's roadway and subdivision projects. It also lies at
the core of the work of Frederick Law Olmsted Jr. in his service on the Brookline
Planning Board. Plans for boulevards and parkways, though mostly not carried
out, guided the town to act in ways that anticipated future growth, especially in
relatively undeveloped tracts south of Beacon Street. Similarly, the subdivision
plans generated by the Olmsted firm worked to preserve the "topographical condition" of the town. Frederick Law Olmsted Sr. and John Charles Olmsted set high
standards, providing their fellow townspeople with an understanding of what was
possible with good planning. By the early twentieth century, as development pressures accelerated with the popularity of the automobile, Frederick Law Olmsted
Jr. aimed to develop sound principles of city planning to regulate growth through
zoning laws.

That Frederick Law Olmsted and his two sons remained at 99 Warren Street
while managing an office with projects throughout the country is testimony to the
appeal of Brookline's suburban character. Because of its close proximity to Boston,

Brookline was experiencing development pressures in the 1880s. By that time the semirural character of the adjacent communities of Jamaica Plain (formerly part of Roxbury) and Brighton had been radically transformed with high-density working-class housing. The legacy of this change is visible today, principally in the survival of three-family housing, particularly the freestanding wood structures popularly known as "three-deckers." The impact of the demand for this type of housing is evident in Brookline, especially along sections of Boylston Street (Route 9) and south of that road on Cypress Street in Brookline Village, although urban renewal projects during the early 1960s erased the full effect of the multitude of three-deckers built in Brookline in the late nineteenth century.[2]

Frederick Law Olmsted's plan for the Riverside suburb of Chicago (with Calvert Vaux) is perhaps the most famous example of his vision of a scenic refuge from urban congestion. Even though no such plan was conceived for Brookline, the system of boulevards the firm worked on endorsed the concept that travel to and from work should afford some relaxation and scenic beauty. Indeed, the very notion recognized the importance of well-designed roads.[3] One way to preserve Brookline's traditional character as a town of predominantly single-family detached homes was to accommodate development in a way that facilitated easy access to and from the city for those who could afford their own means of transportation. In part this required a system of attractive roads leading directly to town. The impact of the streetcar on the suburb was also tested in Brookline, on Beacon Street. The plan by the Olmsted firm was for a boulevard that would include room for pleasure vehicles, not just a highway to enable commuters to travel to work and back.

BROOKLINE BOULEVARDS AND PARKWAYS

Like many of his Brookline neighbors, Olmsted was mindful that unplanned intensive multifamily development was disfiguring what had formerly been scenic suburbs nearby. In the late nineteenth century, Brookline rejected several attempts to incorporate the town as a neighborhood of the city of Boston. The annexation of the formerly independent adjacent towns of Brighton, Roxbury, and West Roxbury fueled Boston's expansion as the largest city in Massachusetts. The citizens of Brookline resisted, even giving up land on the Charles River to provide a bridge between Brighton and Boston along what is now Commonwealth Avenue in 1874. The incorporation of neighboring towns, and the last serious effort to induce annexation, occurred before Olmsted decided to relocate to Brookline.[4] Although the town preserved its independence, by the time he arrived, it was surrounded on three sides by a growing metropolis. Regional suburban expansion with the development of highways, and later trolley lines, inevitably affected the town. The

Olmsted firm played an important role in planning for new arterial roads within the town as well as to the western suburbs, which, like Brookline, were developing as popular residential communities for Boston commuters.

TOXTETH STREET

The firm's earliest boulevard project was located entirely within Brookline. In 1885 the Board of Selectmen engaged the firm of F. L. & J. C. Olmsted to develop a plan to rationalize street layouts in the residential neighborhood between Brookline Village and Longwood Mall. This land had mostly belonged to the Aspinwall family, whose seventeenth-century house stood at the corner of Aspinwall Avenue and St. Paul Street until about 1897. St. Paul's Episcopal Church, completed in 1852 to designs of Richard Upjohn, stood directly across the street. On a lot adjacent to the church, Peabody & Stearns designed a new rectory in 1885. Linden Park and Linden Place, an 1844 planned subdivision (called "the Lindens"), occupied an area to the southwest between Aspinwall Avenue and Brookline Village. To the northeast, bordering Boston at the milldam that crossed Back Bay, David Sears in 1849 had laid out the Longwood neighborhood with several small squares, including Longwood Mall, the famous park with his imported beech trees. This neighborhood extended across Beacon Street, laid out as a county road in 1850, and included a stop of the Boston and Albany Railroad at Chapel Street. A second neighborhood called Cottage Farm, established by Amos A. Lawrence, incorporated much of the Sears property on the north side of Beacon Street (renaming portions of what had all been part of Longwood). Development in both of these neighborhoods was initially restricted to relatives and acquaintances of the Lawrence and Sears families.

By 1885 the continued attraction of the Longwood and Cottage Farm neighborhoods, with their close proximity to Boston, encouraged development of the land west of the Kent Street boundary of Longwood Mall. The growth of the neighborhood led to the construction of the Lawrence School on Francis Street in 1884 and a "chemical fire station" on Monmouth Street in 1886, both designed by Peabody & Stearns. The proposed plan by F. L. & J. C. Olmsted added new streets between Francis Street and Brookline Village, but the major change proposed was a boulevard that would link Longwood with the railroad station in Brookline Village.[5] Toxteth Street, an existing road in the Lindens, was to be extended north from Station Street on an axis with the Brookline Village train station. The road was to be cut through Linden Place and continue on to intersect with Longwood Avenue, one of the streets extending west from Longwood Mall, where large new homes were already being built in 1885. Linden Place, a small square park, was reduced in the Olmsted scheme to an even smaller triangular green in the style of an urban square, inside a Y-shaped traffic intersection where Toxteth Street angled off at one branch of the Y. The boulevard park was a scheme the Olmsted firm often employed in the nineteenth century.

Lack of support from landowners in the neighborhood resulted in only minor street improvements. The failure to create an arterial road out of Toxteth Street left no focus for future development, and although both parks survive, the area around the Lindens neighborhood was subsequently developed for two- and three-family homes. The Lawrence School neighborhood between Aspinwall Avenue and Francis Street saw the construction of single-family homes, but most were not the larger upper-middle-class residences that characterized the expanding Longwood neighborhood. In 1893 the town commissioned Olmsted, Olmsted & Eliot to prepare a plan for improvements to the Longwood Playground, adjacent to the Lawrence School, but it appears that the work was not carried out.[6]

BEACON STREET

In contrast to the failed Toxteth Street scheme, the next major arterial road the firm planned was built and had a major impact on the town. As noted, Beacon Street was a county road established in 1850. In the next thirty-five years only a few homes were built along Beacon Street, mostly in the vicinity of Coolidge Corner. A general store for which Coolidge Corner was named was the only commercial development. Nonetheless, the direct access to Boston provided by this road facilitated the daily commute by horse and carriage for Boston lawyers and merchants. A number of wealthy Boston businessmen had built homes along Beacon Street beyond Longwood and Cottage Farm, but the area west, toward Newton, remained largely undeveloped farmland in 1886. In May of that year the Olmsted firm developed a scheme to widen Beacon Street for the West End Land Company, owned by Beacon Street resident Henry M. Whitney (fig. 6.1). The

Fig. 6.1. "Preliminary Plan for Widening Beacon Street from the Back Bay District of Boston to the Public Pleasure Grounds at Chestnut Hill Reservoir and for Connections with Massachusetts and Commonwealth Avenues," November 29, 1886, F. L. & J. C. Olmsted. Courtesy National Park Service, Frederick Law Olmsted National Historic Site.

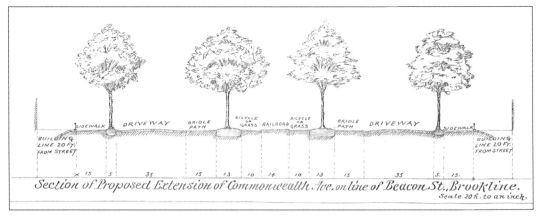

**Fig. 6.2. Detail, "Study of Plan for Extension of Commonwealth Avenue on the Line of Beacon Street"
from "Preliminary Plan for Widening Beacon Street," October 2, 1886, F. L. & J. C. Olmsted.** Courtesy
National Park Service, Frederick Law Olmsted National Historic Site.

plan called for turning the fifty-foot country road into a boulevard two hundred
feet wide. In the center was proposed a "clean" railroad (originally a cable car, but
quickly supplanted by the newly invented electric trolley). On either side of the
fourteen-foot-wide tracks were planned ten-foot-wide sections for either bicycle
paths or grass, and beyond them thirteen-foot-wide tree lines. On the other side
of the tree lines were to be fifteen-foot-wide bridle paths, followed by thirty-five-
foot-wide "driveways." The outside borders were to be five-foot-wide tree lines
and fifteen-foot-wide sidewalks (fig. 6.2). This was transportation planning with
a grand vision. Designed with tree-lined circles at each end (Audubon Circle and
Cleveland Circle in Boston, still extant though the trees were never realized),
the concept clearly projected a link to the parklike Chestnut Hill Reservoir and
the city of Newton beyond. The firm repeated this pattern in a similar boulevard
concept for Commonwealth Avenue in the Brighton section of Boston. A modified
version of that boulevard (without trees) was begun in 1895.[7]

A description of the plan outlined the firm's vision for this underdeveloped
section of Brookline. Fundamental to all the firm's approaches is the belief that
development was inevitable for Brookline, and that it was in the town's interest to
manage that growth. As the *Brookline Chronicle* reported:

This plan is designed to supply certain advantages, the lack of which is
hindering a desirable, and inviting an inadvisable, occupation of the large
and beautiful district lying on each side of Beacon Street for three miles
beyond Back Bay. It assumes that what is now wanting to secure a natural,
suitable, speedy, and profitable outgrowth over this district from the Back
Bay quarter is, first, a spacious direct trunk-line thoroughfare, specially

adapted to pleasure driving, riding, and walking; and second, a means of direct communication between it and the city that shall be always ready for use, convenient, economical, and expeditious.[8]

It is significant that one of the plans was labeled "Study of Plan for the Extension of Commonwealth Avenue on the Line of Beacon Street."[9] The direct link with Commonwealth Avenue in the Back Bay, then the most fashionable address in Boston, was both literal and symbolic. The Olmsted description includes an appeal to the wealthier classes:

> The different means of locomotion, and the several lines of trees provided in this plan are expected to make the avenue attractive, not only because of the unusual convenience secured, but because of the sylvan beauty to be enjoyed in passing over it. As those to be drawn to use it on this account, will form in themselves and by the elegance of their equipage and attire, a pleasing spectacle as they pass by in daily procession, another feature will be gained, tending to make the adjoining building sites particularly attractive to many people.[10]

Notwithstanding descriptions of "sylvan beauty," the Beacon Street plan was never intended to exclude commercial development, which is why it could not be described as a "parkway," as Olmsted defined the term.[11]

Henry M. Whitney had secretly acquired a good deal of land along both sides of Beacon Street before he formed his West End Land Company syndicate in 1886 and went public with his petition to the Board of Selectmen. A number of prominent citizens, including Amos A. Lawrence, Henry Lee, Moses Williams, William Aspinwall, William I. Bowditch, and the architects Robert S. Peabody and John Hubbard Sturgis signed the petition.[12] Opposition coalesced at a public hearing and included several equally influential residents who signed a petition declaring that the project was "unnecessary to the public welfare" and "extravagant." Among the opponents were prominent businessmen such as Henry Varnum Poor, Theodore Lyman, Edward Atkinson, and Edward S. Philbrick.[13] They did not live near Beacon Street, but among several other petitioners who did, and whose residential property would be affected, were Charles H. Stearns, A. W. Benton, and John Wales.[14]

Prior to the public hearing on December 7, the Board of Selectmen consulted with "many citizens and the engineers" to have the planned width of the street cut from 200 feet to 160 feet.[15] The principal concern was to reduce the cost in land taking where Whitney had not secured property for his syndicate. Accordingly the two bicycle paths and one bridle path were eliminated. Construction began in April 1887. As originally laid out in 1850, Beacon Street ran along the base of Corey Hill, on the north side of the road between Harvard and Washington streets, where the Olmsted plan intended to accommodate the change in grade for the outbound driving lanes.[16] In order to avoid cutting into the hill, the plan divided Beacon Street at the foot of Summit Avenue, with the outbound lane rising above the inbound lane before descending to join it again at Washington Street.

In August, George Armstrong began construction of a house on Beacon Street at Coolidge Corner. It was designed by Shepley, Rutan & Coolidge, and the landscape plans were by the Olmsted firm.[17]

In July of the following year Whitney decided to employ new technology for his trolley by petitioning the Board of Selectmen for permission to install and operate an electric-powered line. The one on Beacon Street—now the oldest continually powered electric trolley line in the country—was in operation by the end of 1888. Its success no doubt contributed to the change of character of the street from large single-family homes to middle-class apartment blocks and row houses (fig. 6.3). While some houses with stables were built (such as Armstrong's), as well as a row of brick stables constructed on St. Mary's Court, the popularity of the electric

Fig. 6.3. Beacon Street near Carlton Street, ca. 1910. This view looking west shows the north side of the street with the trolley tracks on the left. The elm trees were part of the original design. Dutch elm disease and automobile parking spoiled much of the original character of the Olmsted design.
Courtesy Brookline Public Library.

trolley encouraged a reliance on public transportation. George Armstrong, with his large Shingle Style house and stable, misjudged his investment. Coolidge Corner rapidly became characterized by row houses, apartment buildings, and small-scale commercial enterprises. The rapidity of this change was demonstrated in 1890, directly opposite Armstrong's property, where Shepley, Rutan & Coolidge designed a row of brick town houses at 1394–1408 Beacon Street.

Although Olmsted's plan for Beacon Street continued to attract several wealthy businessmen who constructed large single-family homes, particularly on Corey Hill, developers of middle-class housing also saw the potential there, and as a result, the new street dramatically altered the character of north Brookline. By extending Beacon Street beyond the Chestnut Hill Reservoir, the road provided a major artery to the western suburbs as well.[18] The firm's Beacon Street plan included a similar boulevard that branched off Brighton Avenue (referred to as "Massachusetts Avenue" in some schemes), which originated at Kenmore Square. The name was later changed to Commonwealth Avenue. Running roughly parallel to Beacon Street, Brighton Avenue and its extension, Commonwealth Avenue, also connected to the Chestnut Hill Reservoir.[19] Located in the city of Boston, where the citizenry were less involved in its development, the Brighton portion of Commonwealth Avenue never experienced the construction of architecture equaling that of Beacon Street, even with regard to the brick row houses that still line much of the latter. Property values in Brighton would never equal those in Brookline, and this is still reflected in the comparative quality of the architecture of both streets today.[20]

The Olmsted firm was called on to develop a similar plan for Boylston Street along with a connector to Beacon Street via Chestnut Hill Avenue. Boylston Street, the other major east-west road through Brookline, was a logical continuation of this system of arterial roads. An older road, it was first built in 1804 as the Worcester Turnpike and had a long history as an east-west highway. As with Beacon Street and the northern part of town, the Olmsted principals must have understood that development in the southern section of Brookline was inevitable and should be managed to encourage the wealthy to continue to reside in older neighborhoods such as Town Green and Green Hill, as well as in the new neighborhoods of Fisher Hill and Chestnut Hill. A citizens' petition signed by one hundred property owners initiated the process in which the Board of Selectmen held public hearings on the matter. Those same citizens hired F. L. Olmsted & Co. to prepare the initial design.[21]

In the 1892 plan Boylston Street was similar to Beacon Street, except that it was not originally conceived to be as wide. Moreover, the earlier construction of homes at the lower end (east of Cypress Street) eliminated that section for consideration as part of the improvements, as it would have been too costly to acquire land where houses stood close to the street. A petition dated April 25, 1892, called for widening the fifty-five-foot road west of Cypress Street to 130 feet and introducing electric streetcars.[22] The signatories in support included architects Edward C. Cabot, Arthur Rotch, and Charles H. Rutan, all of whom lived close enough to use the road on a regular basis, but whose property would not be directly affected. Opposition was led by men such as Augustus Lowell, who lived on Heath Street south of Boylston, and Henry Lee, whose estate was on Fisher Hill opposite the Brookline Reservoir and Boylston Street. Lee's opposition was a clarion call for rearguard action to preserve the old Brookline. He believed that electric trolley lines were "dangerous to man and beast." Moreover, he said, "I deny that rapid transit is the only or the paramount consideration with settlers in the country, and consequently to be sought at all hazards and sacrifices; and I maintain that it interferes with repose and recreation of mind and body; with walking, riding and driving, and with the seclusion which is one charm of country life."[23] Lee's objections articulated the very reason Frederick Law Olmsted had been attracted to Brookline ten years earlier. Olmsted and his sons, however, must have recognized that Brookline could not remain an underdeveloped arcadia. Their planning efforts for major roadways reflected a willingness to work with the changing means of transportation.

Although the plan was publicly discussed in 1892, no action was taken until the matter was brought up for a formal town meeting vote in 1896. At that time modifications were made, including the addition of bicycle paths in response to the huge popularity of cycling. Proponents made a point of illustrating the connection with the road in Newton as well as in Boston. Opponents defeated the plan with a remonstrance signed by major landowners who lived along the road. They also argued that the impetus for the scheme originated with land speculators in Newton who wanted to open their city to suburban development.[24]

The proposed widening was taken up again in 1898. The revised plan called for three different widths. From Cypress Street to Sumner (Buckminster) Road, the corridor would be 110 feet wide. For the section between the Brookline Reservoir and Fisher Hill, it would be 90 feet. This section was narrower on account of the reservoir on the south side and Fisher Hill on the north side (where, incidentally, much of the land was owned by Henry Lee). West from Chestnut Hill Avenue, where more land was available at lower cost, the plan called for a 115-foot-wide road.[25] This effort also failed, and it was not until 1899 (after Lee's death) that the town meeting approved widening the road to 75 feet uniformly. The West End Street Railroad Company was also given permission to construct double tracks along Boylston Street to the Newton line. These changes, however, did not incorporate the Olmsted plan for a wide boulevard with lines of trees separating traffic lanes.[26] Nonetheless, the Olmsted involvement in the initial efforts set the standard and framed the discussion for the citizens of Brookline. Although a trolley line was eventually built to Newton and beyond, it was short-lived, and major changes came with the pressures of automobile traffic in the 1930s and the link with the new Hammond Pond Parkway.

SOUTH BROOKLINE PARKWAYS

The plans to widen Boylston Street attracted the attention of developers interested in opening up the southern part of town to lower-income citizens. In particular, John J. McCormack, one of Brookline's most active real estate developers, acquired the land of the Suburban Club on Clyde Street, opposite The Country Club, which he divided into one hundred parcels to sell unimproved (fig. 6.4). McCormack's development required that the town accept his new streets. The large property owners immediately realized the consequences of McCormack's subdivision. South Brookline would be intensively developed like Brighton or, even worse, nearby Jamaica Plain, with its concentration of three-deckers. Part of McCormack's plan depended on the construction of a new "highway" from Boylston Street at the Brookline Reservoir along the line of the present Lee and Clyde streets to Newton Street. Opposition to the new road, first from the Board of Selectmen and then from the town meeting, put a halt to the development.[27]

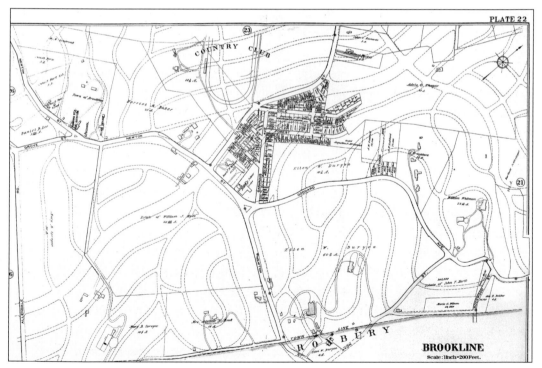

Fig. 6.4. Detail of McCormack's proposed Clyde Street development, 1897, *Atlas of the Town of Brookline* **(1900). Courtesy Brookline Public Library.**

Because of the determined opposition of the area's estate owners and the stagnant economy in 1893, when the lots were initially made available, only one house had been built by 1897 and only sixteen by 1925.[28] The failed project ended McCormack's real estate career.

The large landowners responded to this threat to their neighborhood of country estates by hiring Olmsted, Olmsted & Eliot to design plans for future development that were more to their liking. According to the local newspaper, the firm had been engaged to submit a plan "having in view connecting roads, transportation facilities, public reservations, drainage, and whatever else claims consideration in modern suburban development."[29] A note dated February 13, 1894, of a meeting between John Charles Olmsted and Alfred D. Chandler, "representing five or six landowners in the Clyde Street district," records that for a fee not to exceed $500, the firm was to show "only probable thoroughfares which may be desirable in the future and also such reservations along the water courses as may be desirable to preserve them."[30] The Olmsted, Olmsted & Eliot plans for the proposed roads date from early 1896. Although it is not clear why there was a delay of two years, it may have reflected the enlarged scope of the work, calling for schematic designs that encompassed much more than a response aimed narrowly at the McCormack development.[31] It is not clear who initiated the expansion of the project; perhaps the Olmsted partners pushed for a more comprehensive scheme than one directed against the McCormack development.

That the Olmsted firm was not working to limit development per se, just certain types of subdivisions, is evident in the fully developed portion of the plans in which the neighborhood was to be called "Brookside Roads." Dated September 5, 1894, a "Sketch of Proposed Brookside Roads in Upper Brookline" (fig. 6.5) shows a parkway from Boylston Street along the lines of Lee and Clyde streets to Newton Street with a large playground opposite The Country Club. A branch of this parkway at Dudley and Warren streets extends to Jamaica Pond. Running between the Schlesinger estate and the rear of the houses on Cottage Street, this branch skirts the south side of Sargent Pond. More schematic versions show the extension of this system north of Boylston Street following what became Eliot Street through undeveloped land to Cleveland Circle. There was also a proposed branch extending from Clyde Street just north of The Country Club property to Hammond Street. None of these plans was realized, although a portion for a reservation at Hammond and Newton streets reached the stage of detailed drawings, with Warren Manning the assigned supervisor of plantings and Edward Bolton in charge of construction.[32]

A more comprehensive concept of planning for the development of Brookline south of Boylston Street appears as an overlay in the town's 1897 atlas of streets, properties, and buildings.[33] Although no direct link between this vision

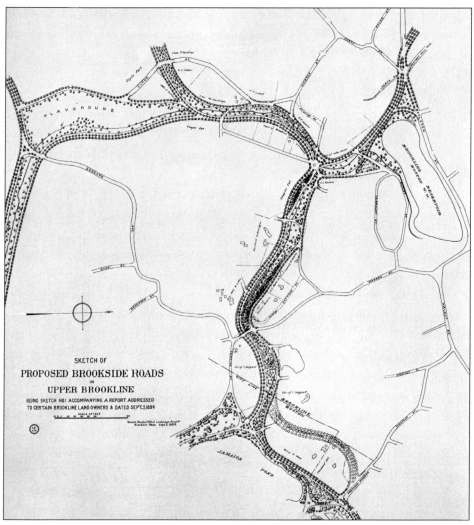

Fig. 6.5. "Sketch of Proposed Brookside Roads in Upper Brookline," September 5, 1894. Olmsted, Olmsted & Eliot. Courtesy National Park Service, Frederick Law Olmsted National Historic Site.

of development and the Olmsted firm has been established, its timing and concept make a connection very plausible. Osborne Howes Jr., in a letter to the *Brookline Chronicle,* had laid out the very same concept in 1893. In his long paean to Frederick Law Olmsted, Howes praised Olmsted's role in the Columbian Exposition and called for the town to hire the firm to prepare a comprehensive plan. "The work thus planned," he wrote. "would not have to be undertaken at once, which would, of course, involve an inordinate outlay; but whenever it became necessary for this town to make a move, or whenever individual property owners desired to develop their own estates, the work should be done in conformity with this general plan."[34]

The last major effort to construct part of the Olmsted, Olmsted & Eliot scheme came in 1901 with the "Chestnut Hill Parkway" proposal. This is not to be confused with the plan to widen Chestnut Hill Avenue as a tree-lined parkway between Cleveland Circle and Boylston Street. Those plans were prepared in 1891 but never realized.[35] The impetus for the parkway project was probably related to the fact that the Brookline Reservoir property was soon to be sold by the City of Boston, as it no longer functioned as part of the municipal water supply system. Constructed in 1848 as part of the first system bringing water from the Cochituate Reservoir, it was also used as a promenade park from the beginning. Once it was no longer used as a reservoir, there was a possibility of filling it in and using the land for development. As the town was reluctant to spend $150,000 for a park with so little recreational potential (only recently a large public "bathhouse" had been built nearby for swimming), the thirty-acre site required public support to be preserved. In order to ensure that the town acquired the reservoir, a number of landowners, including Warren Street resident John Charles Olmsted, raised $50,000 toward the town's purchase of it.

The City of Boston announced the sale of the reservoir property in 1902. It is likely that the plans for the Chestnut Hill Parkway were developed in 1901, when prominent Brookline residents heard of the projected sale of the reservoir. It was not the reservoir alone that was a matter of concern, however. A group of seventy prominent citizens, represented by Alfred D. Chandler, petitioned the town to promote a scheme in which the reservoir would become part of the metropolitan park system, connected to "the public reservations in West Roxbury and Brighton by a parkway which would naturally follow the lines of the improvements for sewerage, drainage, and transportation already being acted upon by Brookline." The broader concern expressed by the petitioners was as follows: "Southwest of Boylston street, between Heath Hill and Jamaica Pond, changes of ownership in estates caused by death or transfers, have forced attention also to the natural main lines of municipal development to be established in that direction, before private construction out of harmony with broad economic views would conflict with public interest."[36]

The Olmsted plan was developed in conjunction with this petition, but there was not sufficient support in either Boston or Brookline to develop the link between Jamaica Pond and the Chestnut Hill Reservoir.[37] The construction of Lee Street from Boylston to Warren was the only linkage to make the reservoir more accessible, as well as improving north-south transit.

Frederick Law Olmsted Jr. later promoted sections of these wide roadways during his long service with the Brookline Planning Board.[38] As chairman of the Board of Municipal Improvements (the predecessor body), he led the effort to persuade the town to accept Lee Street from Warren to Clyde, and Eliot Street from Boylston to Dean Road, as potentially eighty-foot-wide roadways.[39] Elements of the proposed 1894 thoroughfares by Olmsted, Olmsted & Eliot turn up in a map, "Main Thorofares for Southwestern Part of Brookline," published in the annual report of the Brookline Planning Board for 1925.[40] Regional transportation planning was a major concern of the Olmsteds, and it can be assumed that their influence was felt over the years in ways that extend beyond the job files of the firm.

Although many of the proposals were not adopted, the various plans to develop comprehensive systems of roads and parkways contribute to a better understanding of the firm's role in the development of subdivisions in Brookline.

LARGE RESIDENTIAL SUBDIVISIONS

We now turn to the Olmsted firm's involvement with residential subdivisions in Brookline, beginning with the larger developments for wealthier owners.

ASPINWALL HILL

Even before Frederick Law Olmsted settled in Brookline, he was engaged by William Aspinwall and the Aspinwall Land Company to prepare a subdivision plan in the summer of 1880. The Aspinwalls, one of the oldest families in Brookline, had built a "new" family homestead in the Federal style on Aspinwall Hill. The seventeenth-century family residence, a garrison house, stood on Aspinwall Avenue in Brookline Village.[41] The complicated project for an Aspinwall Hill subdivision has been well documented by Cynthia Zaitzevsky, and her analysis appears to be accurate.[42] The main difficulty was that there were two major landowners who were not working in harmony. The Aspinwall family owned much of the top of the hill, while Boston University held title to the north slope above Beacon Street, the major access point from Boston. A third landowner, George Baty Blake on the eastern slope of the hill, was apparently not involved. The Aspinwalls hired Olmsted, while Boston University trustees engaged Ernest Bowditch, the son of another landowner and member of another old Brookline family. Although he was primarily a civil engineer, Bowditch also worked as a landscape designer.[43] The preliminary Olmsted scheme for the hill was in the tradition of Frederick Law Olmsted's work, in which streets and building lots were laid out with respect for the natural topography. Although Beacon Street was only a county road at this time, it provided a direct link between Boston and the Chestnut Hill Reservoir, originally designed like a park and open to the public.

Thomas Aspinwall, William's son, was also a civil engineer in the firm of Aspinwall & Lincoln, the company that had prepared a topographical survey of the hill. He was not happy when Boston University engaged Bowditch, but it was the Aspinwall Land Company that terminated Olmsted's involvement. The final scheme, according to Zaitzevsky, appears to be largely the work of Bowditch.[44] The Olmsted firm later became tentatively involved in the Aspinwall Hill development when, in 1894–95, it did some work for the Blake estate with architects Shepley, Rutan & Coolidge. There was, however, apparently no involvement in the initial efforts to subdivide the estate in 1916 or in subsequent construction during the 1920s.

FISHER HILL

A group of six landowners who held property on Fisher Hill hired Olmsted to develop a plan of roads and building lots which represents a model subdivision of its kind. The difficulties experienced with Aspinwall Hill were not repeated with Fisher Hill. By 1886 Olmsted had settled in Brookline, and the Fisher Hill landowners were his neighbors. Indeed, the firm had already done extensive work for the Joseph H. White estate (see chapter 4). Olmsted suggested the name Brookline Hill for the subdivision, thinking that, like Newton Highlands and Arlington Heights, it would fix the location in the public's mind.[45] It is the most famous and successful subdivision by Olmsted and his son John Charles in Brookline because of its size and intact character.[46] The topography of the hill was maintained in a manner that enhanced the value of the land for single-family development by creating a system of curving roads and generous lots attractive to upper-middle-class homeowners. Rather than altering the site, the Fisher Hill plan of roads was based on designs that worked with the topography, a concept that dated back to Olmsted's Riverside development outside Chicago in 1868. In his Riverside report, Olmsted had advised, "As the ordinary directness of line in town-streets, with its resultant regularity of plan would suggest eagerness to press forward, without looking to the right hand or to the left, we would recommend the general adoption, in the design of your roads, of gracefully-curved lines, generous spaces, and the absence of sharp corners, the idea to suggest and imply leisure, contemplativeness, and happy tranquility."[47]

An advantage of this property over Aspinwall Hill was that Fisher Hill had readily defined physical boundaries. Along the north edge ran the Boston and Albany Railroad tracks. The other boundaries were marked by Cypress Street, Chestnut Hill Avenue, and Boylston Street, then known as the Worcester Turnpike. This made encroachments by less desirable multifamily developments less likely. Another advantage was the existence of two reservoirs on Fisher Avenue, one owned by the town, and one built in 1887 as part of the Chestnut Hill reservoir system.[48] These formed ready-made parks that would contribute to green space on Fisher Hill.

The Olmsted design did not provide much more detail than the schematic plan that was published in lithographic format (fig. 6.6). For one of the clients, Joseph White, Olmsted had already been hired to create more detailed plans, and White continued to be involved as more houses were added to his estate. For Jacob Pierce, another property owner, the firm prepared different plans to subdivide his land on the west end of Fisher Hill above Chestnut Hill Avenue. Pierce, one of the first to initiate development on the hill, hired the architect William R. Emerson to design two houses, but no record of landscape work has come to light.[49]

A third landowner, George A. Goddard, had a special problem with a portion

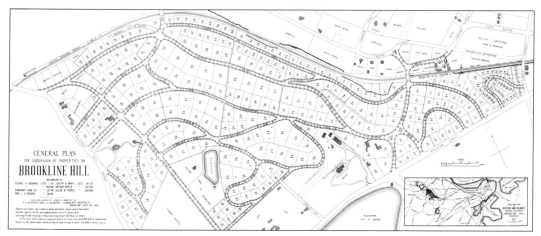

Fig. 6.6. Plan for Fisher Hill (originally tentatively called Brookline Hill), 1886, F. L. & J. C. Olmsted. Copy of lithograph. Courtesy Brookline Public Library.

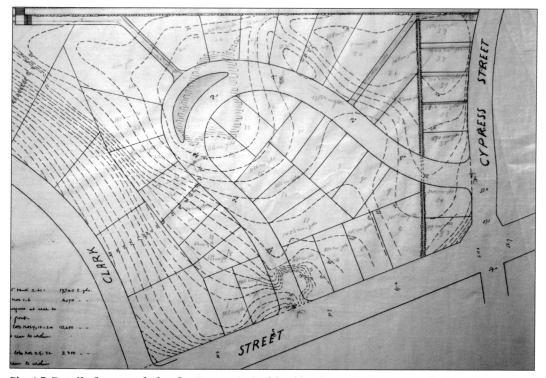

Fig. 6.7. Detail of accepted plan for George A. Goddard land, now Brington Road, 1886, plan. Courtesy National Park Service, Frederick Law Olmsted National Historic Site.

of his land and hired F. L. & J. C. Olmsted to work out a solution for that property in more detail. The Goddard Land Company property at the narrow eastern edge of the development, which was bounded on three sides by Cypress Street, Boylston Street, and the Boston and Albany Railroad tracks, was in closest proximity to potential multifamily or commercial development on Boylston Street. Within a few years, commercial blocks and three-deckers were in fact built at Boylston and Cypress streets, although the housing has since been demolished. This land was in danger of being cut off from the rest of the development, as there was no good way to provide a link to the other roads in the plan. Olmsted prepared a plan for an oxbow street, which was later called Brington Road. His solution (fig. 6.7) was to extend the road in a wide curve from Cypress Street, almost doubling back on itself to Boylston Street. In the curve of the road is a green space hardly large enough to be called a park. At this location the plans show a pedestrian path to the railroad tracks, where there was a crossing to a proposed Brookline Hill station on the other side.[50] The Olmsted firm also provided a separate plan for the train station site, which, had it been built, would have been a significant advantage for this property.[51]

The other three studies for the Goddard land included two that created a cul-de-sac off Cypress Street with a larger oval park (fig. 6.8). The third provided an outlet to Clark Road, the only one with a direct connection to the rest of

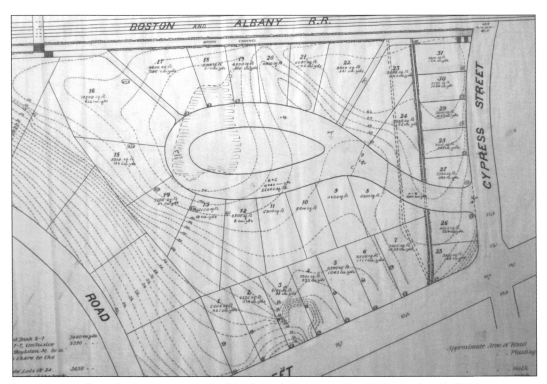

Fig. 6.8. Detail, study for George A. Goddard land (Brington Road), December 7, 1886.
Courtesy National Park Service, Frederick Law Olmsted National Historic Site.

the Fisher Hill plan.[52] In order to promote the development of his land, Goddard hired Shepley, Rutan & Coolidge to design five Shingle Style houses costing about $6,000 each, all of which were built and are still standing. Photographs and plans of several were published in the *Scientific American Builders Edition* for March 1893.[53] To control development initially, Goddard included deed restrictions that expired in 1890. In requesting advice from John Charles Olmsted, Goddard had asked for "reasonable restraints to be put upon my oxbow lots" to "keep objectionable buyers out." At the same time, he acknowledged that the Cypress Street lots should be allowed to develop as "an almost continuous block of stores."[54] Nonetheless, despite these efforts, Brington Road remained a kind of back alley in relation to Fisher Hill.[55]

As the first houses were under construction on Fisher Hill, plans were conceived to extend the development in a similar fashion west of Chestnut Hill Avenue (the western boundary of Fisher Hill as laid out). The consortium of property owners hired Ernest Bowditch to develop a topographical plan, showing buildings and roads, of the land that extended to Reservoir Lane and was bounded on the north by the railroad tracks and on the south by Boylston Street. Although its name is not on the drawing, it can be assumed that the firm provided the colorized

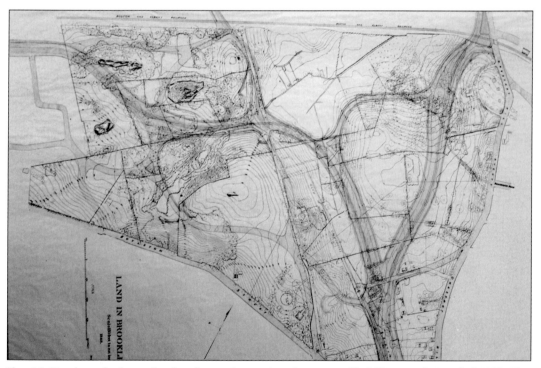

Fig. 6.9. Portion of schematic plan for parkways in what was called "Reservoir Lands," 1888. The Chestnut Hill Reservoir is at the top of the drawing, Boylston Street is at the bottom, and Chestnut Hill Avenue is on the right side. Courtesy National Park Service, Frederick Law Olmsted National Historic Site.

overlay of roads on the Bowditch plan, which is simply labeled "Land in Brookline, Mass.," dated 1888 (fig. 6.9). In the same job file is a notice of a meeting of the property owners set for May 1, 1889, to discuss the plans developed by F. L. & J. C. Olmsted, at which Frederick Law Olmsted was to be present. All of the property owners are listed, along with their lands and the assessed valuations. Nothing further came of this project, and it can be assumed that there was no consensus among the prospective developers.[56]

This unrealized development was different from Fisher Hill in an important way. This scheme included two major parkways. One appears to follow the line of the present Eliot Street from Boylston Street to Cleveland Circle. (By this time the plans for Beacon Street had been completed.) In this plan the road is a parkway with a green reservation between lanes of traffic. A second, similar parkway, possibly with a stream in the reservation, branches off toward Chestnut Hill in Newton (off the drawing to the left). A significant portion of the land is allocated for these parkways, and no proposed building lots are shown. This concept of a regional road system was a logical extension of the Olmsted plans for Beacon Street in Brookline and Commonwealth Avenue in Brighton and received a new life with the 1901 Chestnut Hill Parkway proposal by Olmsted Brothers, but was never built.

With the exception of the White estate, no major landscape designs for individual properties on Fisher Hill have been identified. Warren H. Manning designed the estate for F. C. Fletcher at 34 Philbrick Road in 1914 after he had left the Olmsted firm.[57] The largest Fisher Hill estate, Longyear, at the top of the hill, was apparently the work of other designers. The Longyear property is also the only instance in which a portion of the original street plan was altered (at Hyslop Road). The lack of involvement by Olmsted Brothers in 1904 is surprising because the Longyears had hired the Olmsted firm for their house in Marquette, Michigan, in 1891–92, and again for an addition in 1896. Instead, in 1904 John and Mary Longyear of Chicago hired Benjamin M. Watson, a professor at the Bussey Institute, to prepare landscape plans for their large estate. In 1925–26 the landscape architect Elizabeth L. Strang made substantial changes.[58]

SMALL RESIDENTIAL SUBDIVISIONS

The area north of Beacon Street extending to Commonwealth Avenue grew rapidly after Beacon Street was widened, but prominent developers of middle-class homes such as David McKay and Peter Graffam employed standard grid street layouts on small lots. These neighborhoods of speculative development were not likely candidates for landscape architects. This also appears to have been the case with the area north of Beacon Street between Washington Square and Cleveland Circle (known as Aberdeen for the portion in Boston). More surprising is the Olmsted firm's lack of involvement with Chestnut Hill in Brookline. Specifically, the land bounded by Boylston Street, Reservoir Lane, the Boston and Albany Railroad tracks, and the city of Newton was a prime candidate for an Olmsted plan. The upper-middle-class houses built close to the Newton line in the late 1890s were mostly Shingle Style residences by Chapman & Frazer and Andrews, Jaques & Rantoul. (Both Frazer and Jaques lived in the neighborhood.) The informal, semirural character of this subdivision was exactly the type of development for which the Olmsted firm was often engaged. The available evidence, however, indicates that to the extent the area was planned, it was the work of Joseph H. Curtis, who, like Ernest W. Bowditch, was both a civil engineer and a landscape architect.[59]

PHILBRICK ESTATE

The Olmsteds began to attract commissions from Pill Hill residents, some even before moving to 99 Warren Street. For the estate of engineer Edward Philbrick, the Olmsted firm developed plans for the subdivision of his property (fig. 6.10). His father, Samuel Philbrick, had acquired the Tappan estate on Walnut Street in 1829 and was one of a number of Swedenborgians who were involved with the development of the Brookline Land Company property.[60] After the death of

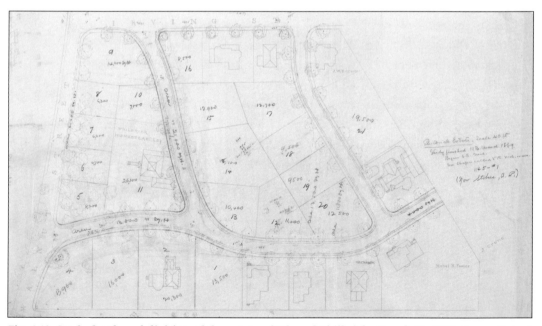

Fig. 6.10. Study for the subdivision of the estate of Edward Philbrick, March 11, 1889. Courtesy National Park Service, Frederick Law Olmsted National Historic Site.

Edward Philbrick, his heirs commissioned Olmsted in 1889 to lay out a small sub-division between High Street and Walnut Street, in which he introduced curving roads to match the topography of the site, but a comprehensive plan for the entire hill was never developed.

COBB ESTATE

Elsewhere on Pill Hill, one large subdivision was only partially realized. For Albert A. Cobb, F. L. & J. C. Olmsted prepared plans for a substantial subdivision in 1886. Cobb lived in an old house on Walnut Street built in 1821. He engaged his son, Chicago architect Henry Ives Cobb, to design two sets of puddingstone row houses—one with five units and the other with four—to be built on either side of his small wood frame residence in 1886–1889 (fig. 6.11).

The projected development included a cul-de-sac that extended between one block of stone houses and Cobb's own residence, which rather awkwardly remained on its site. This road was to have had three more blocks of houses of seven, thirteen, and sixteen units (figs. 6.12 and 6.13).[61] Cobb's plans, had they been fully completed, would have radically altered the neighborhood of Walnut Place to the east, one of the most secluded private ways in Brookline. The plan would also have pushed into a large working-class neighborhood known as Whis-key Point to the southeast.

Fig. 6.11. View of one of two rows of houses constructed by A. A. Cobb and designed by the Chicago firm Cobb & Frost. This photograph was published in *American Architect and Building News*, November 19, 1887. Courtesy Brookline Public Library.

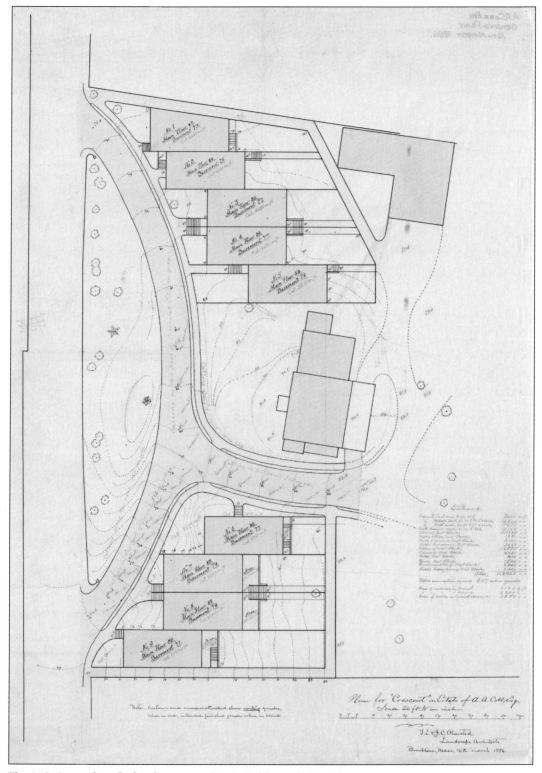

Fig. 6.12. General study for the estate of A. A. Cobb, April 21, 1886. Courtesy National Park Service, Frederick Law Olmsted National Historic Site.

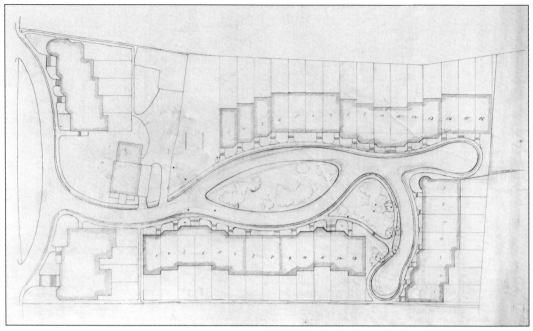

Fig. 6.13. Plan for "Crescent" on the Cobb estate, March 16, 1886. Courtesy National Park Service, Frederick Law Olmsted National Historic Site.

FERNWOOD

While the Olmsted firm received more commissions related to property south of Boylston Street, this work tended to be on individual estates. For example, the Fernwood estate off Clyde Street bounded the north side of The Country Club. Alfred Douglass from New York acquired the property in 1909, demolished the old Gardiner house, and hired Boston architect Charles Patch to design a house, servant's house, and carriage barn. The Olmsted records include extensive plans for work on this estate, with its Tudor Revival–style buildings. According to a promotional brochure for the subsequent subdivision of the property, under the direction of the Olmsted firm, "over three miles of macadam road were built, paths located, the entire property graded, and a section kept moist by a dozen springs transformed into a beautiful pond covering nearly two acres."[62] Douglass evidently ran into financial difficulties and sold the property in 1924. He died early in 1925. The 1922 subdivision projected sixteen large houses on lots of at least two acres (fig. 6.14). The largest lot, over eighteen acres, included a pond. The Douglass mansion became a school. Large single-family homes were not built until the late twentieth century. The new construction seems to have respected much of the intent behind the 1922 plan in the sense that the area has not been intensively developed.[63]

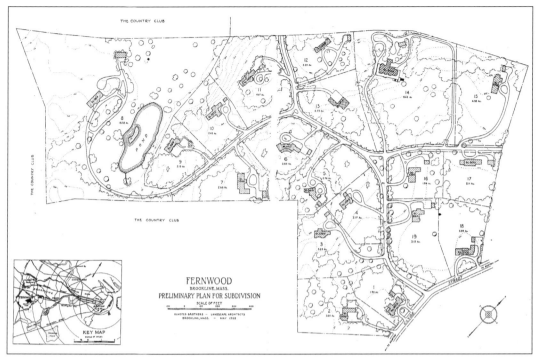

Fig. 6.14. "Fernwood, Brookline, Massachusetts. Preliminary Plan for Subdivision," 1922, Olmsted Brothers. Courtesy Brookline Preservation Commission.

HILLFIELDS

The best example in Brookline of a small subdivision designed by Olmsted Brothers dates to 1926 in another area where the firm had a history of having done work. This was Singletree Hill in the Chestnut Hill area between Heath Street and Boylston Street. In 1885–86, J. Randolph Coolidge built a house on a portion of Singletree Hill which he called "Hillfields." It was designed by C. Howard Walker, and the Olmsted firm was hired for landscape designs.[64] In 1893, on another portion of Singletree Hill, Ruth Cabot Paine constructed a large house designed by Andrews, Jaques & Rantoul. Olmsted, Olmsted & Eliot provided plans.[65] The Olmsted Brothers firm returned for Mrs. Robert Treat Paine II in 1907, and again when Andrews, Jaques & Rantoul extensively remodeled the house for her in 1917 (see chapter 4).[66]

In 1926 the Coolidge estate was sold to a group of businessmen who formed the Hillfields Company, with Arthur B. Nichols as president and Frances R. Boyd as treasurer. The company hired the Olmsted firm to develop a subdivision plan. Initially the subdivision was to be twice as large as it became, consisting of eighty-two building lots.[67] This job provided Olmsted Brothers with a measure of control that accorded with the philosophy of Frederick Law Olmsted Jr., the sole surviving family member.

In 1927 he articulated the requirements for a properly managed subdivision in connection with the Sargent estate, a project with which the firm was not involved. Holm Lea, a close neighbor of the Olmsted home and office at 99 Warren Street, became available for development after Charles Sprague Sargent's death that year. One of the trustees, Cora Codman Ely, sister of Henry Sargent Codman and Philip Codman, who had both worked for the firm, called on Percival Gallagher in the Olmsted office for assistance. She explained that she was under great pressure to begin the subdivision of the estate, and many of Sargent's famous plants were already being sold.[68]

Within a few days Frederick Law Olmsted Jr. wrote Mrs. Ely a long letter of advice, "as a friend of the family, a neighbor and a member of the Planning Board of the Town." He told her:

> Nothing has so much impressed me as the extent to which success in such enterprises[,] especially financial success but also general and lasting success in other respects—depend upon strongly centralized, steady general management, controlling from a single point of view and along a firmly held policy every aspect of the undertaking—including[,] beside the general physical planning, the sales policies, prices, kinds of customers, contractual terms of sales such as covenants governing use of property sold, character and costs of improvements—everything.

He cautioned that he was "loth to undertake any responsibility, however limited, for advising as to the physical plan—the landscape architecture—of any considerable subdivision" unless he had such control.[69] This all-or-nothing demand resulted in no involvement by the firm in general supervision of the subdivision of the Sargent estate.[70] Hillfields, however, did afford a large measure of the control Olmsted advocated.

The plan for Hillfields was developed early in 1926, evidently with the firm's William B. Marquis in charge. The plan (fig. 6.15) was eventually reduced to approximately sixteen acres when a portion of the land was sold to the Christian Science Church for an institutional complex for the training of practitioners. Apparently the Paine family also purchased the eastern half of the subdivision, where the old Coolidge house stood, in order to build a house for Elizabeth Metcalf, the married daughter of Robert Treat Paine II. Franklin King acquired a second lot, and this eliminated the need to extend roads into that section of the development, as both houses were accessed from Boylston Street.[71]

By the summer of 1926 the plan was completed, consisting of lots on Heath Street and three new curvilinear roads, Cary, Randolph, and Jefferson (named after Virginia families in the Coolidge family ancestry). There are two access points into the subdivision from both Heath and Boylston streets. Olmsted Brothers provided plans for two versions of a typical fifty-foot-wide street construction. One had a roadway a little over thirty-three feet wide flanked by granolithic walks; in the other scheme the roadway was to be twenty-eight feet wide, flanked by a five-foot tree lawn and a six-foot cinder sidewalk.[72] The plan with the tree lawn appears to have been used, although only a fragment of the cinder walk survives (fig. 6.16).

The records of the firm reveal the extent of the involvement by Olmsted Brothers for a development that left the landscaping of individual lots up to the owners. Nevertheless, every purchaser of a building lot was required to have the archi-

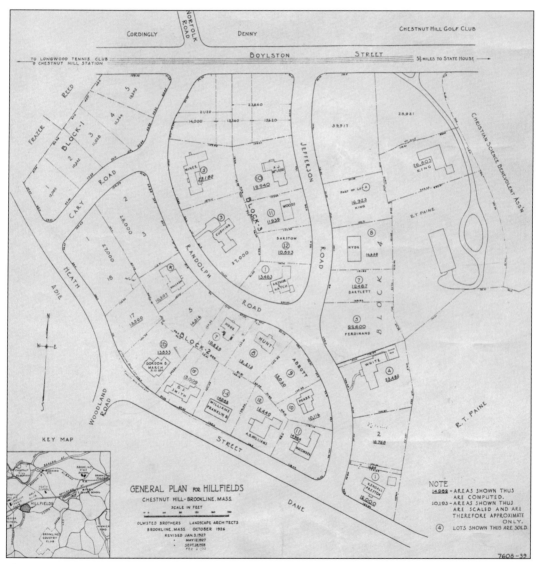

Fig. 6.15. "General Plan for Hillfields, Chestnut Hill, Brookline, Massachusetts," Olmsted Brothers. This is a 1930 update of the original 1926 plan used to monitor progress of the development for buyers.
Courtesy National Park Service, Frederick Law Olmsted National Historic Site.

tect submit a site plan and architectural drawings for approval by the Hillfields Company, and the company consulted Marquis. Letters in the Olmsted job files for Hillfields provide a variety of critiques on the various house projects in the development.

Much of the criticism related to the siting of each house on its lot, particularly its distance from the street and its elevation above the street. Of particular concern was the placement of garages, which the landscape architects preferred be attached, or even in the basement.[73] The placement of appendages as they would affect potential neighbors was also a concern in reviewing site plans.

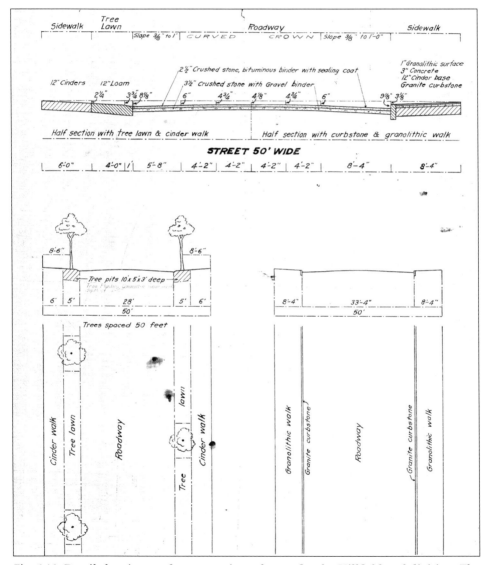

Fig. 6.16. Detail showing road construction schemes for the Hillfields subdivision. The tree-lined proposal on the left was adopted. Courtesy National Park Service, Frederick Law Olmsted National Historic Site.

Marquis strayed into architectural critiques as well. The subjects of the architectural criticism ranged from a large house at 86 Randolph Road which the well-known firm of Little & Russell designed for Richard Paine, to a house designed by a contractor at 9 Cary Road. In regard to the Little & Russell design, a sample of his criticism reads: "The house seems too large for the area; the living room is jammed up against the east line with the adjacent barn very near to it, and with the garage on the Preston lot immediately in front of it. The living quarters of the house are on the east end with the service on the west, which would allow the summer breezes to carry cooking odors, etc. back through the living portion."[74]

For a contractor-designed house on Cary Road, Marquis stated, "We find it very difficult to offer any constructive criticism because the plans are very incomplete as to detail and are very unconvincing as an expression of architectural character." He went on to urge strongly that the owner have the design "overhauled, especially in regard to matters of proportion and details, by an architect of recognized ability." To resolve this problem the owner consulted Royal Barry Wills. The building permit lists as architects the contractor Arthur B. Bernard, with Royal B. Wills "assisting."[75]

Between April 1, 1927, when the first permit for a house was pulled, until 1952, a total of twenty-eight single-family homes were built. Only four appear to

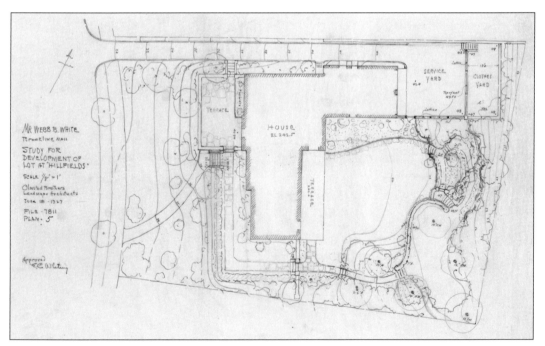

Fig. 6.17. "Study for Development of Lot at Hillfields," June 18, 1927, Olmsted Brothers. This plan for the Webb B. White house created a private sanctuary in the backyard that is not typically associated with small subdivisions like Hillfields. Courtesy National Park Service, Frederick Law Olmsted National Historic Site.

have been constructed as "spec" houses by developers (two by one man, William V. Tripp). The majority are houses built by their first occupants. They were designed by different architects, except for three by Philip Avery (including two for Tripp) and two by Royal Barry Wills (including 9 Cary Road). The Hillfields Company continued to consult Olmsted Brothers for revisions to unsold building lots in an effort to promote more effectively the sale of property during the economic crisis of the early 1930s.

The Olmsted Brothers firm was hired in only one instance, to provide a landscape plan for a single house lot in the Hillfields development; this was for the Webb White house at 78 Randolph Road in 1927 (fig. 6.17). In a second instance, another landscape firm, Loring Underwood & Lawrence Caldwell, was brought in for Mrs. George S. Smith at 401 Heath Street in 1927. Dating from the earliest stages of the development, these two examples suggest that the depression may have discouraged other homeowners from hiring landscape architects.[76]

It should be noted that the Olmsted firm was consulted in another project on Singletree Hill on the other side of the Paine estate. In 1938 the Town of Brookline constructed a large aboveground reservoir to hold 1 million gallons of water. This spherical structure replaced a standpipe. Adjacent to it was a Moderne-style valve house designed by Little & Russell. The original concept was to hire an architect to build a brick wall for screening purposes. As an alternative, Olmsted Brothers was hired to provide plantings (mostly tall trees) to screen the site.[77]

FREDERICK LAW OLMSTED JR. AND BROOKLINE TOWN PLANNING

Frederick Law Olmsted Jr. contributed his expertise to Brookline through his service on public boards during the period of rapid development in the early twentieth century (fig. 6.18). Notwithstanding the demands on him as head of the firm after John Charles's death in 1920, Rick made a substantial contribution to the planning process for over a quarter century, particularly as a member of the Planning Board from 1914 to 1938. His work in this area directly related to the various plans for boulevards, parkways, and subdivisions.

Frederick Law Olmsted Jr. was born on Staten Island in 1870. Originally named Henry Perkins Olmsted, he was renamed after his father owing to what biographers consider an intense desire on the part of Frederick Law Olmsted Sr. to have his name carried on. A graduate of Harvard in 1894, young Rick entered the firm in December 1895 after having spent thirteen months working with his father on the enormous Biltmore estate in Ashville, North Carolina. He became a partner with his half brother, John Charles, in 1897 after his father's retirement.

Fig. 6.18. Frederick Law Olmsted Jr. Courtesy National Park Service, Frederick
Law Olmsted National Historic Site.

Olmsted Jr. gained extraordinary experience in city planning with his appointment by the U.S. Senate, in 1901, to the Park Improvement Commission for the
District of Columbia, the so-called McMillan Commission, named after its chief
sponsor, Senator James McMillan of Michigan. This commission developed the
"McMillan Plan," a report that helped to ensure that the city would be developed
along the lines of the original L'Enfant plan for Washington, D.C.[78]

In 1911 Brookline established the Board of Municipal Improvements, an advisory body charged with guiding the town in matters that later fell under the pur-
view of a planning board. Olmsted Jr. served as chairman with architect Walter
H. Kilham, along with attorneys Leslie C. Wead and Amos L. Hathaway, and
Michael J. O'Hearn, a contractor, all of whom subsequently were appointed to
the first Brookline Planning Board in 1914. He also served as its first chairman,
a position he held until 1926. With his background in the new field of city planning, Olmsted was a natural candidate to serve the town in these capacities. In
1910 he led the effort to establish the first national organization of city planners,
the National Conference on City Planning. He also served on the executive board
of the Massachusetts Federation of Planning Boards when that body issued its first
Bulletin in May 1916.[79] This led to the establishment of the American City Planning
Institute, which he helped found in 1917. In addition to his service to Brookline,
Olmsted contributed time to public service at a national level and was for many
years a key adviser to the National Park Service.[80]

In its first recommendation, the Board of Municipal Improvements supported plans by a property owner, represented by attorney Alfred Chandler, to construct an extension of Cypress Street through to Harvard Street. Although the plan was not carried out, this road would have improved circulation in Brookline Village. The board also advised the Board of Selectman to consider widening Pleasant Street between Beacon Street and Commonwealth Avenue in response to the large buildings under construction at both ends of that street. The board also endorsed the advocacy of "cross-town thoroughfares" when it promoted the development of the large tract of land between Boylston Street, Chestnut Hill Avenue, Reservoir Road, and the Boston and Albany Railroad (now the D, or Riverside, Line) by building a "main thoroughfare" from Boylston Street to Dean Road.[81] This road had its inception in 1888 with a plan for the development of this area of Brookline, mentioned earlier. In 1912 the town accepted this road as an eighty-foot-wide thoroughfare called Eliot Street. Significantly, it joined Boylston Street opposite Lee Street, portions of which were also endorsed as an eighty-foot-wide roadway in 1910 and 1912, although only a section was actually built that wide.[82] These recommendations were in line with the parkway projects of 1896 and 1901. For example, Eliot and Lee streets were envisioned as wide thoroughfares in the Olmsted, Olmsted & Eliot plans developed in 1896.

As one of five members on the Brookline Planning Board, Olmsted certainly exerted a direct impact on various policies and decisions, although his specific role is difficult to document. Nevertheless, his vast experience in city planning issues no doubt ensured that his views carried great weight, and office records reflect his leading role as chairman. His views would have been known to the selectmen as outlined in his article "The Basic Principles of City Planning," published in 1910.[83] Written while he was serving as a professor of landscape architecture at Harvard University, the article outlined three basic concerns for city planning. The first was to improve the means of transportation and circulation within a community and to surrounding towns, a major issue for the Board of Municipal Improvements. The second was the creation and maintenance of public spaces, not as important a matter for Brookline, where land was expensive and much of the town was in close proximity to the Boston municipal park system. The third area of concern was the use of private land "in so far as it is practicable for the community to control or influence such development." All three categories would have been areas of expertise of the Olmsted firm. Moreover, his work on the Brookline Planning Board would have provided experience with urban planning issues on a much smaller scale than in Washington, D.C., and other cities where the Olmsted Brothers firm was active.

One important city planning problem addressed by Frederick Law Olmsted Jr. was the need to rationalize building lines on major thoroughfares in the town. In his article on the basic principles of city planning, he stated that street planners tended "to give quite inadequate attention to the need of the public for various types of main thoroughfares laid out with sole regard to the problems of transportation, and to permit the supposed interests of landowners and fear of heavy damages to limit the width of thoroughfares and force them out of the best lines in order to conform to the owners' preferences as to land subdivision."[84] Many of Brookline's older roads were historically narrow and could not accommodate increased traffic, especially with the advent of the streetcar and the automobile. Street widening involved considerable public expense to acquire property, especially where buildings had been constructed right up to the street. This had not been a problem on Beacon Street in the 1880s, as there was little commercial development before it was widened. The efforts to improve Boylston Street at that time, however, had been more problematical. The town decided that it could not afford to widen the street, which would have been necessary to prevent, for example, a wagon parked at the curb from blocking passage by a streetcar.

The failure to widen Boylston Street was cited in a report to the Board of Selectmen prepared by Olmsted Brothers in 1910, a notable early example of their involvement in town planning. The firm (presumably Rick in this case) advocated the creation of a committee to recommend the establishment of setback restrictions on properties. A contingency fund would be made available to compensate owners. This technique was then in practice in Washington, D.C. (well known to Olmsted Jr.) and in Europe. It is an instance of the firm's efforts to introduce concepts of modern city planning to Brookline.[85]

When Brookline authorized its Planning Board in 1914, the members, with Olmsted Jr. as chairman, announced that their primary directive was to study "matters which are less immediately pressing but are of grave importance for the future of the town." In their first annual report, published in 1915, the board members stated that they had been examining conditions in the town, both public improvements and "the probable ultimate need of a more complete system of main thoroughfares and of a more systematic subdivision of some of the large blocks where a well utilized margin surrounds a comparatively inaccessible interior." This need for new roads to accommodate subdivisions had been a long-standing concern of the Olmsted firm. In 1916 Frederick drafted a letter to the planning boards in Boston, Newton, Needham, and Dedham outlining issues and suggestions for "cross-town thoroughfares."[86]

The other issue that occupied the attention of the board in its first year was "developments on private property as affecting the public welfare, and especially . . . the present and retrospective conditions in and around rented dwellings." This was a clear reference to the alarm felt in some neighborhoods over the accelerated construction of "three-apartment wooden dwellings," now known as three-deckers. On Fisher Hill an agreement among property owners resulted in deed restrictions preventing their construction. Using the safety provision of the building law, a town-wide ban on their new construction was imposed in 1915. In response to a petition from several residents of Corey Hill, the Planning Board recommended the prohibition of "third class buildings" (those with wooden exterior walls) for three or more families. Until zoning legislation was authorized in Massachusetts (and upheld by the United States Supreme Court in 1926 in *Euclid, Ohio v. Amber Realty Co.*), however, the only way to regulate the construction of tenements was through amending the building safety laws. The Brookline Planning Board voted 4–1 in support of an amendment reading, "No tenement house hereafter erected shall be a building of the third class." The dissenting vote came from Michael O'Hearn, the building contractor.[87] Opposition from men like O'Hearn ensured that the 1915 ban would be only temporary, and that revisions to the building code would not be as effective as zoning in regulating use.

That year the architect J. Randolph Coolidge Jr. joined the board. The addition of a second architect must have bolstered Olmsted's efforts to focus on the issue of regulating building setback lines in town. Although facilitating street widening to prevent congestion was a concern of the Planning Board, the issue of urban design took precedence when the board lamented "the disregard of the customary setbacks which has hitherto maintained a margin of cheerful green between the buildings and the sidewalks." Addressing Beacon Street as an example, the board noted, "If the building setback remains purely voluntary the present character of the street will be destroyed at an increasingly rapid rate by the projection of one-story stores and new apartments forward to cover the space between the present voluntary building line and the legal street line." The board pointed out that, except for Coolidge Corner and Washington Square, where there were concentrations of stores, developers had originally provided fifteen- or twenty-foot setbacks from the property line, "giving the sides of the street a generous, dignified appearance in keeping with its general layout." Later builders began to construct right up to the sidewalks. The Planning Board, under Olmsted's leadership, felt so strongly about this issue that their published report featured extensive photographs (fig. 6.19) to illustrate the aesthetic decline resulting when new apartment blocks were built right up to the street by builders who "have refused to do their share toward maintaining this quality in the street, although realizing upon the value which its existence at the expense of others has helped to give to their own properties."[88]

Aesthetic concerns dominated the 1916 annual report, when the board took up the matter of the "entrances" to Brookline from Boston, specifically Brookline Avenue and Washington Street where they intersected Boylston Street in Brookline Village. "The locality as a whole," the report stated, "is characterized by many old and shabby wooden buildings, and by a general appearance

By E.C.W. 22nd Nov. 1915 1310-36

STORES AT WASHINGTON SQUARE NORTH CORNER

By E.C.W. 11-15 1310-31

PARKMAN STREET LOOKING WEST

By E.C.W. 11-15 1310-23

GARRISON ROAD FROM TAPPAN STREET
(SEE NO. 37)

Fig. 6.19. Images from annual report for 1915 of the Brookline Planning Board, showing figs. 3, 7, and 8 with original captions. Courtesy National Park Service, Frederick Law Olmsted National Historic Site.

suggestive of stagnation and decadence." Again using photographs to illustrate their case (fig. 6.20), the board recommended that property owners be provided with incentives to construct a higher class of dwellings.[89] In a letter to Vincent Byers, editor of the *Brookline Townsman,* Olmsted complained of the "notoriously unprepossessing appearance of the entrance to the town by way of the Village."[90] Although the area included a variety of housing stock, including eighteenth-century dwellings, the solution was not, in Olmsted's view, simply to build new streets and parks. The only lasting effective response would be to improve the quality of buildings. In 1917 the Planning Board commissioned a report on the attitudes of the property owners toward forming a consortium to develop the properties on Washington Street and Brookline Avenue. The response was not encouraging for those in favor of redesigning the "entrance" to Brookline at this location. Many property owners were satisfied with the return on their rentals and expressed little interest in the potential for greatly enhanced property values offered in a grander vision.[91]

The town appropriated $1,500 to prepare plans for improvements to this area of Brookline, but with the United States' entry into World War I, no firm

By H. D. Perkins   Dec. 1916   1310-70
PRESENT TENEMENTS BETWEEN POND AND BROOKLINE AVENUES.

Fig. 6.20. The Olmsted office made extensive photographs of both positive and negative conditions in Brookline for the Planning Board to study. These included images of three-deckers and wooden tenements. Courtesy National Park Service, Frederick Law Olmsted National Historic Site.

was hired, and nothing more was done. During the war, Frederick Law Olmsted Jr. was working in Washington and did not participate in Planning Board activities. Also, architect J. Randolph Coolidge moved to Boston and resigned from the board. During this hiatus, however, those interested in controlling and directing development were given important tools when, in 1918, the Massachusetts constitution was amended to allow for the regulation of advertising within the public view and the restriction of buildings according to their use and construction.

In 1920, with the death John Charles Olmsted, Frederick became senior partner of the firm. Notwithstanding the additional responsibilities to his practice, his major contribution may have occurred in the years immediately after the war. Enabling legislation to allow communities to establish zoning was passed in 1920, and Brookline passed a zoning bylaw in 1922 (fig. 6.21). For the next several years Olmsted, as chair of the Planning Board, presided over the implementation of the new law and responded to petitions for changes and amendments. A recommendation from the Board of Selectmen that consideration be given to establish districts allowing the construction of three-deckers was rejected.[92] The board also focused on the development of a more attractive entrance into Brookline from adjacent Boston at Brookline Village in its early planning. In 1923 Olmsted's old ally Walter Kilham moved out of Brookline and resigned from the Planning Board. He was replaced for a few years by another architect with whom the Olmsted firm had worked, J. Lovell Little. In the mid-

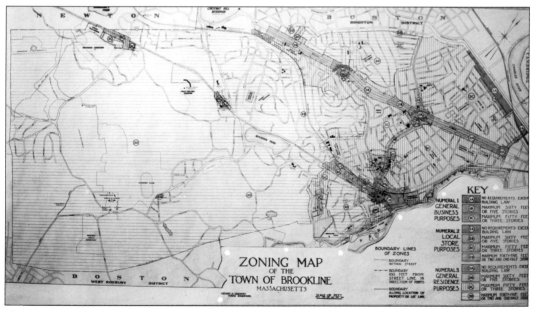

Fig. 6.21. Zoning map for the Town of Brookline, January 1922. Courtesy National Park Service, Frederick Law Olmsted National Historic Site.

1920s attention was given to increased development in south Brookline. The Planning Board worked with the Walnut Hill Realty Company to improve the construction of new roads in that part of town.[93]

In 1925 the board's annual report included a map showing "Main Thorofares for Southwestern Part of Brookline" (fig. 6.22), illustrating the need to plan for the rapid development of that portion of town. In response to requests by the Metropolitan Planning Board, the Brookline Planning Board revived the old Olmsted, Olmsted & Eliot scheme for a "wide thoroughfare" from Cleveland Circle to Jamaica Pond. This road would have passed south of Sargent Pond before continuing along the creek bed behind the former H. H. Richardson house on Cottage Street and across the Schlesinger estate.[94] This proposal was finally laid to rest with the construction of Hammond Pond Parkway in 1929.

Frederick Law Olmsted Jr. stepped down from the chairmanship of the Planning Board in 1927. He continued to work on revisions to the zoning bylaw, and in 1931 he took a very active interest in the efforts to make major improvements to Boylston Street, which was to be improved in conjunction with the construction of Hammond Pond Parkway and the removal of the trolley line. In a ten-page typed,

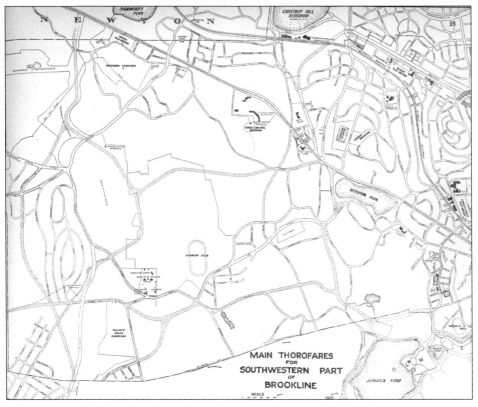

Fig. 6.22. **"Main Thoroughfares for Southwestern Part of Brookline."** Report of the Brookline Planning Board, 1925.

single-spaced report, he outlined his recommendations for widening Boylston Street, calling for two ten-foot-wide lanes in each direction.[95]

In 1938 Olmsted submitted his resignation from the Planning Board, noting his prolonged absences owing to illness and work commitments. Leon Zach from the Olmsted firm was appointed in his place.[96] Although Olmsted continued to be consulted by his former Planning Board colleagues in 1939, office records suggest that this ceased in the final ten years before his retirement in 1949. Nevertheless, under his guidance the first zoning laws were passed, and he served as chairman of the Planning Board that enforced them in its first decade.[97] In this respect his impact on Brookline during the formative years of urban planning, especially the establishment of zoning, was enormous.

Residential subdivision development in Brookline during the early twentieth century had changed radically in the sixty years since Frederick Law Olmsted's seminal design for Riverside outside Chicago. The changes were evident as early as 1886 in the design for Fisher Hill. Although the basic design features associated with Riverside, such as curving roads conforming to the existing topography and houses set back on spacious lots of varied sizes, also guided Fisher Hill, the high price of land dictated the loss of more subtle amenities. Lot sizes tended to be smaller, and the introduction of curbing and sidewalks eroded the picturesque rural character that had been associated with Riverside. The impact of the automobile on suburban development in the early 1900s was also increasingly evident. Concrete "tracks" leading to a garage in the rear of the yard gradually evolved into broad paved driveways with garages attached to the house.

Comprehensive designs for mixed-income residential suburbs with commercial and recreational amenities guided the thinking of Frederick Law Olmsted Jr. and many other leading landscape architects in this country, although for him, Brookline did not afford opportunities to explore concepts of the "English garden suburbs" that influenced other landscape architects in the early twentieth century. He nevertheless employed garden suburb concepts elsewhere, at Forest Hills on Long Island (1910–11) and Guilford in Baltimore (1912). This interest in garden suburb development probably explains why he expressed a reluctance to become involved in the subdivision development of the Sargent estate unless his firm was given complete control of the design. In any case, the high cost of land in Brookline may have discouraged cost-conscious developers from hiring the Olmsted firm for assistance in the residential developments in south Brookline along Hammond Pond Parkway, Brookline's "last frontier." The one exception is the firm's involvement in the Federal Housing Administration–funded garden apartment development called Hancock Village. Located along West

Roxbury Parkway in Brookline and West Roxbury, Hancock Village included a commercial shopping center as well as onsite parking without driveways, but it was begun in 1947, after Olmsted's retirement.

As much as any single individual involved with town planning, Frederick Law Olmsted Jr. guided Brookline through the major development pressures weighing on the town during the first half of the twentieth century.

Seven

THE INSTITUTIONAL CONTEXT

Beyond the armature of the major boulevards, subdivisions, and park systems, the Olmsted office influenced the development of Brookline through key institutional projects. These reinforced traditional patterns in the religious, political, and social life of the community, facilitated planned growth, and engaged central questions about the role of suburbanization in both Brookline and the nation at large. The commissions that the Olmsted firm executed for the First Parish Church, Brookline's park and school systems, the Boston and Albany commuter railroad stations, The Country Club, and the Free Hospital for Women are representative of broad issues that progressive communities addressed to define their uniqueness and their relationship to the central city.[1] It was not just the role of economics that determined the shape of this and other suburbs. The use of politics to control the exurban space, questions of ethnicity, and the dominant role of gender in relation to residential development can all be observed in these commissions. As with the dominant matrix of wealth, Brookline both engaged broader national patterns and set its own course.

As previously noted, when the Olmsted family and office moved to 99 Warren Street, they relocated to the historical center of the town of Brookline. A short walk up Warren Street from Fairsted is the First Parish Church of Brookline, the fourth building for the congregation, which was established in 1711, six years after the incorporation of the town. The original building, completed in 1718, stood across Warren Street from the current stone church. The colonial meetinghouse served the parish until 1806. At that time a new structure, designed by the English-born architect Peter Banner, was erected on the site of the existing building.[2] After surviving the disestablishment of the Congregational Church in 1833, First Parish negotiated the conflict between Unitarian and Trinitarian ideals, retaining both factions under the diplomatic ministry of the Reverend John Pierce. In 1848 the parish built a new Gothic Revival building to the designs of Edward C. Cabot, architect of the Boston Athenaeum at that time and whose family had Brookline connections.[3] In the 1880s the congregation began to consider erecting a larger building for their needs. At first Robert Swain Peabody and John Goddard Stearns Jr., both of whom were Brookline residents and possibly members of the parish, were interested in obtaining the commission.[4] Ultimately, H. H. Richardson's successor firm, Shepley, Rutan & Coolidge, was given the opportunity to design the new church.[5]

The site plan of the previous church had been recorded in 1887 by civil engi-

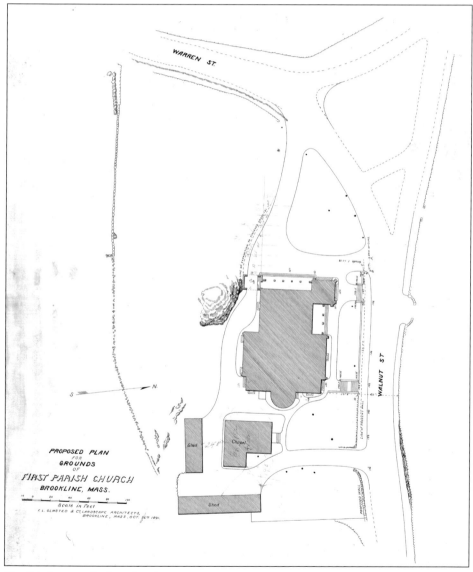

Fig. 7.1. Proposed plans for the grounds, First Parish Church, October 26, 1891.
Courtesy National Park Service, Frederick Law Olmsted National Historic Site.

neering students at the Massachusetts Institute of Technology under the direction of Professor A. E. Burton. Since the Richardson office, a short walk from the church, had functioned as an informal advanced study center for former students from MIT who had joined the firm, it is not surprising to see students recording a building in the neighborhood. The earliest architectural plan by the Shepley office is dated October 15, 1891; the Romanesque Revival design of granite with brownstone trim was completed in 1893. As early as October 15, 1891, the Olmsted office wrote to Shepley, Rutan & Coolidge about the firm's proposals for the church, noting: "As we have not been employed by the building committee and as we were not consulted by you until after the plans of the church had been adopted, we do not wish to be held professionally responsible for the plan of the grounds. We trust, however, that the arrangements shown on our plan will be satisfactory, and will be found to be the best that can be done under the circumstances."[6] Obviously the close working relationship that Olmsted enjoyed with Richardson had not continued as smoothly in the coordination with the successor firm on this particular project. The Olmsted recommendations focused on the approach to the church from Walnut Street and the relationship of the building to the cliff rising behind the proposed structure, part of which would have to be blasted away to provide the necessary space. The earliest landscape plan (fig. 7.1) from the Olmsted office is dated October 26, 1891, followed by a revised plan on November 9, 1892.[7] At that point the Olmsted firm had still not been awarded a contract for work on the project, but by autumn 1893 they were in charge of developing the grounds (fig. 7.2). By this time Moses Williams was the chairman of the building committee. He had hired Peabody & Stearns to design his house in 1885 at 30 Warren Street, opposite the church site, and commissioned the Olmsted office to develop the grounds in 1885–86.[8]

Initial work in grading and some planting proceeded that fall, and by February 1, 1894, Olmsted, Olmsted & Eliot wrote to Williams with the following offer:

> As two members of our firm belong to the parish, and as we are all in hopes that our work at the church will have been a public benefit, we wish to make a contribution to the building fund of the charge of our services and expenses, amounting to $282.14 for which we enclose a receipted bill.
>
> Mr. Frederick Law Olmsted has paid for the plants, with the exception of the ivies ordered by the committee, and desires that the amount, $80.39, should be considered as a contribution to the building fund.[9]

The work of clearing, grading, and blasting, and the construction of a road, paths, steps, and a terrace, had all been completed by this time. The two members of the firm referred to were Frederick Law Olmsted Sr. and John Charles Olmsted,

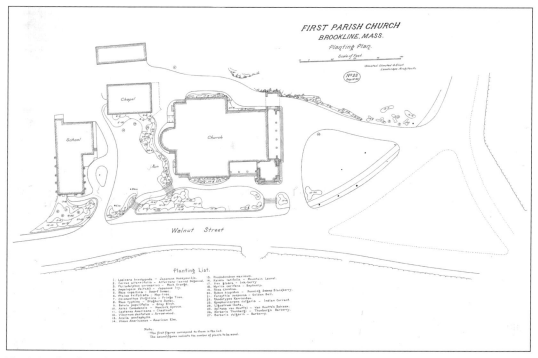

Fig. 7.2. Planting plan, First Parish Church, September 15, 1893. Courtesy National Park Service, Frederick Law Olmsted National Historic Site.

who became members of the parish at least as early as 1890.[10] Frederick Law Olmsted had been raised in the traditions of Connecticut Congregationalism, but he resisted the established church throughout his life and rarely attended services.[11] Although Charles Eliot, whose brother was one of the leading Unitarian ministers in Massachusetts, had joined the firm the previous year, he did not move from Milton to Brookline until late April 1894, three months after this letter was written.[12] Connections between the First Parish Church and the Olmsted office remained close and cordial over the next three decades. In 1901 the Reverend W. H. Lyon, who replaced the Reverend Howard M. Brown as the minister of First Parish, called on the Olmsted firm to handle the planting of hemlocks along the eastern side of his residence to screen a prospective neighboring house.[13] Lyon turned to the firm again in 1906, when a wing was built connecting the church to the adjacent original Brookline Town Hall, built in 1825 and renamed Pierce Hall in honor of John Pierce, the parish's long-serving minister from the early nineteenth century. The new wing replaced a freestanding chapel and a wooden wing to Pierce Hall designed in 1881 by William Ralph Emerson, which had been destroyed by fire in 1901. Charles Collens of the firm of Allen & Collens designed this connecting structure. Frederick Law Olmsted Jr. inspected the changes and reassured the cash-strapped building committee that the landscape alterations were so minor that a contract and specifications would not be necessary.[14] The work (fig. 7.3), which ultimately did require specifications and a contract, included the construction of a carriage drive and turn between the church and Pierce Hall; regrading of paths; and pruning, moving, and planting bushes between the buildings. The work continued into April 1907, when the parish clerk sent Olmsted Brothers a letter registering a vote of thanks "for the valuable professional services which you had freely given to the Parish during the past year."[15]

In 1936–37, at the instigation of Lewis I. Prouty, on whose neighboring property Olmsted Brothers were also working, a review of the landscaping of the church complex was undertaken. Mr. Prouty had volunteered to pay for this work.[16] By October–November 1937 the plans were already well advanced when a member of the firm—probably Edward Whiting, who was attending to the church project—wrote to Mrs. Abbot Peterson, chairwoman of the buildings committee, "To me the fundamental objection to things as they are now is the more or less general atmosphere of wildness—one might almost say neglect—throughout much of the church grounds."[17] A second memo advised, "I should like to see the Church with practically nothing around it but grass and trees, because I have a feeling that that may give just the right character . . . as to delimit rather clearly the amount and kind of new planting."[18] As an indication of the long-term connections between the Olmsted family and the parish, the committee chaired by Mrs. Peterson wrote to

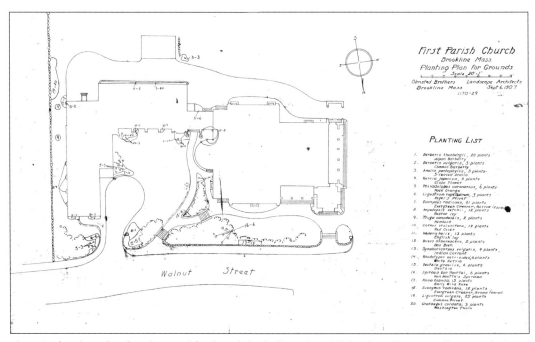

Fig. 7.3. Planting plan for First Parish Church including the addition by Allen & Collens, and Pierce Hall, the former town hall, September 6, 1907. Courtesy National Park Service, Frederick Law Olmsted National Historic Site.

"Mrs. John C. Olmsted and the Misses Olmsted" in January 1938 inviting their contributions to help pay for this work:

> Our committee hopes to raise this amount [$900] from a limited number of our parishioners who we think would be interested and willing to subscribe.
>
> The fact that Olmsted Brothers have designed the changes and will superintend the work gives us assurance that the result will be appropriate, and, we believe, generally satisfactory.[19]

John Charles Olmsted having died in 1920 and Frederick Law Olmsted Jr. having moved to California in 1936, Mrs. John C. Olmsted was the matriarch of the family in Brookline. This exchange ended a four-decade-long connection between the Olmsted office and family and the First Parish Church, the symbol of the original religious and political focus of the town. The various stages of this relationship demonstrate how intimately involved the Olmsteds became with one of the key institutions of the local established order and upper-class Brookline society as men like Moses Williams, Lewis Prouty, and W. H. Lyon invited the Olmsted office to handle developments at their homes and at their church.

Just as the Reverend John Pierce had maintained the centrality of the First Parish Church throughout the antebellum period in Brookline, so too did he connect the church to the evolving political realm of the community. In like manner, the Olmsted office capitalized on the political and public sphere of Brookline, working through organizations such as the School Committee, the Parks Commission, and the Planning Board.

During the nineteenth century, the public schools of Brookline provided one of the most important if contentious tools for maintaining an established worldview. The first high school was founded in 1843 in the town hall (1824) adjacent to the First Parish Church (and later incorporated into the church as a building for education, named Pierce Hall). The Reverend Pierce served as the chairman of the school committee as well. By 1856, however, a special committee had been established to consider the location for a new purpose-built school, which was completed at the corner of School and Prospect streets to the designs of Joseph R. Richards.[20] By 1862, however, the number of students exceeded the number of seats by thirty. The demographic explosion was the result of both the immigration of Irish Catholic working-class families with children and the success of upper-income residential subdivision. The response to this increasing overcrowding was extremely slow, with new wings finally added to the high school by Peabody & Stearns in 1884 and George A. Clough in 1891.

As soon as the second wing was completed, a committee was formed to suggest a location for a new building. George Blake sold land to the town at the intersection of Greenough and Tappan streets, and the local architectural firm of Andrews, Jaques & Rantoul was selected to design the building after a limited competition.[21] Olmsted, Olmsted & Eliot were invited to supervise the site development and landscape design.[22] The site overlooked the existing Cypress Street Playground, acquired by the town, along with the Brookline Avenue Playground, in 1871. These two may have been the earliest municipal playgrounds in the nation.[23] By February 1894, Olmsted, Olmsted & Eliot had developed a scheme (fig. 7.4) for enlarging the Cypress Street playground as a fitting foreground for the new high school.[24] Constructed of eastern red brick and Maynard sandstone, the school was three stories tall over a high basement with a central tower facing the playground. The original landscape plans (fig. 7.5) date from 1895, and the correspondence with the architects, engineer, and school committee address issues of approach, lighting, and year-round use of play areas. An August 19, 1895, letter to William H. Lincoln, representative of the school committee, summarized the firm's intentions:

> We have arranged the planting so as not to interfere with the light of the windows, and also to carry out the suggestions made by the architects

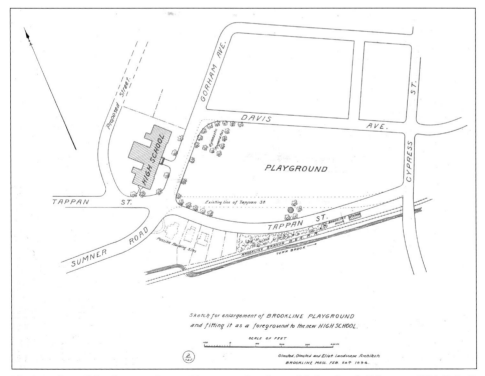

Fig. 7.4. Plan of the Cypress Street Playground and new high school, February 1894, F. L. & J. C. Olmsted. Courtesy National Park Service, Frederick Law Olmsted National Historic Site.

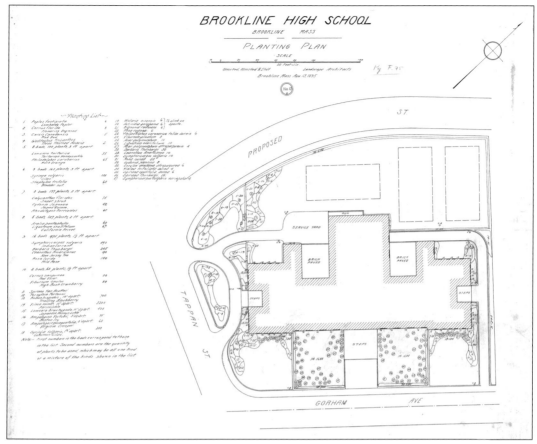

Fig. 7.5. Planting plan, Brookline High School, August 13, 1895, showing massed plant material flanking the entrance at bottom center and the year-round play surfaces. Courtesy National Park Service, Frederick Law Olmsted National Historic Site.

in their elevations, which showed a high mass of foliage near the line of the eaves. We used for this light foliage Gleditchia, three-thorned Acacia, which will grow rapidly and not make too dense a shade for windows of the rooms of the second story; besides this we have used Normandy poplars and the Red-bud or Judas tree. . . . It is our intention to have the surface of the two square enclosed areas to the right and left of the steps in front of the building covered with ground covering or shrubs, and not to have any grass used. These plants will be planted close enough to cover the ground in the course of one or two years, so that little or no further attention will be required.[25]

The building committee remained concerned about the poplar trees blocking light to the classrooms, so they were eliminated. The architects reacted strongly to the idea of massed plantings in the two square areas flanking the steps.[26] These schemes were considered in rapid order as all parties raced to complete the building and its plantings in time for an October 1, 1895, opening of the school. The interiors of the building were handsomely decorated, including works of art that were financed by a special gift from a Brookline resident. Clearly the structure was intended to represent the high standards of the community and the emphasis placed on the role of education.

The purchase of additional land in 1921 allowed for the expansion of the school in several phases throughout the 1930s, with the guidance of the Olmsted firm on each occasion. Kilham, Hopkins & Greeley were selected to design these additions and alterations. These units were designed in 1921–22, 1931, 1937–38, and 1940, with the 1937 campaign replacing the original sections of the building following a fire. These wings formed an interior courtyard, for which the Olmsted firm designed an outdoor theater in 1938 (fig. 7.6).[27] In this case, J. F. Dawson approached the town on behalf of the Olmsted office about providing landscape designs for the new building, part of a more proactive attitude toward attracting clients during the depression. In a June 3, 1938, memo to the file, Dawson reviewed the development of the courtyard theater idea:

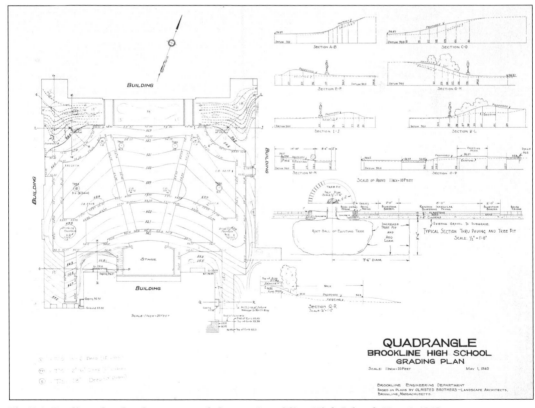

Fig. 7.6. Grading plan for the courtyard theater, Brookline High School, May 1, 1940. Courtesy National Park Service, Frederick Law Olmsted National Historic Site.

A few days ago I drove by the new Brookline High School and it seemed to me a great pity that the grounds of this fine group of buildings could not be properly planted. . . . It occurred to me that Mr. Hamilton's connection with the Town's affairs might help the Town (and perhaps us) in having this work done. . . . Mr. Hamilton telephoned me and asked me to come to the Town Hall at once to meet with the Superintendent of Schools, Mr. Ernest Caverly, with whom he had arranged an appointment. . . . Mr. Caverly said that he had a lot of ideas for the possibilities for the inside court, one of which was to have entertainments and gatherings out-of-doors and I told him in an off-hand way how the development of the so-called open-air theater at Mr. Vanderbilt's School at Scarborough came about and he seemed much interested in that. . . . I hope that something will come out of this.[28]

In this campaign, the Olmsted firm also replaced the original plantings along Cypress and Tappan streets, using honey locusts to frame the main elevations. The firm also lobbied for the closing of Greenough Street in front of the high school to allow students to move between the playing fields and the building without crossing traffic. The replacement sections by Kilham, Hopkins & Greeley were built of red brick with cast stone trim in a Georgian Revival manner, for which the architects had become widely recognized in many public buildings throughout the Boston area.[29]

Near Brookline High School is the Brookline Hill MBTA stop, one of two commuter rail stations on which the Olmsted office worked in coordination with Shepley, Rutan & Coolidge. As the gateway to Brookline for the outer world and for those traveling to and from the city on a daily basis, the suburban railroad station was an important and symbolic institution. Indeed, commuter stations of the Boston and Albany Railroad were among the most widely recognized and lauded elements of suburbanization in the Boston area.

As with other institutional frameworks for the Olmsteds' work in Brookline, personal and professional connections were central to these commissions. The Olmsteds' Green Hill neighbor Charles Sprague Sargent was a director of the Boston and Albany Railroad.[30] In 1882 the B & A purchased track rights of the New York and New England Railroad to create a suburban loop, called "The Circuit," through Brookline and Newton, which officially opened in 1886. Soon after becoming a director in 1880, Sargent joined the building committee.[31] In 1885 he was responsible for commissioning his neighbor H. H. Richardson to design the first of nine railroad stations that he would create for the line. Following Richardson's death in 1886, his successor firm, Shepley, Rutan & Coolidge, would execute twenty-three stations for the line, although most of these would perpetuate the models developed by Richardson: a rectangular mass with a low hipped roof, generally built of granite or puddingstone with brownstone trim.

More important for the line than Richardson and his successors was the involvement of Olmsted, whom Sargent invited to consult on siting and landscape issues. Beginning in 1881, E. A. Richardson (not related to the architect) started to develop the grounds around the Newtonville station, where he was the stationmaster. Sargent was so impressed by this effort that he proposed a comprehensive scheme for landscape enrichment of all of the B & A facilities. Ultimately, sixty stations received some form of landscape embellishment, including the corridors between stations as well. Two of the stations on which the Olmsted office consulted in Brookline were the Longwood station, the earliest commuter rail station on the line, and the Cypress Street or Brookline Hill station, near their work on the Brookline High School.[32] Both were undertaken with Shepley, Rutan & Coolidge; Olmsted's collaboration with Richardson occurred at stations beyond Brookline.

Builder O. W. Norcross constructed the earlier of the two stations at Brookline Hill, originally called the Cypress Street station, in 1891–92.[33] Built of pink granite with brown sandstone trim and measuring sixty by twenty-five feet, it became a model for several later projects.[34] The Olmsted office coordinated the location and planning of this station with local landowners on Fisher Hill for whom they were working in subdivision and private estate projects at this time. As early as 1886, the F. L. & J. C. Olmsted firm's general plan for the adjacent Fisher Hill subdivision incorporated the proposed Brookline Hill station as a northern extension of the plan on the opposite side of the tracks. The station had to serve as an entry to one of the key public nodes of the community—the high school and adjacent designed neighborhoods—and serve the anticipated buyers of lots in the Fisher Hill development that Jonathan H. White, the Goddard family, and others were proposing with Olmsted's assistance.[35]

In terms of landscape development, the station complex at Longwood was more extensive and more widely recognized as a design worthy of emulation. In 1848 Longwood had become the first commuter rail stop in Brookline, and this complex was the second station for the site, actually combining the earlier Chapel and Longwood stations. The simple mass with central door and symmetrical fenestration supported a broadly extending hipped roof supported by brackets on all four sides. Sited below the Longwood Chapel, created by David Sears for his private community, the station was extended with planting along the rail lines in both directions (fig. 7.7). The new station had been anticipated as early as 1886, when an article in the *Brookline Chronicle* announced the project:

> We now hear that the Boston & Albany Railroad Company is ready to erect
> as handsome a station at Longwood, between the two present stations, as

Fig. 7.7. Longwood station at left with Sears Chapel on hillside above and the Riverway of the Boston park system in the foreground. Courtesy Brookline Public Library.

it has anywhere on its main line of track. If the citizens will encourage them by agreeing upon the site, and that a paper is soon to be circulated for signatures in support of this long needed improvement in that section of the town. If some of those near Chapel station, and some of those near Longwood station object to this, as it may be expected some will, it should not be forgotten that the traveling public have rights, and we assume that those having the matter in charge will ask for signatures not in the Longwood section alone, but from Brookline, Newton, Needham, and even beyond there.[36]

Not just the local press applauded the design. Articles in *Garden and Forest* (admittedly edited by Charles Sprague Sargent), *Architectural Record, Suburban Life,* and *House and Garden* brought national attention to this commission and others for the B & A. Perhaps the most enthusiastic champion of this landscape and architecture program was Charles Mulford Robinson, who referred to this work as "the Railroad Beautiful," a variant of the City Beautiful movement inspired by the World's Columbian Exposition in Chicago. Of the Longwood station Robinson wrote:

The railroad touches it on a curve, and, as usual in the avoidance of grade crossings throughout the suburbs, the tracks are depressed. The slopes of the cut are thickly planted with low growing shrubs. . . . The low stone station of the Richardson type nestles beside the track in a clearing of lawn; and up and down the line of the road, the vista, once the train has passed, is as beautiful and peaceful as a country lane all flower-bordered. The day I made the round of stations, the air was sweet with the perfume of wild roses, which, in orderly disorder, climbed the banks on either side.[37]

This program of station architecture and landscape development represented both elegant introductions to the town for the commuter and visitor and one of the symbols of Brookline for the larger world.

If the commuter railroad was intended to facilitate connections with the metropolis, not all residents of Brookline believed that these institutions were assets to their community. The southern half of Brookline, the area south of the Boston and Albany commuter line and Boylston Street, remained open in farming and estate development into the early twentieth century and beyond. Here resided the Brahmin elite, whose life was divided between Boston and Brookline—and occasionally a summerhouse in Newport or Nahant as well. The emblem of this highest level of Brookline society was The Country Club, the place where the right people met the right people to enjoy socializing and recreation.

The Boston area was a national leader in developing athletically oriented social clubs in the periphery of the city.[38] The Eastern Yacht Club, founded in 1870 at Marblehead on the North Shore of Massachusetts Bay, was among the earliest, constructing a clubhouse at Marblehead Neck by 1881. A more relevant ancestor to The Country Club in Brookline was the Myopia Club, organized in 1879 in Winchester, approximately eight miles northwest of Boston. Boston lawyer Frederick O. Prince established this two-hundred-acre club on his private estate. The facilities included a clubhouse with a dining room and bedrooms, a tennis court, and space for baseball, horse racing, and fox hunting.[39] Located in an upper-middle-class railroad suburb, the club proved too distant for many members.

In 1882, under the leadership of J. Murray Forbes, several members of the Myopia Club organized to establish a new club with similar purposes at Clyde Park in Brookline, approximately half the distance from central Boston and in the estate district where many potential members lived. As the organizers explained, "The general idea is to have a comfortable clubhouse for the use of members with their families, a simple restaurant, bed-rooms, bowling-alley, lawn tennis grounds, etc.; also, to have race-meetings and, occasionally, music in the afternoon, and it is probable that a few gentlemen will club together to run a coach out every afternoon during the season, to convey members and their friends at a fixed charge."[40]

Fig. 7.8. Aerial view of The Country Club complex with the original clubhouse in the upper left corner. Courtesy National Park Service, Frederick Law Olmsted National Historic Site.

Most scholars see The Country Club at Brookline as representing the fullest early statement of this new type of social institution. It became a central fixture in the structure and cohesiveness of elite society not just of Brookline but of the Boston area at large. In the words of one insider, the members "played with each other and not with others; they competed with each other, and not with others; above all, they married each other."[41]

The club purchased Clyde Park, the former estate of Dr. William Spooner, converting and expanding the 1802 house for club purposes. The Country Club (fig. 7.8) was founded the year before Frederick Law Olmsted moved to Brookline, but he joined in 1882 as one of the earliest members.[42] Not surprisingly, the club consulted him on plans for development as the institution increased in popularity.[43] The land for the club was originally leased from Francis E. Bacon, one of the incorporators of the institution. As the club grew in popularity and membership, the directors sought to purchase the land before the expiration of the lease. Olmsted became involved at this stage. Bacon realized that the land had become very valuable and sought a high price for the property. J. Murray Forbes, the driving force behind the club project, later recalled the efforts to purchase the property: "During the first years it was considered most important to purchase the original property from Mr. Bacon but he was very stiff in price. Thereupon I and four other members bought the Faulkner Farm, not far distant, putting up $25,000 and obtaining a large mortgage. This succeeded in bringing Mr. Bacon to our terms when he saw he was likely to lose the Club as a tenant or purchaser. We were fortunate to get out even on our purchase of Faulkner Farm."[44] While this second site was under consideration, the purchasers commissioned the Olmsted office to develop proposals for racetracks at Faulkner Farm in 1886 (fig. 7.9). The firm's proposed designs for the eastern, western, and three-quarter-mile tracks in July 1886 were never executed because Bacon agreed to sell the leased land across Newton Street. The original riding track for horse races and steeplechases was built southeast of the clubhouse in 1882 and replaced in 1904 and 1926 by more substantial grandstands.[45]

While the Olmsted firms were consulted at various stages about changes in the landscape development of The Country Club through 1946, the most important period was the 1930s, when they produced a very useful composite plan of the property and various proposals for landscaping around the new locker room building. The plan of The Country Club from 1934 (fig. 7.10) shows the complex of buildings around an oblong driveway at the center bottom, the still surviving racecourse and grandstand to the left of the clubhouse and associated buildings, and various playing fields, skating ponds, and rinks scattered throughout the golf

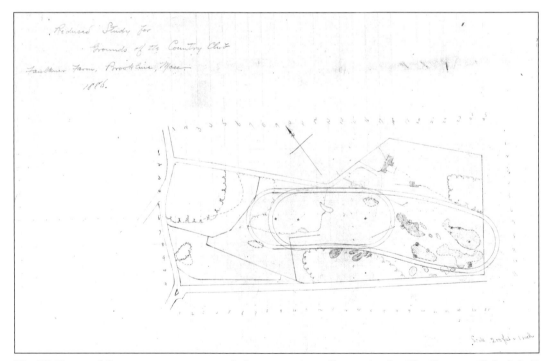

Fig. 7.9. Proposal for eastern, western, and three-quarter-mile racetracks, The Country Club, July 7, 1886. Courtesy National Park Service, Frederick Law Olmsted National Historic Site.

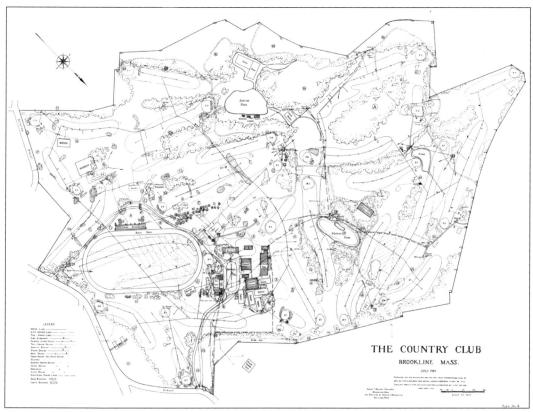

Fig. 7.10. Detail of the clubhouse and associated buildings and race course on the 1934 plan of The Country Club. Courtesy National Park Service, Frederick Law Olmsted National Historic Site.

courses, which had become a major early focus of the club's activities.[46] The Olmsted firm became specialists in golf course and country club design, starting here.[47] As with almost every element of the life of Brookline as a designed suburb, they were periodically consulted by The Country Club as it evolved.

Although Frederick Law Olmsted joined the club briefly, he was "clubbable" in a different way, preferring groups that were less important for their location or building than for what they represented in networks.[48] In 1883, the year he moved to Brookline, Olmsted was invited to join one of the most prestigious intellectual clubs in Boston, the Saturday Club.[49] Founded in 1855 by Oliver Wendell Holmes and James T. Fields, editors of the *Atlantic Monthly,* the club met originally for lunch on the fourth Saturday of each month at the Parker House hotel, two blocks from the offices of the publishing firm of Ticknor and Fields, which published the work of many early members. The matrix of members was expanded to include important academics—especially college presidents—scientists, historians, diplomats, and leaders in a variety of fields. The original members represented the Olympian gods of Boston and American literary culture: Ralph Waldo Emerson, Nathaniel

Hawthorne, Oliver Wendell Holmes, Henry Wadsworth Longfellow, Henry David Thoreau, John Greenleaf Whittier, and William Dean Howells.[50] Among Olmsted's friends, Charles Eliot Norton, the first professor of art history at Harvard College, and Edwin Lawrence Godkin, with whom Olmsted had worked in founding the *Nation* in 1856, may have nominated him for membership.[51] The admission of both Richardson and Olmsted in the same year, the first members of the prestigious club from their respective professions, signals an expansion of the interests of the group into the larger society. Given Olmsted's exhausting travel schedule for his practice and the lack of club records, it is not known how often he was able to attend the luncheons. Charles William Eliot, who was invited as a very young man to join the Saturday Club in 1870, one year after his ascension to the presidency of Harvard College, did record meetings with Olmsted at the club during which he discussed the interests of his son Charles in pursuing a career in landscape architecture (see chapter 3), conversations that led to an invitation to the young Eliot to become the first intern in the Olmsted office at Fairsted.[52] Olmsted supported the offer of club membership to his Brookline neighbor Charles Sprague Sargent in 1896. By that time, however, Olmsted had retired from his practice and was experiencing bouts of mental instability that would plague him for the remainder of his life. Appropriately, Sargent wrote the biography of Olmsted for the 1927 history *The Later Years of the Saturday Club.*[53] Sargent persistently refers to him as a landscape gardener rather than as a landscape architect as Olmsted would have preferred, but he does conclude: "Time proves that Olmsted was not only the greatest landscape gardener the world has known, but the greatest of all American artists, and that his genius has added enduring pleasure and given health to the increasing millions of the urban population of the United States. He deserved all the honors that any could bestow on him. His greatness will be realized and appreciated as the centuries pass."[54] From 1883 until his retirement in 1894, Olmsted enjoyed the congeniality and intellectual stimulation of this group of men who were known and admired throughout the nation.

At a more parochial level, Olmsted also participated to a limited extent in the activities of the Brookline Club. At the invitation of club president William Estes, Olmsted gave a talk to the club that was reported in the *Brookline Chronicle* on Saturday, March 2, 1889.[55] His topic was the development of roads and parkways. After commenting on the problems and characteristics of roads in northern Europe, Rome, Paris, and London, he turned to American conditions. The reporter summarized, "The fashion in vogue in this country of building detached houses with open spaces about them he commended, making a special reference to the restrictions placed upon land of the Brookline and Aspinwall Land companies against the placing of buildings within twenty-five feet of the roadway."[56] Olmsted then reminisced about his reasons for moving from New York City to Brookline, commenting on his having observed during a visit the removal of snow by town workers on a Saturday morning under the supervision of a selectman, which he considered an indication of the high level of local civilization.

The majority of his remarks were focused on planning for the future of the town. The problems and solutions, as reported by the newspaper, were these:

> How to preserve the topographical condition of the town is the most critical question. No house should be built within a reasonable distance of the street and other restrictions might well be fixed. To exempt from taxation all roadside lands might be a desirable thing, and land unavailable for building purposes might also be exempted. The question had been asked whether the town ought not to acquire something for a park but he thought it ought not. It might be profitable, he said, to secure small tracts in various parts of the town, for example a lot on Pond Avenue, and a half acre on the summit of Corey Hill; and a triangle like that near St. Paul's church might be expanded to advantage. In considering the development of the town, Mr. Olmsted laid particular stress to the importance of laying out streets with an eye to the future and in advance of present needs.

He also felt that mechanisms used to control private land development should be extended to public policy. Several prominent citizens responded to Olmsted's remarks. William Aspinwall urged town planning for wider roads. Desmond Fitzgerald discussed his "efforts to beautify the grounds of the Chestnut Hill Reservoir," and Albert L. Lincoln Jr. reiterated the possibility of seeking "special legislation with reference to exempting from taxation a definite area of lands fronting upon the street when kept open for public use."

Although ladies could only be guests of the all-male Brookline Club, another local institution did represent their interests. The Free Hospital for Women introduces other major elements of the Brookline suburban story and how these relate to national and regional trends. For many cultural and social historians, the suburb is associated with the world of women in contrast to the male-dominated sphere of the city. That broad characterization has perhaps greater relevance in the middle-class suburb, something that Brookline was not. Nevertheless, the general argument runs that the suburb was designed as a safe and healthy world in which women could nurture the next generation of middle- and upper-class American children.[57] Of course, this same ambition was embraced by women among minorities and immigrant populations as their incomes allowed them to participate in the project known as suburbanization.

The Free Hospital for Women, on which the firm of Olmsted, Olmsted & Eliot advised on grading and the creation of roads and paths, provides an opportunity to consider the issues of the suburb as a feminine domain and of professionalism in Brookline. Dr. William Henry Baker established the hospital in 1875 in Boston to treat poor women suffering from female health problems.[58] The institution's focus on gynecology provided a match to the Boston Lying-In Hospital's role in obstetrics for the poor.[59] Soon after its founding, the Free Hospital became the first teaching hospital associated with the Harvard Medical School.[60] After moving among several sites in the central city, the institution in 1889 began to seek a larger space in suburban Brookline. The following year the hospital purchased a lot at the corner of Marion and Park streets, but the resistance of surrounding neighbors was so intense that the town denied a building permit.[61] The trustees of the Free Hospital sold that land and in 1892 purchased another property, bounded by Pond Road, Cumberland Avenue, Highland Road, and Glen Road, from the Brookline Land Company, one of the earliest residential subdivision companies in Brookline. When the Free Hospital relocated to suburban Brookline in 1895, it anticipated a move of the Harvard Medical School and other associated hospitals to the Longwood section of Boston, across the Muddy River from Brookline, a decade later. The land overlooked the Muddy River improvement to the Boston park system, then being developed by the Olmsted firm. Architects Shaw & Hunnewell designed a chateauesque building in yellow brick with limestone trim for the hospital. An octagonal louvered ventilator topped the central pavilion, and an arcaded passageway bordered the first floor on the view side of the building. The architects and landscape architects positioned the hospital above Leverett Pond, one element of the emerging park system. Having the Olmsted firm consult on the landscape development allowed for a natural continuity between the public parkland and the private hospital (fig. 7.11).

Fig. 7.11. Free Hospital for Women seen from Leverett Pond. Courtesy Tim Sullivan.

In the end, the Olmsted office did relatively little to embellish the grounds of the hospital. Their initial focus, necessarily, was on the grading of the east-facing slope and the lowering of Glen Road, which was the main access to the property from the adjacent subdivision. Most of the correspondence surrounding this first stage of development concerns the frustrating effort to get grass to grow successfully on the sloping site.[62] Although some trees were cut down, and Olmsted, Olmsted & Eliot may have planted others, the actual development of the landscape became the domain of Charles Sprague Sargent, whose wife was a member of the corporation of the hospital.[63] In October 1895 Sargent volunteered to oversee the planting of the grounds.[64] The hospital being located relatively near his large estate, Holm Lea, and along the parkway circuit that would lead to the Arnold Arboretum, of which he was the first director, Sargent was eager to supervise the selection, planting, and maintenance of trees and plants for the hospital trustees into the 1910s.

A free hospital devoted to the gynecological needs of poor patients provides an opportunity to consider the role of women in the concept of the ideal suburb. The provision of private rooms for recuperation from surgery and with views out over the surrounding landscape could be seen as reflecting a feminine attitude toward the treatment of women patients.[65] The curative value of nature, however, was a principle that Olmsted and others had long advocated for in the siting and development of mental hospitals.[66] While the hospital staff included at least one leading woman doctor, it remained a facility primarily run by men for women,[67] although the appointment of women, such as Mrs. Charles Sprague Sargent, to the board of trustees and as advisers gave women increased agency within this suburban institution.

Catharine Beecher had been one of the most influential voices on the role of women in the mid-nineteenth century. In an article titled "How to Redeem Woman's Profession from Dishonor" in the November 1865 issue of *Harper's* magazine, she argued:

Woman, as well as man, was made to work; her Maker has adapted her body to its appropriate labor. The tending of children and doing house-work exercise those very muscles which are most important to womanhood; while neglecting to exercise the arms and trunk cause dangerous disability in most delicate organs. . . .

It is believed that the remedy for all these evils is not in leading women into the professions and business of men, by which many philanthropists are now aiming to remedy their sufferings, but to train woman properly for her own proper business, and to secure her the honor and profit which men gain in their professions. . . .

When houses are built on *Christian principles* women of wealth and culture will *work themselves, and train their children to work,* instead of having ignorant foreigners to ruin their food in a filthy kitchen, and ruin their children in the nursery.[68]

Here and elsewhere, Beecher lobbied for American Protestant women to take control of their lives and their homes, running them themselves, without servants, as sites of suburban feminine perfection. While Brookline's elite women would certainly have heard these arguments, their situation was radically different from the one that Beecher envisioned. In 1870, at a time when 40 percent of the Brookline population consisted of poor Irish Catholics, one out of three Brookline households had servants. Women servants constituted 93 percent of this workforce, with only the wealthiest Brookline families employing male servants.[69] Far from being servant-less, Brookline households had a higher number and a larger percentage of servants than any other suburb of Boston. Thus, the women who were married to clients of the Olmsted firm or were clients themselves were functioning as domestic professionals, running households with substantial budgets and a comfortable workforce. They were not trying to create a radical feminine zone in Brookline, as Beecher had been proposing. The wives of the elite and upper-middle class tended to support the worldview of their husbands. For example,

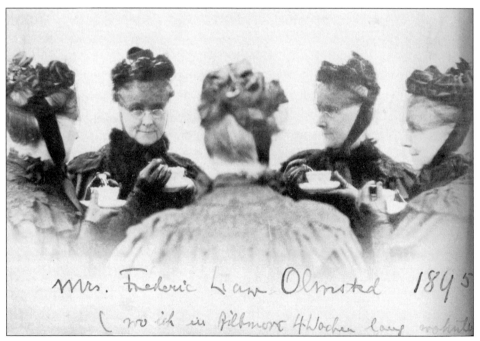

Fig. 7.12. Mary Perkins Olmsted, 1895. Courtesy National Park Service, Frederick Law Olmsted National Historic Site.

Mrs. Frederick Law Olmsted (fig. 7.12), Mrs. Charles S. Sargent, Mrs. Henry M. Whitney, Mrs. Francis Lawrence, Mrs. Alfred D. Chandler, Mrs. Henry Lee, Mrs. Theodore Lyman, and Mrs. James Codman, among others, supported an anti-suffrage campaign launched in 1902 in Brookline.[70]

The hospital was also a natural neighbor to the professional residential district that was being developed on the hilltop and land to the east. This area has come to be known as Pill Hill because of the large number of physicians who chose to live there. When Harvard University built a new medical school campus in the nearby Longwood district of Boston in 1906, it became a magnet for a series of specialty teaching hospitals that were built around it, adding to the migration of doctors and their work environment to this area. Not only physicians saw the Brookline Land Company property as a desirable area for their residences. Clients of the Olmsted firm in the Pill Hill neighborhood included architects, engineers, and lawyers as well as doctors. Indeed, the upper middle class of professionals and businessmen became the individuals running the town government and serving on important boards and committees from the late nineteenth century on. The Olmsteds themselves were representatives of this class.

Eight

THE NEIGHBORHOOD CONTEXT

To understand fully the deep impact that the Olmsted family and firm had in the development of Brookline at large, we need to consider the microcosm of the Fairsted neighborhood in which they chose to live and work. Here they interacted with neighbors, many of whom sought their professional services, while others contributed to the knowledge and experience of the Olmsted office. (figs. 8.1 and 8.2) Few other areas of the town would have been more receptive or responsive to the professional and personal interests of the Olmsteds. And few other towns would have been as eager for their advice and expertise or as useful in providing a continuous stream of lucrative clients. In moving to Brookline, they entered a world of social and economic privilege that was typical of other members of the professional class there. They joined The Country Club in 1882, when it was founded as the first such organization in the nation.[1] They achieved listing in the Boston edition of the *Social Register* from its first publication in 1890 onward.[2] In short, the Olmsted family and firm members became part of the social network they served and whose properties they shaped.

By moving to 99 Warren Street, Frederick Law Olmsted also established himself in the most historic section of Brookline. The First Parish Church—the religious and governmental focus of the community throughout the eighteenth and early nineteenth centuries—stood at the top of the hill at the intersection of Walnut and Warren streets (see chapter 7). Most of the surrounding territory was originally divided into large land grants, from south to north, for Thomas Oliver (1638 and 1641), Thomas Leverett (1638 and 1641), and the Reverend John Cotton (1638), all representative of the acquisition of Brookline farmland by key figures in the Massachusetts Bay Company.[3] In 1667 these large parcels, among the largest in the community, remained intact, now owned by John White, Thomas Gardner, and the heirs of John Cotton, respectively. By 1693 the White lands had been divided between John and Benjamin White; the Gardner lands were partitioned among Joshua, Thomas, and Andrew Gardner, with smaller sections acquired by Thomas Boylston and John White; while the heirs of John Cotton still retained all of the original grant. This central core near where the meetinghouse would be built in 1711 had thus become an area of agricultural estates of substantial size.

After the establishment of the town of Brookline in 1705 and the erection

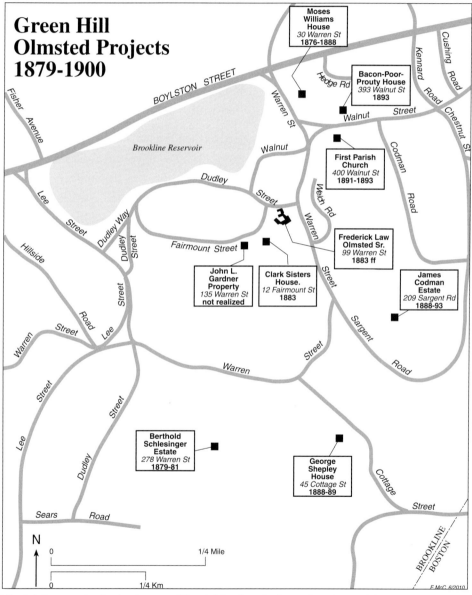

Fig. 8.1. Properties in the Green Hill neighborhood where the Olmsted firm worked 1880–1900. Map by Eliza McClellen.

of the meetinghouse, the land around this community focal point became more desirable and valuable. By 1747 the number of landholders had been expanded, although the number of families owning land remained relatively small. Samuel Clark had acquired the property previously owned by John White. The Reverend James Allen held a narrow, long parcel adjacent to the town land where the meetinghouse stood. The Gardner and Boylston families shared the land farther north and west. This ownership pattern was only slightly modified by 1796, when the

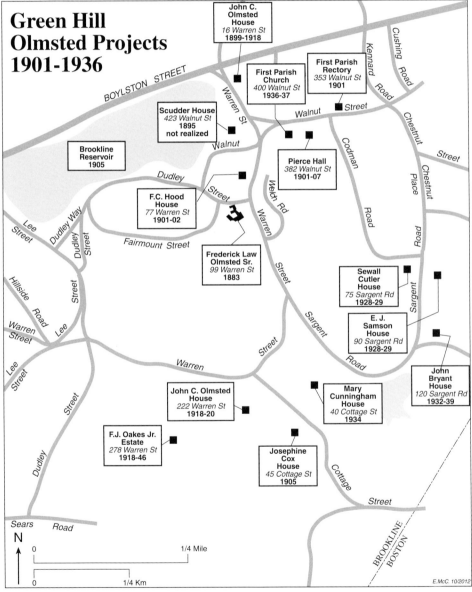

Fig. 8.2. Properties in the Green Hill neighborhood where the Olmsted firm worked, 1901–36. Map by Eliza McClellen.

long-term subsistence agricultural patterns of Brookline began to be challenged by new arrivals from Boston and beyond.

As detailed by Tamara Thornton in *Cultivating Gentlemen,* the invasion of Brookline by wealthy merchants intent on creating summer country residences for experimental agriculture and horticulture began in the period following the American Revolution and had become a marked phenomenon in the federal period. Important for the Fairsted area was the purchase by Richard Sullivan of the former

Fig. 8.3. Plan of the Sargent-Codman estate as drawn by students of engineering at MIT, 1885. Courtesy National Park Service, Frederick Law Olmsted National Historic Site.

Gardner-Hyslop estate at the top of the hill, north of the meetinghouse. Sullivan, one of the most energetic and loyal members of the Massachusetts Society for Promoting Agriculture, was the leading figure of a small colony of newcomers in the neighborhood of the meetinghouse.[4] Another concentration of wealthy outsiders who sought country estates where they could enjoy the pleasures of the soil was established a half-mile south of the town center by George Cabot, an early convert to the rural beauty of Brookline. He eventually tired of raising potatoes and sold off sections of his nine-acre farm in 1803 to the Boston merchants Stephen Higginson Jr., Thomas Coffin Amory Jr., Thomas Handasyd Perkins, and Stephen H. Perkins, among others.[5] The Sullivan and Cabot colonies, if we can call them that, bracketed the property that Olmsted would eventually purchase and defined this section of Brookline as the territory of wealthy Bostonians who sought a genteel refuge from the pressures of business.

The major change that occurred in the neighborhood between the early nineteenth century and the arrival of Olmsted in 1883 was the development of a large and horticulturally sophisticated estate south of Warren Street, south of the property that had been held by George Cabot. In 1845 Ignatius Sargent purchased the first of three parcels that would be combined to form his estate, Holm Lea. In 1858 a second parcel was acquired as a house site for his daughter Henrietta and her husband, James McMaster Codman, who was keenly interested in agriculture and animal husbandry. Sargent added a third adjacent property in 1871, acquiring the twenty-acre estate of Henry Lee, which had been much praised by Andrew Jackson Downing in his seminal *Treatise on the Theory and Practice of Landscape Gardening Adapted to North America*.[6] The horticultural collections of Henry Lee augmented the specimens Sargent collected and displayed. His son Charles Sprague Sargent took over the management of Holm Lea (fig. 8.3) in 1868, by which time the estate had grown to nearly 150 acres, stretching almost to the shores of Jamaica Pond. He became the first director of Harvard College's Arnold Arboretum in nearby Jamaica Plain in 1873, a position he held until his death in 1927, and in which capacity he enlisted Olmsted's assistance before the family and office moved to Brookline (see chapter 5).

Thus, when Olmsted arrived in Brookline in 1883, he entered a rarefied world in which agriculture, horticulture, landscape design, and open space conservation were all community values. He also joined a wealthy, well-educated, well-connected group of neighbors who could ease his entry into Brookline and Boston society. In addition, he was attracted to this town and neighborhood by the presence of his close friend from New York, Henry Hobson Richardson, who had made his home (fig. 8.4) on nearby Cottage Street in 1874 (see chapter 3). It is hard to imagine an environment in which he would have been happier or more engaged. The personal and professional retreat to suburban Brookline from New York City,

Fig. 8.4. The E. W. Hooper house, rented by H. H. Richardson, 25 Cottage Street, Brookline, 1874–1886. Photograph by Jean Bear O'Gorman. Courtesy James F. O'Gorman.

however, did little to lessen the demand on Olmsted's services. Indeed, this community was in need of a professional with his experience, and the Olmsted office found in Brookline a ready supply of commissions on many levels.

For the purposes of this discussion, the Fairsted neighborhood can be described as a combination of the Town Green district to the east and the Green Hill district to the west and south of 99 Warren Street. In some ways it is very difficult to define the boundaries of this neighborhood or sphere of influence because the projects by the various iterations of the Olmsted firm extended out from Fairsted in almost all directions throughout Brookline. To retain manageable and appropriate boundaries, we will look at the interaction of the Olmsted office with clients whose properties lay south of Boylston Street and Lee Street, down to the border with the Roxbury section of Boston.

Even before deciding to move to Brookline, and specifically to Warren Street, Frederick Law Olmsted received a commission from one of his future neighbors. Barthold Schlesinger had come to the United States as a diplomat from Germany, then married a member of Boston society and gone into business there. As lovers of music and collectors of art, the Schlesingers became prominent in Boston and Brookline social circles, and their new Brookline estate, a showplace. In 1879 Olmsted began studying the twenty-eight-acre property at 278 Warren Street (fig. 8.5) in coordination with George Harney, the New York architect Schlesinger hired to design the house (1880–81), a Jacobean Revival pile in brick with stepped gables and towers.[7] Perhaps H. H. Richardson, Schlesinger's neighbor at 25 Cottage Street, had recommended his New York friend Olmsted. Although South-wood, as the Schlesingers named their estate, lacked a natural vista, Olmsted developed a pond from a stream running through the front of the property and created expansive lawns marked by an impressive variety of trees (fig. 8.6).

Mrs. Schlesinger assumed a central role in developing the estate. Harney

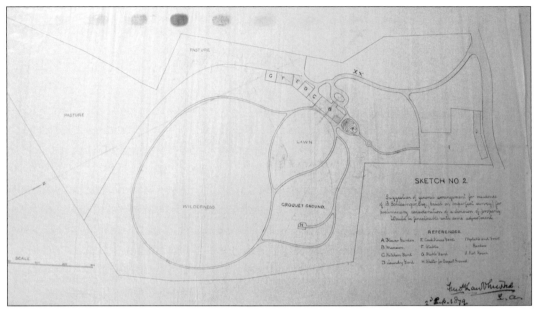

Fig. 8.5. Southwood, Barthold Schlesinger estate, sketch no. 2 for property, 1879. Even though this is not the final plan for the estate, it shows the various components with which Olmsted was working: pasture, wilderness, croquet ground, and lawn. In the final scheme, the stable wings extended from the south end of the house. Courtesy National Park Service, Frederick Law Olmsted National Historic Site.

Fig. 8.6. Barthold Schlesinger estate. Courtesy Frances Loeb Library, Harvard Graduate School of Design.

warned Olmsted in advance of a visit to Brookline: "Be prepared to answer all sort of questions about the position of the house. Mrs. Schlesinger insists upon it that you have it a trifle to S. Easterly to get the sun and S. Westerly windows late in the day. A *round* house would have been the thing to build."[8] Olmsted turned over to his son John Charles the responsibility for developing the plan, but he remained involved in the oversight of this large estate, both approving the scheme and offering advice on modifications. One of the major design issues was the transition of the house into the landscape. Mrs. Schlesinger wrote to Olmsted concerning her preference for the treatment of a "platform" or terrace around the house: "I sent you word by Telephone yesterday, through Kelly, that we had decided to take down the Tree at the North side and finish the slope from it as proposed by you. Also that we adopt your new design for the finish of the South Front including your design for the Platform, the lines of which pleased Mr. Schlesinger better than those sketched by Mr. Harney."[9] The Olmsted office continued to offer advice on landscape matters at Southwood through the mid-1890s.

Barthold Schlesinger died in 1900, and his widow continued to live at Southwood until 1917, when Francis J. Oakes Jr. acquired the bulk of the property. He hired Bigelow & Wadsworth to remodel the interior of the house extensively, using Jacobean combinations of wood and cast stone. From 1918 on, the Olmsted office served as the advisers for changes in the estate, especially in 1920–21.[10] A member of the Boston Park Commission, Oakes added specimen trees to the estate. Today the estate comprises only nineteen acres, and Southwood has become the Holy Transfiguration monastery, which allows access to the grounds and some of the ground-floor rooms of the mansion.

While the planning and execution of the grounds at Southwood proceeded, Olmsted was involved in negotiating for himself the purchase of a neighboring property, the two-acre Joshua Clark house at 99 Warren Street (fig. 8.7). The Olmsteds had to provide an incentive for the Clark sisters, descendants of one of the oldest Brookline families, to sell their home on land held by their family since the colonial period. Economic need was a key motivation, but the most important carrot was the offer to build a new house for the sisters at the northern edge of the property where they could live rent free for the remainder of their lives. John Charles Olmsted designed this handsome if modest shingled cottage (fig. 8.8), perhaps in response to Richardson's proposal for a house for the Olmsteds on land next to his on Cottage Street.[11] The very competent residence demonstrates the range of the younger Olmsted's design talent. It also allowed the remaining members of this old Brookline family the security of living out their lives on their ancestral land. Between the original Clark house and

Fig. 8.7. The former Joshua Clark house, acquired by the Olmsted family in 1883 and renamed Fairsted. Courtesy National Park Service, Frederick Law Olmsted National Historic Site.

the new cottage built for the unmarried sisters, the Olmsted family and office expanded the Fairsted complex to accommodate the growth of the practice over time (fig. 8.9).

From this new home base the Olmsted family and firm began to expand into the social and professional networks of their new neighborhood. Their immediate neighbors to the west at 135 Warren Street were Mr. and Mrs. John Gardner. As with the Schlesingers farther down the street, Mrs. Gardner—Isabella Stewart Gardner—was the driving force in the development of this estate, known as

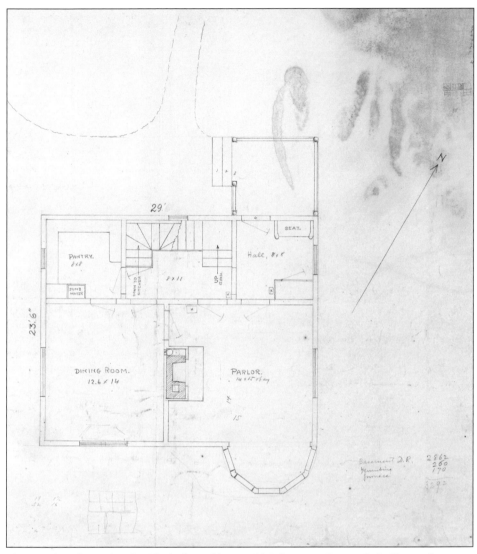

Fig. 8.8. First-floor plan for Clark sisters' house, 99 Fairmount Street, J. C. Olmsted. Courtesy National Park Service, Frederick Law Olmsted National Historic Site.

Green Hill (fig. 8.10). Captain Nathaniel Ingersoll had lost his fortune shortly after he built this country home in 1806 and was compelled to sell the property. Ingersoll had constructed a house whose two-story veranda was, like its neighbor Old Green Hill, in the style of a West Indies plantation house. The arcaded lattice-work between the posts, however, makes the portico on Green Hill much more elaborate.

John Lowell Gardner, who acquired the property in 1842, introduced major horticultural improvements to the estate. His famous daughter-in-law, Isabella Stewart Gardner, made alterations to the house and added an Italian garden (fig.

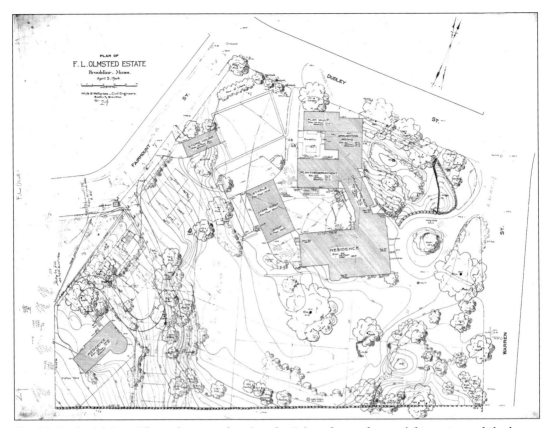

Fig. 8.9. Frederick Law Olmsted estate, showing the Fairsted complex at right center and the house for the Clark sisters in the lower left corner. Courtesy National Park Service, Frederick Law Olmsted National Historic Site.

Fig. 8.10. Green Hill, constructed in 1806 by Nathaniel Ingersoll and purchased by John L. Gardner in 1842. Courtesy Historic New England.

8.11), a Japanese garden, and extensive iris beds to the grounds.[12] Although virtually all evidence of her gardens, as well as most of the outbuildings, has been lost with the subdivision of the property in recent years, the family donated a corridor of land along Warren Street to the Nature Conservancy, which transferred the land in 2001 to the National Park Service. The Park Service–owned land now preserves the historic view of the house, with its commanding position on the hillside.

Despite having the nation's most respected landscape architect as her next-door neighbor, Mrs. Gardner preferred to rely on her own counsel. She did correspond once with Olmsted concerning plant material, but she designed her gardens without professional advice. Her husband, however, sought the assistance of the Olmsted firm about land that he owned at the northwest corner of the Green Hill estate, at the intersection of Dudley and Fairmount streets.[13] This was north of where John Charles Olmsted had recently placed the house for the Clark sisters at 99 Fairmount. The drawings in the Olmsted firm archive from 1886–87 are topographical plans and profiles of existing conditions rather than a specific pro-

Fig. 8.11. The "Italian Garden," Green Hill, Isabella Stewart Gardner, 1885.

posal for development of this land. Mr. Gardner also called on the Olmsteds for assistance with plant material, asking through his foreman William Thatcher to purchase box edging from the "Jamaica Park," presumably the Jamaica Pond area of the Boston park system.[14]

To the east and north of Fairsted, across Dudley Street, the adjacent neighbor, Frederick Clarke Hood, called upon the Olmsted Brothers in 1901–2 for assistance with the grounds of his new house. Hood was the treasurer of the Hood Rubber Company, based in Watertown, Massachusetts, and a resident of Brookline from 1892 on. He moved into his new house in 1900; Ernest Bowditch developed the original landscape scheme. Well known as a businessman who avoided employing union workers, Hood was very careful in his expenditures on the grounds, always asking about the price of each suggestion and trying to find less costly ways to achieve his ends.[15] As a new-money industrialist, he added another element to the social landscape of the Fairsted environs.

Thus the immediate neighbors of the Fairsted property were individuals of great prominence in their various fields and usually of substantial personal wealth (fig. 8.12). Frederick Law Olmsted, his partners, and family could walk to the residence of H. H. Richardson, arguably the country's leading architect in the years before his death; the estate of Isabella Stewart Gardner, the nation's first female art collector of prominence and the founder of Fenway Court (now the Isabella Stewart Gardner Museum, overlooking the Fenway section of Olmsted's Boston park system); or that of Charles Sprague Sargent, the nation's premier horticulturalist. He had businessmen neighbors as clients, from the old-money Brahmin John Gardner to the German Jewish immigrant Barthold Schlesinger to the new-money industrialist F. C. Hood. Two of his neighbors were members of park commissions—Sargent in Brookline and Oakes in Boston. The surrounding properties included estates that had been nurtured and pruned since the colonial era and new suburban residences carved out of larger properties. Throughout the district, however, and in part through the efforts of the Olmsted offices, the Green Hill neighborhood maintained the semi-rural charm that initially attracted Olmsted to Brookline.

Farther up Warren Street, overlooking the town green and the First Parish Church, the Olmsted firm helped with the development of at least three properties. As we saw in the preceding chapter, there was a close relationship between some of these private property owners and First Parish, and they were concerned for the appearance of the landscape around the church.

After the Schlesinger estate, the next major project that the Olmsted firm undertook in the Fairsted neighborhood was the development of the residence for Moses Williams at 30 Warren Street. A lawyer, legislator, and president of the State Street Trust Company, Williams had attended the Brookline public schools before entering Harvard. In 1877 he purchased the Gardner-Gridley-Hulton

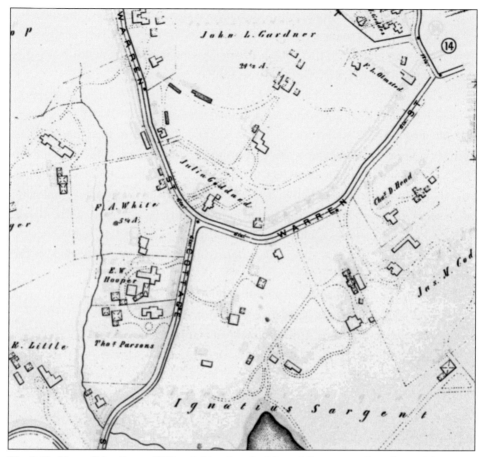

Fig. 8.12. Map of the Green Hill neighborhood of Brookline. Note the Olmsted house in the upper right corner, the Gardner estate in the top center of the plan, the Ignatius Sargent estate across the bottom of the page, the Richardson house (E. W. Hooper) at left center, and the Schlesinger estate unmarked on the top left side of the plan. *Atlas of the Town of Brookline* (1884). Courtesy Brookline Public Library.

estate, which dated from 1740. In 1885 he commissioned Peabody & Stearns to design a new house for the property in coordination with the landscape developed by Olmsted.[16] The challenge of this site was to retain the earlier house, stable, and roads while sequencing the construction of a new house, stable, and landscape to replace them (fig. 8.13).

The work of the Olmsted office began in March 1885 and continued into the following spring. To aid in determining the placement of the house, a cutout of the ground-floor configuration was developed as early as June 1883, which could be moved around the site plans to demonstrate the relative merits of each location.[17] A plan from December 1885 (fig. 8.14) shows the potential development of the rear of the property, with lots for future development and the inscription: "This is a mere diagram as a basis of discussion showing a possible method of subdivision into building sites. Neither the road and yards nor the location of the house are as my father would recommend but are merely to give you an idea of general disposition and size." Despite the creation of an ideal suburban setting, including tennis court and formal gardens, Moses Williams sold the house after a decade and a half. The *Brookline Chronicle* for January 5, 1901, reported, "Residents of Brookline expressed much regret when Mr. Moses Williams, who had been born and had always lived in the town, sold his estate and removed to Boston, and are now correspondingly pleased to learn that he has purchased the John E. Thayer estate." W. D. Hunt bought the property, which was widely regarded as among the most handsome of its scale, so much so that *Country Life* published an article titled "A Suburban Place of Four Acres: A Brookline Home with the Landscape Art of a Great Estate" in August 1903.

Just north of the town green and diagonally across Warren Street from the Williams-Hunt property, John Charles Olmsted discussed a much more modest house and landscape with a Mr. Scudder. In a memo dated June 27, 1896, he provided the following summary:

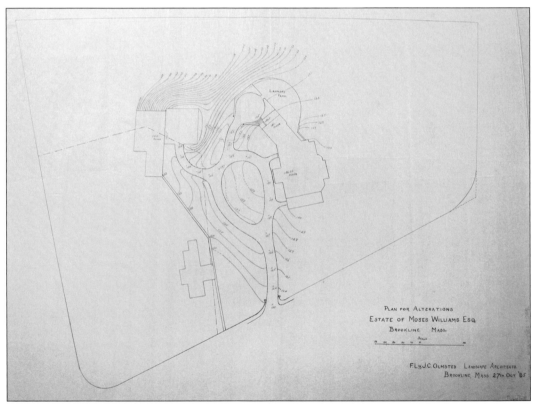

Fig. 8.13. Plan of the Moses Williams estate, October 1885, showing the relationship of the original house and stable on the left of the plan to the new house and stable to the right. Courtesy National Park Service, Frederick Law Olmsted National Historic Site.

Mr. Scudder has advised with me once before about a lot on Warren Street, opposite the church. Sketch for house I then gave him won't quite go on lot. He bought lot of Ernest Bowditch, paying, I think, 75 cents a foot and facing on church triangle, because his sister who is to keep house for him wants to be where she can see people go by from her windows and dislikes retirement. They also bought on account of trees, elevation—

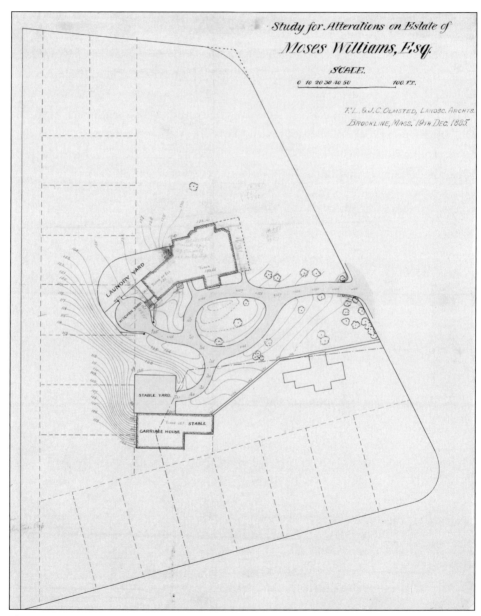

Fig. 8.14. Plan of the Moses Williams estate showing the possible location of lots for development along the northern and western edges of the property, December 1885. Courtesy National Park Service, Frederick Law Olmsted National Historic Site.

highest above road, old neighbors, new neighbors and hope to get some glimpse of the reservoir. . . . There is a prominent little knoll near north side of lot, which determined shape and location and should determine placing of house so a corner or bay shall seem to grow out of the knoll. He had this time two sketches on the scale of the land plan (30'—1") one about like this.[18]

It is unclear whether John Charles Olmsted had been proposing a house of his own design (fig. 8.15). In any case, the Scudder property was never realized. The importance of being in the center of village life and having a view of the reservoir, if restricted, helps explain some of the popularity of the Town Green neighborhood. This particular quadrant of the neighborhood was being developed at this point with three houses dating from 1896: 37 Warren Street (Winslow & Wetherell), 45 Warren Street (Hartwell & Richardson), and 49 Warren Street (F. Manton Wakefield).[19]

Back down Walnut Street opposite the First Parish Church was the Bacon-Poor-Prouty house, originally built in 1852, making it one of the earliest houses to survive in this neighborhood. In 1913 it was dramatically remodeled in the Federal Revival style. The Olmsted firm began to work on the redevelopment of the Lewis I. Prouty property that same year, when the house was altered. While they completed substantial work in 1913–14, the Olmsted firm members continued to make changes and additions to the landscape from 1929 to 1937. By the latter

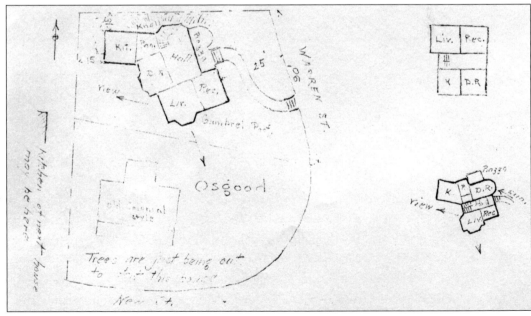

Fig. 8.15. Proposal for the Scudder house, July 27, 1896. Olmsted Associates Papers, series E, Manuscript Division, Library of Congress.

date, Prouty was also supporting the Olmsted office in making landscape improvements to the First Parish Church across the street. (The Olmsted firm's long-term involvement with First Parish is discussed in chapter 7.)

One of the important projects for the neighborhood at large was the preservation of the Brookline Reservoir, just north of the Town Green district, as a public open space after it was no longer needed for water supply. In 1844 the city of Boston constructed a receiving reservoir for its new Cochituate water system in what was marshland just north of Brookline's old town common. At the corner of Warren and Boylston streets stands the building designed in 1848 by Charles E. Parker to house the distribution chamber for the reservoir. The Brookline Reservoir doubled as a picturesque promenade and park, making the immediate neighborhood more attractive for residential development. In 1902 Boston decided to sell the reservoir land. Neighbors John Charles Olmsted, Walter Channing, Henry Lee, Amy Lowell, and others contributed $50,000 toward the price of $150,000 for the town to purchase the reservoir and preserve it as a park.[20] Walter Channing, of course, was H. H. Richardson's only Brookline commission—for a house at the corner of Chestnut Hill Avenue and Boylston Street, at the northern edge of the reservoir. Henry Lee was his neighbor to the south and a staunch opponent to development in this section of Brookline. He lived in the Boylston-Hyslop house, begun around 1738, and was keenly aware of the historic importance of his property and of the character of the neighborhood. When developers assisted by the Olmsted firm proposed a widening of Boylston Street, Lee countered that the road was as worthy of preservation as the Old State House and Old South Church.[21]

Closer to Fairsted, the Olmsteds were involved with projects for themselves and their close associates. John Charles Olmsted lived at various sites around the neighborhood until he purchased the house in 1899 at 14 Warren Street, near the Brookline Reservoir and across from the future project for Moses Williams. The previous year he had married Sophia White, whose parents lived at Cliffside, the estate at 222 Warren Street, between the Schlesinger and Richardson properties. Originally built around 1844 for Samuel Perkins, the first house at 222 Warren burned in 1852 and was replaced in 1857 by the mansard-roofed residence for Nathaniel Goddard. Perkins had gained a reputation for his cultivation of fruit trees and bushes, often in competition with his brother Thomas Perkins, who lived at 450 Warren Street.[22] Francis A. White purchased the property in 1858 and lived there until his death in 1910. In 1918 John Charles and Sophia Olmsted purchased her childhood home, an equally easy walk from Fairsted, and began to work on their own landscape.[23] After John Charles's death in 1920, Philip Richardson, son of the architect, became the next owner of Cliffside and continued the tradition of horticultural enrichment of the property.

Farther down Cottage Street at number 45, a property on which the Olmsted firm worked from 1888 through 1902, lived the architect George Shepley.[24] The Olmsted office remained intimately involved with this property. In October 1902 Shepley called the Olmsted office and "begged" Arthur Shurtleff to meet with Mrs. Shepley the following Friday to discuss her garden.[25] On November 4 Shurtleff reported, "Mr. Dawson and myself worked at the Shepley estate from 7 in the morning until 5 at night, with 5 laborers from contractor Kelley," regrading the arbor terrace and steps, remodeling the garden, adding turf, and planting substantial groups of lilacs and vines. He ends by noting: "At a former meeting I told Mrs. Shepley that the probable cost of the whole day's work would not exceed $25.00. At the time I assumed mentally that we would make no professional charge for professional services."[26] Mrs. Shepley was the former Julia Richardson, the daughter of H. H. Richardson. Obviously the professional and familial relationship between the Olmsted office and the members of the former Richardson office remained strong.[27]

At the northern edge of the Fairsted neighborhood, near The Country Club, the lawyer Sherman Whipple asked the assistance of the Olmsted firm in developing a small subdivision at the end of Warren Street between Lee and Clyde streets. The scheme required the collaboration of the Town of Brookline and Moses Williams, both of whom owned land nearby. Although this area did not develop as Whipple wished and as the Olmsteds suggested, it does represent another element of the changing real estate and property ownership patterns of Brookline at this time.

Mr. and Mrs. Whipple first approached John Charles Olmsted on June 7, 1896, about developing a scheme for this fifteen-acre parcel that they were considering buying. Olmsted noted, "In the absence of nearby electric cars and of sewers and considering the heavy cost of drainage and filling, I did not advise the purchase."[28] The Whipples backed away from this project temporarily, but Mr. Whipple was considering a related scheme by January 1904 and again came to John Charles Olmsted for assistance. He recorded:

> Whipple would like me to . . . advise him what would best be done in this matter and also advise him as to planting trees that will eventually add to the attractiveness of the land for a millionaire to build a house where the little red house is and facing down the meadow towards the reservoir. He now owns the Goldsmith property and would like to get Williams to give up his old lane out to Clyde Street. Thus, Whipple would have an uninterrupted frontage of about two-thirds of a mile. He also wants the

town to sell him the tract it owns partly as a gravel pit and dump and partly for a future playground. He thinks the town should buy a large playground in the McCormack low land.[29]

The proposal suggests the degree of private and public maneuvering that was typical of Brookline real estate development and speculation in these years. There may be a note of disdain in discussing the needs of "a millionaire" who would demolish "the little red house . . . facing down the meadow towards the reservoir." The "McCormack low land" was a parcel that had been proposed for development as small lots with multiple-family housing very near the entrance to The Country Club, something that estate owners such as Whipple were attempting to thwart. This proposal related to the debate over the opening of a wide boulevard with trolley service in this section of Brookline. As John Charles Olmsted admitted in another memo one month later, the reason for a playground in this area was

> to benefit the Country Club by clearing out all the cheap houses and lots in that locality and to throw the 80-foot street near the high ground east of the playground, thus diverting any future electric car line from Boylston Street by west end of Brookline Reservoir to Newton Street away from Clyde Street, if in latter it would be decidedly objectionable to the Country Club people. I understand that representatives of the Country Club are trying to buy and get options on the various houses and small lots and wish the matter kept very quiet.[30]

A year later Whipple was still pursuing this possibility. In January 1905 Olmsted confessed that Whipple "seemed to be thoroughly imbued with a speculative spirit with regard to land in this vicinity. He said he paid 30 cents a foot for the Hamlin place on which he is living at the corner of Warren and Clyde Streets. He said he wanted us to make a subdivision plan for the land along Warren and Clyde Streets, so he could determine intelligently what trade to make with Mr. Williams."[31]

The Olmsted proposal shows the current lines of Lee and Clyde streets, between which the house lots were created, but the public playground between Clyde and Dudley streets was never developed (fig. 8.16). This more intensive development was in stark contrast to the large estate stretching from Holm Lea and the Schlesinger properties to the south up to The Country Club. Even if Whipple was trying to control or eliminate McCormack's middle- or working-class development, he was also altering the character of the estate district surrounding The Country Club. By 1916 there were forty-seven lots proposed for sale in this development, and the Clyde Street Playground was still incorporated in the scheme. This May 3, 1916, revision of a plan developed the previous October

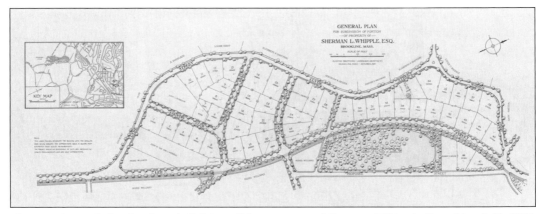

Fig. 8.16. General plan for the subdivision of the property of Sherman Whipple, Esq., March 22, 1905.
Courtesy National Park Service, Frederick Law Olmsted National Historic Site.

also shows a proposed parkway from Jamaica Pond, cutting through the southern section of Holm Lea and the rear of lots on Cottage and Warren streets, including the Schlesinger estate. Certainly this idea posed a direct threat to the district's estate owners and would have had a personal effect on Fairsted and John Charles Olmsted's own residence. Although the general street pattern of the Whipple plan was eventually accepted and implemented, neither the playground nor the parkway was ever realized.

The most dramatic change to the neighborhood around Fairsted occurred after the death of Charles Sprague Sargent in March 1927. His heirs, led by Cora Codman Ely, first approached the firm for advice in May. A May 11, 1927, telephone message recorded that Mrs. Ely wanted to know "if we have old plan of Sargent estate made when Mr. Codman member of firm. She thinks there was a plan by FLO, Sr., showing tentatively what could be done with place if they ever decided to cut it up."[32] The following day Henry Gallagher made a visit to Mrs. Ely and reported:

> As a result of a conversation with Mrs. Ely, she having called again on the telephone, I called on her with the plan made in 1894 for that section of Brookline and the 1897 town atlas which showed a proposed system of roads through the Sargent Estate. . . .
>
> She told me there has been a tremendous pressure to sell the property and she is anxious as, I understood, a trustee to sell off nothing except in accordance with some general scheme. Henry Richmond of Guy Lowell's office is now studying the problem.
>
> Mrs. Ely is the sister of Henry Sargent Codman and Phillip Codman, and she remembered that her brothers had given some study to the

question and she had therefore turned to us for whatever information we might have. She thinks that what she remembers was the plan of 1894 for the parkway scheme, but she was very much interested to see the atlas, although I could not tell her how that scheme of development came about.[33]

Four days later, while in New York en route to California, Frederick Law Olmsted Jr. sent Mrs. Ely a seven-page letter discussing the issues of subdivision of Holm Lea in great detail. Addressing her as "Dear Cora," Olmsted begins parenthetically, "(It is so long since I have written you or seen you that I instinctively use the form of address harking back to boyhood)," continuing, "I need hardly tell you that, both as a friend of the family and also as a neighbor and a member of the Planning Board of the Town, I am deeply interested in any steps that may be taken which will determine, for better or for worse, the *manner* of the (presumably inevitable) conversion of the Sargent-Codman Estate into smaller units." Remarking, "I am so much interested that I shall venture to thrust some general advice upon you," he goes on:

> Nothing has so much impressed me as the extent to which success in such enterprises—especially financial success but also general and lasting success in other respects—depend upon strongly centralized, steady general management controlling from a single point of view and along a firmly held policy every aspect of the undertaking—including beside the general physical planning, the sales policies, prices, kinds of customers, contractual terms of sales such as covenants governing use of property sold, character and costs of improvements, everything. No matter how skillful and able may be the individual advisers and helpers whom the Trustees may bring to their aid—landscape architects, architects, engineers, real estate dealers, lawyers, etc.—unless their respective points of view are welded firmly together at all stages of the undertaking by some one responsible and indefatigable head, . . . there is almost certain to be great waste of opportunity and likely to be serious waste of funds.

Olmsted bases his plea for this level of control on his "observation of the successes and failures of many real estate undertakings with which I have come in contact in the last thirty years or so."[34] Cora Ely replied to this lecture with a note inviting "Rick" to visit when he was next in Brookline so that they could renew their friendship.

The relationship between the Olmsted, Sargent, and Codman families was indeed long and deep. Charles Sprague Sargent had invited Frederick Law Olmsted Sr. to assist with the planning of the Arnold Arboretum as early as 1874. Despite an initially cool response, Olmsted embraced the project with enthusiasm from 1878 onward, just as the Boston Park Commission was also turning to him for advice. Beyond this long-term professional engagement at the arboretum, there were other family ties as well. Sargent's sister Henrietta married James McMaster Codman, and two of their sons eventually worked for the Olmsted office. Henry Sargent Codman collaborated on the plans for the Arnold Arboretum while an intern in the Olmsted office. Later made a partner in the firm, he died suddenly in January 1893, following an appendicitis operation, while supervising the landscape work for the World's Columbian Exposition in Chicago for the Olmsted office. His younger brother Philip followed him as an apprentice in the Olmsted office. The firm played only a minor role in developments within the former Sargent-Codman estate itself. In 1888 several studies were made for a new entrance drive from the bend in Warren Street to the Codman house, which is not surprising since Henry Codman would become a partner in the firm the following year. Cora Codman Ely was the sister of Henry and Philip.

Despite their close ties and the frank recommendations of Frederick Law Olmsted Jr., the trustees of the Sargent-Codman property did not turn to the Olmsted office to control the redevelopment of Holm Lea. The firm of architect and landscape architect Guy Lowell, a son-in-law of Charles Sprague Sargent, was selected instead. Nevertheless, the Olmsted firm received multiple commissions from those who bought property within the Sargent estate, as it is still called today.

Among the earliest was Sewall Cutler, the secretary of the Eastern Drug Company in Boston, who proposed to move with his sister from 310 Walnut Street into the Sargent estate. They chose the Olmsted office to design the gardens. In a note to the file, E. C. Whiting of the Olmsted office summarized the project: "The lot is about 1 acre, the house being built on the foundations of an old barn. Strickland, Blodgett & Law are architects. . . . Space is to be provided for a laundry yard, and if we can work it out, for a small vegetable and cutting garden. The main development of the scheme, however, should be a sort of lawn garden development in the old barn which is now immediately south of the house. I think it should be rather formal but no definite requirements have been laid down. Of course, we should save and utilize old walls as far as possible."[35] Within the formal garden the Olmsted office was attempting to respond to the English character of the converted barn-house. The garden shed for tools was a charming case in point (fig. 8.17). Whiting advised the client:

The tool and garden house is a queer looking thing on plan, but here also I think you would not notice the queerness when it is built. My idea was to

Fig. 8.17. Elevation drawing for garden house and tool shed, Sewall Cutler house, Sargent estate.
Courtesy National Park Service, Frederick Law Olmsted National Historic Site.

make a little octagonal shelter in the corner of the lawn garden and then to tack on a small extension to the west for tools. Perhaps this is all larger than you need and the octagonal building alone might serve your purpose. In that case I would suggest a short grape arbor where the tool house is now shown. It would give height and strength in the design and would be an interesting feature at the end of the cutting garden.[36]

While the Cutler project preserved some of the character and even the physical fabric of the Holm Lea property, other commissions were more substantial.

On the opposite side of the Sargent estate, at 40 Cottage Street, Mrs. Alan Cunningham commissioned the Olmsted firm to design a new formal garden and border screen planting east of her house in the fall of 1934. She initially approached the firm "because she liked Mrs. Ketchum's plantings and wants to see what she should do."[37] Henry Hubbard developed the design (fig. 8.18). The following June, however, a landscape architect identified as Miss Harrison called to ask whether the Olmsted firm had finished their project for the Cunningham estate as she had been commissioned to continue the work.[38] The domination of Brookline garden making by the Olmsted firm was beginning to be challenged.

Further commissions within the former Sargent estate include a project for Dr. John Bryant from 1932 to 1939 at 120 Sargent Road.[39] Bryant was the son of Dr. John Bryant Sr. and Charlotte Olmsted, daughter of Frederick Law Olmsted Sr. Married in 1878, they commissioned Richardson and Olmsted to design a summer

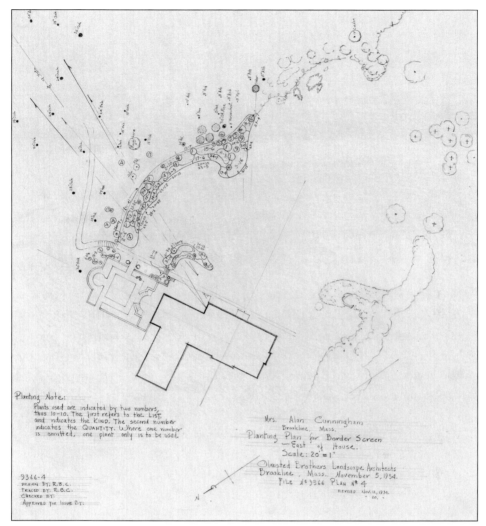

Fig. 8.18. The Alan Cunningham estate, 40 Cottage Street, showing the formal flower garden to the left of the house and the border screen planting above. Courtesy National Park Service, Frederick Law Olmsted National Historic Site.

house for them at Cohasset, Massachusetts, in 1880. John, their first son, born in 1880 at Cohasset, became a physician like his father and grandfather. He married Adelaide Whitney Barnes in 1910 and moved to this property in the former Sargent estate in 1932, inviting his grandfather's firm to design the grounds. He died on September 20, 1935, but Mrs. Bryant continued to work with the Olmsted office on the development of the property.

To summarize what this neighborhood looked like and what it represented to those who lived and worked here, we can turn to a contemporary source. F. Manton

Wakefield, a Brookline native who was trained as an architect in the office of H. H. Richardson on Cottage Street, provided a full review of the neighborhood around the Olmsted office in his essay "Suburban Homes" for *Brookline Magazine* in 1897:

> We have here many fine examples of the modern home in its larger and ampler expression, some of them on a very broad and liberal scale. It would be impossible here even to make mention of the many beautiful homes which go to make up the Brookline of today. A few notable examples, taken almost at random, must suffice.
>
> No one needs to be told of "Holm Lea," the beautiful place of 100 acres, the home of Professor Sargent, which spread out over hill and valley, meadow and woodland, in undulating freedom, composed and enriched by the most skillful art. Here, skirting the pond at the foot of one of the broad meadows, the rhododendrons annually celebrate their gorgeous festival; yet they are only part of the floral pageant. While not modern, in that it has occupied its place in local history for generations, it is very truly so in its development. The same may be said for the Gardner place, directly to the west and in its way one of the most charming. In the same region is the Schlesinger estate, also on a large scale, with its great sheltering pines bordering the valley which sweeps romantically away into the shadow.
>
> Nearby, on a rocky eminence stands the new Wright house. Nature had done so much for this beautiful place that there seems to have been nothing else than to fall in with her happy mood.
>
> Returning nearer the center of the town we find the White mansions, overlooking the old Brookline Reservoir the one of Roxbury stone in English Gothic, the other of brick. The use of the broken ledge stone, so full of life and color[,] is particularly suited to our rural work, and has been widely employed—in this instance with telling effect; while in the landscape treatment of the houses—the massing of shrubbery accentuating the open stretches of green—is obtained broad values and diversity of interest.
>
> A little further, still near the reservoir, is the Williams Place, which with its banks of flowering shrubs, the comfortable-looking house half-hidden in the trees, the whole protected by a rustic vine-clad wall, suggesting privacy and repose, we must acknowledge an expression of how charming and domestic the out-of-town home may be.[40]

Without ever mentioning Olmsted—or any architects either—Wakefield provides a thorough tour of the Fairsted neighborhood, briefly extending north across Lee Street and Boylston Street. With the exception of the earlier houses that had helped to define the character of the neighborhood—such as the Gardners' Green

Hill or the Sargents' Holm Lea—all of the other properties were ones on which the Olmsted firm was hired to develop the grounds. Wakefield emphasizes the importance of the landscapes but presents them as if they were just the natural condition of Brookline. The various generations of the Olmsted office would have been pleased to have their work thought of as so inconspicuous, so much a part of the Brookline character. They had been drawn to the physical beauty and active market of suburban Brookline and reveled in the opportunity to enrich this landscape inheritance.

Aerial photograph of Brookline, 1930. Courtesy Brookline Historical Commission.

CONCLUSION
LANDSCAPE INTO TOWNSCAPE

In the half century after his removal from Manhattan to Brookline, Frederick Law Olmsted, his family, and successor firms manipulated the landscape of suburban Brookline through privately financed commissions and public planning efforts. For "the richest town in the world," the Olmsteds provided the professional guidance that made the community the envy of and model for many other suburbs. Their new hometown became a laboratory in which they pursued ideas and practices that reflected the national changes in landscape architecture and town planning. Several broad patterns can be observed from this evolution.

Unlike the comprehensive plans that the Olmsted office created for highly regarded new towns such as Riverside, Illinois (1869), and Forest Hills Gardens, New York (1908), Brookline was a town that grew incrementally in response to new development opportunities, changing demographics, economic evolution, transportation innovations, and expanding models of governmental control. As such, it typified patterns of growth seen across much of the country. Because of the Olmsted firm's exceptionally large client base and range of projects, Brookline offers interlocking examples of both development for and resistance to suburban change. These shifts can be viewed through the limited but increasing public preparation for expansion, institutional networks that provide an armature for the private residential background of the town, and advances in circulation and transportation that could be either embraced and manipulated or repelled and diverted.

The largest change that occurred through these decades was the expansion of landscape architecture into the field of city, town, and regional planning. Just as Frederick Law Olmsted had named and defined the practice of landscape architecture from the 1850s onward, his heirs and successors were leaders in the developing academic programs in landscape design and in the related profession of town planning. In particular, Frederick Law Olmsted Jr. provided direction in the growth of this larger sphere of community planning in the opening decades of the twentieth century. The office at Fairsted served as the first training center for landscape architects, beginning with the apprenticeship of Charles Eliot in 1883. In some ways Olmsted was duplicating a tradition established by his friend and neighbor Henry Hobson Richardson, who provided training for young architects, often educated first in MIT's school of architecture, replicating somewhat the Parisian atelier where he had studied in the 1860s. For landscape architects, however, there was no formal academic education available, so the internships at Fairsted became a dress rehearsal for the ultimate founding of the first academic program in landscape architecture, at Harvard in 1900. Two members of the Olmsted office—Frederick Law Olmsted Jr. and Arthur Shurcliff—established the curriculum and shaped the future development of landscape architecture education at Harvard and nationally.

An important early component of the training was the incorporation of city planning into the curriculum. After Frederick Law Olmsted Jr. participated in the development of the McMillan Commission plan for Washington, D.C., in 1901–2, he became the principal landscape architect shaping the most visible and prominent development in city planning, generally referred to as the City Beautiful movement. He quickly realized, however, that the making of grand plans to reshape cities in a radical and aesthetic manner did not correspond to the normal character of community development, a lesson he observed growing up in Brookline, within the Olmsted office.

Olmsted served as the first president of the National Conference of City Planning in 1909 and accepted commissions to provide city planning advice to Brookline and communities across the country. When in 1916 his former student John Nolen, a graduate of the Harvard program and a recognized early practitioner of urban planning, attempted to craft a manual for this new enterprise, titled *City Planning,* he turned to Frederick Law Olmsted Jr. to write the introduction.[1] Here Olmsted defines city planning as "the attempt to exert a well-considered control on behalf of the people in a city over the development of their physical environment as a whole." He continues: "The new and significant fact on which this new term 'city planning' stands is a growing appreciation of a city's organic unity, of the interdependence of its diverse elements, and of the profound and inexorable manner in which the future of this great organic unit is controlled by the actions and omissions of today."[2]

As the planning historian Jon Peterson has noted:

In his insightful essay on the historical roots of city planning published in 1914, Frederick Law Olmsted Jr. likened the movement to a "river . . .

composed of a number of streams of varied origin and character still running side by side without quite loosing their identity, and for the most part traceable through independent courses far back to 1890." The streams to which he referred—public street planning, sewerage, water supply, parks, and civic architecture—represented "converging lines" that had come together after 1890 and especially after 1900. . . . Olmsted in effect argued that the special purpose forms of planning that predate the Progressive Era had mingled, becoming components of the new approach.[3]

These "special purpose" plans were the building blocks of the Olmsted office's work in Brookline from 1880 onward. While each project may have been considered in relation to other adjacent uses and opportunities, they represented separate streams, each with its own inherent logic. In Brookline, the Olmsted office undertook designs for private estates, residential subdivisions, institutional landscapes, transportation corridors, and public parks, generally as separate enterprises.

In his public park work Frederick Law Olmsted Sr. consistently pushed for the integration of individual units through parkway connectors and municipal systems. In Brookline he pursued these ideals in both the public domain, as seen in the Muddy River development of the Boston park system, and the private sphere, as represented by the tree-lined Beacon Street corridor. Given the careful control and substantial development of Brookline when he arrived, Olmsted never had the liberty of planning a new town comprehensively here. Rather, through residential subdivision plans such as the Fisher Hill development, he created templates that could be connected to adjacent developments. One only needs to wander down from the crown of Fisher Hill through the subdivision master plan, to adjacent individual properties the firm designed for the White families, and then past the Brookline Hills railroad station and onto the grounds of Brookline High School, all separate Olmsted firm designs, to comprehend the model of parallel rivers flowing into that organic whole later discussed by his son.

From Fairsted, Olmsted firm partner Charles Eliot added to the mix of ideas a campaign for regional planning as represented by his leadership work with the Boston Metropolitan Park Commission in the 1890s. Although there were opportunities to consider connecting Brookline to this larger regional matrix, those efforts were thwarted by the determination of Brookline at large, and especially the private property owners of the southern half of the town, to remain independent and in control of its land, destiny, and fellow citizens.

Frederick Law Olmsted Jr., Nolen, and other contemporaries saw planning in the early twentieth century as more of a process than a single product. Brookline provided the Olmsted firm a microcosm in which to observe and coordinate the larger patterns described in Olmsted's introductory essay. Yet his holistic approach to planning as process was derived from the kinds of commissions consistently sought by the Olmsted firm, especially those pursued in Brookline and beyond after its removal from New York.

As the younger Olmsted ascended to prominence in the firm, then moved beyond to a position of national leadership in the opening decade of the twentieth century, he was basing his understanding of planning in part on the experience of growing up in Brookline and in the firm. When Massachusetts passed enabling legislation, Brookline was one of the first communities to establish a town planning commission, appointing him to chair that effort. As a result, he was able to experiment in his home territory, while cities and towns from across the country sought his advice on planning issues.

Not surprisingly, Brookline embraced town planning but accepted the new efforts on the community's own terms. In 1917 a national survey of planning commissions throughout the country revealed how miserly most communities were in their support for these efforts. Brookline, by contrast, allocated $2,500 for planning, a handsome sum when seen against the $6,480 in neighboring Boston, particularly compared to national standards.[4] True to his evolving philosophy of the meaning of planning as process, Olmsted and his fellow commission members focused on principles of setback and building typology rather than advancing specific plans for new development. In many ways, Brookline by the opening decade of the twentieth century had absorbed the incremental lessons provided by various projects from the Olmsted office and now primarily needed adjustments rather than radical new development. In this respect, Brookline had proved a testing ground for the Olmsted firm's evolution in addition to advancing and refocusing its direction from the creation of discrete landscapes to the professional management of the townscape.

The Olmsted office helped Brookline to grow from a fairly homogeneous population of approximately eight thousand in 1880 to more than five times that number by the 1930s. Always fiercely aware of its identity as a place apart, Brookline was assisted by the members of the Olmsted office in maintaining its unique landscape character even as it faced the pressure of metropolitan expansion and demographic change.

The influence from those few years that Frederick Law Olmsted and Henry Hobson Richardson shared as Green Hill neighbors rippled out across the country and beyond as they established patterns of architecture and landscape design. Equally important but less well recognized was the mutual support provided by Charles Sprague Sargent and Olmsted as they attempted to improve their respective professional fields and their surrounding environment. Surely the Green Hill neighborhood in the heady days of the 1880s could not be equaled for the design professions by any other place in the country. Sargent, who had preceded Richardson and Olmsted in Brookline, upheld and consolidated the shared interests of the three men, in part because he significantly outlived them, not dying until 1927.

As Olmsted, with age and failing health, necessarily relinquished his control over the office, the Olmsted partnership, as constantly redefined over the next four decades, remained at the heart of both Brookline's and the nation's evolution. Certainly Charles Eliot's schemes for the Boston metropolitan park system, as they matured during his brief tenure at Fairsted, launched a radically new and larger framework through which to analyze growth patterns and the need for public landscape in expanding urban areas. That Brookline resisted joining those efforts does not undermine their transformative influence in the country at large.

The educational model of the Fairsted internship from which Eliot emerged was transformed after his death by his pupil Arthur Shurcliff and his mentor's namesake, Frederick Law Olmsted Jr., in the establishment of Harvard's professional program in landscape architecture. And just as his father had named and defined the profession from the 1850s onward, the son took the training at Fairsted and his experience of growing up in Brookline as a foundation for his own expansion of the profession at the beginning of the twentieth century into the domains of city and regional planning. Number 99 Warren Street was not just a family home and business address. It provided the nurturing environment and experimental laboratory that allowed Brookline to stand out as the consummate community shaped by design.

Olmsted Design Projects in Brookline

Almy, William. Job no. 07703. Plans: 1, 1909; correspondence: 1926–27.

Apthorp, H. O. Job no. 07462. Plans: none; correspondence: 1925.

Arborway-Jamaicaway-Riverway complex. Job no. 10239. Plans: none; correspondence: 1896.

Armstrong, George W. Job no. 01077. Plans: 16, 1887–1901; correspondence: 1888–1889 and 1902–3.

Aspinwall Avenue Housing Project. Job no. 10068. Plans: none; correspondence: 1894.

Aspinwall Hill (Aspinwall, Thomas). Job no. 00622. Plans: 30, 1880–81; correspondence: 1880–1886.

Baker, Edith School. Job no. 01312. Plans: 12, 1935–1942; correspondence: none.

Beacon Street Widening. Job no. 01172. Plans: 87, 1886–87; correspondence: 1884–1887.

Beamis, John W., and Wilson, W. R. Job no. 02285. Plans: 1, 1896; correspondence: 1896.

Beck, Fred. Job no. 02069. Plans: 2, 1895–1898; correspondence: 1898–99.

Beck, Frederick. Job no. 02069. Plans: none; correspondence: 1889 and 1898–1900.

Belcher, John. Job no. 01436. Plans: 4, 1895; correspondence: 1895–96.

Bennett, Louis. Job no. 07506. Plans: 18, 1925–26; correspondence: 1925–26.

Bigelow, Albert (Sewell Park). Job no. 07807. Plans: none; correspondence: 1927.

Bigelow, Prescott. Job no. 01324. Plans: 5, 1892; correspondence: 1892–1896 and 1902–1905.

Blake, A. W., cemetery. Job no. 01322. Plans: 5, 1892–1899; correspondence: 1892–93.

Blake estate. Job no. 01019. Plans: 44, 1882–1886; correspondence: 1878 and 1886–1890.

Boston and Albany Railroad. Job no. 00647. Plans: 95, 1880–1884; correspondence: 1883–1897 and 1921.

Boylston Street widening. Job no. 01301. Plans: 19, 1882–1896; correspondence: 1891–1901.

Brimmer, Martin. Job no. 12037. Plans: none; correspondence: 1882 and 1886.

Brookline Avenue Playground. Job no. 01303. Plans: 1, 1897; correspondence: 1884.

Brookline Cooperative Civic Progress Association, School Street Improvement. Job no. 09371. Plans: 1, 1935; correspondence: 1935.

Brookline Education Society. Job no. 01319. Plans: none; correspondence: 1903–1908.

Brookline High School. Job no. 01205. Plans: 120, 1894–95 and 1921–1944; correspondence: 1894–1896.

Brookline Hills R.R. Station. Job no. 12056. Plans: none; correspondence: 1884.

Brookline Land Company / Chandler, Alfred D. Job no. 01321. Plans: 3, 1894; correspondence: 1882, 1888, and 1894–95.

Brookline Parkway. Job no. 12051. Plans: none; correspondence: 1892.

Brookline Public Library. Job no. 01302. Plans: 11, 1903–4; correspondence: 1896 and 1904–1907.

Brookline Reservoir. Job no. 00105. Plans: none; correspondence: 1901–2.

Brookline School Museum Association. Job no. 02937. Plans: none; correspondence: 1904–5.

Brookline Soldiers Monument. Job no. 01309. Plans: none; correspondence: 1911–12.

Brookline streets. Job no. 12042. Plans: 1, 1894; correspondence: 1884, 1891, and 1895–96.

Brookline Town Planning Board. Job no. 01310. Plans: 3, 1915–1920; correspondence: 1894–1896 and 1913–1943.

Brookline Village Square, Brookline Village. Job no. 01304. Plans: 4, 1894–95; correspondence: 1904–5.

Brown, George R. Job no. 09397. Plans: 81, 1927–1946; correspondence: 1936–1946.

Bryant, Dr. John / Sargent estate. Job no. 09320. Plans: 15, 1932–1935 and 1939; correspondence: 1932–1939.

Cabot, Henry B. Job no. 07296. Plans: 1, 1924; correspondence: 1924.

Cabot Hill Reservoir. Job no. 03222. Plans: 41, 1906–1924; correspondence: 1906–1908 and 1916–1922.

Chandler, A. D. et al. Job no. 01074. Plans: 3, 1894; correspondence: 1887–1894.

Channing, Dr. Walter. Job no. 02230. Plans: 4, 1899; correspondence: 1891–1899.

Chestnut Hill Ave. widening. Job no. 01078. Plans: 40, 1886–1891; correspondence: 1891–92.

Chestnut Hill Parkway. Job no. 01306. Plans: 8, 1892–1902; correspondence: 1893 and 1901–1907.

Clark, Paul F. Job no. 09483. Plans: 105, 1936–1944; correspondence: 1937–1944.

Cliffside / White, Francis / Olmsted, J. C., estate. Job no. 00632. Plans: 599, 1914–1918 and 1959; correspondence: 1916–17 and 1959.

Clyde Street Playground. Job no. 01307. Plans: 1, 1903–4; correspondence: none.

Cobb, A. A. Job no. 01049. Plans: 25, 1886; correspondence: 1886.

Cobb, Clarence. Job no. 09555. Plans: 8, 1936; correspondence: 1936–1969.

Coffin, F. S. Job no. 00226. Plans: 8, 1902; correspondence: 1902–3.

Colby, Charles. Job no. 10039. Plans: 22, 1935, 1965, and 1967; correspondence: 1956 and 1966.

Coolidge, J. R., Jr. / Coolidge, J. Randolph. Job no. 00323. Plans: 63, 1885–1926; correspondence: 1886–1895, 1903, and 1911.

Corbett, F. A. Job no. 06921. Plans: none; correspondence: 1921.

Corey Hill Hospital. Job no. 02383. Plans: 7, 1902–3; correspondence: 1902–1907 and 1917.

The Country Club. Job no. 01048. Plans: 37, 1886–1946; correspondence: 1888–89 and 1937–1947.

Cousens, Dr. J. A. Job no. 07790. Plans: 8, 1912–1927; correspondence: 1927.

Curran, Joseph F. Job no. 07775. Plans: 5, 1927; correspondence: 1927.

Curtis, Mr. & Mrs. / Parsons, Ernst M. Job no. 09009. Plans: 24, 1928–29; correspondence: 1929–30 and 1936.

Cutler, Sewell / Sargent estate. Job no. 07992. Plans: 18, 1927–28; correspondence: 1928–29.

Davis, Dr. David. Job no. 09454. Plans: 3, 1936; correspondence: 1936.

Davis, Mary S. Job no. 02953. Plans: 1, 1899; correspondence: 1899.

Doliber, Thomas. Job no. 01132. Plans: 33, 1889–90; correspondence: 1890–1898.

Dorr, Henry G. Job no. 12047. Plans: none; correspondence: 1891.

Douglas, Alfred (Fernwood). Job no. 04010. Plans: 164, 1909–1934; correspondence: 1910–1914, 1922–1926, and 1937.

Duryea, Herman B. and Ellen W. Job no. 04010. Plans: 2, 1897–1899; correspondence: 1897–1899.

Eaton, Charles S. Job no. 01046. Plans: 36, 1886–87; correspondence: 1886–1903.

Elliot, G. F. Job no. 07634. Plans: 6, 1926; correspondence: 1926.

Estey, Clarence H. Job no. 02993. Plans: 2, 1904; correspondence: 1904.

Fabyan, George F. Job no. 02281. Plans: 8, 1901; correspondence: 1901–2.

Fahey, Frank J. (Fisher Hill residence). Job no. 07266. Plans: 63, 1923–1928; correspondence: 1924–1930.

Faulkner, Dr. J. M. Job no. 09151. Plans: 72, 1929–1951; correspondence: 1921–1931.

Fine, Dr. Jacob. Job no. 09388. Plans: 13, 1935–1937; correspondence: 1935–1937.

First Parish Church. Job no. 01178. Plans: 23, 1887–1938; correspondence: 1889–1894, 1900–1907, 1917, and 1936–1938.

Free Hospital for Women. Job no. 01342. Plans: 12, 1892–93; correspondence: 1893–1897.

Gardner, John L. Job no. 01044. Plans: 17, 1886–87; correspondence: 1895.

Goddard estate. Job no. 01043. Plans: none; correspondence: 1884–1894.

Goddard Land Co. / Brookline Hill. Job no. 01012. Plans: 74, 1884–1889; correspondence: 1884–1894.

Hamlen, N. P. Job no. 12067. Plans: none; correspondence: 1882, 1896, and 1899.

Hartt, Arthur W. Job no. 03796. Plans: 13, 1896–1934; correspondence: 1909–1911, 1927–1929, and 1934.

Harwood, John H. Job no. 07380. Plans: 10, 1924–1929; correspondence: 1924–1929 and 1937.

Heath Square. Job no. 01308. Plans: 4, 1910; correspondence: 1890 and 1910.

Hillfields subdivision. Job no. 07608. Plans: 119, 1926–1938; correspondence: 1926–1938.

Holdsworth, Frederick. Job no. 09026. Plans: 7, 1928–29; correspondence: 1929.

Hood, Donald / Hood, H. P. / Tripp, W. V. / Brooks estate. Job no. 09646. Plans: 23, 1927 and 1942–1946; correspondence: none.

Hood, F. C. Job no. 02276. Plans: 2, 1901; correspondence: 1901–2.

Hopkins, C. A. Job no. 01166. Plans: 15, 1906; correspondence: 1890–1893 and 1906.

Howe, Albert S. Job no. 06971. Plans: 9, 1921; correspondence: 1921–22.

Hunt, W. N. estate. Job no. 00465. Plans: none; correspondence: none.

Jacques, Herbert. Job no. 12512. Plans: 2, n.d.; correspondence: none.

Jenney, Charles S. Job no. 09490. Plans: 79, 1937–1950; correspondence: 1937–1940.

Jenney, Malcolm. Job no. 09538. Plans: 12, 1928–1939; correspondence: 1938–1940.

Kennard, Martin P. Job no. 01125. Plans: 8, 1894–95 and 1911; correspondence: 1894–95.

King, Franklin / Hillfields subdivision. Job no. 09349. Plans: 37, 1933–1934; correspondence: 1934–1937.

Kingsbury, J. F. (Kingsbury estate). Job no. 01161. Plans: 11, 1889–90; correspondence: 1890–1898.

Lapham, Henry G. / Louis Cabot Place. Job no. 06435. Plans: 110, 1916–17; correspondence: 1916–1921.

Lee, George. Job no. 00270. Plans: 8, 1899–1900; correspondence: 1899–1900.

Linden Park. Job no. 10199. Plans: 29, 1893 and 1965–1967; correspondence: none.

Livermore-Nickerson estate / Nickerson-Livermore / Livermore-Nickerson estate. Job no. 01806. Plans: 9, 1895; correspondence: 1892–1896.

Longwood Playground. Job no. 00924. Plans: none; correspondence: 1893 and 1895.

Longwood R.R. Station. Job no. 12046. Plans: none; correspondence: 1890–91.

Lord, H. C. Job no. 06195. Plans: none; correspondence: 1915.

Loring, Atherton. Job no. 05496. Plans: 70, 1912–1930; correspondence: 1912–1916, 1921–1923, and 1928–1935.

Maddock, A. F. Job no. 02885. Plans: none; correspondence: 1904.

Mailman, Charles. Job no. 07096. Plans: 9, 1922; correspondence: 1922.

McKittrick, Dr. Leland S. Job no. 09778. Plans: 7, 1931, 1947, and 1952; correspondence: none.

Mitton, George W. Job no. 07820. Plans: 42, 1926–1929; correspondence: 1927–28.

Morss, Charles A. Job no. 03215. Plans: 12, 1907–1926; correspondence: 1907 and 1920.

Nash, E. R. Job no. 07358. Plans: 14, 1913–1925; correspondence: 1924–1929.

Nelson, Arthur T. Job no. 09776. Plans: 77, 1925 and 1947; correspondence: none.

Oakes, F. J., Jr. (Schlesinger estate). Job no. 06625. Plans: 30, 1918–1946; correspondence: 1918–1922.

Olmsted, F. L. (99 Warren Street). Job no. 00673. Plans: 160, 1880–1968; correspondence: 1883–1899, 1904–1907, and 1918–1950.

Olmsted, F. L., miscellaneous / Olmsted, Frederick Law, Jr. Job no. 02919. Plans: 14, 1911–1928; correspondence: 1896–1952.

Olmsted, John C. Job no. 01030. Plans: none; correspondence: 1899 and 1926.

Paine, Frederick W. Job no. 01363. Plans: 3, 1895 and 1926; correspondence: 1895–1898 and 1926.

Paine, L. C. Job no. 01364. Plans: 1, 1893; correspondence: 1893.

Paine, R. T. Job no. 03341. Plans: 7, 1893–1907; correspondence: 1907 and 1917.

Park School. Job no. 09197. Plans: 2, 1884 and 1930; correspondence: 1930.

Parks, F. R. Job no. 05659. Plans: 5, 1903–1913; correspondence: 1912–13.

Pierce, J. W. / Goddard estate. Job no. 06057. Plans: 6, 1884–1914; correspondence: 1914.

Prouty, Lewis I. Job no. 05889. Plans: 136, 1913–1936 and 1950; correspondence: 1912–13 and 1927–1943.

Prouty-Oakes burial lots. Job no. 09513. Plans: 12, 1937–1950; correspondence: 1937–1974.

Reservoir Lane lands. Job no. 01057. Plans: 10, 1888–89; correspondence: 1901–1905.

Reuter, Henry H. Job no. 01230. Plans: 4, 1891–1894; correspondence: 1893–94.

Rice, Dana Hall. Job no. 03556. Plans: none; correspondence: 1908.

Richardson, G. K. Job no. 10180. Plans: none; correspondence: 1893.

Rogers, A. M. / Rogers, A. H. Job no. 05514. Plans: 3, 1912; correspondence: 1912.

Rogers, Mr. & Mrs. E. W. Job no. 10398. Plans: 1, 1972; correspondence: 1892–1895 and 1972.

Ruhl, Edward / Curtis, Mrs. R. W. Job no. 06280. Plans: 3, 1905; correspondence: 1915–16.

Rutan, Charles H. Job no. 03044. Plans: 1, 1905; correspondence: 1905–1908.

St. Paul's Church. Job no. 00687. Plans: 19, 1885; correspondence: 1898–1903.

Samson, E. J. Job no. 07901. Plans: 10, 1928–29; correspondence: 1929.

Sanger, Sabin B. Job no. 06264. Plans: 2, 1915; correspondence: 1915–1917.

Sargent, Adelaide. Job no. 09508. Plans: 3, 1937; correspondence: 1937–38.

Sargent estate. Job no. 01056. Plans: 20, 1885–1893; correspondence: 1927.

Schlesinger, Barthold. Job no. 00614. Plans: 116, 1880–81; correspondence: 1879–1890.

Shaw, Francis G., Jr. Job no. 09584. Plans: 10, 1939–1962; correspondence: 1930–1971.

Shepard, John III. Job no. 09845. Plans: 14, 1928, 1929, 1948, and 1949; correspondence: 1929–1950.

Shepley, George. Job no. 01055. Plans: 11, 1888–1902; correspondence: 1888–89 and 1937–1947.

Sloane, Dr. & Mrs. Robert / Rangeley Road. Job no. 10324. Plans: none; correspondence: 1893–94.

Snow, William B. Job no. 07899. Plans: 8, 1927–28; correspondence: 1927–1929.

Sprague, C. F. Job no. 00299. Plans: 19, 1886–1895; correspondence: 1893–1895.

Stokes, A. P. / Philbrick estate. Job no. 01145. Plans: 30, 1956–57; correspondence: 1889 and 1956–1960.

Stone, Galen L. Job no. 03675. Plans: 14, 1909–10; correspondence: 1909–1912.

Stone, Galen L., subdivision. Job no. 07310. Plans: 2, 1924; correspondence: 1924–25 and 1931.

Stone, Robert G. Job no. 09053. Plans: 13, 1929–1931; correspondence: 1929–1931.

Storrow, Charles. Job no. 00629. Plans: 36, 1882; 1886; correspondence: 1882–1884 and 1917.

Stuart, Dr. Harold. Job no. 07421. Plans: 7, 1925; correspondence: 1925.

Sullivan, Mrs. John B., Jr. Job no. 09388. Plans: 21, 1926 and 1935–1939; correspondence: 1935–1938.

Tavern Club. Job no. 02981. Plans: none; correspondence: 1904.

Thompson, R. E. Job no. 07719. Plans: 72, 1923–1929; correspondence: 1928–1931.

Town of Brookline. Job no. 01300. Plans: 53, 1884–1922; correspondence: 1888–1920.

Tripp, W. V. Job no. 09380. Plans: 20, 1932–1935; correspondence: 1935.

Tripp, W. V. Job no. 09645. Plans: 1, 1937; correspondence: none.

Wardwell, Mrs. Sheldon E. Job no. 10193. Plans: none; correspondence: 1893.

Washburn / Taylor estate. Job no. 00460. Plans: none; correspondence: 1902.

Watts, John R. Job no. 06686. Plans: 3, 1920–21; correspondence: 1919–1922.

Welch, Francis W. Job no. 02237. Plans: 1, 1900; correspondence: none.

Whipple, Sherman L. Job no. 02881. Plans: 15, 1902–1919; correspondence: 1894–1896 and 1904–1921.

Whitcomb, Arthur. Job no. 07291. Plans: none; correspondence: 1924.

White, John H. Job no. 01079. Plans: 42, 1887–88; correspondence: 1887–1895.

White, Jonathan. Job no. 00463. Plans: none; correspondence: 1883 and 1895.

White, Joseph H. / Stone, Galen L. Job no. 06626. Plans: 122, 1880–81; correspondence: 1880–1886.

White, Webb B. (Hillfields). Job no. 07811. Plans: 22, 1927–1941; correspondence: 1927.

Whitney, Henry M. Job no. 12167. Plans: none; correspondence: 1890–1898.

Wightman, George H. Job no. 00223. Plans: 15, 1901–2 and 1921; correspondence: 1901–1911 and 1921–22.

Wightman, George H. Job no. 04019. Plans: 7, 1907–1911; correspondence: 1910–11.

Willetts, George F. / Willetts, George F. Job no. 02392. Plans: 1, 1903; correspondence: 1904–1907.

Williams, Moses. Job no. 00464. Plans: 38, 1875–1886; correspondence: 1886–1890.

Williams, Moses. Job no. 01023. Plans: none; correspondence: 1888.

Wilson, W. R. / Beamis, John. Job no. 01438. Plans: 5, 1898; correspondence: 1896–1898.

Worthley, George H. Job no. 00457. Plans: none; correspondence: 1901.

Wright, Dr. George. Job no. 07651. Plans: 14, 1926–1931; correspondence: 1926 and 1931–1934.

Wright, Dr. George H. / Faulkner / Wright, George. Job no. 09068. Plans: 1, 1929; correspondence: 1929.

Wright, Mr. J. G. Job no. 00224. Plans: 19, 1895–1909; correspondence: 1895–1909.

APPENDIX B

Architects and Landscape Architects in Brookline

Structures are extant except where noted.

Andrews, Robert D. 50 Fisher Ave., 1906–1928.

Bowditch, Arthur H. 12 Maple St., 1893–1941.

Bowditch, Ernest. Tappan St. (father's house; not extant), late 1870s, early 1880s.

Cabot, Edward C. 232 High St. (not extant), 1857–1901.

Coolidge, J. Randolph, Jr. 1014 Boylston St. (not extant), 1895–96; 24 Cottage Farm Rd, 1905–1909; Warren St. nr. Cottage St. (exact location unknown), 1910–1919.

Dabney, William H. 153 Dean Rd., 1894–1897.

Eliot, Charles. Western end of Warren St. (not extant), 1895–1897.

Frazer, Horace S. 471 Heath St., 1890–1931.

Jaques, Herbert 50 Dunster Rd. (not extant), 1887–1916.

Kilham, Walter H. 2 or 12 Monmouth Court, 1899–1908; 33 Edgehill Rd., 1909–1922.

Law, Alexander. 99 Fairmount St., 1923–1941[+?].

Little, J. Lovell. 75 Goddard Ave., 1900–1927.

Lowell, Guy. 20 Chestnut Place (not extant), 1901–1927.

Manning, Warren. Fairmount St. nr. Dudley St. (exact location unknown), 1889–1898; Richmond Court., Beacon St., 1899–1902; 15 Dwight St., 1903–1905; 29 Colbourne Crescent, 1908–1916.

Olmsted, Frederick. 99 Warren St., 1895–1949.

Olmsted, John C. 16 Warren St., 1899–1920; 222 Warren St., 1918–1920.

Peabody, Robert S. 50 Edgehill Rd., 1876–1900.

Richardson, H. H. 25 Cottage St., 1874–1886.

Richardson, Philip. 11 Welch Rd., 1916–1919.

Rotch, Arthur. 70 Hyslop Rd., 1888–1894.

Rutan, Charles H. 109–111 Davis Ave., 1889–1914.

Shepley, George. 45 Cottage St. (not extant), 1889–1903.

Stearns, John G., Jr. 24 Pleasant St. (not extant), 1868–1917.

Strickland, Sidney. 43 Hedge Rd., 1916–1921; 170 Dudley St., 1921–1933.

Wakefield, F. Manton. 99 High St., 1902–1905; 31 Allerton St., 1906; 36 High St., 1907–1913.

Statement as to Professional Methods and Charges, 1902

John Charles Olmsted.   **Fredrick Law Olmsted Jr.**

OLMSTED BROTHERS,

LANDSCAPE ARCHITECTS
———————

BROOKLINE, MASS.

STATEMENT AS TO PROFESSIONAL METHODS AND CHARGES.

———————

Our business is the supplying of professional advice with respect to the arrangement of land for use, and the accompanying landscape for enjoyment. We design or revise the arrangement of private grounds and gardens, public parks and squares, suburban neighborhoods, town sites, streets, and parkways. We consult with owners, architects, engineers, and gardeners concerning the placing of buildings, the laying out of roads, the grading of surfaces, and the treatment of new or old plantations. In general we advise as to the arrangement of land and the objects upon it for any purpose whatsoever where the appearance of the result is worth consideration.

PRELIMINARY VISIT.

The first step in our employment is a preliminary visit to the ground and a consultation with the client. This visit binds neither party to any further dealings with the other. Verbal suggestions of considerable value can often be made on the spot; while if plans, designs, or written reports are called for, the preliminary visit enables us to acquire much of the general information upon which these can be based. When it appears that a topographical map is needed for the proper study of the problem, instructions as to the making of the survey are prepared by us without extra charge. We ourselves are not surveyors. If the client knows in advance that he desires from us a design drawn to a scale, the necessary surveyors map should be made ready for our use on the occasion of our first visit.

PRELIMINARY AND GENERAL PLANS.

Upon the basis of the topographical map we design a preliminary plan embodying the ideas suggested at the preliminary visit, with such other ideas as closer study or additional visits may have evolved. The preliminary plan is intended to be examined, criticized, and discussed, in order that a better solution of the given problem may, if possible, be reached. If changes prove to be desirable, a revised preliminary plan is prepared. In case the problem is concerned with any buildings, our preliminary plan should be made in advance of the building plans, and our subsequent drawings should include the results of consultations with the architect of the buildings.

After the principal suggestions of our preliminary plan have been approved, the next step is the making of a general plan showing the outlines of the visible constructions, the controlling figures of elevation, the general disposition of plantations, and the more important modifications of existing wood or ground cover. The general plan is accompanied in important cases by an explanatory report, describing its principal points and setting forth the essential elements of the design which might not otherwise be fully recognized. In many cases the preliminary plan, or a revision of it, serves as a general plan. The general plan can be carried out by any one possessed of suitable technical training, but its designed results in detail are rarely to be attained without occasional visits and more or less other assistance from the designers.

WORKING DRAWINGS AND SUPERVISION.

Some of our clients commit the interpretation and execution of our general plans to their own superintendents, engineers, or gardeners. On the other hand, we are always prepared to make detailed or working drawings, to write specifications, and to supervise days' work or contract work, if we are desired to do so. Such working drawings show the positions, shapes, and sizes of every important construction, and the designed modeling of earthwork. The specifications describe whatever cannot be readily shown upon the drawings, and indicate the quality of materials and the kind of workmanship required. When all is ready, we attend to the procuring of bids from reliable contractors. We do not undertake the business management of work as contractors, nor do we act as surveyors or engineers. In supervising work done, either by contract or by the day, our practice precisely corresponds to that of architects.* We assume no pecuniary responsibility for the qualities and quantities of material used, or for workmanship. Our visits are made primarily with reference to matters of design, and are necessarily only occasional; but we act as a check on the contractor, and he is entitled to the payment of no bills until the claims made in them have been examined and approved by us. Large undertakings should have the constant supervision of a competent resident superintendent.

PLANTING PLANS AND SUPERVISION.

Precisely as we are always ready to supervise the execution of such parts of our general plans as call for grading, road building, or other earthwork, so we are always ready to advise our clients concerning the execution of that part of our plans which calls for changes in existing vegetation, whether such changes are to be effected by the use of the axe or by planting. When asked to do so, we make planting plans in all necessary detail, and when our plans are approved, it is our custom to order for our clients the required trees, shrubs, and herbaceous plants. We are systematically at much pains to ascertain where all classes of plants needed for the carrying out of planting plans can be obtained to the best advantage, and as our orders are often large, we are able to secure plants at the lowest wholesale rates, of which our clients get the advantage. We are not gardeners, nor are we dealers in plants, and we take no commissions on purchases. We are not responsible for errors of nurserymen, or for the miscarriage or damage of plants in transportation, or for their failure to grow. We are advisors and designers only; but as such, we are accustomed to direct such gardeners or contractors as may be employed as to the proper interpretation to be put upon our plans, and the best methods to be employed in their execution, exactly as architects do in the case of buildings.

With whatever care plantations may be designed and executed, they need to be intelligently thinned and

---

Extract from the "Schedule of Minimum Charges" of the American Institute of Architects: —

"The supervision or superintendence of an architect (as distinguished from the continuous personal superintendence which may be secured by the employment of a clerk of the works), means such inspection by the architect, or his deputy, of a building or other work in process of erection, completion or alteration, as he finds necessary to ascertain whether it is being executed in conformity with his designs and specifications or directions, and to enable him to decide when the successive instalments or payments provided for the contract or agreement are due or payable. He is to determine in constructive emergencies, to order necessary changes, and to define the true intent and meaning of the drawings and specifications, and he has authority to stop the progress of the work and order its removal when not in accordance with them."

otherwise revised every year, and we are always glad to advise our clients year after year in this important matter and to send our trained assistants to attend to the details of such work.

CHARGES.

For a Preliminary Visit our fee (which may, if desired, be agreed upon in advance) is ordinarily $100.00, but it varies from $50.00 to $500.00, depending upon the importance and difficulty of the problem put before us, and upon whether it is or is not expected that we should report in writing. The traveling and subsistence expenses of ourselves and our assistants are always to be refunded to us by our clients; but when visits are made to several places in the course of a tour, these expenses are divided.

If Preliminary and General Plans are desired, our charge is generally made up of a professional fee (often agreed upon in advance, and varying from $50.00 for a small building lot to some thousands of dollars for a large public park), plus expenses.

Expenses as used in this circular include all special disbursements by us required in connection with the clients' work, such as traveling expenses, telegrams, expressage, sunprints, photographs, and the like, and also the cost of elaborating and draughting all plans made in our office, collecting needed information not furnished by the surveyor's maps, estimating, selecting, and ordering plants, visiting the work or nurseries, and in general the cost of all we may have done for the client by means of our assistants, as distinguished from our own personal services, for which we are paid by the professional fee. As about half of the expenses in connection with our assistants' services are of a general nature difficult to subdivide precisely among our several clients without an extravagantly elaborate system of bookkeeping, our method is to charge double the actual amounts paid to assistants for the hours when they are engaged exclusively upon the work of each client.

Our plans are based on topographical maps and other needed information furnished us free of expense; and they are made in the form of tracings, which remain in our possession, and from which we obtain, by sunprinting, as many copies as may be needed by our clients and the engineers, architects, contractors, foresters, or gardeners, who may be concerned.

For Grading and Construction Plans, specifications, and supervision of construction, we charge a professional fee for our personal attention to designing and supervision, plus expenses.

Similarly for Planting Plans, estimating and ordering plants and supervision of planting, we charge a professional fee, plus expenses.

For subsequent supervision of planting we charge a comparatively small annual professional fee, plus expenses.

We are always ready to stop with either the Preliminary Visit, the Preliminary and General Plans, the Grading and Construction Plans, or the Planting Plans, and we do not usually proceed to any subsequent stage until we are authorized to do so.

BROOKLINE, MASS., JANUARY 1st, 1902.

Collaborative Projects of H. H. Richardson and F. L. Olmsted Sr.

For further information about these commissions, listed here alphabetically, consult Jeffery Karl Ochsner, *H. H. Richardson: Complete Architectural Works* (Cambridge: MIT Press, 1982); and Lucy Lawliss, Caroline Loughlin, and Lauren Meier, eds., *The Master List of Design Projects of the Olmsted Firm, 1857–1979*, 2nd ed. (Washington, D.C.: National Association for Olmsted Parks and National Park Service, Frederick Law Olmsted National Historic Site, 2008). The date following the building name or location of the commission is the construction date for the building or structure. The plans and correspondence dates refer to material in the Olmsted Associates Papers or Frederick Law Olmsted Papers, Manuscript Division, Library of Congress. Unless otherwise noted, all sites are in Massachusetts.

Ames family commissions, Olmsted job no. 00649, 7 plans (1881–1884); correspondence 1881–1887, 1902–3, 1977:

F. L. Ames Gate Lodge, North Easton, 1880–81
F. L. Ames Ice House project, North Easton, ca. 1880–81
Oakes Ames Memorial Town Hall, North Easton, 1879–1881
Oliver Ames Free Library, North Easton, 1877–1879

Alexander Dallas Bache Monument, Congressional Cemetery, Washington, D.C., 1867; no Olmsted job no.

Boston & Albany Railroad stations, Olmsted job no. 00647, 95 plans (1880–1884); correspondence 1883–1897, 1921:

Auburndale (1881; demolished 1960s)
Chestnut Hill (1883–84; demolished 1960)
Palmer (1881–1885)

Boston Park Commission, Muddy River Improvement, Olmsted job no. 00927; 171 plans (1882–1893); correspondence 1882–1899, 1907, 1970–1980:

Back Bay Fens bridges: Charlesgate West, 1880–1883; demolished 1965; Boylston Street, 1880–1884
Stony Brook Gate House, Back Bay Fens, 1880–1882

Dr. John Bryant House, Cohasset, Mass., 1880–81; Olmsted job no. 12187; 0 plans; correspondence 1880–1882, 1894.

Buffalo Park Commission, Buffalo, New York, Olmsted job no. 00700:

Civil War Memorial project, Buffalo, 1874–1876

Buffalo State Hospital, Buffalo, New York, 1869–1880 (1895); Olmsted job no. 12035; 0 plans; correspondence, 1876–77

Converse Memorial Public Library, Malden, 1883–1885; Olmsted job no. 00292, 5 plans (1885); correspondence 1884–85.

Crane Memorial Public Library, Quincy, 1880–1882; Olmsted job no. 00624; 22 plans (1881–1913); correspondence 1881–82, 1891, 1913–1918, 1923, 1977.

William E. Dorsheimer House, Buffalo, New York, 1868–1871; no Olmsted job no.; Olmsted simply provided an introduction to the client.

New York State Capitol, Albany, New York, 1867–1899. Olmsted job no. 00608; 35 plans (1875–1878); correspondence 1864, 1877–1899.

Old Colony Railroad Station, North Easton, 1881–1884. Olmsted job no. 00670; 3 plans (1883); correspondence 1883.

Robert Treat Paine House, Waltham, 1883–1886. Olmsted job no. 00677; 13 plans (1884–85); correspondence 1884–1887, 1892–1898, 1975–1980.

Collaborative Commissions of the Olmsted Office in Brookline

The Olmsted job number is listed in parentheses.

COLLABORATIVE COMMISSIONS WITH SHEPLEY, RUTAN & COOLIDGE

1887, 1892, 1900
George Armstrong, 1405 Beacon St. (01077)

1888
Boston & Albany R.R., Reservoir Station (00647)

1889
Charles Rutan, 111 Davis Street (03044)

1892
Boston & Albany R.R., Brookline Hills (00647)

1892, 1897
Boston Park Commission, Riverway (00930)

1893, 1901
First Parish Church, 382 Walnut St. (01178)

1894
Boston & Albany R.R., Longwood (00647)
Joseph H. White, 104 Buckminster Rd. (06626)

1899
Arthur Blake, 450 Washington St. (01019)

1901
George Wightman, 43 Hawes St. (00223)

1905, 1917
George Wightman, 26 Monmouth St. (00223)

1916

Mrs. R. L. Pope, 16 Monmouth St. (04019)

COLLABORATIVE COMMISSIONS WITH PEABODY & STEARNS

1880

Joseph H. White, 535 Boylston St. and 62 Buckminster Rd. (01079)

1885

Moses Williams, 30 Hedge Rd. (00464)

COLLABORATIVE COMMISSIONS WITH ANDREWS, JAQUES & RANTOUL

1892, 1916

Herbert Jaques, 50 Dunster Rd. (12512)

1893, 1899, 1905

Robert Treat Paine II, 325 Heath St. (03341)

1894, 1915, 1916–17

Brookline High School, Greenough St. (01205)

1900, 1902, 1915, 1916

The Country Club, off Clyde St. (01048)

Brookline Projects of Shepley, Rutan & Coolidge

Structures are extant except where noted.

ca. 1885
Rutan, Charles F., 31–33 Elm St. Double house.
Rutan, Charles F., 35–37 Elm St. Double house.

1887
Armstrong, George W., 1405 Beacon St. House and carriage barn (demolished).
White, Jonathan H., 531 Boylston Street.

1888
Boston & Albany R.R., Reservoir station (demolished).
Seamans, James M., 256 Washington St. Commercial block.

1889
Rutan, Charles F., 111 Davis Ave. House.

1890
Williams, Samuel, 48 Park St. Barn (demolished).

1891
Wason, Mary J., 1394–1408 Beacon St. Block of nine houses (partially demolished).

1892
Boston & Albany R.R., Brookline Hills station (demolished).
Boston Park Commission, Riverway Park Bridge.
Goddard, George A., 26 Brington Rd. House.
Goddard, George A., 41 Brington Rd. House.
Goddard, George A., 42 Brington Rd. House.
Goddard, George A., 53 Brington Rd. House.
Goddard, George A., 64 Brington Rd. House.
Rutan, Charles F., 111 Davis Ave. Carriage barn.
Perkins, Charles F., 73 Seaver St. House.

1893

Brookline Artificial Ice Co. Unknown ice house (demolished).

First Parish Church, 382 Walnut St. Church.

Harvard Congregational Society, 210 Harvard St. Chapel.

Williams, Samuel, 46 Park St. House and stable alterations (demolished).

1894

Boston & Albany R.R., Longwood station (demolished).

Brookline Park Commission. Service yard building (demolished).

White, Joseph H., 104 Buckminster Rd. Gardener's cottage.

White, Joseph H., 80 Seaver St. House (for Batchelder).

1897

Brookline Park Commission. Riverway Park bridge.

1899

Blake, Arthur W., 450 Washington St. House alterations (demolished).

Leyden Congregational Church, 1835 Beacon St. Chapel.

1900

Armstrong, George W., 1405 Beacon St. House additions (demolished).

1901

Town of Brookline, Newton St. Contagious Hospital (demolished).

First Parish Church, 382 Walnut St. Church additions.

Wightman, George H., 43 Hawes St. House.

Seamans, James M., 256 Washington St.

1905

Bremer, Theodore G., 42 Fisher Ave. House.

Leyden Cong. Church, 1835 Beacon St. Church.

Wightman, George H., 26 Monmouth St. House (for Reynolds).

1908

Williams, Samuel, 46 Park St. Stable alterations (demolished).

1910

Wightman, George H., 16 Monmouth St. House (for Pope).

1913

Bremer, Theodore G., 42 Fisher Ave. Garage.

Leyden Congregational Church, 1835 Beacon St. Chapel alterations.

1916

Pope, Mrs. R. L., 16 Monmouth St. Piazza enclosure.

1917

Wightman, George H., 26 Monmouth St. House alterations.

Brookline Projects of Peabody & Stearns

Structures are extant except where noted. AABN = American Architect and Building News.

1871
Wells, J., 98 Colchester St. (demolished). Source: *AABN.*

1872
Rooney, J., 7 Kent St.(?). Source: Plans.

1874
Town of Brookline, Francis St. (demolished). Source: Town reports, plans.
Stearns, John G., Jr., 24 Pleasant St. (demolished). Source: Tax lists.

1875
Curtis, Charles, 100 Longwood Ave. (demolished). Source: Plans.
Town of Brookline, Fisher Ave. Source: Town reports.

1876
Quinlin, M. W., Hight St. (demolished). Source: Plans.
Peabody, R. S., 50 Edgehill Rd. Source: Newspaper.

1877
Storey, Moorfield, 44 Edgehill Rd. Source: Plans.
Wiggins, G. W., Unknown. Source: Plans.
Stearns, Charles H., 265 Harvard St. (demolished). Source: Plans.

1879
Town of Brookline, Cypress St. (demolished). Source: Town reports, plans.

1880
St. Mary's Church, 3 Linden Place. Source: Plans, newspaper.
White, Joseph H., 535 Boylston St. Source: Plans, newspaper.
St. Paul's Church, 104 Aspinwall Ave. Source: Church records.

1881
Town of Brookline, Boylston St. (demolished). Source: Town reports, plans.

1882

Town of Brookline, Boylston St. (demolished). Source: Town reports.

1883

Mills, Arthur, 22 Irving St. Source: Plans.
Town of Brookline, Walter St. (demolished). Source: Town reports.

1884

Rooney, J., 7 Kent St.(?). Source: Plans.
Town of Brookline, School St. (demolished). Source: Town reports, plans.

1885

St. Paul's Church, 130 Aspinwall Ave. Source: Newspaper.
Williams, Moses B., 30 Hedge Rd. Source: Plans.
Grant, Stephen M., 135 St. Paul St. Source: Plans.
Town of Brookline, Francis St. (demolished). Source: Town reports, plans.

1886

Town of Brookline, 599 Brookline Ave. Source: Town reports, plans.
Town of Brookline, Marion St. (demolished). Source: Town reports, plans.
Town of Brookline, 86 Monmouth St. Source: Town reports, newspaper.
Town of Brookline, Walter St. (demolished). Source: Town reports.
Stearns, Chas. and William, 101–105 Longwood Ave. Source: Plans.

1888

Town of Brookline, Wasington St. (demolished). Source: Town reports, plans.
Town of Brookline, Holden St (demolished). Source: Town reports, plans.
J. H. White, 62 Buckminster Rd. Source: Plans.
Kay, J. Murray, Gardner Rd. (demolished). Source: Plans, newspaper.
Davis, L. Shannon, 36 Sumner Rd. Source: Plans.

1889

Cross, Charles R., 100 Upland Rd. Source: Plans.
Lamb, Henry, High St.(?) (not built?). Source: Permits.

1890

Lamb, Henry, Cumberland Ave. (demolished). Source: Permits, plans, newspaper.

1891

Brookline Gas & Light Co., Brookline Ave. (demolished). Source: Permits.
Stearns, James P., Pleasant St. (demolished). Permits.
Cummings, Prentis, Gardner Rd. (demolished). Source: Permits.
Peabody, R. S., 50 Edgehill Rd. Source: Drawings.

1892

Edwards, Misses, Longwood Ave. (demolished). Source: Permits.

1893

Foster, C. H., 78 Upland Rd. Source: Permits.
Dexter, George, 5 Maple St. Source: Permits, drawings.
Page, George and Mary, 17 Hawthorn Rd. Source: Permits.
Page, George and Mary, 21 Hawthorn Rd. Source: Permits.

1894

French, Alexis, Washington St. (demolished). Source: Permits.

1895

Stearns, Miss Elizabeth, John St. (demolished). Source: Permits.

1898

Town of Brookline, 237 Cypress St. (demolished). Source: Permits, plans.
Stearns, James and John, 10 Pleasant St. (demolished). Source: Permits, plans.
Stearns, James and John, 14 Pleasant St. (demolished). Source: Permits, plans.
Stearns, William B., 43 Pleasant St. (demolished). Source: Permits, plans.

1899

Davis, L. Shannon, 36 Sumner Rd. Source: Permits.
Town of Brookline, Cypress St. (demolished). Source: Permits, drawings.
Hunt, W. D., 58–60 Hedge Rd. Source: Permits.

1900

Davis, L. Shannon, 36 Sumner Rd. Source: Permits.
Boit, R. A., 19 Colchester Rd. (demolished). Source: Permits.
Quinlin, M. W., Hight St. (demolished). Source: Permits.

1901

Town of Brookline, Druce Rd. (demolished). Source: Permits.
Stearns, J. P., 31 Pleasant St. (demolished). Source: Permits.

1902

Brookline National Bank, 1, 3, 5 Harvard St. Source: Permits, plans.
Howe, Henry St., 165 Ivy St. (demolished). Source: Permits, plans, *AABN*.
Rogers, Robert and Agnes, 35 Gardner Rd. Source: Permits, plans.
Town of Brookline, Eliot St. (demolished). Source: Town reports, plans.

1903

Boit, R. A., 29 Colchester Rd. Source: Permits.

1906

Boit, R. A., 19 Colchester Rd. Source: Permits, drawings.

1909

Hunt, W. D., 30 Warren St. Source: Permits, drawings.

1911

Hunt, W. D., 30 Warren St. Source: Permits, drawings.
Boston Elevated R.R. Co., 19 Webster St. Source: Permits.

1915

Cooper, Almon F., Marion St. (demolished). Source: Permits.

1917

Quinlin, M. W., 27–29 Boylston St. (not built?). Source: Permits.

The Brookline Commissions of Andrews, Jaques & Rantoul

Structures are extant except where noted.

1887
Jaques, Herbert, 50 Dunster Rd. (demolished). Source: Newspaper.

1889
Cox, William E., 70 Woodland Rd. Source: Permits.
Cox, William E. (farm barn,) Woodland Rd. Source: Permits.
Cox, William E., 400 Heath St. Source: Permits.
Cox, William E. (stable), 319 Heath St. Source: Tax lists.

1890
Town of Brookline. Fire station. Boylston St. (demolished). Source: Permits.
Chapman, Mary, 52 Upland Rd. Source: Permits.
Head, Lydia C., 56 Upland Rd. Source: Permits.
Barry, Michael, 1244 Boylston St. (demolished). Source: Permits.

1891
Cox, William E., 39 Heath St. Source: Permits.
Cushing, Livingston, 63 Perry St. Source: Permits.
Cushing, Livingston, 66 Toxteth St. Source: Permits.

1892
Jaques, Herbert (stable), 50 Dunster Rd. Source: Permits.
Thomas Estate, 63 Francis St. Source: Permits.
Thomas Estate, 67 Francis St. Source: Permits.
Thomas Estate, 71 Francis St. Source: Permits.
Woodworth, Herbert G., 101 Ivy St. Source: Permits.
Raymond, Henry, 133 Salisbury Rd. Source: Permits.

1893
Cushing, Livingston (club house), 49 Francis St. Source: Permits.
Paine, Robert Treat, 325 Heath St. Source: Permits.
Robert, Henry E. (stable), 133 Salisbury Rd. Source: Permits.

1894

Town of Brookline (high school), Greenough St. (demolished). Source: Permits.

1896

Cushing, Livingston (club house addition), 49 Francis St. (demolished) Source: Permits.

1898

Miller, Charles, 30 Norfolk Rd. Source: Permits.

1899

Dodge, Edward W., 26 Circuit Rd. Source: Permits.
Paine, Robert Treat (stable), 325 Heath St. (demolished). Source: Permits.

1900

Miller, Charles, 30 Norfolk Rd. Source: Permits.
The Country Club (addition), 191 Clyde St. (extant?) Source: Permits.

1902

The Country Club (stable), 191 Clyde St. (extant?). Source: Permits.

1903

Paine, Robert Treat (addition) 325 Heath St. Source: Permits.

1905

The Chestnut Hill Riding Club (school and stable) (demolished). Source: Permits.
Dane, E. B. (auto stable), 312 Heath St. Source: Permits.
Dane, E. B. (addition), 400 Heath St. Source: Permits.
Paine, Robert Treat (house addition), 325 Heath St. Source: Permits.

1906

Dane, E. B. (house alteration), 400 Heath St. Source: Permits.
Dana, E. S., 42 Beech Rd. Source: Permits.
Dane, E. B. (servants' house), 308 Heath St. Source: Permits.

1907

Dane, E. B. (cow barn), off Woodland Rd. Source: Permits.

1908

Dane, E. B. (greenhouse), off Woodland Rd. (demolished). Source: Permits.

1909

Dane, E. B. (Music room addition), 400 Heath St. Source: Permits.

1910

Sagendorph, George A., 107 Crafts Rd. Source: Permits.

1912

Johnson, Franklin R., 64 Sumner Rd. Source: Permits.

1913

Howe, Dudley, 22 Worthington Rd. Source: Permits.

1915

Dane, E. B. (stable alteration), 310 Heath St. Source: Permits.

Dane, E. B. (garage alteration), 312 Heath St. Source: Permits.

The Country Club (locker house), 191 Clyde St. Source: Permits.

Town of Brookline (high school alteration), Greenough St. (demolished). Source: Permits.

1916

Dane, E. B. (organ room), 400 Heath St. Source: Permits.

Dane, E. B. (servant house addition), 70 Woodland Rd. Source: Permits.

The Country Club (stable and squash court), 191 Clyde St. (extant?). Source: Permits.

Town of Brookline (high school alteration), Greenough St. (demolished). Source: Permits.

Jaques, Herbert (house alteration), 50 Dunster Rd. (demolished). Source: Permits.

1917

Dane, E. B. (cow barn silo), off Woodland Rd. Source: Permits.

Paine, Robert Treat (house addition), 325 Heath St. Source: Permits.

Town Green and Green Hill Properties
with Olmsted Connections

353 Walnut Street, the First Parish Church Rectory, 1856.
The Reverend W. H. Lyon invited the Olmsted office in 1901 to advise on landscape plantings to screen a prospective neighbor.

382 Walnut Street, Pierce Hall; Olmsted job number 01178.
Built in 1824 as the first town hall of Brookline after disestablishment, it was acquired in 1890 by the First Parish Church when a new town hall was constructed on the Washington Street near Brookline Village. The church used the building, renamed in honor of the Reverend John Pierce, as an education and meeting space. It was eventually connected to the adjacent church through a wing designed in 1901 by Charles Collens. The Olmsted firm oversaw the landscape development of the new wing and Pierce Hall. Work was completed in 1907.

393 Walnut Street, Bacon-Poor-Prouty house, 1852, architect unknown; Olmsted job number 05889.
In 1893 Ben Prouty invited the Olmsted office to provide a design for the grounds of the house. The previous owner had been Nathaniel Poor, creator of the Standard & Poor's Index.

400 Walnut Street, First Paris Church, designed 1893, Shepley, Rutan & Coolidge, architects; Olmsted office job number 00134.
The Olmsted firm was invited to advise on landscape development beginning in 1891, after the site of the building had been determined. A contract was signed in 1893, with Moses Williams, an Olmsted client and neighbor, serving as the head of the building committee. In a memo to Williams, the office first volunteered to donate their services since two members of the firm belonged to the parish. Frederick Law Olmsted Sr. donated most of the plant material. They also provided designs for the landscape treatment in relation to the construction of a new wing in 1906. Lewis I. Prouty, on whose property the Olmsted firm also worked, volunteered to pay for modification in the landscape in 1936–37, which the firm oversaw.

Warren and Boylston Street, the Brookline Town Reservoir, 1851; Olmsted job number 00105.
As part of the Cochituate Reservoir project of the City of Boston, this reservoir was developed as a holding tank for water pumped from a larger reservoir farther to the west. When the reservoir was no longer needed by the City of Boston, John Charles Olmsted was one of the neighborhood residents who donated money to purchase the property and donate it to the Town of Brookline, preventing its development, in 1905.

16 Warren Street, 1851–1852, architect unknown; Olmsted job number 01030.
John Charles Olmsted lived here from 1899 to 1918, a short walk from his office at 99 Warren Street. It is not

surprising that he took an active role in the campaign to secure the Brookline Reservoir from development in 1905, given how close his residence was to the future park site.

30 Warren Street, 1885, the Moses Williams house, Peabody & Stearns architects; Olmsted job numbers 00464 (1875–1886) and 01023 (1888).
Williams, an attorney and state representative, was a frequent client of the Olmsted office. In addition to seeking the advice of the firm on the development of the grounds for his new house in 1885, he also asked them to project how the property could be subdivided if he chose to develop the land more intensely. In 1905, he paid for improvements to the First Parish Church property when he was the head of the property committee. He was frequently involved with possible real estate development projects in Brookline and often advocated for the plans of friends and neighbors before the Brookline Town Council.

423 Walnut Street, 1896, Joseph Chandler, architect.
John Charles Olmsted had corresponded in 1895 with the owner of this property, a Mr. Scudder, about the potential development of the site. See figure 122 for the sketch plan he developed that was never realized.

77 Warren Street, Frederick Clarke Hood House, Chapman & Frazer, architects, Olmsted job number 02276, 1901–1902.
F. C. Hood moved to 77 Warren Street in 1900. He was then serving as the treasurer of the Hood Rubber Company, which he had founded with his brother in 1896. In 1901–2 he invited the Olmsted firm to make alterations and extensions to the original landscape scheme by Ernest Bowditch.

99 Warren Street; Frederick Law Olmsted Home and Studio, Olmsted job number 00673.
Fairsted is the hinge between the Town Green National Register Historic District and the Green Hill National Register Historic District to the south and west. The property has been studied in several reports issued by the National Park Service and is not included in the mission of this project.

12 Fairmount Street, 1883, John Charles Olmsted, architect; included in Olmsted job number 00673.
Designed for the Clark sisters as their new residence after they sold the Fairsted property to the Olmsted family and firm. A two-and-a-half-story shingled cottage, it is sited at the rear of the Clark property and overlooks the family's former home, now the Olmsted property. John Charles Olmsted may have been inspired by the simple Shingle Style cottages that H. H. Richardson and other architects were designing in these years. The family sold the property in 1915 after the deaths of both Clark sisters.

Corner of Fairmount and Dudley streets.
While a member of the Olmsted office, from 1889 to 1898 Warren Manning lived in a house across Fairmount Street from the Clark sisters' home. The street number is not known. From 1899 onward, he lived in the Coolidge Corner and then Aspinwall Hill areas of Brookline. He left the firm in 1903, when he developed an independent practice of national scope as a landscape architect and horticulturalist.

135 Warren Street, 1806, unknown architect.
Originally built for Nathaniel Ingersoll, Green Hill was acquired by John Lowell Gardner in 1846. His daughter-in-law Isabella Stewart Gardner dramatically changed the landscape from the 1880s on, adding an early Italian garden, a Japanese garden, greenhouses, and elaborate iris beds. Her husband worked with the Olmsted office on consideration of possible development for land along the Fairmount edge of the property in 1886–87. The Olmsted job number for this work is 01044. Strangely, Mrs. Gardner did not capitalize on the advantage of having the nation's leading landscape architect as her next-door neighbor.

278 Warren Street, 1880, George Harney, architect; Olmsted job numbers 00614 (1879–1881) and 06625 (1918–1946).
Barthold Schlesinger commissioned Frederick Law Olmsted Sr. to develop the landscape of his estate, Southwood, in 1879, before the office had been moved from New York to Brookline. Completed between 1880 and 1890, the grounds were among the largest in this section of Brookline and established the reputation of the firm in Brookline. F. J Oakes Jr. next acquired the property and invited the Olmsted office to make changes between 1918 and 1922. Now the Holy Transfiguration Monastery, the property has been substantially reduced in scale but maintains the character of the landscape developed by the firm through two clients.

222 Warren Street, 1857, architect unknown; Olmsted job number 06323.
An earlier house designed for Samuel Perkins was constructed around 1845 but burned down in 1852. Nathaniel Goddard next acquired the property and built a new residence in 1857, which he called Cliffside. In 1858 Francis A. White, a partner in the tanning business of Guild & White, purchased the house and lived here until his death in 1910. One of his daughters was Sophia Buckland White, who married John Charles Olmsted in 1898. The Olmsteds acquired the property for their residence in 1918 and lived here for two years, until his death in 1920.

25 Cottage Street, late eighteenth century, 1804, architect unknown.
Built by Samuel G. Perkins in the manner of West Indian plantations with a two-story colonnade of slender columns along the front and sides, the house passed to Ned Hooper, who rented the property to H. H. Richardson from 1873 until his death in 1886. When Olmsted decided to move to this area of Brookline, Richardson proposed to design and build a shingled cottage for the Olmsted family on the land that he rented. The property served as both the Richardson family home and the office for the Richardson architectural firm. Here many important architects learned their craft in the atelier-like environment of the Richardson office. Olmsted never consulted on landscape development for the property, which is not surprising since Richardson never owned the house. His widow was given the property after the architect's death. His son Henry H. Richardson II, a highly praised horticulturalist, winning the first prize of the Massachusetts Horticultural Society for the development of the plant material on this site, next acquired the house.

45 Cottage Street.
George Shepley lived in the previous house on this site from 1889 until 1903. The Olmsted office designed the gardens of the Shepley house in 1888–89, when the Shepleys first moved to this property. The Olmsted job number is 01055. Mrs. Shepley, the daughter of H. H. Richardson, had lived before her marriage in the adjacent house at 25 Cottage Street. George Shepley led Richardson's successor architectural firm, Shepley, Rutan & Coolidge. Following Shepley's death, Josephine Cox commissioned the architects Chapman & Frazer to design a new house on this site and the one at 75 Cottage Street and invited the Olmsted firm to develop the grounds of her new residence.

209 Sargent Road, 1845, attributed to Richard Upjohn, architect; Olmsted job number 01056.
Ignatius Sargent may have commissioned Upjohn in 1845 to build this Italianate villa in red sandstone, which still survives. After Sargent's death in 1884, his daughter and son-in-law Mr. and Mrs. James M. Codman Jr. inherited the property. They consulted the Olmsted firm on approach drives to property in 1888. Mrs. Codman was the sister of Charles Sprague Sargent, whose own estate sat adjacent. Two of the sons of the Codman family—Henry Sargent Codman and Philip Codman—trained in the Olmsted office. H. S. Codman entered the office as an intern in 1884 and, after spending two years studying with Édouard André in Paris, returned to become an important member of the firm. He was given central responsibility for the World's Columbian Exposition, on which he was working when he died following an appendectomy on January 13, 1893. Philip Codman graduated from Harvard in 1889 and then traveled in Europe for two years before beginning a course at the Bussey Institute and the Arnold Arboretum. He became a student of F. L. Olmsted in 1892, entered the firm, and, like his brother, died suddenly, from pneumonia, on October 30, 1896.

The Sargent estate (Olmsted job number 01056) was begun by Ignatius Sargent in 1845, when he built his residence and began to acquire adjacent landscape for garden and agricultural development. He added properties in 1858 and in 1871, the latter the former estate of Henry Lee, which was highly praised for its horticultural collection. In 1868 Sargent's son, Charles Sprague Sargent, became the manager of the property, which he continued to refine into one of the most widely admired private landscapes in the United States. In 1872 Harvard University appointed him the first director of the Arnold Arboretum, on land located in nearby Jamaica Plain. He requested the assistance of Frederick Law Olmsted with the development of the arboretum beginning in 1875. In addition to the attraction of his friend H. H. Richardson living nearby at 25 Cottage Street, Sargent's estate was another strong magnet for the relocation of Frederick Law Olmsted from New York to Brookline. Over the remainder of their careers, Olmsted and Sargent were frequent collaborators and learned much from each other. At his death in 1927, Sargent's heirs subdivided the estates. Although the Olmsted office had developed a possible scheme for the residential development of the estate as early as 1895, the heirs did not choose to follow that template in the development of this large property. Nevertheless, the

Olmsted office was invited by several of the new owners of parts of the Sargent property to develop their estates. These included:

Sewall Cutler, 75 Sargent Road, 1928–29, Strickland Blodgett & Law, Olmsted job number 07992. The architects and landscape architects redeveloped a barn foundation from the Sargent estate as a new residence and walled garden. The one-acre property incorporated a formal garden in the former barnyard.

E. J. Samson, 90 Sargent Road, 1928–29, Olmsted job number 07901.

Dr. John Bryant, 120 Sargent Road, 1932–1939, Olmsted job number 09320. Dr. Bryant's parents (his mother was Charlotte Olmsted, daughter of Frederick Law Olmsted Sr.) commissioned Richardson and Olmsted to design a summer house at Cohasset, Massachusetts, in 1880. Beginning in 1883, Charlotte experienced emotional problems that led to her institutionalization until her death in 1908. John, their first son, was born in 1880 at Cohasset; he became a physician, like his father and grandfather. He married Adelaide Whitney Barnes in 1910 and moved to this property in the former Sargent estate in 1932, inviting his grandfather's firm to design the grounds. He died on September 20, 1935, but Mrs. Bryant continued to work with the Olmsted office on the development of the property. (The source for this information is the obituary files of the Brookline Room, Brookline Public Library. We are deeply grateful to Anne Clark of the Brookline Public Library for finding this file. Strangely, the Bryants are not listed in the normal Brookline directories for these years.)

Mrs. Mary Cunningham, 40 Cottage Street, 1934, Olmsted job number 09366. Mrs. Cunningham contacted the firm in 1934 about the plantings at her house. The following year a landscape architect named Miss Harrison contacted the firm to say that she would be taking over the further development of the property.

Later Olmsted projects in the former Sargent estate that postdate the scope of this study include:

The William Tripp property, 36 Codman Road, 1938, Olmsted job number 09549.

Two projects for Charles E. Mason at 21 Sargent Crossways, Olmsted job numbers 09582 (no date) and 09853 (1949).

Notes

INTRODUCTION

1. See Becky Nicolaides and Andrew Wiese, eds., *The Suburb Reader* (New York: Routledge, 2006). This anthology of essays on a range of issues concerning the creation and meaning of suburbs is a convenient source for reviewing current scholarship and the historiography of the topic of American suburbia.

2. Sam Bass Warner, *Streetcar Suburb: The Process of Growth in Boston, 1870–1900* (Cambridge: Harvard University Press, 1962).

3. Ronald Dale Karr, "The Evolution of an Elite Suburb: Community Structure and Control in Brookline, Massachusetts, 1770–1900" (Ph.D. diss., Boston University, 1981). Karr published several useful articles drawn from the research in his dissertation. See "Brookline: The Evolution of an Elite Suburb," *Chicago History,* Summer 1984, 36–47; "The Transformation of Agriculture in Massachusetts, 1770–1885," *Historical Journal of Massachusetts* 15.1 (January 1987): 33–49; "Brookline Rejects Annexation, 1873," in *Suburbia Re-examined,* ed. Barbara M. Kelly (New York: Greenwood Press, 1989), 103–10; and "Two Centuries of Oligarchy in Brookline," *Historical Journal of Massachusetts* 13.2 (June 1985): 117–28.

4. Henry C. Binford, *The First Suburbs: Residential Communities on the Boston Periphery, 1815–1860* (Chicago: University of Chicago Press, 1985).

5. Kenneth T. Jackson, *Crabgrass Frontier: The Suburbanization of the United States* (New York: Oxford University Press, 1985). Also of note during this period was Robert Fishman, *Bourgeois Utopias: The Rise and Fall of Suburbia* (New York: Basic Books, 1987), which expands on the context of the suburb to include English and Continental contributions.

6. David Hackett Fischer, ed., "Brookline: The Social History of a Suburban Town, 1705–1850," *Chronos: A Journal of Social History* 3 (Fall 1984): 2. Our thanks to Douglass Shand-Tucci for bringing this source to our attention.

7. Michael Rawson, *Eden on the Charles: The Making of Boston* (Cambridge: Harvard University Press, 2010), esp. chap. 3, "Inventing the Suburbs."

8. David Schuyler, "Frederick Law Olmsted's Riverside Drive," *Planning History Present* 7.2 (1993): 1–5.

9. Susan L. Klaus, *A Modern Arcadia: Frederick Law Olmsted Jr. and the Plan for Forest Hills Gardens* (Amherst: University of Massachusetts Press in association with the Library of American Landscape History, 2002). See also Catherine Joy Johnson, *Olmsted in the Pacific Northwest: Private Estates and Residential Communities, 1873–1959* (Seattle: Friends of Seattle's Olmsted Parks, 1997).

10. Cynthia Zaitzevsky, "Frederick Law Olmsted in Brookline: A Preliminary Study of His Public Projects," in *Proceedings of the Brookline Historical Society for 1975–1978* (Brookline: Brookline Historical Society, 1979), 42–65. This essay is especially important for the discussion of the public park movement in Brookline and adjacent Boston. See also Zaitzevsky's magisterial *Frederick Law Olmsted and the*

Boston Park System (Cambridge: Belknap Press of Harvard University Press, 1982), the most important book to date on the work of Olmsted in Boston.

11. Jackson, *Crabgrass Frontier,* 79.

12. Frederick Law Olmsted severed his relationship with Calvert Vaux in 1872, nearly a decade before his relocation to Brookline. The name of the firm evolved over the years as follows: 1872–1884, Frederick Law Olmsted; 1884–1889, F. L. & J. C. Olmsted; 1889–1893, F. L. Olmsted & Company; 1893–1897, Olmsted, Olmsted & Eliot; 1897–1898, F. L. & J. C. Olmsted; 1898–1957, Olmsted Brothers. See Johnson, *Olmsted in the Pacific Northwest,* 65–66. The firm received more than three hundred Brookline commissions before closing in 1979.

1. BROOKLINE BEFORE OLMSTED

1. For general information on the development of the town, consult *A History of Brookline, Massachusetts, from the First Settlement of Muddy River until the Present Time, 1630–1906* (Brookline: Brookline Press Company, 1906). For a more concise and visually reinforced history, see Greer Hardwicke and Roger Reed, *Images of Brookline* (Charleston, S.C.: Arcadia Publishing, 1998). Also valuable is David Hackett Fischer, ed., "Brookline: The Social History of a Suburban Town, 1705–1850," *Chronos: A Journal of Social History,* no. 3 (Fall 1984). This anthology of five essay by Brandeis University undergraduates was produced under the direction of Fischer, who wrote the introduction.

2. Ronald Dale Karr, "The Evolution of an Elite Suburb: Community Structure and Control in Brookline, Massachusetts, 1770–1900" (Ph.D. diss., Boston University, 1981), 29. Although the Winchester family did not maintain its privileged position after the American Revolution, descendants of the Gardners and the Whites would remain prominent landowners and members of the upper-class community in Brookline into the time of Frederick Law Olmsted. Indeed, the landscape architect would undertake planning and design projects for representatives of both families in the late nineteenth century.

3. Ibid., 18–19.

4. Karr points to the construction of the first greenhouse in New England on the estate of Henry Hulton in 1766 as an indication of farms becoming genteel estates. Ibid., 61–64.

5. Thomas C. Amory, *Memoir of the Hon. Richard Sullivan* (Cambridge: John Wilson and Son, 1850), 16, quoted in Tamara Plakins Thornton, *Cultivating Gentlemen: The Meaning of Country Life among the Boston Elite, 1785–1860* (New Haven: Yale University Press, 1989), 106. See John Gould Curtis, *History of the Town of Brookline, Massachusetts* (Boston: Houghton Mifflin, 1935); Samuel Aspinwall Goddard, *Reflections of Brookline, Being an Account of the Houses, the Families and the Roads in Brookline in the Years 1800 to 1810* (Birmingham, England: E. C. Osborne, 1873); and Theodore F. Jones and Charles F. White, *Land Ownership in Brookline from the First Settlement* (Brookline: Riverside Press, 1923), esp. maps 5–8.

6. Among the more distinctive early estates was the group of country houses on Warren and Cottage streets with two-story arcades, possibly influenced by plantation architecture of the Caribbean. This was the neighborhood into which Frederick Law Olmsted would move in the early 1880s.

7. Thornton, *Cultivating Gentlemen,* 116.

8. In addition to the excellent and comprehensive treatment by Tamara Thornton in *Cultivating Gentlemen,* see also Charles Hammond, "'Where the Arts and Virtue Unite': Country Life near Boston, 1637–1864" (Ph.D. diss., Boston University, 1982), which contains a wealth of relevant information on this phenomenon but overlooks the leading role of Brookline landowners.

9. In addition to the histories of the Horticultural Society published in the nineteenth and twentieth centuries, see also Tamara Plakins Thornton, "Horticulture and American Character," and Walter T. Punch, "The Garden Organized: The Public Face of Horticulture," both in *Keeping Eden: A History of Gardening in America,* ed. Walter T. Punch (Boston: Little, Brown, 1992), 189–203 and 219–40.

10. Karr, "Evolution of an Elite Suburb," chap. 3.

11. Uriah Cotting, the leader of the milldam project, purchased the three hundred–acre Sewell farm in 1815. Upon his death in 1819, three associates—David Sears, Ebenezer Francis, and Israel Thorndike— divided the property. Eventually, Sears and Francis built houses there.

12. See Karr, "The Railroad Suburb," in "Evolution of an Elite Suburb," esp. 147–57.

13. For information on earlier suburban experimentation in England, see Robert Fishman, *Bourgeois Utopias*

(New York: Basic Books, 1987); and Robert A. M. Stern, *The Anglo-American Suburb* (London: Architectural Design, 1981).

14. Quoted in "Historic Neighborhood Brochure: The Lindens," Brookline Preservation Commission, 1996.

15. Karr, "Evolution of an Elite Suburb," 264–65.

16. Although the evolution of these two developments is not simple, the area north of Beacon Street has come to be known as Cottage Farm, while Longwood is consider the district to the south, both at Brookline's eastern boundary with Boston.

17. The property was named on a whim after Sears saw the key to Longue Bois exhibited in a museum in Paris during one of his many trips there. Sears was an admirer of Napoleon, having experienced the apogee of Napoleonic power during his wedding trip to Paris in 1811, including meeting the empress Josephine, whom he found exceedingly charming. Sears had the letter *N* inscribed in various architectural details of his Alexander Parris–designed Beacon Street mansion. John W. Sears, interview with Elizabeth Hope Cushing, May 22, 2008.

18. Linda Olson Pehlke, "Longwood and Cottage Farm," www.brooklinehistoricalsociety.org/history/longwood.asp (originally published in *Our Town Brookline,* 2005).

19. Charles Sprague Sargent, "David Sears, Tree Planter," *Horticulture,* April 15, 1925, 164.

20. Ibid. According to Karr, such development frequently included homes for family members, friends, and colleagues. Sears's streets and squares were laid out by Alexander Wadsworth. The squares remained in private use until 1902, when Sears's heirs gave the four squares to the town of Brookline for public parks. Before 1885, save for a few syndicates of investors, development in Brookline was carried out almost entirely by "farmers, hereditary owners, or resident Brahmins" such as Sears. Karr shows that the growth of the Longwood area was carefully controlled by Sears, including the construction of roads and buildings. By 1885, "after nearly forty years of development, only three-score houses were found throughout all of Longwood, and the neighborhood was among the most prestigious in Brookline." Karr, "Evolution of an Elite Suburb," 259, 255–56, 260.

21. Quoted in Sargent, "David Sears, Tree Planter," 64.

22. They consisted originally of "magnificent specimens of the typical green-leafed tree" with "three or four of the purple-leafed variety." Charles Sprague Sargent "Beech-trees," *Bulletin of Popular Information,* July 2, 1925, 50.

23. Cornelia Hanna McMurtrie, "The Beech in Boston," *Arnoldia,* Winter 1982, 38.

24. Anne Wardwell, "Longwood" and "Cottage Farm," in *Victorian Boston Today: Ten Walking Tours,* ed. Pauline Chase Harrell and Margaret Supplee Smith (Boston: New England Chapter, Victorian Society in America, 1975), 56–69, cited in Karr, "Evolution of an Elite Suburb," 265.

25. Lawrence, who was active in the movement to abolish slavery, added a chapel wing to his house in 1865 commemorating the fall of Richmond and memorializing President Lincoln.

26. The research file at the Brookline Historical Commission includes a reference to a restriction in a deed of October 1, 1849, stating that "no building shall be placed within 20 feet of any of the streets or avenues laid out on said Fairmount prior to the 1st day of June 1864." We were unable to find that reference in the Norfolk County deeds.

27. For example, in 1859 Ignatius Sargent built a house at 39 Fairmount, where in 1861, James Dudley, a coachman, and John Power, a gardener, lived as tenants. These men were probably employed by Sargent.

28. Karr, "Evolution of an Elite Suburb," 177. By 1870, 48 percent of Brookline households were headed by foreigners, and three-quarters of these were from Ireland.

29. In 1850 the population was 2,514, a figure that had grown to 9,000 by 1885. See the population growth chart in Karr (ibid., 154).

30. Ibid., 225. No member of the expanding ethnic working class was admitted to a position of responsibility in the public sphere throughout the nineteenth century.

31. Cited ibid., 235.

32. Ibid., 220.

33. Jackson, *Crabgrass Frontier,* 100. Articles in the local press and national journals repeatedly referred to Brookline as "the richest town in the world."

34. For a discussion of Olmsted's efforts to control the use of his parks as early as Central Park, see Roy

Rosenzweig and Betsy Blackmar, *The Park and the People: A History of Central Park* (New York: Cornell University Press, 1992), chap. 12 and passim.

2. OLMSTED BEFORE BROOKLINE

1. Before he was formally requested to view the proposed Boston park system in 1875, Olmsted was informally solicited as early as 1869 by individual citizens of Boston, who were evincing a growing interest in a public park system.

2. Severe sumac poisoning at age fifteen affected his eyesight, precluding formal higher education (specifically Yale College, where he had anticipated matriculating). All his life the sensitive, high-strung Olmsted was to do battle with various physical ailments as well as bouts of depression. Eventually, in 1864, Olmsted was given the honorary degree of A.M. from Harvard. Later, in 1893, he received an honorary LL.D. from Yale.

3. Olmsted's mother, Charlotte Law (Hull) Olmsted, died when he was three years old; John Olmsted married Mary Ann Bull two years later. John Hull Olmsted, Frederick's younger brother, was an infant when their mother died. The brothers remained devoted friends throughout their lives.

4. Mariana Griswold Van Rensselaer, "Frederick Law Olmsted," *Century Magazine,* October 24, 1893, 861.

5. Ibid., 860.

6. William Gilpin (1724–1804) and subsequently Uvedale Price (1747–1829), with his *Essay on the Picturesque, as Compared with the Sublime and the Beautiful* (1794), drew away from the neoclassical style and the gardenless simplicity of Capability Brown (1716–1783), shepherding in, through their writings, the Romantic style in landscape design, known as the picturesque. See Nikolaus Pevsner, *The Picturesque Garden and Its Influence outside the British Isles* (Washington, D.C.: Dumbarton Oaks, 1974); and John Dixon Hunt, *Gardens and the Picturesque* (Cambridge: MIT Press, 1992).

7. Charles Capen McLaughlin, introduction to *The Papers of Frederick Law Olmsted,* vol. 1, *The Formative Years, 1822–1852,* ed. Charles Capen McLaughlin and Charles E. Beveridge (Baltimore: Johns Hopkins University Press, 1977), 5. Barton had formerly served as a civil engineer for the Coast Survey.

8. Olmsted's interest in such a voyage is not as improbable as it might first appear. Three of his great-uncles made their living on the sea. See Van Rensselaer, "Olmsted," 860.

9. In 1851 he wrote an article for the *American Whig* titled "A Voice from the Sea," reflective of Richard Henry Dana (1815–1882) and his "voice from the forecastle" in *Two Years before the Mast* (1840). Both men were highly critical of the inhumane treatment of seamen, as was Herman Melville (1819–1891).

10. McLaughlin, introduction, 8.

11. A. J. Downing, *A Treatise on the Theory and Practice of Landscape Gardening, Adapted to North America; with a View to the Improvement of Country Residences* (1865; reprint, New York: Dover Publications, 1991), 51.

12. McLaughlin, introduction, 8.

13. David Schuyler, *Apostle of Taste: Andrew Jackson Downing, 1815–1852* (Baltimore: Johns Hopkins University Press, 1996), 348–49, quoting Downing's 1851 essay "The New-York Park."

14. Emerson (1803–1882) was the leader of the Transcendental movement as well as a philosopher, poet, and essayist. Carlyle (1795–1881) was a Scottish essayist, satirist, and historian. Macaulay (1800–1859) was an English poet, essayist, historian, and politician. All three men had enormous influence on the intellectual currents of their time. Emerson and Carlyle were correspondents. Emerson's writings in particular would have resonated with Olmsted's sensibilities. His famous essay "Nature," published anonymously in 1836, includes the declaration: "To the body and mind which have been cramped by noxious work or company, nature is medicinal and restores their tone. The tradesman, the attorney comes out of the din and craft of the street, and sees the sky and the woods, and is a man again. In their eternal calm, he finds himself." *The Complete Essays and Other Writings of Ralph Waldo Emerson,* ed. Brooks Atkinson (New York: Random House, 1940), 9–10.

15. Interestingly, Olmsted recorded nothing of his travels on the Continent, either in letters home or in the book he later wrote about the trip.

16. Frederick Law Olmsted, *Walks and Talks of an American Farmer in England* (1852; reprint, Amherst: Library of American Landscape History, 2002), 98–99.

17. Autobiographical fragment, n.d., quoted in Laura Wood Roper, *FLO: A Biography of Frederick Law Olmsted* (Baltimore: Johns Hopkins University Press, 1973), 70.

18. Olmsted, *Walks,* 407.

19. Frederick Law Olmsted to William Platt, February 1, 1892, Frederick Law Olmsted Papers, Manuscript Division, Library of Congress, Washington, D.C.

20. Frederick Law Olmsted to A. J. Downing, November 23, 1850, in *Frederick Law Olmsted, Landscape Architect, 1822–1903,* ed. Frederick Law Olmsted Jr. and Theodora Kimball (New York: G. P. Putnam's Sons, 1922), 90.

21. Creator of the famous 1851 Crystal Palace for England's Great Exhibition, Paxton (1802–1865) was a landscape gardener and a famous glasshouse designer who dedicated his later life to urban planning projects.

22. Olmsted, *Walks,* 91.

23. Ibid., 93.

24. Roper, *FLO,* 69.

25. Olmsted, *Walks,* 87.

26. Roper, *FLO,* 78.

27. Ibid., 89.

28. *The Papers of Frederick Law Olmsted,* vol. 2, *Slavery and the South, 1852–1857,* ed. Charles E. Beveridge and Charles Capen McLaughlin (Baltimore: Johns Hopkins University Press, 1981), 263.

29. Ibid., 261.

30. Ibid., 265.

31. These were *A Journey in the Seaboard Slave States, A Journey through Texas,* and *A Journey through the Back Country.*

32. Among other things, Olmsted was sent abroad in 1856 to negotiate with English publishing firms on the rights to publish their works in America.

33. See Roy Rosenzweig and Elizabeth Blackmar, *The Park and the People: A History of Central Park* (Ithaca: Cornell University Press, 1992), for a thorough discussion of the creation of the park. Also see Morrison H. Heckscher, "Creating Central Park," *Metropolitan Museum of Art Bulletin,* Winter 2008.

34. Roper, *FLO,* 130.

35. There were few practitioners of the art of landscape design at the time: New York's André Parmentier (1780–1830), the predecessor of A. J. Downing; the architect A. J. Davis (1803–1892), who designed Llewellyn Park in New Jersey in 1857; and Horace W. S. Cleveland (1814–1900), who practiced individually and with Robert Morris Copeland (1833–1874) in the Boston area. Downing was an early advocate of a public park for New York City.

36. Charles S. Sargent, "Frederick Law Olmsted, 1822–1903," in *Later Years of the Saturday Club, 1870–1920,* ed. M. A. DeWolfe Howe (Boston: Houghton Mifflin, 1927), 184.

37. Van Rensselaer, "Olmsted," 867.

38. Olmsted was serving as a landscape consultant to the commission by that time. A carriage accident in 1860 had left him with a severe limp, and his continual sporadic ill health made it impossible for him to serve in battle.

39. McLaughlin, introduction, 26.

40. Roper, *FLO,* 237.

41. Henry Whitney Bellows to Frederick Law Olmsted, August 13, 1863, Frederick Law Olmsted Papers.

42. Roper, *FLO,* 236.

43. In 1905, owing to lack of proper maintenance by the state of California, the two properties were returned to the federal government.

44. Roper, *FLO,* 284.

45. Ibid., 315–16.

46. McLaughlin, introduction, 35.

47. Witold Rybczynski, *A Clearing in the Distance* (New York: Scribner, 1999), 273.

48. Ibid.

49. *The Papers of Frederick Law Olmsted: Supplementary Series,* vol. 1, *Writings on Public Parks, Parkways, and Park Systems,* ed. Charles E. Beveridge and Carolyn F. Hoffman (Baltimore: Johns Hopkins University Press, 1997), 19.

50. Frederick Law Olmsted, "Preliminary Report upon the Proposed Suburban Village at Riverdale Near Chicago by Olmsted, Vaux & Co., Landscape Architects," *Landscape Architecture,* July 1931, 275.

51. Rybczynski, *Clearing, 293.*

52. They collaborated twice more, on an 1887 report for the creation of a Niagara Falls reservation, and for a park in Newburgh honoring the man who had mentored them both, Andrew Jackson Downing.

53. Frederick Law Olmsted to Whitelaw Reid, November 26, 1874, Whitelaw Reid Papers, Manuscript Division, Library of Congress, Washington, D.C. Note the Downingesque quality of the statement.

54. See Elizabeth Cromley, "Riverside Park and Issues of Historic Preservation," *Journal of the Society of Architectural Historians,* October 1984, 238–49, for a description and history of the park.

55. This was the year John Charles Olmsted (1852–1920) was given an interest in the firm, where he had been working as an apprentice since his graduation from the Sheffield Scientific School at Yale in 1875. In 1884 he was made a partner. He proved an invaluable member of the firm, eventually playing a large role in the development of the Boston park system.

56. Olmsted had known the Irish-born Godkin since the latter immigrated to New York in 1856. Elizabeth Stevenson, *A Life of Frederick Law Olmsted* (New York: Macmillan, 1977), 347.

57. Sargent also became the director of the Arnold Arboretum (see chapter 4).

58. Norton asked Olmsted to draw up a plan for the subdivision of his thirty-four-acre estate, Shady Hill, in Cambridge. It was through Godkin, in his role as editor of the *Nation,* that Olmsted met Norton, who would be an important friend after his move to Brookline. Stevenson, *A Life of Frederick Law Olmsted,* 357.

59. Sylvester Baxter, "How Boston Has Systematized Its Parks," *Century Magazine,* May 1897, 952.

60. See Cynthia Zaitzevsky, *Frederick Law Olmsted and the Boston Park System* (Cambridge: Belknap Press of Harvard University Press, 1982), for an excellent in-depth discussion of the making of the Boston park system.

61. Eventually 120 acres of the original tract were lost to city institutions, and the meadowland was turned into an eighteen-hole golf course.

62. Zaitzevsky, *Frederick Law Olmsted and the Boston Park System,* 44.

63. After the city suffered the Great Fire of 1872, then finances were again wracked by the Panic of 1873; funds available for developing the park system diminished drastically.

64. Cynthia Zaitzevsky and Zaitzevsky Associates, *Fairsted: A Cultural Landscape Report for the Frederick Law Olmsted National Historic Site,* vol. 1, *Site History* (Boston: Olmsted Center for Landscape Preservation, National Park Service and Arnold Arboretum of Harvard University, 1997), 9. Zaitzevsky refers to a conversation between Frederick Law Olmsted Jr. and Laura Wood Roper in *FLO,* xiv.

65. Interview with Frederick Law Olmsted Jr., n.d., quoted by Roper in *FLO,* 383.

66. Frederick Law Olmsted to Charles Loring Brace, March 7, 1882, Frederick Law Olmsted Papers.

67. "The Brookline Club," *Brookline Chronicle,* March 2, 1889.

68. Zaitzevsky et al., *Fairsted,* 146.

69. *Brookline Chronicle,* March 2, 1889.

70. H. H. Richardson to F. L. Olmsted, February 6, 1883, Olmsted Papers, cited in Zaitzevsky, *Olmsted and the Boston Park System,* 128 and fig. 93. Richardson was renting the house from a college friend, Edward William Hooper.

71. The household at that time consisted of Mary and Frederick Olmsted, their daughter Marion, and son Frederick Law Olmsted Jr. John Charles joined them when the move was complete. Two trusted apprentices, Henry Sargent Codman and Charles Eliot, were added to the Brookline firm.

72. Peter B. Wight, obituary of H. H. Richardson, *The Inland Architect and Builder,* May 1886, 61. See Mary Alice Molloy, "Richardson's Web: A Client's Assessment of the Architect's Home and Studio," *Journal of the Society of Architectural Historians,* March 1995, 8–23, which describes the seventy-six-page account of Richardson's home and studio written by his Chicago client John Jacob Glessner (1843–1936). The Richardson-trained architect Charles A. Coolidge, in Howe, *Later Years of the Saturday Club,* characterizes Richardson's combined home and workplace as "not an office in the present sense, but an atelier where one lived and thought art, and hours did not count" (194).

73. Hazel G. Collins, "Landscape Gardening in Brookline," 1903, Brookline Public Library.

74. Frederick Law Olmsted to John Charles Olmsted, December 25, 1877, Frederick Law Olmsted Papers.

75. Waverly Keeling, "Home of Frederick L. Olmsted, Landscape Artist of the World's Fair," *Chicago Inter-Ocean,* 1896, clipping in Brookline Public Library.

76. Codman died in 1892 at the age of twenty-nine and Eliot in 1897 at the age of thirty-seven.

77. Frederick Law Olmsted Jr. joined the firm in 1897. After his father retired and Charles Eliot died unex-

pectedly, John Charles asked his stepbrother to join him as partner. They formed Olmsted Brothers. Successor firms continued at Fairsted until 1980.

78. Two of his largest projects, the Chicago World's Columbian Exposition of 1893 and his long-term association with the George W. Vanderbilt estate Biltmore in Asheville, North Carolina (from 1889 onward), were worked on during this time.

79. See Van Rensselaer, "Olmsted," for a discussion of Olmsted's self-perceived "deficits" in training.

80. Roper, *FLO,* 388. Although the arboretum was owned by Harvard University, thanks to Olmsted and Sargent, an ingenious long-term lease allowed the property to become part of the metropolitan park system in 1882. According to Zaitzevsky, Olmsted "took endless pains" on Franklin Park because he considered it "the most critical part of the whole park system" (*Boston Park System,* 65).

81. Zaitzevsky, *Boston Park System,* 44.

82. Charles E. Beveridge and Paul Rocheleau, *Frederick Law Olmsted: Designing the American Landscape* (New York: Universe Publishing, 1998), 44.

83. Ibid.

84. Baxter, "How Boston Has Systematized Its Parks," 952.

85. Beveridge and Rocheleau, *Frederick Law Olmsted,* 44.

86. Zaitzevsky, *Boston Park System,* 92–93.

87. Keeling, "Home of Frederick L. Olmsted."

3. HENRY HOBSON RICHARDSON

1. Mariana Griswold Van Rensselaer, *Henry Hobson Richardson and His Works* (1888; reprint, New York: Dover Publications, 1969), 118–19. Van Rensselaer was a friend to Olmsted, Richardson, and their neighbor Charles Sprague Sargent. The dedication of her 1893 book *Art Out-of-Doors* to them as her "Friends in Brooklyn" was changed to her "Friends in Brookline" in the 1925 edition.

2. Laura Wood Roper, *FLO: A Biography of Frederick Law Olmsted* (Baltimore: Johns Hopkins University Press, 1973), 368.

3. Mariana Griswold Van Rensselaer, "Landscape Gardening.—III," *American Architect and Building News,* January 7, 1888, 4.

4. James F. O'Gorman, *H. H. Richardson and His Office* (Cambridge: Harvard College Library, 1974), 30. Their collaboration included the Buffalo State Hospital, the Buffalo Civil War Memorial, the Albany State Capitol, fourteen railroad stations, the Malden Public Library, the Robert Treat Paine and John Bryant houses, the Blake-Hubbard estate, the Quincy (Mass.) Library, Memorial Town Hall in North Easton (Mass.) and Richardson's numerous projects for the Ames family there, and the bridges in the Fens in Boston.

5. Witold Rybczynski, *A Clearing in the Distance* (New York: Scribner, 1999), 349–50.

6. In 1871 Richardson and Olmsted joined with Elisha Harris and J. M. Trowbridge to publish for the Staten Island Improvement Corporation their *Report of a Preliminary Scheme of Improvements, Presented January 10th, 1871* (New York, 1871). See James F. O'Gorman, *H. H. Richardson: Architectural Forms for an American Society* (Chicago: University of Chicago Press, 1987), 143.

7. Jeffery Karl Ochsner, *H. H. Richardson: Complete Architectural Works* (Cambridge: MIT Press, 1982), 41; *The Century Yearbook, 2006* (New York: The Century Association, 2006).

8. We are grateful to Russell Flinchum, archivist of the Century Association Archives, for providing information on club nominations for both Olmsted and Richardson. Personal correspondence, May 12, 2010.

9. Richardson and Gambrill inaugurated an eleven-year partnership in October 1867. Richardson was rapidly inserted into the life of the club when, from 1867 to 1869, he and Gambrill oversaw plans for an art gallery addition to the clubhouse at 42 East Fifteenth Street in New York. See Ochsner, *Richardson: Works,* 41. Surprisingly, Richardson resigned from the Century the following year (Flinchum correspondence). See also James F. O'Gorman, *Living Architecture: A Biography of H. H. Richardson* (New York: Simon & Schuster, 1997), 77.

10. For a discussion of Olmsted's park work in Buffalo, consult Francis R. Kowsky, "Municipal Parks and City Planning: Frederick Law Olmsted's Buffalo Park and Parkway System," *Journal of the Society of Architectural Historians* 46.1 (March 1987): 49–64.

11. From 1874 through 1876 Richardson worked on the design for a Civil War memorial to be placed in the center of Niagara Square, one of the more formal elements of Olmsted and Vaux's Buffalo park system. Although it was never built, the massive structure is another indication of Olmsted's admiration for Richardson as a designer. Two Richardson clients, Dorsheimer and Mrs. A. P. Nichols (for whom Richardson proposed a Buffalo house that was also never constructed), were backers of the memorial project. See Ochsner, *Richardson: Works,* 144–45; and James F. O'Gorman, "H. H. Richardson and the Civil War Monument," *Nineteenth Century* 23 (Fall 2003): 3–9.

12. Francis R. Kowsky, "The William Dorsheimer House: A Reflection of French Suburban Architecture in the Early Work of H. H. Richardson," *Art Bulletin* 62 (March 1980): 134–47. Kowsky, with Andrew Zarmeba, then the librarian of the Century Association, also worked out the chronology and sponsorship of the Century Club nominations for Olmsted, Richardson, and Dorsheimer (ibid., 137n8). Kowsky, however, refers incorrectly to Olmsted's father-in-law, Charles L. Perkins, as Dr. Parmly.

13. Ibid., 134–47.

14. The Olmsted job number for the Buffalo State Hospital is 00612. For further information, see Carla Yanni, *The Architecture of Madness: Insane Asylums in the United States* (Minneapolis: University of Minnesota Press, 2007).

15. Frances R. Kowsky, "A Towering Masterpiece: H. H. Richardson's Buffalo State Hospital," *Buffalo Spree,* March–April 2000; text available online at *Buffalo as an Architectural Museum,* http://buffaloah.com/a/forest/400/statekowsky/index.html.

16. For further information on all of these mental hospitals and the most recent and comprehensive treatment of asylum design, see Yanni, *Architecture of Madness,* esp. chap. 4.

17. The Olmsted job number for the New York State Capitol is 00608.

18. Ochsner, *Richardson: Works,* 87. A committee was formed March 28, 1870, to study the possibility of erecting a new town hall. Sixteen competition entries were received, including one from Gambrill and Richardson. Designed by S. F. J. Thayer, the new town hall was dedicated on February 22, 1873.

19. O'Gorman, *H. H. Richardson and His Office,* 3.

20. Peter B. Wight, obituary for H. H. Richardson, *Inland Architect and Builder,* May 1886, 59.

21. Frederick Law Olmsted Jr. to Laura Wood Roper, September 16, 1951, Frederick Law Olmsted Jr. Retirement Correspondence, box 2, folder 2, Frederick Law Olmsted National Historic Site, National Park Service, Brookline.

22. Robert F. Brown, "The Aesthetic Transformation of an Industrial Community," *Winterthur Portfolio* 12 (1977): 35–64.

23. The Olmsted job number for the Crane Library is 00624.

24. The Olmsted job number for the Converse Library is 00292.

25. For the definitive study of all of the Richardson public libraries, see Kenneth A. Breisch, *Henry Hobson Richardson and the Small Public Library in America: A Study in Typology* (Cambridge: MIT Press, 1997).

26. For all of the projects in North Easton, consult Larry Homolka, "Henry Hobson Richardson and the 'Ames Memorial Buildings'" (Ph.D. diss., Harvard University, 1976), and also Homolka, "Richardson's North Easton," *Architectural Forum* 124 (May 1966): 72–77.

27. Even the building material changes from granite and sandstone on the first level to brick at the second and half-timbering in the front gable dormer.

28. Richardson played no known role in this element of the commission. See Brown, "Aesthetic Transformation," 45–48 and fig. 13. The Olmsted job number is 00649.

29. Ibid., 45–47.

30. For a detailed examination of this aspect of the relationship between Olmsted and Richardson, see O'Gorman, *H. H. Richardson: Architectural Forms,* chap. 5, "Ruralism," 91–111; and James F. O'Gorman, "Man-Made Mountain: 'Gathering and Governing' in H. H. Richardson's Design for the Ames Monument in Wyoming," in *The Railroad in American Art,* ed. Susan Daly and Leo Marx (Cambridge: MIT Press, 1988), 113–26.

31. An undated design for an icehouse on the Langwater estate was published by Mariana Griswold Van Rensselaer in *Henry Hobson Richardson and His Works,* 117. In his Harvard dissertation Larry Homolka suggests that this project was replaced by the gate lodge when Ames's plans for this end of the property changed.

32. There are two Olmsted job numbers for this property: 01224 (1891–92) and 01326 (1887–1891).

33. The Olmsted job number is 00670; three plans are dated 1883.

34. For a study of the suburban railroad stations of Richardson and Olmsted, see Jeffrey Karl Ochsner, "Architecture for the Boston & Albany Railroad: 1881–1894," *Journal of the Society of Architectural Historians,* 47.2 (June 1988): 109–31.

35. Richardson's Charlesgate West Bridge (1880–1883) in the Back Bay Fens was demolished in 1965. Cynthia Zaitzevsky has written extensively on the interactions of Olmsted and Richardson in the creation of the Back Bay Fens. See her "Frederick Law Olmsted and the Boston Park System" (Ph.D. diss., Harvard University, 1975); *Frederick Law Olmsted and the Boston Park System* (Cambridge: Belknap Press of Harvard University Press, 1982); and "The Olmsted Firm and the Structures of the Boston Park System," *Journal of the Society of Architectural Historians* 32 (May 1973): 167–74; also Ochsner, *Richardson: Works,* 221–23. The Olmsted job number for the Back Bay Fens is 00916.

36. A portion of the Boston park system extends into the town of Brookline, but the masonry work there, such as the Longwood Avenue Bridge, was completed later by Shepley, Rutan & Coolidge, Richardson's successor firm. See the discussion later in this chapter.

37. The Vale was created from 1793 onward and became one of the premier country estates of the Boston area, especially noted for its landscape development and horticultural sophistication.

38. Margaret Henderson Floyd, "H. H. Richardson, F. L. Olmsted, and the House for Robert Treat Paine," *Winterthur Portfolio* 18.4 (Winter 1983): 227–48. Paine's wife was the former Lydia Williams Lyman.

39. The Olmsted job number for the Paine estate is 00677.

40. The Bryant house is job number 12187 in the Olmsted archives. The initial correspondence between John Bryant and Frederick Law Olmsted is dated August 26, 1880. The original work was completed by 1882, although Bryant again requested the help of the firm in changes made to the property in 1894.

41. Sadly, the joy of the Bryant household was shattered by the emotional breakdown of Charlotte Olmsted Bryant in 1883 after the birth of their third child. She spent the remainder of her life in an asylum, where she died in 1908. Elizabeth Stevenson, *A Life of Frederick Law Olmsted* (New York: Macmillan, 1977), 356–57, citing a letter from Calvert Vaux to Frederick Law Olmsted, October 7, 1883, Frederick Law Olmsted Papers, Library of Congress, Washington, D.C. For other connections to the medical community in Brookline, see the discussion of the Free Hospital for Women and the residences of physicians in the area known as Pill Hill, near the adjacent hospital district in Boston.

42. The job number for the Channing project is 02230.

43. Greer Hardwicke and Roger Reed, *Images of America: Brookline* (Charleston, S.C.: Arcadia, 1998), 80.

44. For the evolution of the subdivision of Channing's land, see drawings 02230-1 and 02230-5 in the Olmsted archives, Brookline.

45. For Richardson and the École, see Richard Chaffee, "Richardson's Record at the École des Beaux-Arts," *Journal of the Society of Architectural Historians* 36 (October 1977): 175–88.

46. Hunt had been the first American to attend the École des Beaux-Arts (1846–1852) and therefore the first to bring that pedagogy and experience to bear on architectural practice in the United States. Of course, there was no reason for Richardson, on his return from Paris, to seek the training that Hunt provided to a number of young American architects. Indeed Richardson's partner, Charles Gambrill, had been one of the informal students who entered the Tenth Street Studio. For information on this group, see Alan Burnham, "The New York Architecture of Richard Morris Hunt," *Journal of the Society of Architectural Historians* 11.2 (May 1952): 9–14.

47. For the development of the architecture program at MIT, see J. A. Chewning, "William Robert Ware at MIT and Columbia," *Journal of Architectural Education* 33.2 (November 1979): 25–29.

48. James F O'Gorman, *H. H. Richardson and His Office, A Centennial Of His Move To Boston, 1874: Selected Drawings* (Cambridge: Dept. of Printing and Graphic Arts, Harvard College Library, 1974), 4–13, provides the fullest discussion of the education and work culture within the Richardson office.

49. *American Architect and Building News* 16 (December 27, 1884): 304, quoted in Mary M. Woods, *From Craft to Profession: The Practice of Architecture in Nineteenth-Century America* (Berkeley: University of California Press, 1999), 108.

50. Mary Alice Molloy, "Richardson's Web: A Client's Assessment of the Architect's Home and Studio," *Journal of the Society of Architectural Historians* 54.1 (March 1995): 8–23.

51. Frederick Law Olmsted Jr. to Laura Woods Roper, June 16, 1952, Frederick Law Olmsted Jr. Retirement Correspondence, box 2, folder 3.

52. Herbert Langford Warren became the director of the School of Architecture at Harvard, and John Galen Howard joined the faculty of the University of California, Berkeley.

53. The basic source on the life and career of Charles Eliot is his father, Charles W. Eliot's, *Charles Eliot: Landscape Architect* (1902; reprint, Amherst: University of Massachusetts Press for the Library of American Landscape Architecture, 1999), with a new introduction by Keith N. Morgan.

54. Ibid., 34. Charles Eliot Norton, the first professor of art and architectural history at Harvard College, was the cousin of President Eliot. He had taught young Charles at Harvard.

55. For a synopsis of the places Eliot visited with Olmsted, the projects on which he worked, and his thoughts about the Olmsted firm, see ibid., 36–44. Eliot's journals are divided between the Loeb Library, the Harvard Graduate School of Design, and the papers held by Alexander Yale Goriansky, Eliot's grandson, for the family of Carola Eliot Goriansky.

56. For a thorough discussion of the apprentices and junior members of the Olmsted office, see Zaitzevsky, *Olmsted and the Boston Park System,* 131–35.

57. See chapter 5 for the significance of Sargent and horticulture in the collaborations among the three men.

58. Frederick Law Olmsted to Mariana Van Rensselaer, August 11, 1886, Papers of Frederick Law Olmsted, Manuscript Division, Library of Congress, Washington, D.C., quoted in Carla Yanni, "'The Richardson Memorial': Mariana Griswold Van Rensselaer's *Henry Hobson Richardson and His Work,*" *Nineteenth Century* 27 (Fall 2007): 28–29. See also Cynthia Kinnard, "The Life and Works of Mariana Griswold Van Rensselaer" (Ph.D. diss., Johns Hopkins University, 1977), 138.

59 Yanni points out that Sargent saw the book not only as a tribute to his friend but also as a lucrative commercial opportunity; he received $1,304.21, half of the profits from publication. Yanni, "The Richardson Memorial," 30.

60. Ethan Carr, "*Garden and Forest* and Landscape Art," www.loc.gov/preserv/prd/gardfor/essays/carr.html.

61. One way in which Olmsted did not influence Richardson was in his business dealings and love of luxury. "H. H. Richardson died intestate and, as it turned out, insolvent, on 27 April 1886. . . . Itemized creditors included F. L. Olmsted, Norcross Brothers, A. H. Davenport, and Henry Poole, the architect's London tailor." James F. O'Gorman, "Documentation: An 1886 Inventory of H. H. Richardson's Library, and Other Gleanings from Probate," *Journal of the Society of Architectural Historians* 41.2 (May 1982): 150. Norcross was a builder with whom Richardson frequently worked; Davenport was a furniture maker.

4. THE DESIGN COMMUNITY

1. See appendix B for a list of the architects, landscape architects, and engineers who resided in Brookline during the period of this study, 1883–1936.

2. Arthur Rotch lived from 1888 to 1894 at 70 Hyslop Road, and Dabney resided at 153 Dean Road from 1894 to 1897.

3. "Circular as to Professional Methods and Charges," January 1894, and "Statement as to Professional Methods and Charges," January 1, 1902, National Park Service, Frederick Law Olmsted National Historic Site. For the full text of the 1902 version see appendix C. The name of the firm changed several times over the period covered by this book: 1872–1884, Frederick Law Olmsted; 1884–1889, F. L. & J. C. Olmsted; 1889–1893, F. L. Olmsted & Company; 1893–1897, Olmsted, Olmsted & Eliot; 1897–1898, F. L. & J. C. Olmsted; 1898–1961, Olmsted Brothers Landscape Architects. At each stage various partners and principals directed the work of the firm. For further information on firm members at each stage, see Catherine Joy Johnson, *Olmsted in the Pacific Northwest: Private Estates and Residential Communities, 1873–1959* (Seattle: Friends of Seattle's Olmsted Parks, 1997).

4. The Richardson circular is published as appendix V in Mariana Griswold Van Rensselaer, *Henry Hobson Richardson and His Works* (1888; reprint, New York: Dover Publications, 1969), 147. All quotations in this discussion are from this source. There is no indication of the date when this circular was first developed.

5. Mary Woods, *From Craft to Profession: The Practice of Architecture in Nineteenth-Century America* (Berkeley: University of California Press, 1999), 110.

6. Surprisingly little has been written about the firm, which is still in business today in Boston under the

name of Shepley Bulfinch, one of the oldest American architectural offices in continuous operation. Julia Heskel, *Shepley Bulfinch Richardson and Abbott: Past to Present* (Boston: Shepley Bulfinch Richardson and Abbott, 1999); and J. D. Forbes, "Shepley, Bulfinch, Richardson & Abbott: An Introduction," *Journal of the Society of Architectural Historians* 17.3 (Autumn 1958): 19–31.

7. For a list of the forty-two projects undertaken by Shepley, Rutan & Coolidge in Brookline, see appendix F. The archives of Shepley Bulfinch Richardson & Abbott provide further documentation of these commissions.

8. George F. Shepley to C. A. Coolidge, December 19, 1886, cited in Heskel, *Shepley Bulfinch,* 19.

9. The early-nineteenth-century house at 45 Cottage Street was demolished in 1905 to make way for the house that still stands today.

10. The project is job number 01055. On one planting list, 01055-Z2, notes appear to be in Olmsted's hand.

11. For a discussion of the Beacon Street development, see chapter 6 and Cynthia Zaitzevsky, "Frederick Law Olmsted in Brookline: A Preliminary Study of His Public Projects," in *Proceedings of the Brookline Historical Society for 1975–1978* (Brookline: Published for the Society, 1979), 59.

12. "George Wightman Dies in Brookline," *Brookline Chronicle,* April 20, 1937; "A Longwood Mansion," *Brookline Chronicle,* November 29, 1902. As always, the authors are grateful to Greer Hardwicke and the staff of the Brookline Preservation Commission for sharing their files.

13. The only surviving plan for the Hawes Street Wightman house is job number 04019-34, a study for the proposed profile of the boundary of property along Hawes Street. Photographs of the property exist in the collections of the Loeb Library, Graduate School of Design, Harvard University.

14. See plan number 04019-3, which was received by the Olmsted office on June 4, 1910. The plan notes that the property to the east, 26 Monmouth Street, was owned by Flora W. Reynolds, a project controlled by Wightman with a house designed by Shepley, Rutan & Coolidge in 1905.

15. Wheaton Holden, "The Peabody Touch: Peabody and Stearns of Boston, 1870–1917," *Journal of the Society of Architectural Historians* 32.2 (May 1973): 115–16.

16. For information on Gridley J. F. Bryant, see Roger Reed, *Building Victorian Boston: The Architecture of Gridley J. F. Bryant* (Amherst: University of Massachusetts Press, 2007).

17. For the development of the architecture program at MIT, see J. A. Chewning, "William Robert Ware at MIT and Columbia," *Journal of Architectural Education* 33.2 (November 1979): 25–29; and Kimberly Alexander-Shilland, "Ware and Van Brunt: Architectural Practice and Professionalism, 1863–1881" (Ph.D. diss., Boston University, 1991).

18. Robert Day Andrews, "Conditions of Architectural Practices Thirty Years and More Ago," *Architectural Review* 5.11 (November 1917): 237–38.

19. For a discussion of the relationship between the Olmsted firm and Ernest Bowditch, see the section in chapter 6 on landscape architects and civil engineers.

20. Holden, "The Peabody Touch," 120–22.

21. For the Lenox commissions, see Richard S. Jackson Jr. and Cornelia Brooke Gilder, *The Architecture of Leisure: Houses of the Berkshires, 1870–1930* (New York: Acanthus Press, 2006); Ann Williams Swallow, "The Eclecticism of Peabody and Stearns in Lenox, Massachusetts, 1881–1905" (M.A. thesis, University of Virginia, 1984); and Anne Robinson, *Peabody and Stearns: Country Houses and Seaside Cottages* (New York: W. W. Norton, 2010).

22. For a list of the seventy-two projects that Peabody & Stearns planned and executed in Brookline, see appendix G. In 1892 the Peabodys moved to 22 The Fenway, another house that the architect designed for himself, this time overlooking Olmsted's Back Bay Fens.

23. The house was badly remodeled in 1964; the original west porch was eliminated, and a new two-story glass entrance was cut into the west facade. At this writing, new owners were planning to restore the building to something closer to Peabody's intentions.

24. This paper was published in *American Architect and Building News,* April 28, 1877, 133–34.

25. Robert S. Peabody, "Georgian Houses of New England, I," *American Architect and Building News* 2 (October 20, 1877): 338–39; "Georgian Houses of New England, II," *American Architect and Building News* 3 (February 16, 1878): 54–55.

26. "Dry Goods Establishment of R. H. White, Boston, Mass.," *American Architect and Building News* 2 (May 1877): 148.

27. The firm also designed the substantial stable complex for this property at 545 Boylston Street, which

White named Elmhurst. The image in figure 4.9 was published in *L'Architecture Américaine,* the first photographic anthology of contemporary American architecture, published in Paris in 1886 and republished as *American Victorian Architecture* (New York: Dover, 1975), with a new introduction by Arnold Lewis and notes by Keith Morgan.

28. The Joseph H. White job number is 00626; this is plan number 26.

29. See plan numbers 00626-18-TP6 and 00626-Z-10.

30. The other property holders were the Goddard Land Company, Mrs. L. S. Rogers, Arthur Rotch, and Jacob W. Pierce.

31. See plan number 00626-z19.

32. Many of the Jonathan H. White plans are intermixed with the Joseph H. White files of the Fairsted Collections. See plan number 00626-33. The "line of continuation of walk opposite dwelling of Mr. Joseph H. White" marked on this plan shows an interconnection of the White properties from an early stage.

33. An unidentified building permit was pulled for the house in 1891.

34. According to the *Brookline Chronicle,* November 28, 1891.

35. According to Brookline atlases, the house was demolished sometime between 1921 and 1925.

36. See Charles W. Eliot, *Charles Eliot: Landscape Architect* (1902; reprint, Amherst: University of Massachusetts Press for the Library of American Landscape Architecture, 1999), 37: "He also prepared not infrequently what he called 'show maps,' that is, maps intended to interest prospective buyers in estates it was proposed to cut up into house-lots."

37. The Stones' changes in the gardens west of the house are detailed in plan number 00626-8, dated September 28, 1931. The Stones moved here from a house at 149 Buckminster Road, designed for them by Chapman & Frazer, who remodeled the interiors of the White house for the Stones.

38. Among other services rendered to Richardson by Herbert Jaques was to serve as his traveling companion on a rapid tour of Europe in the summer of 1882. See James F. O'Gorman, "On Vacation with H. H. Richardson: Ten Letters from Europe, 1882," *Archives of American Art Journal* 19.1 (1979): 2–14.

39. The Brookline Historical Commission survey form lists five estates in this neighborhood, owned by Randolph Coolidge, Walter Cabot, Robert Treat Paine, William Cox, and Theodore Lyman.

40. Paine was the grandson of his namesake, who had been the chairman of the building committee for Richardson's Trinity Church and had commissioned Richardson and Olmsted to develop his country estate, Stonehurst, in Waltham. The same firm designed a stable for the estate in 1899 and added to the house in 1903.

41. The initial plan in the Paine drawings, job number 03341, is for the estate of Walter C. Cabot, drawn by Joseph H. Curtis, "landscape engineer and gardener," in December 1893.

42. We are deeply grateful to Greer Hardwicke of the Brookline Preservation Commission for sharing her unpublished study of the Boylston Street Corridor in Brookline. The Olmsted office job number for the Coolidge project is 00323.

43. The Charles Storrow property is job number 00629 in the Olmsted archives. Interestingly, Cabot & Chandler won the competition for Johns Hopkins Hospital in Baltimore in 1889, which became the model for pavilion hospital plans, the new paradigm in medical practice. It is not surprising that they were also working for doctors on Pill Hill in Brookline, even though Storrow was not a physician.

44. The Olmsted job number for the J. G. Wright estate is 00224. The property was located between Hammond and Heath streets with the entrance from Heath near Woodland Road.

5. CHARLES SPRAGUE SARGENT

1. James F. O'Gorman, "On Vacation with H. H. Richardson: Ten Letters from Europe, 1882," *Archives of American Art Journal* 19.1 (1979): 4; Peter B. Wight, obituary of H. H. Richardson, *The Inland Architect and Builder,* May 1886, 61.

2. See Ronald Dale Karr, "The Evolution of an Elite Suburb: Community Structure and Control in Brookline, Massachusetts, 1770–1900" (Ph.D. diss., Boston University, 1981), for a thorough discussion of the socioeconomic development of Brookline.

3. Ibid., 81–82.

4. Tamara Plakins Thornton, *Cultivating Gentlemen: The Meaning of Country Life among the Boston Elite, 1785– 1860* (New Haven: Yale University Press, 1989), 60.

5. Ibid., 163.

6. Harriet F. Woods, *Historical Sketches of Brookline, Mass.* (Boston: Robert S. Davis and Co., 1874), 359.

7. Andrew Jackson Downing, *Landscape Gardening and Rural Architecture* (1865; reprint, New York: Dover Publications, 1991), 38.

8. Marshall Pinckney Wilder, "The Horticulture of Boston and Vicinity," in *The Memorial History of Boston Including Suffolk County, Massachusetts, 1630–1880* (Boston: James R. Osgood and Co., 1881), 626.

9. Woods, *Historical Sketches,* 357–58.

10. Perkins was a subscriber to Audubon's *Birds,* purchasing one set for himself and one for Boston's chief private library, the Boston Athenaeum.

11. Thornton, *Cultivating Gentlemen,* 150.

12. Carl Seaburg and Stanley Paterson, *Merchant Prince of Boston: Colonel T. H. Perkins, 1764–1854* (Cambridge: Harvard University Press, 1971), 391–92. Robert Manning wrote in his *History of the Massachusetts Horticultural Society* (Boston: Rand, Avery, 1880) that among the most interesting accounts written in the late 1820s, *New England Farmer and Horticultural Journal* (1822–1842) was "of the method of heating hothouses and graperies with hot water, by Samuel G. Perkins and Thomas H. Perkins, this method having been just introduced" (207).

13. Wilder, "Horticulture of Boston and Vicinity," 625.

14. H. A. S. Dearborn, address to the Society at the Boston Athenaeum, September 19, 1830, quoted in Manning, *History of the Massachusetts Horticultural Society,* 219–20.

15. Downing, *Landscape Gardening and Rural Architecture,* 39–40. Jamaica Lake is now called Jamaica Pond.

16. Harriet Manning Whitcomb, *Annals and Reminiscences of Jamaica Plain* (Cambridge: Riverdale Press, 1897), 15.

17. Charles Knowles Bolton, *Brookline: The History of a Favored Town* (Brookline: C. A. W. Spencer, 1897), 96.

18. Woods, *Historical Sketches,* 363.

19. Downing, *Landscape Gardening and Rural Architecture,* 40.

20. Manning, *History of the Massachusetts Horticultural Society,* 122.

21. His full name was Joseph Augustus Peabody Lowell. The Lowell Institute is an educational foundation established by members of the Lowell family in 1799 in order to provide "free lectures on scientific, literary, and religious themes." Whitcomb, *Annals and Reminiscences of Jamaica Plain,* 16.

22. Richard Hunt, "Amy Lowell: A Sketch of Her Place in Contemporary Fiction," Houghton Library, Harvard University, 1917.

23. Percival Lowell, "Augustus Lowell," *Journal of the Proceedings of the American Academy of Arts and Sciences,* 1901, 2.

24. Ibid.

25. Among the children were Abbott Lawrence Lowell (1856–1943), president of Harvard University; the poet Amy Lowell (1874–1925); Percival Lowell (1855–1916), the iconoclastic astronomer who discovered Pluto; and Guy Lowell (1870–1927), architect and landscape designer, married to Henrietta Sargent, Charles Sprague Sargent's daughter. Guy Lowell later headed the landscape architecture course at the Massachusetts Institute of Technology.

26. Thomas Wentworth Higginson, *Life and Times of Stephen Higginson* (Boston: Houghton, Mifflin, 1907), 235. Stephen Higginson was a member of the Massachusetts Society for Promoting Agriculture. He was also a kinsman and close friend of Augustus Lowell's grandfather, the Roxbury horticulturist John Lowell (49).

27. Amy Lowell, "Sevenels," in *Florence Asycough and Amy Lowell: Correspondence of a Friendship,* ed. Harley Farnsworth MacNair (Chicago: University of Chicago Press, 1945), 248. This essay gives a detailed description of the garden during Amy Lowell's residence in the house (1900–1919).

28. P. Lowell, "Augustus Lowell," 6. Percival Lowell was a member of the Massachusetts Horticultural Society from 1863, joining just before he left for his sojourn in Europe.

29. Ibid.

30. A. Lowell, "Sevenels," 248. The following quotations are from this page.

31. Ibid., 248, 249.

32. Downing, *Landscape Gardening and Rural Architecture,* 37.

33. Ibid., 41.

34. Karr, "Evolution of an Elite Suburb," 224.

35. "Drives about Boston: Brookline and Chestnut Hill," in *Boston and Its Suburbs* (Boston: Stanley & Usher, 1888), 103–4.

36. S. B. Sutton, *Charles Sprague Sargent and the Arnold Arboretum* (Cambridge: Harvard University Press, 1970), 6.

37. *Gardener's Monthly and Horticulturist,* October 1884, 318.

38. Karr, "Evolution of an Elite Suburb," 310.

39. Ida Hay, *Science in the Pleasure Ground: A History of the Arnold Arboretum* (Boston: Northeastern University Press, 1995), 67.

40. Downing, *Landscape Gardening and Rural Architecture,* 34. Fishkill Landing is now Beacon, New York. The name Wodenethe, according to Sargent, was drawn from two Saxon words, *woden* and *ethe,* meaning "woody promontory."

41. J. J. Smith, "Visits to Country Places," no. 3, "About New York: The North River," *Horticulturist,* 1856, 29.

42. William Howard Adams, "Breaking New Ground: Twentieth-Century American Gardens," in *Keeping Eden: A History of Gardening in America,* ed. Walter Punch (Boston: Bulfinch Press, 1992), 63.

43. Hay, *Science in the Pleasure Ground,* 66.

44. J. E. Spingarn, "Henry Winthrop Sargent and the Landscape Tradition at Wodenethe," *Landscape Architecture,* October 1938, 32. Sargent contributed articles to Downing's *Horticulturist* and to C. M. Hovey's English *Magazine of Horticulture;* his most significant contribution to the field of horticultural literature, however, is probably his supervision of the sixth edition of Downing's *Landscape Gardening* (published in 1859, after Downing's death), which included an extensive supplement written by Sargent that describes his own estate as well as that of his cousin H. H. Hunnewell.

45. Hunnewell's estate had twelve greenhouses and numerous gardens for flowers, fruits, and vegetables. He planted native and exotic trees along the estate's many avenues. Thornton, *Cultivating Gentlemen,* 153. He named it Wellesley to honor his wife's family, the Welleses.

46. Allyson M. Hayward, "Private Pleasures Derived from Tradition: The Hunnewell Estates Historic District," *Arnoldia* 64.4 (2006): 33.

47. Henry Winthrop Sargent spent from 1847 to 1849 traveling in Europe and the Levant, studying landscape and park design as well as acquiring plant material. Spingarn, "Henry Winthrop Sargent," 33.

48. Ibid., 39.

49. M. G. Van Rensselaer, "A Suburban Country Place," *Century Magazine,* May 1897, 6.

50. For a thorough discussion of Sargent's development of Holm Lea, see Natalie Wampler's Boston University graduate paper "Holm Lea, the Sargent Estate in Brookline," May 1, 2007, Brookline Historical Commission.

51. M. C. Robbins, "A Tree Museum," *Century Magazine,* April 1893, 873.

52. Stephen A. Spongberg, "C. S. Sargent: Seeing the Forest and the Trees," *Orian Nature Quarterly,* Autumn 1984, 6.

53. Walter Muir Whitehill, "Francis Parkman as Horticulturist," *Arnoldia,* May 1973, 177.

54. This included remodeling the taxonomic beds following Bentham and Hooker; removing overgrown, duplicate, and misplaced trees and shrubs; and adding grass walks in order to facilitate student and visitor access. An extant rock garden was rebuilt and substantially enlarged. Every specimen was labeled with its scientific and common name, as well as its place of origin. Hay, *Science in the Pleasure Ground,* 73.

55. Ibid., 37.

56. Charles Sprague Sargent, "Arnold Arboretum: What It Is and Does," *Garden Magazine,* November 1917, 3. Ultimately the arboretum incorporated 265 acres, 40 of them given by the City of Boston.

57. Ibid., 4.

58. Robbins, "Tree Museum," 871.

59. Harvard University required that a fund of at least $150,000 be accumulated before it would agree to the existence of an arboretum under its auspices. Eventually the goal was reached in 1879.

60. Frederick Law Olmsted to Charles Sprague Sargent, July 8, 1874, Frederick Law Olmsted Papers, Library of Congress, Washington, D.C.

61. Sargent, "Arnold Arboretum," 4.

62. Sheila Connor Geary and B. June Hutchinson "The Original Design and Permanent Arrangement of

the Arnold Arboretum as Determined by FLO and CSS," August 1979, rev. April 1981, 6, Arnold Arboretum Archives, Harvard University. This reference suggests that the renowned botanist Asa Gray collaborated on early plans for the arboretum.

63. Ibid.

64. E. H. Wilson, *America's Greatest Garden: The Arnold Arboretum* (Boston: Stratford Co., 1925), 94–95.

65. Whitcomb, *Annals and Reminiscences of Jamaica Plain,* 52–53.

66. Wilder, "Horticulture of Boston and Vicinity," 632.

67. Judith Leet, "The Hunnewell Pinetum: A Long-Standing Family Tradition," *Arnoldia,* Fall 1990, 35.

68. "Report of the Director of the Arnold Arboretum to the Boston Park Commission," 1875, Arnold Arboretum Archives.

69. "Report of the Director of the Arnold Arboretum to the President and Fellows of Harvard College for the Year Ending August 31, 1878," Arnold Arboretum Archives.

70. Wilder, "Horticulture of Boston and Vicinity," 618.

71. William Trelease, "Biographical Memoir of Charles Sprague Sargent," *National Academy of Sciences of the United States of America Biographical Memoirs,* 1928, 250.

72. Robbins, "Tree Museum," 876.

73. Mariana Griswold Van Rensselaer, *Art Out-of-Doors* (New York: Charles Scribner's Sons, 1925), 434.

74. See Mariana Griswold Van Rensselaer, *Accents as Well as Broad Effects: Writings on Architecture, Landscape, and the Environment, 1876–1925,* ed. David Gebhard (Berkeley: University of California Press, 1996), for examples of her landscape writings.

75. Charles S. Sargent, "A Garden of Trees," *Youth's Companion,* March 15, 1917, 147.

76. Beatrix Farrand, "Contemplated Landscape Changes at the Arnold Arboretum," *Arnoldia,* November 1, 1946, 45.

77. Cynthia Zaitzevsky, *Frederick Law Olmsted and the Boston Park System* (Cambridge: Belknap Press of Harvard University Press, 1982), 63.

78. Van Rensselaer, *Art Out-of-Doors,* 445.

79. Jane Brown, "Lady into Landscape Gardener: Beatrix Farrand's Early Years at the Arnold Arboretum," *Arnoldia,* Summer 1991, 7. Codman was Sargent's nephew and one of Olmsted's most prized protégés.

80. Ibid.

81. Beatrix Farrand, "Beatrix Farrand, 1872–1959," *Reef Point Gardens Bulletin* 1, n.d. (Farrand wrote her own obituary before she died.)

82. Beatrix Farrand to Paul C. Mangelsdorf, May 15, 1946. Jane Brown writes of Farrand's work at the arboretum in a two-part article for *Arnoldia,* "The Lady as Landscape Gardener: Beatrix Farrand at the Arnold Arboretum, Part 1," Summer 1991, 3–10, and "Part 2," Winter 1992, 9–17.

83. From 1882 on, Charles Edward Faxon (1846–1918), a Jamaica Plain botanical illustrator, was in charge of the herbarium and the library there. He was an invaluable member of the arboretum staff.

84. C. S. Sargent, "The Greatest Garden in America: The Arnold Arboretum," *Home Acres,* February 1927, 95. Sargent, a member of the Massachusetts Horticultural Society from 1870 on, also contributed a significant number of pamphlets, both domestic and foreign, to the society's library. Albert Emerson Benson, *History of the Massachusetts Horticultural Society* (Boston: Massachusetts Horticultural Society, 1929), 431.

85. Van Rensselaer, *Art Out-of-Doors,* 435.

86. Sargent, "Arnold Arboretum," 5.

87. Trelease, "Biographical Memoir of Charles Sprague Sargent," 252.

88. Albert Emerson Benson, *History of the Massachusetts Horticultural Society* (Boston: Massachusetts Horticultural Society, 1929), 507–8.

89. Dismayed that the price of the volumes ($25 each) made them inaccessible to the general public, in 1905 Sargent published an abbreviated version, *Manual of the Trees of North America.*

90. Spongberg, "C. S. Sargent," 9. The landscape architect Bremer W. Pond (1884–1959) confirmed in 1950 that *Garden and Forest* was "widely read." Bremer W. Pond, "Fifty Years in Retrospect: A Brief Account of the Origin and Development of the ASLA," *Landscape Architecture,* January 1950, 59.

91. Norman T. Newton, *Design of the Land: The Development of Landscape Architecture* (Cambridge: Belknap Press, 1971), 320. For a discussion of Eliot's contributions, see Keith N. Morgan's introduction to the

reprint edition of Charles W. Eliot, *Charles Eliot: Landscape Architect* (1902; Amherst: University of Massachusetts Press in association with Library of American Landscape History). The Trustees of Public Reservations is currently known as the Trustees of Reservations.

92. Mary Sargent Potter, "Silhouettes: My Mother—My Father," *Spur Magazine,* n.d., 6. Potter (Mrs. Nathanial Bowditch Potter) was one of the four children who lived to adulthood in the Sargent family. The other three were Henrietta (Mrs. Guy Lowell), Charles S. Sargent, and Alice Sargent, who lived at home with her parents, then with her father upon Mrs. Sargent's death in 1919. Andrew Robeson Sargent died in 1918.

93. Ibid., 3.

94. Alfred Rehder, "Charles Sprague Sargent," *Journal of the Arnold Arboretum,* 1927, 73.

95. Ernest H. Wilson, "Charles Sprague Sargent," *Harvard Graduates Magazine,* June 1927, 614.

96. Ibid., 112, 80–81.

97. Nancy Zaroulis, "The Man Who Invented Mars," *Boston Globe Magazine,* April 27, 2008, 31.

98. Wilson succeeded Sargent as "Keeper of the Arboretum" (a title he insisted on rather than director) until his untimely death three years later in 1930.

99. Walter Muir Whitehill, "Father of the Arboretum," *Boston Sunday Herald Traveler,* December 6, 1970, 2.

100. Walter T. Punch, "The Garden Organized: The Public Face of Horticulture," *Keeping Eden: A History of Gardening in America,* ed. Walter Punch (Boston: Little, Brown, 1992), 225.

101. *Plantae Wilsonianae: An Enumeration of the Woody Plant Collection in Western China for the Arnold Arboretum of Harvard University during the Years 1907, 1908, and 1910* was the full title.

102. Dawson (1841–1916) eventually became an American citizen.

103. Sheila Connor Geary and B. June Hutchinson, "Mr. Dawson, Plantsman," *Arnoldia,* March 1980, 55.

104. Parkman's house "stood on rising ground, close to the shore of Jamaica Pond. Here he had his gardens and green-houses, and here he came early in the spring, and remained late in the autumn every year," wrote his friend and Harvard classmate Edward Wheelwright. Quoted in Whitehill, "Francis Parkman," 173-174, 176. In 1866 Parkman published *The Book of Roses.* Ill health caused Parkman to serve at the institute for only one year.

105. In 1886 he and his growing family moved to the Lewis farmhouse, initially leased from the Adams Nervine Asylum, where a small greenhouse and an acre for plant propagation were provided. Between 1924 and 1927 Sargent negotiated its purchase for the arboretum. See Boston Landmarks Commission, "The Lewis-Dawson Farmhouse at the Arnold Arboretum: Study Report, June 2007." Arnold Arboretum Archives, for a full discussion of the history of the property.

106. Quoted in Geary and Hutchinson, "Dawson," 57.

107. Ibid., 60.

108. "In Memoriam: Jackson Thornton Dawson," 1916, Arnold Arboretum Archives.

109. Benson, *History of the Massachusetts Horticultural Society,* 466–67.

110. Cynthia Zaitzevsky, "Frederick Law Olmsted in Brookline: A Preliminary Study of His Public Projects," *Proceedings of the Brookline Historical Society,* Fall 1977, 42.

111. Zaitzevsky, *Frederick Law Olmsted and the Boston Park System,* 82. The problem, in part, was a result of the filling of the Back Bay, which reduced the tidal flow.

112. Ibid.

113. Charles E. Beveridge and Paul Rocheleau, *Frederick Law Olmsted: Designing the American Landscape* (New York: Rizzoli, 1995), 86.

114. The other two members were Francis W. Lawrence and Theodore Lyman, eventually replaced by William H. Lincoln and Henry M. Whitney.

115. Zaitzevsky, *Frederick Law Olmsted and the Boston Park System,* 83.

116. Ibid., 83. Zaitzevsky provides a thorough discussion of the system's evolution.

117. Frederick Law Olmsted, "Suggestions for the Improvement of Muddy River," in *Annual Reports of the Town Officers of Brookline, for the Year Ending January 31, 1881* (Brookline: Chronicle Steam Press, Arthur & Spencer, 1881), 169, 172.

118. Ibid., 173.

119. Ibid., 174–75.

120. "Report of the Park Commissioners," in *Reports of the Town Officers of Brookline for the Year Ending January 31, 1884* (Brookline: Chronicle Press, C. A. W. Spencer, 1884), 218.

121. "Report of the Park Commissioners," in *Town Records and Reports of the Town Officers of Brookline, Massachusetts, for the Year Ending January 31, 1885* (Brookline: Chronicle Press, C. A. W. Spencer, 1885).

122. "Report of the Park Commissioners," in *Town Records and Reports of the Town Officers of Brookline, Massachusetts, for the Year Ending January 31, 1886* (Brookline: Chronicle Press, C. A. W. Spencer, 1886).

123. "Report of the Park Commissioners," in *Town Records and Reports of the Town Officers of Brookline, Massachusetts, for the Year Ending January 31, 1887* (Boston: Franklin Press, 1887), 153.

124. "Report of the Park Commissioners," in *Town Records and Reports of the Town Officers of Brookline, Massachusetts, for the Year Ending January 31, 1888* (Brookline: Chronicle Press, C. A. W. Spencer, 1888), 255.

125. "Report of the Park Commissioners," in *Town Records and Reports of the Town Officers of Brookline, Massachusetts, for the Year Ending January 31, 1889* (Brookline: Chronicle Press, C. A. W. Spencer, 1889), 301.

126. Ibid., 303.

127. F. L. Olmsted and Co. to Francis W. Lawrence, Esq., "Report of the Park Commissioners," in *Town Records and Reports of the Town Officers of Brookline, Massachusetts, for the Year Ending January 31, 1890* (Brookline: Chronicle Press, C. A. W. Spencer, 1890), 258.

128. Ibid., 259.

129. "Report of the Park Commissioners," in *Town Records and Reports of the Town Officers of Brookline, Massachusetts, for the Year Ending January 31, 1891* (Boston: Cashman, Keating & Co., 1891), 278. The new station was subsequently abandoned as "impracticable" without damaging the park.

130. The Boston Park Commission had set aside eight and a half acres, situated on the banks of the river, for a "Fresh-Water Zoological Garden" sponsored by the Boston Society of Natural History. See *Town Records and Reports for the Year Ending January 31, 1890, 263.*

131. Ibid., 264.

132. Ibid., 269.

133. *Town Records and Reports for the Year Ending January 31, 1891,* 281.

134. Zaitzevsky, *Frederick Law Olmsted and the Boston Park System,* 85.

135. "Report of the Park Commissioners," in *Town Records and Reports of the Town of Brookline, Massachusetts, for the Year Ending January 31, 1892* (Brookline: Chronicle Press, C. A. W. Spencer, 1892), 305.

136. Newton, *Design of the Land,* 301.

137. Alexis H. French, "Report of the Engineer," in *Town Records and Reports of the Town Officers of Brookline, Massachusetts for the Year Ending January 31, 1893* (Brookline: Chronicle Press, C. A. W. Spencer, 1893), 355.

138. Zaitzevsky, *Frederick Law Olmsted and the Boston Park System,* 196. See her "Appendices: Lists A. and B.: Brookline and Boston, 1892–1893" for the full list of plants and the one edited by Sargent, both of which are still in the files of the Olmsted National Historic Site.

139. H. S. Codman to John Olmsted, April 7, 1892.

140. Zaitzevsky, *Frederick Law Olmsted and the Boston Park System,* 197.

141. Ibid.

142. *Town Records and Reports for the Year Ending January 31, 1892,* 305–6.

143. "Report of the Engineer," in *Town Records and Reports for the Year Ending January 31, 1893,* 355.

144. Charles Sprague Sargent, "Prospect Park," *Garden and Forest,* July 4, 1888, 218.

145. *Brookline Chronicle,* January 1, 1876, quoted in Karr, "Evolution of an Elite Suburb," 253.

146. "The Brookline Club," *Brookline Chronicle,* March 2, 1889.

147. Paul M. Hubbard and Richard C. Floyd, "Report of the Park Commissioners," in *222d Annual Report of the Town Officers of Brookline, Massachusetts, and the Town Records for the Year Ending December 31, 1927* (Newton, Mass.: Garden City Press, 128), 239.

148. Van Rensselaer, "Suburban Country Place," 3, 6.

149. Ibid., 5.

150. Wampler, "Holm Lea, the Sargent Estate in Brookline," 10.

151. Wilhelm Miller, "The Sargent Home Near Boston," *Country Life in America,* March 1903, 202. According to Miller, the greenhouses comprised "some three or four thousand feet of glass" (206); they were used for growing cut flowers for winter and also for unusual plants.

152. Wampler, "Home Lea," 12. According to Wampler, Sargent's granddaughter Cora Codman Wolcott said that the apples were used to provide cider in winter for the various Sargent households.

153. Miller, "Sargent Home," 202.

154. Hazel Collins, "Landscape Gardening in Brookline."

155. Van Rensselaer, "Suburban Country Place," 9.

156. Miller, "The Sargent Home Near Boston," 201.

157. Quoted in Sutton, *Charles Sprague Sargent and the Arnold Arboretum,* 156, 157–58.

158. John Muir, "Sargent's Silva," *Atlantic Monthly,* July 1903, 9.

159. Philip H. Weld, "Rockweld: A Boy's Eden," *Sloan,* Winter 1985, 21. See Elizabeth Hope Cushing, "Historic Landscape Report for the MIT Endicott House, Dedham, Massachusetts," March 2003, MIT Endicott House, for a discussion of the Rockweld gardens. Weld was one of the contributors toward Ernest Wilson's explorations in China.

160. Potter, "Silhouettes," 7.

161. W. L., "Mary Robeson Sargent," *Boston Transcript,* August 20, 1919.

162. Wilder, "Horticulture of Boston and Vicinity," 626.

163. Trelease, "Biographical Memoir of Charles Sprague Sargent," 257.

164. He was a member of the National Academy of Sciences, the American Academy of Arts and Sciences, and the American Philosophical Society. He was the rare foreign member of the Linnaean Society of London, the Royal Society of Ireland, the Société Nationale d'Agriculture de France, the Royal Horticultural Society of England, the Société Nationale d'Acclimatation de France, the Deutsche Dendrologischen Gesellschaft, the Scottish Arboricultural Society, the English Arboricultural Society, and the Oesterreichische Dendrologischen Gesellschaft.

165. Hubbard and Floyd, "Report of the Park Commissioners," in *222d Annual Report,* 239.

166. Benson, *History of the Massachusetts Horticultural Society,* 508.

167. Frederick Law Olmsted [Jr.], "Charles Sprague Sargent," December 15, 1927, John Charles Olmsted Collection, Frances Loeb Library, Harvard Graduate School of Design.

168. Hay, *Science in the Pleasure Ground,* 197.

169. Phyllis Andersen, "Sargent, Charles Sprague," in *Pioneers of American Landscape Design,* ed. Charles A. Birnbaum and Robin Karson (New York: McGraw-Hill, 2000), 324.

170. Rehder, "Charles Sprague Sargent," 73.

6. THE PLANNING CONTEXT

1. "The Brookline Club: Members and Ladies Entertained with a Paper by Frederick Law Olmsted," *Brookline Chronicle,* March 2, 1889.

2. The areas on both sides of Route 9 in Brookline Village, as well as sections along Boylston Street below Cypress Street, were cleared of housing in the 1960s.

3. Charles E. Beveridge and Paul Rocheleau, *Frederick Law Olmsted: Designing the American Landscape* (New York: Universe Publishing, 1998), 102–3.

4. Annexation attempts occurred in 1873, 1875, 1879, and 1880.

5. Plan number Z-5, job number 01300, Frederick Law Olmsted National Historic Site, National Park Service, Brookline. There is no written information on the plan. In the same file, "Plan #10" is an unlabeled plot plan for the area between the Brookline Village railroad station and Longwood Avenue, signed Alexis E. French, C.E., January 25, 1885.

6. *Town Records and Reports of the Town Officers of Brookline, Massachusetts, for the Year Ending January 31, 1894* (Brookline: Chronicle Press, 1894), 345–46. The published report includes the plan, dated October 25, 1893. This is one of several plans for small parks. The others are found in job number 01300, Town of Brookline, Frederick Law Olmsted National Historic Site. Probably none of these schemes was carried out.

7. F. L. & J. C. Olmsted, Landscape Architects, "Preliminary Plan for Widening Beacon Street from the Back Bay District of Boston to the Public Pleasure Grounds at Chestnut Hill Reservoir and for Connection with Massachusetts and Commonwealth Avenues," November 29, 1886, plan number 1172-1, copy in Brookline Public Library.

8. "The Beacon Street Plan," *Brookline Chronicle,* December 4, 1886.

9. Plan 1172-33, copy in Brookline Public Library. This plan can be found in the Frederick Law Olmsted National Historic Site under job number 00944, which deals mostly with Commonwealth Avenue in Boston.

10. "The Beacon Street Plan."

11. Cynthia Zaitzevsky, *Frederick Law Olmsted and the Boston Park System* (Cambridge: Belknap Press of Harvard University Press, 1982), 31.

12. *Brookline Chronicle,* August 7, 1886.

13. Edward Atkinson also had an impact on H. H. Richardson's career. His writings on fireproof mill construction influenced the architect's design for the Marshall Field wholesale store in Chicago. See James F. O'Gorman, "The Marshall Field Wholesale Store," *Journal of the Society of Architectural Historians* 37 (October 1978), 175–94; and Jeffery Karl Ochsner, *H. H. Richardson: Complete Architectural Works* (Cambridge: MIT Press, 1981), 255. We are grateful to James F. O'Gorman for bring this connection to our attention.

14. *Brookline Chronicle,* December 11, 1886. Stearns was related to Peabody's partner John Goddard Stearns. The family owned land around Coolidge Corner. The Charles Stearns house remarkably survived until the 1930s. Benton and Wales were Boston businessmen. Benton's Beacon Street house had to be moved around the corner on Marion Street, while Wales constructed a new house on Carlton Street, farther from Beacon Street.

15. Moses Williams, Counsel for the Town, and Clement K. Fay, Counsel for the West End Land Company, *Beacon Street: Its Improvement in Brookline by Connection with Commonwealth Avenue* (Brookline: Chronicle Press, 1887).

16. It is important to note that the Olmsted firm did not develop a plan for Corey Hill, just for the Beacon Street corridor along the base of Corey Hill.

17. See chapter 5 for the house and chapter 3 for the landscape plans.

18. Originally the trolley line followed development and extended up Harvard Street from Beacon Street to Allston. The Cleveland Circle section of the line followed a few years later.

19. The Newton portion of Commonwealth Avenue was begun in the 1890s.

20. Job number 00944, Olmsted Associates Papers, Manuscript Division, Library of Congress, Washington, D.C., is a file relating to Commonwealth Avenue; most of the letters, however, concern Commonwealth Avenue in the Back Bay. Frederick Law Olmsted Sr. and Charles Sprague Sargent had advised the city on tree plantings for the mall in 1880, and Frederick Law Olmsted Jr. gave additional advice in 1907–1915. The Olmsted firm apparently did not provide any supervision for the construction of Commonwealth Avenue in Brighton in the 1890s but was again solicited by the city for advice on tree plantings.

21. *Brookline Chronicle,* June 4, 1892, including as a supplement the "Preliminary Plan for Widening Boylston Street from Chestnut Hill Avenue to Cypress Street" by F. L. Olmsted & Co., March 25, 1892.

22. Ibid. Actually the Chestnut Hill segment predated this as a proposal. See F. L. Olmsted & Co., Landscape Architects, "Preliminary Plan for Widening Chestnut Hill Avenue," June 4, 1891, published in a supplement to the *Brookline Chronicle,* June 20, 1891.

23. Lee also objected to the effect the road widening would have on his historic Boylston-Hyslop House: "Dr. Boylston built the present house in 1736, the year before the Hancock House. It is one of the few examples left of the handsome houses of that era which have never been surpassed, or in my opinion, equaled." *Brookline Chronicle,* May 28, 1892. Augustus Lowell, father of architect Guy Lowell, poet Amy Lowell, and astronomer Percival Lowell, expressed sentiments similar to Lee's.

24. *Brookline Chronicle,* February 8, 15, 22, 1896.

25. *Brookline Chronicle,* March 19, 1898.

26. *Annual Report of the Town Officers of Brookline, for the Year Ending December 31, 1899,* 63–72, 112–13.

27. Ronald Dale Karr, "The Evolution of an Elite Suburb: Community Structure and Control in Brookline, Massachusetts, 1770–1900" (Ph.D. diss., Boston University, 1981), 339–49. McCormack mounted a lively defense of his plans with long letters in the local newspaper, often in response to unsigned attacks. See, for example, *Brookline Chronicle,* July 22, 1893. The land was eventually developed for middle-class housing (mostly single-family homes) in the mid-twentieth century. Known as Button Village, it was home to many policemen and firemen. Only one three-decker was actually built opposite The Country Club, coincidentally for the father of the renowned amateur golfer Francis Ouimet. Ironically, Francis Ouimet was a poor boy who learned golfing by serving as a caddy and, in 1913, won a major tournament at the same exclusive Country Club.

28. Casey McNeill, "John J. McCormack and the Struggle for Moderate Housing in South Brookline" (History

of Art and Architecture Department, Boston University, 2011), 22. We are grateful to Casey McNeill for exploring the fascinating career of John J. McCormack and for allowing us to use her research.

29. *Brookline Chronicle,* July 7, 1894. This article identifies the petitioners as "Joseph Hubbard and thirteen others."

30. Olmsted Associates Papers, box E-4, 196. Included in job number 01300 is a "Plan #4," job number 01074, showing the land around the McCormack property and marked "A. D. Chandler," which may relate to the original smaller scope of this project. That the McCormick scheme was considered a continued threat was evident in an unrealized plan for a "Clyde Street Playground," dated May 1, 1903. This concept by Alexis French, the town engineer, shows the boundary of a proposed playground encompassing almost the entire McCormick development. French's notation in red pencil, "The plan to be kept *very private,*" is testimony to its sensitive nature. Job number 01307, Frederick Law Olmsted National Historic Site.

31. Zaitzevsky, *Frederick Law Olmsted and the Boston Park System,* 119, fig. 89. For a fuller description of the report, which Zaitzevsky credits to Charles Eliot, see her "Frederick Law Olmsted in Brookline: A Preliminary Study of His Public Projects," in *Proceedings of the Brookline Historical Society for 1975–1978* (Brookline: Brookline Historical Society, 1979), 60–61.

32. See the following plans under job number 01300, Town of Brookline, at the Frederick Law Olmsted National Historic Site: plan number 7, "Proposed Layout of Streets, Olmsted, Olmsted & Eliot, January 16, 1896; plan number 10, "Study for a Reservation between Heath & Newton Streets West of Hammond Street," Olmsted, Olmsted & Eliot, February 17, 1895; plan number 11, "Plan for Reservation for Brooks, Playgrounds, School Houses, and Park Purposes," Olmsted, Olmsted & Eliot., February 19, 1896, Warren A. Manning, supervisor of plantings, and Edward D. Bolton, supervisor of construction; plan number 13, "Map of the Town of Brookline," Olmsted, Olmsted & Eliot, February 25, 1896. Also related in this group are plan number 1, sheets 1–5; plan number 6; and plan number 18, sheets 1 and 2. It is not clear from available records how the project was funded to a point where staff was assigned to supervise work.

33. French & Bryant, Civil Engineers, *Atlas of the Town of Brookline* (Brookline: French & Bryant, 1897). The overlay was probably the work of French & Bryant, but it seems highly likely that there was input from the Olmsted firm, which had a close working relationship with the engineers.

34. "Development of Brookline," *Brookline Chronicle,* July 15, 1893. Osborne Howes Jr. (1846–1907) served as secretary of the Boston Board of Fire Underwriters and was on the boards of the Boston Chamber of Commerce, the Rapid Transit Commission, and the Metropolitan District Commission. He built a house at 45 Woodland Road in Brookline in 1892.

35. "Preliminary Plan for Widening Chestnut Hill Avenue."

36. Alfred D. Chandler, "The Proposed Brookline Parkway Including the Reservoir," *Brookline Chronicle,* December 27, 1901.

37. Job number 01306, Chestnut Hill Reservoir, Frederick Law Olmsted National Historic Site. See in particular plan number 7, Olmsted Brothers, Landscape Architects, "Preliminary Plan for Chestnut Hill Parkway to Connect the Park at Chestnut Hill Reservoir and Proposed Park at Brookline Reservoir with Jamaica Park," November 1901, Frederick Law Olmsted National Historic Site. The town undertook minor improvements to the Brookline Reservoir Park area, including, at the behest of park commissioner and Brookline resident Charles Sprague Sargent, improving the triangular gravel pit at Dudley Street and the newly built Lee Street with plants and trees. *Annual Report to the Town Officers . . . for the Year Ending January 31, 1904* (Brookline: Riverdale Press, 1904), 276.

38. See "Thoroughfare Problems, 1916–1937," in job file 1310, Frederick Law Olmsted National Historic Site.

39. Only Lee Street was eventually widened to four lanes, and not until the 1950s. *207th Annual Report of the Town Officers of Brookline . . . for the Year Ending December 31, 1912* (Brookline, E. L. Grimes Co., 1913), 211; *208th Annual Report of the Town Officers of Brookline . . . for the Year Ending December 31, 1913* (Brookline, E. L. Grimes Co., 1914), 186.

40. *Annual Report of the Town Officers of Brookline . . . for the Year Ending December 31, 1925* (Brookline: E. L. Grimes Co., 1926), 124. The National Register nomination for Hammond Pond Parkway credits the design to Olmsted, Olmsted & Eliot. This is an error, as the road did not follow the 1894 plans and in any case was built long after the passing of all three men.

41. Both houses have been demolished, although Thomas Aspinwall built a copy of the Federal style house in 1892 on Hawthorn Road in the Pill Hill neighborhood.

42. Zaitzevsky, "Frederick Law Olmsted in Brookline," 42–65.

43. Ernest W. Bowditch (1850–1918) was a partner of Robert Morris Copeland in the design of the Walnut Hills Cemetery in Brookline in 1874–75. Copeland and Bowditch both developed plans for a metropolitan park in advance of Olmsted's Boston park system. See Zaitzevsky, *Frederick Law Olmsted and the Boston Park System,* 38–39. Bowditch was also involved in the layout of the Beaconsfield development at Beacon and Tappan streets in the 1890s, but his work as a landscape architect, as opposed to a civil engineer, remains insufficiently documented.

44. Initially, Aspinwall Hill was developed as intended, with large houses designed by firms such as William G. Preston, Cram & Ferguson, Harwell & Richardson, Cabot & Chandler, and Peabody & Stearns. By the early 1900s, however, many of those houses had been replaced by inexpensive one- and two-family houses and apartment blocks.

45. J. C. Olmsted to George A. Goddard, September 23, 1884, Olmsted Associates Papers. It is not known why it was named after Francis Fisher, as he was not one of the first residents on the hill.

46. "General Plan for Subdivision of Proposed Brookline Hill," December 1884, plan number 7, job number 01012, Frederick Law Olmsted National Historic Site.

47. Olmsted, Vaux & Co., "Report on the Proposed Suburban Village at Riverside," cited in Charles E. Beveridge and Paul Rocheleau, *Frederick Law Olmsted: Designing the American Landscape* (New York: Universe Publishing, 1998), 103–4.

48. The town reservoir was covered over in 1903. Water has been drained from both reservoirs. Plans were in progress at this writing to develop the town site for housing, while the state property will be used for recreational purposes.

49. See, for example, "Study for Pierce Estate," September 30, 1884, Plan number Z-5, job number 1012, Frederick Law Olmsted National Historic Site. The Emerson-designed houses, one of which still stands at 195 Fisher Avenue, were described in "Boston Sketches: Suburban Work," by C. H. Blackall, published in *The Inland Architect and News Record,* April 1889, 53–54.

50. F. L. & J. C. Olmsted Landscape Architects, "George A. Goddard Study for Layout: Land between Clark Road and Railroad," December 7, 1886, plan number Z-1 TC3, job number 01012, Frederick Law Olmsted Historic Site. There are several drawings showing this scheme.

51. F. L. Olmsted Landscape Architects, "Proposed Clifton Station, Brookline," July 18, 1884, plan number 6, job number 01012, Frederick Law Olmsted National Historic Site; plan number Z-10, dated July 24, 1884, is a larger drawing of the same scheme, Frederick Law Olmsted Historic Site. In the event, the path in this location led to two stables, one still standing and converted for a single-family house.

52. For the other three versions, there are several drawings in different mediums. See, for example, plan number Z-15, dated January 3, 1887; plan number Z-1 TC-1, dated December 7, 1886; and plan number Z18A, dated December 7, 1886 Frederick Law Olmsted National Historic Site.

53. The houses are at 26, 41, 42, 53, and 64 Brington Road.

54. George Goddard to John Charles Olmsted, February 19 and March 20, 1889, job number 01012, Olmsted Associates Papers.

55. Two Shingle Style houses were built at 77 and 78 Brington Road (close to Boylston Street) in 1889–90, but the rest of the street remained undeveloped until the 1920s. This portion of the Olmsted plan was not included in the Fisher Hill National Register nomination.

56. Job number 01057, Frederick Law Olmsted National Historic Site. The "Reservoir Lands" file for the same job number in the records of Olmsted Associates contains a typed text of the 1888 agreement. There is also a report of a conversation between John Charles Olmsted and J. W. Lund, dated June 27, 1901, which explains why one of the major landowners opposed the plan.

57. Photographs of the now demolished house and plans are in the collections of Historic New England, Boston. The house was designed by Chapman & Frazer and is now the site of the Maimonides School.

58. John and Mary Longyear, disciples of Mary Baker Eddy, acquired eight lots and had their Michigan house dismantled and moved to Brookline for reconstruction. Letters from John Longyear in the Olmsted files do not suggest dissatisfaction with the earlier project in Michigan. Job number 00059, Olmsted Associates Papers.

59. *Town Records and Reports of Town Officers of Brookline for the Year Ending January 31, 1894,* 150. It is noted that

Joseph H. Curtis, C.E., built Circuit and Middlesex roads under contract, and his name is on the plans in the town's engineering department.

60. Greer Hardwicke and Roger Reed, *Images of America: Brookline* (Charleston, S.C.: Arcadia Publishing, 1998), 52–53. The Olmsted office job number for the Philbrick property is 01145. Later, Episcopal bishop Anson Phelps Stokes commissioned the Olmsted office to make changes to part of this property.

61. Job number 01049, plan number 10, sheet 1, Frederick Law Olmsted National Historic Site. The plans do not include planting schedules, but the specifications for job number 01049 survive in the Frederick Law Olmsted Papers, Library of Congress. The houses are at 236–242 and 254–258 Walnut Street. In 1903 Oakland Road was cut through between the two stone blocks approximately where the cul-de-sac would have gone. The old Cobb house and carriage barn (converted for residential use) were turned to face that new street. Parking spaces have subsequently been added in front of the stone buildings on Walnut Street.

62. "Fernwood Brookline," promotional brochure, ca. 1922, copy in the archives of the Brookline Preservation Commission.

63. Job number 04010. The Country Club acquired the large eighteen-acre lot.

64. Job number 00323.

65. Job number 01364.

66. Job number 03341.

67. Job number 07608, plan number 1, "Boyd-Nichols-Morrison Land Preliminary Study for Subdivision," February 4, 1926; plan number 16, "Revised Preliminary Study for the Subdivision of the Boyd, Nichols & Morrison Land," Olmsted Brothers, June 18, 1926, job number 7608, plan number 39, Frederick Law Olmsted National Historic Site.

68. "Report on Visit by Mrs. Ely to Mr. Gallagher," May 12, 1927, job number 01056, Olmsted Associates Papers. She was shown the 1894 Olmsted, Olmsted & Eliot plan (see fig. 6.5), as well as the 1897 atlas with its projected street overlay.

69. Frederick Law Olmsted Jr. to Mrs. Cora Codman Ely, May 16, 1927, job 01056, Olmsted Associates Papers.

70. The Olmsted Associates Papers do include work on the following individual properties: job numbers 07901 (90 Sargent Road), 07992 (75 Sargent Road), 09320 (120 Sargent Road), 09549 (36 Codman Road), 09582 (21 Sargent Crossways), and 09853 (21 Sargent Crossways).

71. Job number 09345 for Franklin King involved developing a driveway approach off Boylston Street. See plans at the Frederick Law Olmsted National Historic Site.

72. "General Plan for Hillfields," Olmsted Brothers Landscape Architects, October 1926, revised to February 3, 1930, job number 07608, plan number 39, print 2; "Street 50' Wide," not dated, job number 07609, plan number 19, Frederick Law Olmsted National Historic Site.

73. A good example of the firm's critique in this regard is a letter to Arthur B. Nichols concerning 359 Heath Street, January 21, 1928, Olmsted Associates Papers.

74. WBM (carbon copy of unsigned letter) to Francis R. Boyd, Hillfields Company, April 16, 1930, job number 07608, Olmsted Associates Papers.

75. WBM (carbon copy of unsigned letter) to Arthur B. Nichols, May 28, 1930, job number 7608, Olmsted Associates Papers. The Town of Brookline building permit for 9 Cary Road, dated June 5, 1930, identifies the involvement of Royal Barry Wills.

76. For Webb White, see job number 07811, Frederick Law Olmsted National Historic Site, which also includes architectural plans by Philip Avery. It appears that the landscape plan was carried out, although the recent addition of a swimming pool makes that difficult to ascertain without a field inspection. For the Underwood and Caldwell landscape plans, see job number 07608, plan number 76, Frederick Law Olmsted National Historic Site.

77. See job number 01311, Frederick Law Olmsted National Historic Site. The records of the firm's correspondence in the Olmsted Associates Papers and the drawings in the Frederick Law Olmsted Historic Site provide extensive documentation for this job.

78. Susan L. Klaus, "Frederick Law Olmsted, Jr.," in *Pioneers of American Landscape Design,* ed. Charles A. Birnbaum and Robin Karson (New York: McGraw-Hill, 2000), 273–76. Olmsted later served on the Commission of Fine Arts (1910–1918) and the National Capital Park Planning Commission (1926–1932) and worked on several of the major Washington, D.C., parks and monuments. See also "Frederick

Law Olmsted, Jr." by Susan L. Kraus on the National Association of Olmsted Parks website (www. olmsted.org).

79. "The Functions of Massachusetts Planning Boards," bulletin no. 1, May 1916.

80. Klaus, "Frederick Law Olmsted, Jr."

81. Board of Municipal Improvements to Board of Selectmen, November 28, 1911, Olmsted Associates Papers. As an advisory board, this group met in comfortable surroundings: the St. Botolph Club, 2 Newbury Street, Boston. Also in attendance were John C. Olmsted and Brookline's premier civil engineer, Alexis French.

82. *208th Annual Report of the Town Officers of Brookline . . . for the Year Ending December 31, 1913* (Brookline: E. L. Grimes Co., 1914), 186. The report stated, "The balance of the entire width of eighty feet may be utilized for a part of a street car location, a wider roadbed or walk when they are required." Lee Street was not widened until the 1950s.

83. Frederick Law Olmsted Jr., "The Basic Principles of City Planning," *The American City* 3.2 (August 1910): 67–72.

84. Ibid., 68. The town, however, did not create a separate committee to recommend the establishment of building restrictions on properties.

85. "Olmsted Brothers Propose Plan for Building Lines," *Brookline Chronicle,* March 26, 1910.

86. Frederick Law Olmsted Jr. to Planning Boards, January 1, 1916, folder 9, Olmsted Associates Papers.

87. Typed report amending Section 4 of Article XVII of the building law and signed by Frederick Law Olmsted (chairman) and board members Walter H. Kilham, Amos L. Hatheway, and Leslie C. Weed, folder 7, job file 1310, Olmsted Associates Papers.

88. *Annual Report of the Planning Board of Brookline, Massachusetts, for the Year Ending December 31, 1915* (Brookline: Riverdale Press, 1916), 349–51.

89. *Annual Report of the Planning Board of Brookline, Massachusetts, for the Year Ending December 31, 1916* (Brookline: Riverdale Press, 1917), 338.

90. Frederick Law Olmsted Jr. to Vincent Byers, August 25, 1916, Olmsted Associates Papers.

91. James Lynch to Frederick Law Olmsted Jr., December 4, 1917, Olmsted Associates Papers. This document provides an interesting window on the attitudes of these property owners by transcribing individual responses. The town's recent "Village Gateway" plans are only the latest of many efforts to improve the "entrance" to Brookline.

92. For a consideration of the attitude of planning boards and architects in metropolitan Boston toward three-deckers, see Diane Jacobsohn, "Boston's 'Three-Decker Menace': The Building, the Builders, and the Dwellers, 1870s–1930" (Ph.D. diss., Boston University, 2004).

93. There is no record that the Olmsted firm was involved.

94. *Annual Repot of the Town . . . for the Year Ending December 31, 1925* (Boston: Chapple Publishing Co., 1915), 125.

95. "Considerations Related to Widening of Boylston Street, Brookline, Massachusetts," June 7, 1931, folder 9, Olmsted Associates Papers. Since his proposals for widening Boylston Street were not implemented, it is difficult to gauge Olmsted's influence in providing guidance for town officials and public opinion over a long period of years while the road was under discussion.

96. Frederick Law Olmsted Jr. to Gorham Dana, October 3, 1938, and Henry Ware, November 23, 1938; Dana to Olmsted, December 6, 1938, Olmsted Associates Papers, job number 01310.

97. A thorough study of the career and influence of Frederick Law Olmsted Jr. is badly needed.

7. THE INSTITUTIONAL CONTEXT

1. These are not the only institutional projects that the firm executed in Brookline, but they have been chosen for the range of issues and institutional types they represent. Other potential candidates for this list would be the Edith Baker School, the Brookline Public Library, Corey Hill Hospital, Heath Square, and the Chestnut Hill pumping station.

2. Banner is perhaps best known as the architect of the Park Street Church in Boston, finished in 1810.

3. Cabot designed the Boston Athenaeum in 1846–1849 in collaboration with George Dexter, architect of two important houses in the Cottage Farm section of Brookline. See chapter 1.

4. Two letters in the Olmsted Associates Collection, Manuscript Division of the Library of Congress,

Washington, D.C., relate to the interest of Peabody & Stearns in a possible building for the First Parish Church. These are very difficult to read, but they are clearly dated July 20, and the year may be 1891. One letter is to the Reverend Howard M. Brown, the rector of First Parish, in response to a letter from him requesting that the Olmsted firm meet with Peabody at the site of the church. The second letter is addressed to Peabody & Stearns, enclosing a copy of the letter to Brown and responding to one from the architects. Both suggest that Peabody & Stearns had a proposal that was under consideration by the rector, who had firm views on the orientation and siting of a new church.

5. For information on the Brookline residences of members of both of these architectural firms, consult chapter 4.

6. F. L. Olmsted to Shepley, Rutan & Coolidge, October 15, 1891, Olmsted Associates Papers, series A (Letterbooks).

7. The job number for the First Parish Church plans is 01178.

8. See chapter 8 for a discussion of the Olmsted firm's work for Moses Williams.

9. Olmsted, Olmsted & Eliot to Moses Williams, February 1, 1894, Olmsted Associates Papers, Series A (Letterbooks). *The Church of the First Parish in Brookline, Massachusetts* (Brookline: Riverdale Press, 1901) lists the members of the parish at the time and when they joined. No member of the Olmsted firm is listed for that year. It was certainly possible for someone to consider himself or herself a member without officially joining the church.

10. *First Parish in Brookline Yearbook: 1890* (Boston: Press of George H. Ellis, 1890), 14. I am deeply grateful to William Dwyer, a member of First Parish in Brookline with a strong interest in the parish's history, who reviewed the membership books for the parish and found no signatures of Olmsted family members. He found the two published yearbooks for 1890 and 1919. Frederick Law Olmsted Sr. and John Charles Olmsted were listed in the first year, while Mrs. John C. Olmsted was listed as a member of the First Parish sewing club in 1919. *First Parish in Brookline Yearbook: 1919* (Brookline: Riverdale Press, 1919), 7. Both yearbooks are in the collections of the First Parish Church.

11. Charles E. Beveridge, "Frederick Law Olmsted: The Formative Years, 1822–1865" (Ph.D. diss., University of Wisconsin, 1966), 47–54, 68–73, 82–87, 106–11.

12. Charles W. Eliot, *Charles Eliot: Landscape Architect* (Boston: Houghton Mifflin, 1902), 418. Eliot's Brookline house was near the intersection of Warren and Dudley streets.

13. A. P. Wyman, memo to file, April 9, 1901, Olmsted Associates Papers, Series A (Letterbooks).

14. Frederick Law Olmsted Jr., memo to file, October 25, 1906, Olmsted Associates Papers, Series B (Letterbooks).

15. Parish Clerk to Olmsted Brothers, April 24, 1907, Olmsted Associates Papers, Series B (Letterbooks).

16. Telephone message from Mr. Prouty to Mr. Whiting, October 6, 1936, Olmsted Associates Papers, Series B (Letterbooks). The message includes information on both Prouty's house and the church, "this church work to be billed to Mr. Prouty."

17. Olmsted Brothers to Mrs. Abbot Peterson, October 30, 1937, Olmsted Associates Papers, Series B (Letterbooks). Lack of maintenance had resulted in a landscape that was an embarrassment to both the neighbors and the Olmsteds.

18. Olmsted Brothers to Mrs. Abbot Peterson, November 16, 1937, Olmsted Associates Papers, Series B (Letterbooks).

19. Mrs. Abbot Peterson to Mrs. John C. Olmsted, January 14, 1938, Olmsted Associates Papers, Series B (Letterbooks). There is no record indicating whether they made a contribution to this project.

20. Research summary on the history of Brookline High School provided by the Brookline Historical Commission.

21. Eleven firms competed. Boston City Architect Edmund March Wheelwright, a specialist in public school architecture, and Professor Francis Ward Chandler from MIT also advised on the competition. See "New High School Building," *Brookline Chronicle,* October 14, 1893; and "Proposed New High School Building," *Brookline Chronicle,* January 20, 1894, which includes a photograph of the proposed building.

22. Olmsted job number 01305. The correspondence for this project begins in May 1895.

23. Greer Hardwicke and Roger Reed, *Images of America: Brookline* (Charleston, S.C.: Arcadia Publishing, 1998), 68. Two years after beginning the work on Brookline High School, Olmsted proposed his first playground at Charlesbank, an active recreation site he designed for a stretch of the Charles River shore

in the West End of Boston. See Cynthia Zaitzevsky, *Frederick Law Olmsted and the Boston Park System* (Cambridge: Belknap Press of Harvard University Press, 1982), 96–99.

24. Job number 01305, drawing 2, February 1894, "Sketch for Enlargement of Brookline Playground and Fitting It as a Foreground for the New High School."

25. Olmsted, Olmsted & Eliot to William H. Lincoln, August 19, 1895, Olmsted Associates Papers, Series A (Letterbooks).

26. The architects responded to the planting suggestions: "The more we reflect about the planted court in front of the High School, the more we are convinced that if it is simply filled in with shrubs, without any evidence of design in their arrangement and planting and the spaces of ground left between them, if there is no greensward at all, and if the whole place looks simply like a wild tangled shrubbery, we do not possibly see how it can be a success." Andrews, Jaques & Rantoul to Olmsted, Olmsted & Eliot, September 18, 1895, Olmsted Associates Papers.

27. In a letter dated September 16, 1938, to Francis J. Oakes Jr., Olmsted Associates Papers, Series B (Letterbooks), the Olmsted office responded to a telephone call of the previous day inquiring as to how much it would cost for the office to develop and supervise a landscape scheme for the new high school. Oakes had purchased the former Barthold Schlesinger estate at 278 Warren Street. The Olmsted firm oversaw the development of that estate for both Schlesinger and Oakes. Whether Oakes was serving on the building committee for the new high school or was considering making a gift of the firm's services needs to be determined.

28. J. F. Dawson, "Report of Visit," Brookline High School, June 3, 1938, Olmsted Associates Papers, Series B (Letterbooks). The school to which Dawson refers is the Scarborough School, financed by Frederick A. Vanderbilt in Scarborough, New York, on which the Olmsted firm worked from 1916 to 1927 (job number 06427).

29. Greer Hardwicke, "Town Houses and the Culture of Recall: Public Buildings and Civic Values in Massachusetts and the Architectural Firm of Kilham, Hopkins and Greeley, 1900–1930" (Ph.D. diss., Boston College, 1985).

30. The essential analysis of the Boston and Albany Railroad stations is provide by Jeffrey Karl Ochsner, "Architecture for the Boston and Albany Railroad: 1881–1894," *Journal of the Society of Architectural Historians* 47.2 (June 1988): 109–31. This railroad was initially chartered as the Boston and Worcester Railroad in 1831 and completed in 1835; the western section was completed to Albany by 1842. The two sections were incorporated in 1867. Ibid., 110–11.

31. The extensive campaign of buildings and landscapes were the response to the success of the B & A, which had become the largest railroad in New England by the late nineteenth century. The Massachusetts legislature had placed a 10 percent cap on the income the railroad could receive from its investments, so the building projects were part of an effort to dispose of excess profits. Ibid., 109.

32. The Olmsted office job numbers for these projects were 12046 (Longwood, 1884–1891) and 12056 (Brookline Hills, 1889–1894). In addition, Olmsted provided designs for the landscapes of stations at Brookline Reservoir, Brookline Junction, Allston, Brighton, Auburndale, Newton, Palmer, Wellesley, Wellesley Hills, and Charlton.

33. O. W. Norcross Builders worked on many projects for H. H. Richardson, beginning with the high school in their hometown of Worcester, Massachusetts. See James F. O'Gorman, "O. W. Norcross, Richardson's 'Master Builder': A Preliminary Report," *Journal of the Society of Architectural Historians* 32.2 (May 1973): 104–13.

34. *Brookline Chronicle,* November 21, 1891.

35. See chapter 6 for a discussion of the Fisher Hill (originally Brookline Hill) subdivision.

36. "New Longwood Station," *Brookline Chronicle,* August 28, 1886.

37. Charles Mulford Robinson, "The Railroad Beautiful," *House and Garden,* November 2, 1892, 567, cited in Ocshner, "Architecture for the Boston and Albany Railroad," 121.

38. Earlier suburban clubs included the Philadelphia (1854), Germantown (1855), and Merion (1865) cricket clubs in Pennsylvania. James M. Mayo, *The American Country Club: Its Origins and Development* (New Brunswick: Rutgers University Press, 1998), 65.

39. Ibid., 63–64.

40. Frederick H. Curtiss and John Heard, *The Country Club, 1882–1932* (Boston: Little, Brown, 1932), 14–16.

41. See Benjamin G. Rader, *American Sports: From the Age of Folk Games to the Age of Spectators* (Englewood Cliffs, N.J.: Prentice Hall, 1990), 75–101, and "The Quest for Subcommunities and the Rise of American Sport," *American Quarterly* 29 (Fall 1977): 355–69.

42. David Allan Mittell, *The Country Club: Physical Evolution, 1882–2001* (1882; reprint, Attleboro, Mass.: Colonial Lithograph, 2001). Mittell calls Olmsted (whose name he misspells) "an original member of the Club" (26). By the time of the 1888 edition of this publication, Olmsted had resigned his membership in The Country Club. We appreciate the assistance of Charline Lawless with verification of information at The Country Club. Olmsted's frequent collaborators Richardson and Sargent were also members.

43. Elmer Osgood Cappers, *Centennial History of The Country Club, 1882–1982* (Brookline: The Country Club, 1981), 16. Membership reached 536 in its second year and a long waiting list existed by 1885. The Olmsted job number for The Country Club is 01048. The firm was consulted on later occasions in the 1910s, 1930s, and 1940s as well.

44. Ibid., 16. Congressman Charles Sprague purchased Faulkner Farm and developed it as a private estate. He initially invited the Olmsted firm to lay out the grounds but fired them and hired a young landscape architect named Charles Platt to design the gardens in 1897–98.

45. Hardwicke and Reed, *Images of America,* 44.

46. "The first six holes [at The Country Club] were laid out in March, 1893, by Messrs. Hunnewell, Curtis and Bacon. Then Scott Willie Campbell was hired as the professional in 1894 and helped to oversee the expansion of the course to nine holes that summer." GolfClubAtlas.com.

47. Lucy Lawliss, "Country Club, Resorts, Hotels, and Clubs," in *The Master List of Design Projects of the Olmsted Firm, 1857–1979,* 2nd ed. (Washington, D.C.: National Association for Olmsted Parks, 2008), 275–83, lists more than 150 projects in this category for the firm.

48. As discussed in chapters 2 and 3, Olmsted was a member of the Century Association in New York City, which had provided important introductions to prominent individuals. He joined this prestigious club for men in the arts and letters in 1859, twelve years after it was founded. *The Century Club Yearbook, 2008* (New York: The Century Association, 2008), 552. Although he never became a member, Olmsted conceived of the idea for the Union League Club in New York City while serving as the secretary-general of the United States Sanitary Commission in 1863. "Olmsted fluently supplied rules, admissions procedures, guidelines for the kinds of men to be admitted, and significantly stressed the need to search out persons of talent and promise in the arts as well as of good family and money." Elizabeth Stevenson, *Park Maker: A Life of Frederick Law Olmsted* (New York: Macmillan, 1977), 239.

49. For the history of the Saturday Club, consult Edward Waldo Emerson, *The Early Years of the Saturday Club* (Boston: Houghton Mifflin, 1918); and M. A. DeWolfe Howe, ed., *The Later Years of the Saturday Club, 1870 to 1920* (Boston: Houghton Mifflin, 1927).

50. For a taste of the old days of the Saturday Club, read Oliver Wendell Holmes's poem "At the Saturday Club," published in 1884 in *The Autocrat of the Breakfast Table,* in which he remembers the club members who have died.

51. Although Godkin joined the Saturday Club in 1875, he had left the Boston area by 1881, when he joined Carl Schurz and Horace White in purchasing the *New York Evening Post.* Howe, *Later Years of the Saturday Club,* 88.

52. Eliot, *Charles Eliot,* 34. The architect Robert Swain Peabody, who would later become a member of the Saturday Club, also introduced Eliot to Olmsted that spring. Peabody, Eliot, and Norton were all related to one another as well.

53. Howe, *Later Years of the Saturday Club,* 183–87.

54. Ibid., 187. Sargent's laudatory but sober assessment of Olmsted is in stark contrast to the memoir of Richardson by Charles A. Coolidge for the same history of the club, in which he tells at great length an anecdote concerning the death by drowning of the Richardson children's pet donkey, Betsy Edward, and the efforts to remove her rotting corpse from the pond behind the Richardson house that ended with two crazed horses dragging the donkey across the road and into the cold frames of Holm Lea, the Sargent estate. Ibid., 196–98.

55. All quotations are from this source. See also Cynthia Zaitzevsky, "Frederick Law Olmsted in Brookline: A Preliminary Study of His Public Projects," in *Proceedings of the Brookline Historical Society for 1975–1978* (Brookline: Published by the Society, 1979), 42–65.

56. His presentation to "the members and ladies" of the Brookline Club had occurred the previous Monday.

57. Catherine Beecher was one of the first to define the suburb as an ideal feminine sphere in her writings from the 1840s through the 1860s. For more recent discussions of this argument, see Gwendolyn Wright, *Building the Dream: A Social History of Housing in America* (New York: Pantheon Books, 1981); and D. Arnold Lewis, *An Early Encounter with Tomorrow: Europeans, Chicago's Loop, and the World's Columbian Exposition* (Urbana: University of Illinois Press, 1997).

58. The Francis A. Countway Library of Medicine at the Harvard University Medical School holds a scrapbook related to the Free Hospital for Women, which is also accessible online at http://nrs.harvard,edu/urn-3:HMS.COUNT:680593.

59. Boston Lying-In Hospital was established in 1832 and occupied multiple sites in Boston before moving to the area of the new Harvard Medical School in Longwood in 1921–22, the two hospitals eventually merging with other institutions to form Brigham and Women's Hospital.

60. For general information on the Free Hospital, consult Elmer O. Cappers, *History of the Free Hospital for Women* (Boston: Boston Hospital for Women, 1975); and Greer Hardwicke, Carla Benka, and Roger Reed, "Boston Free Hospital for Women: Form B" (1995), Massachusetts Historical Commission, Boston.

61. Ibid., 26–27.

62. The firm of Jameson Brothers of Brookline was hired to do the grading of the site, paths, and road and to install topsoil and seed the lawns. From May 1894 through September 1895, multiple letters and memo from both E. D. Bolton and J. C. Olmsted to the trustees and the contractor detail the ongoing dissatisfaction with the quality of the grass. Eventually legal action was threatened.

63. In the *Twentieth Annual Report of the Free Hospital for Women, 1894–95* (Boston: Washington Press, 1895), 4, Mrs. C. S. Sargent is listed as an active member of the corporation. From the 1895–96 annual report forward, she is listed as an associate member of the Board of Lady Visitors. Since Holm Lea is located so close to the hospital, one wonders whether either Mr. or Mrs. Sargent played a role in the hospital's purchasing this land.

64. "The grounds about the building were unfinished and remained so until October 1895 when 'Mr.' Charles S. Sargent of Brookline, as the Secretary's minutes designate that world-famous professor, offered to care for the trees and plant shrubs in the Hospital grounds." Cappers, *Free Hospital*, 31.

65. Placing patients in a landscape setting to recover from various illnesses had been part of the environmental response to disease from the time of A. J. Downing and his contemporaries forward. Olmsted had been involved with similar earlier projects, such as the designs for the Buffalo Asylum for the Insane, on which he collaborated with H. H. Richardson, or in choosing the new rural site for the McLean Asylum of Massachusetts General Hospital in Belmont, where Olmsted would spend his final years. In the case of the Free Hospital for Women, however, Olmsted was responding to the work of others rather than defining the philosophy of therapy.

66. See Carla Yanni, *The Architecture of Madness: Insane Asylums in the United States* (Minneapolis: University of Minnesota Press, 2007), passim.

67. It is important to note that the Free Hospital for Women pioneered in the treatment of cancer with radiation and in the development of the birth control pill.

68. Catharine Beecher, "How to Redeem Woman's Profession from Dishonor," *Harper's*, November 1865, quoted in *The Suburb Reader*, ed. Becky Nicolaides and Andrew Wiese (New York: Routledge, 2006), 47–48.

69. Ronald Dale Karr, "The Evolution of an Elite Suburb: Community Structure and Control in Brookline, Massachusetts, 1770–1900" (Ph.D. diss., Boston University, 1981), 177, 202–3.

70. Ibid., 332. Nearly every woman on this list was married to someone who commissioned the Olmsted firm to undertake planning or landscape projects. The fullest discussion of Mary Cleveland Bryant Olmsted appears in appendix B of Laura Roper, *FLO: A Biography* (Baltimore: Johns Hopkins University Press, 1973), 478. Roper paints her as "tart" and "intolerant."

8. THE NEIGHBORHOOD CONTEXT

1. Frederick Law Olmsted was a member of The Country Club from 1882 through 1885. Correspondence with Charlene Lawless, The Country Club, Brookline, July 15, 2009.

2. *Social Register, Boston* (New York: Social Register Association, 1890). Frederick Law Olmsted Sr. was listed as a member of the Century Association and Union League Club in New York and of the St. Botolph Club in Boston. John Charles Olmsted's clubs included the Union Boat Club and the Athletic Club in Boston; Frederick Law Olmsted Jr. was a member of his brother's two clubs and was listed as an 1894 graduate of Harvard College.

3. Charles F. White, *Land Ownership in Brookline from the First Settlement* (Brookline: Brookline Historical Society, 1923), map 1, 1636–1641. This pamphlet and the associated ten maps trace the evolution of landownership from 1636 to 1916.

4. Thomas C. Amory, *Memoir of the Hon. Richard Sullivan* (Cambridge: John Wilson and Son, 1850), 16.

5. Ronald Dale Karr, "The Evolution of an Elite Suburb: Community Structure and Control in Brookline, Massachusetts, 1770–1900" (Ph.D. diss., Boston University, 1981), 83.

6. Andrew Jackson Downing, *A Treatise on the Theory and Practice of Landscape Gardening Adapted to North America,* 4th ed. (New York: Putnam, 1850), 56. See chapter 5 for further information on this estate.

7. The Olmsted job number for the Schlesinger commission is 00614. Correspondence between Harney and Olmsted began on September 1, 1879, with the architect sending the landscape architect an initial plan for the house. On September 13 Harney invited Olmsted to meet Barthold Schlesinger and him at the property to review the proposals. A previous house stood on this site, as documented in a landscape plan by Grendel & Grendel in the drawing collection (Z84) of the Olmsted National Historic Site, Brookline.

8. G. E. Harney to F. L. Olmsted, "16th, 188[?]," Frederick Law Olmsted Papers, General Correspondence, Manuscript Division, Library of Congress.

9. Mrs. Schlesinger to F. L. Olmsted, "Nahant, Sunday," n.d., Frederick Law Olmsted Papers,. This letter probably dates from the summer of 1882, when the development of the grounds was proceeding quickly. Kelly was the landscape contractor for the project.

10. The Olmsted job number for the Oakes projects at Southwood is 06625, dating from 1918 through 1957.

11. The Clark sisters' project is contained in the files for Fairsted, whose Olmsted job number is 00673. These plans also include floor plans for the house the Olmsteds purchased before it was modified to meet their needs. On May 16, 1915, the house and land of the Clark sisters at 99 Fairmount was conveyed to Lillian Hastings Thompson, both Clark sisters having died.

12. For information on Mrs. Gardner's interests in landscape design and horticulture, see Mary L. Cornille, "Isabella Stewart Gardner as Landscape Gardener" (M.A. paper, Boston University, 1985); and Keith N. Morgan, *Charles A. Platt: The Artist as Architect* (Cambridge: MIT Press for the Architectural History Foundation, 1985), 52–53.

13. The Olmsted job number for the Gardner project is 01044. The drawings at the Olmsted National Historic Site date from 1886–87.

14. Olmsted, Olmsted & Eliot to George F. Clarke, September 14, 1895, Olmsted Associates Papers, Series A (Letterbooks), Manuscript Division, Library of Congress.

15. F. C. Hood and his brother Arthur Needham Hood founded the Hood Rubber Company in 1896. Their factory in Watertown finally closed in 1969. The *Harvard Crimson* announced a lecture by Hood to the Engineering School Society on December 14, 1923, noting, "He is one of the few men to have successfully employed non-union men exclusively throughout this period of labor troubles." Many of those workers were Armenian immigrants.

16. The Olmsted job number for the Williams estate is 00464.

17. Plan number 00646-Z4, drawing collection, Olmsted National Historic Site. The cutout of the ground floor is also preserved in the drawing collection.

18. J. C. Olmsted, memo to file, June 27, 1898, Olmsted Associates Papers, Series A (Letterbooks).

19. The house designed by F. Manton Wakefield for Elias Bliss at 49 Warren Street sits on the lot that had previously been owned by Scudder.

20. Greer Hardwicke, "Built by Brookline: A Survey of Buildings and Properties Built and Owned by the Town of Brookline" (available at the Brookline Preservation Commission), 32–33. Walter Channing was a client of the Olmsted firm whose property overlooked the reservoir, as did the estate of Henry Lee.

21. Cynthia Zaitzevsky, "Frederick Law Olmsted in Brookline: A Preliminary Study of His Public Projects,"

in *Proceedings of the Brookline Historical Society for 1975–1978* (Brookline: Brookline Historical Society, 1979), 60.

22. Carla Benka, Green Hill Area Form, Massachusetts Historical Commission, 1983.

23. The Olmsted job number for the house is 01030.

24. This commission is also discussed in chapter 4.

25. A. A. Shurtleff to file, October 28, 1902, Olmsted Associates Papers. Shurtleff changed his name to Shurcliff in 1930.

26. A. A. Shurtleff to file, November 4, 1902, Olmsted Associates Papers.

27. After George Shepley died in 1903, the property was sold to Josephine Cox, who demolished the house and commissioned Chapman & Frazer to build a new residence for her.

28. The Whipples wanted to use "two or three acres of it for a house lot and sell the rest in ½ acre and acre lots." J. C. Olmsted to file, June 7, 1896, Olmsted Associates Papers, series E, box E-6.

29. J. C. Olmsted, memo to file, January 10, 1904, Olmsted Associates Papers, series B.

30. J. C. Olmsted, February 17, 1904, Olmsted Associates Papers, series B.

31. J. C. Olmsted to file, January 6, 1905, Olmsted Associates Papers, series B.

32. Telephone message from Cora Codman Ely, May 11, 1927, Olmsted Associates Papers, series B.

33. Henry Gallagher, report of visit to Mrs. Ely, May 12, 1927, Olmsted Associates Papers, series B. Gallagher also advised Mrs. Ely to consult the town engineer. She was "pleased" to discover that Olmsted was a member of the town Planning Board.

34. Frederick Law Olmsted Jr. to Cora Codman Ely, May 16, 1927, Olmsted Associates Papers, series B, "Copied from Mr. Olmsted's manuscript and signed in his absence."

35. Report of Conference by E. C. Whiting, August 27 and 28, 1928, Olmsted Associates Papers, series B. The Olmsted job number for the Cutler project is 07992; the project was under development from 1927 through 1929.

36. E. C. Whiting to Sewall Cutler, February 1, 1929, Olmsted Associates Papers, series B.

37. Telephone message from Mrs. Alan Cunningham, September 28, [1934], Post-1949 Correspondence, Frederick Law Olmsted National Historic Site. The Olmsted job number for the Cunningham project is 09366. The Phillips Ketchum commission in Natick is Olmsted job number 09357, undertaken from 1932 to 1935.

38. This Miss Harrison was probably Dorothea Harrison, who was an instructor in the Lowthorpe School of Landscape Architecture in 1929 and a member of the American Society of Landscape Architects in 1932. She lived in Concord, Massachusetts, during the 1930s. See Catherine R. Brown, "Women and the Land," typescript, n.d., Special Collections, Loeb Library, Graduate School of Design, Harvard University. We are grateful to Betsy Igleheart for bringing this source to our attention.

39. Olmsted job number 09320.

40. F. Manton Wakefield, "Suburban Homes," *Brookline Magazine,* 1897, 40–41. In addition to the Schlesinger estate and the Williams estate discussed in this chapter, refer to chapter 4 for further information on the two White properties. The J. G. Wright house, where the firm worked from 1895 to 1909, was Olmsted job number 00224.

CONCLUSION: LANDSCAPE INTO TOWNSCAPE

1. An excellent analysis of this new field is provided by Jon A. Peterson, *The Birth of City Planning in the United States, 1840–1917* (Baltimore: Johns Hopkins University Press, 2003).

2. Frederick Law Olmsted Jr., introduction to John Nolen, *City Planning: A Series of Papers Presenting the Essential Elements of a City Plan* (1915; reprint, New York: D. Appleton and Company, 1929), 1.

3. Peterson, *Birth of City Planning,* 12.

4. Ibid., 273.

Index

theater, *185*, 185–86; Fisher Hill development as template for, 229; Olmsted and Kilham & Hopkins collaborate at, 90; plan of Cypress Street Playground and, *183*; planting plan for, *184*

Brookline Land Company, 15, 156, 193, 195, 198

Brookline Park Commission: in Muddy River improvement, 122, 123, 124, 126; as response to Boston Park Act of 1875, 121; Sargent serves on, 110, 121, 129, 135, 211

Brookline Planning Commission: annual report of 1915, *170*; annual report of 1925, 173; on Brookline Village, 169, 171; establishment of, 230; Olmsted Jr. resigns from, 173; Olmsted Jr. serves on, 89–90, 137, 149, 165, 166, 167, 168, 172, 230; and South Brookline parkways, 149–50; three-deckers restricted by, 168–69; zoning law overseen by, 172

Brookline Reservoir: Fairmount development south of, 13; in Green Hill neighborhood, *66*, *200*, *201*; in McCormack's development plan, 146; minor improvements to, 276n37; in popularity of Town Green neighborhood, 215; preserving as public space, 216; sale of, 149, 216, 253; White brothers build houses overlooking, 81, 82, *82*, 84, 224

Brookline Town Hall, 47, 180

Brookline Village: colonial bridge over Muddy River at, 7; as commercial core of Brookline, 14; condition of wooden buildings in, 169, 171; developing more attractive entrance to Brookline from, 172; omnibus and railroad connection to Boston, 9; and proposed Cypress Street extension, 167; three-deckers in, 138; and Toxteth Street development, 139

Brown, Howard M., 180, 280n4

Brown, Jane, 115, 271n82

Bryant, Adelaide Whitney Barnes, 223, 256

Bryant, Charlotte Olmsted, 28, 54, 222–23, 256, 265n41

Bryant, Gridley J. F., 54, 79

Bryant, John, Jr., *201*, 222–23, 256

Bryant, John, Sr., 54, 222

Buffalo park system, 31, 45

Buffalo State Hospital, 45–47, *46*

Burton, A. E., 179

Bussey, Benjamin, 110, 112

Bussey Institute (Harvard University), 60, 110, 119, 120

Byers, Vincent, 171

Cabot, Edward Clark, 87–89; Boston Athenaeum designed by, 178, 279n3; and Boylston Street development, 145; First Parish Church designed by, 178; home of, *68*, 69, 237

Cabot, George, 8, 203

Cabot, Walter Channing, 87

Cabot & Chandler, 87–89, 268n43

Caldwell, Lawrence, 165

Carlyle, Thomas, 23, 260n14

Carnes, George W., 16–17

Central Park (New York City), 26–28, *28*, 30, 32, 39

Century Association, 43–44, 263n9, 284n2

Chandler, Alfred D., 147, 149, 167

Chandler, Mrs. Alfred D., 198

Chandler, Frank W., 79, 87–89

Channing, Walter, 55–56, *56*, 216, 284n20

Chapman & Frazer, 89, 156, 254, 255

Chestnut Hill: and Fisher Hill development, 155; and Hillfields subdivision, 160, 162; Olmsted and Vaux lay out, 5; Olmsted firm's lack of involvement in, 156; the wealthy continue to reside in, 144

Chestnut Hill Avenue, 55, 144, 149, 151, 154–55, 167, 216

Chestnut Hill Land Company, 15

Chestnut Hill Parkway, 149, 155

Chestnut Hill Reservoir: in Beacon Street widening plan, *140*, 141, 144; in Chestnut Hill Parkway plan, 149; and Fisher Hill development, 151, *154*; Olmsted's efforts to beautify, 194; as park, 150, 151

Christ's Church, Longwood, 12, 126

Church of Our Saviour, 12

"Circular as to Professional Methods and Charges" (Olmsted, Olmsted & Eliot), 69–71, 92

City Beautiful movement, 188, 228

City Planning (Nolen), 228

Clark, Joshua, 206, *207*

Clark, Samuel, 201

Clark, William S., 118

Clark sisters house, 206–7, 254; Gardner property near, 210; location of, *200*, *209*; Olmsted builds, 36, 206; plans for, *208*, 284n11

Cleveland, Horace W. S., 261n35

Clough, George A., 182

Clyde Street, *146*, 146–47, 159, 217, 218

Cobb, Albert A., *157*, 157–58, *158*, *159*

Cobb, Henry Ives, 157

Codman, Henry Sargent: in Arnold Arboretum planning, 112, 221; death of, 61, 115, 221, 255, 262n76; home in Green Hill neighborhood, *66*, 68; and Muddy River improvement, 128; in Olmsted firm in Brookline, 37, 61, 255, 262n71; and Sargent estate subdivision, 161, 219, 221

Codman, James McMaster, *200*, 203, 221, 255

Codman, Mrs. James McMaster, 198, 203, 221, 255